COERCIVE BRAIN-READING IN CRIMINAL JUSTICE

Emerging neurotechnology offers increasingly individualised brain information, enabling researchers to identify mental states and content. When accurate and valid, these brain-reading technologies also provide data that could be useful in criminal legal procedures, such as memory detection with EEG and the prediction of recidivism with fMRI. Yet, unlike in medicine, individuals involved in criminal cases will often be reluctant to undergo brain-reading procedures. This raises the question of whether coercive brain-reading could be permissible in criminal law. *Coercive Brain-Reading in Criminal Justice* examines this question in view of European human rights: the prohibition of ill-treatment, the right to privacy, freedom of thought, freedom of expression, and the privilege against self-incrimination. The book argues that, at present, the established framework of human rights does not exclude coercive brain-reading. It does, however, delimit the permissible use of forensic brain-reading without valid consent. This cautionary, cutting-edge book lays a crucial foundation for understanding the future of criminal legal proceedings in a world of ever-advancing neurotechnology.

Sjors Ligthart is an assistant professor in the Department of Criminal Law at Tilburg Law School and a postdoctoral researcher at the Willem Pompe Institute for Criminal Law and Criminology at Utrecht University. His research interests include human rights over the mind and the legal implications of brain-reading, neurointerventions, virtual reality, and persuasive technologies in criminal justice. He is the co-editor of *Neurolaw: Advances in Neuroscience, Justice & Security* (2021).

LAW AND THE COGNITIVE SCIENCES

Law and the Cognitive Sciences publishes book monographs exploring connections between law and the cognitive sciences. The books will be of interest to academics, students, and practitioners, and in particular to the scholars in the fields of legal theory, philosophy of law, psychology of law, the theory of law and artificial intelligence, general theory of private and criminal law, and evidence.

Coercive Brain-Reading in Criminal Justice

AN ANALYSIS OF EUROPEAN HUMAN RIGHTS LAW

SJORS LIGTHART
Tilburg University
Utrecht University

CAMBRIDGE
UNIVERSITY PRESS

CAMBRIDGE
UNIVERSITY PRESS

University Printing House, Cambridge CB2 8BS, United Kingdom

One Liberty Plaza, 20th Floor, New York, NY 10006, USA

477 Williamstown Road, Port Melbourne, VIC 3207, Australia

314–321, 3rd Floor, Plot 3, Splendor Forum, Jasola District Centre, New Delhi – 110025, India

103 Penang Road, #05–06/07, Visioncrest Commercial, Singapore 238467

Cambridge University Press is part of the University of Cambridge.

It furthers the University's mission by disseminating knowledge in the pursuit of education, learning, and research at the highest international levels of excellence.

www.cambridge.org
Information on this title: www.cambridge.org/9781009252430
DOI: 10.1017/9781009252447

First published 2022

A catalogue record for this publication is available from the British Library.

ISBN 978-1-009-25243-0 Hardback

Contents

Tables

Acknowledgements

I would like to thank Tijs Kooijmans and Gerben Meynen for their excellent support, refreshing perspectives, and valuable comments on earlier versions of this book. I also wish to thank the Oxford Uehiro Centre for Practical Ethics of the University of Oxford for their hospitality. Furthermore, my gratitude goes to the Tilburg Law School for their financial support. The finalisation of this book has been funded by the Dutch Research Council (NWO), as part of the project Law and Ethics of Neurotechnology in Criminal Justice (project number VI.C.201.067).

Abbreviations

ANS	autonomic nervous system
CCTV	closed-circuit television
CFR	Charter of Fundamental Rights of the European Union
CIT	concealed information test
CPT	European Committee for the Prevention of Torture and Inhuman or Degrading Treatment or Punishment
CT	Computed tomography
ECHR	European Convention for the Protection of Human Rights and Fundamental Freedoms
EComHR	European Commission of Human Rights
ECtHR	European Court of Human Rights
EEG	electroencephalography
ERP	event-related potential
EU	European Union
fMRI	functional magnetic resonance imaging
GDPR	General Data Protection Regulation
GKT	guilty knowledge test
HR	Dutch Supreme Court
ICCPR	International Covenant on Civil and Political Rights
MRI	magnetic resonance imaging
PET	positron emission tomography
Rb.	*Rechtbank* (Dutch District Court)
SPECT	single-photon emission computed tomography
UDHR	Universal Declaration of Human Rights
UN	United Nations
UNCAT	United Nations Convention against Torture and Other Cruel, Inhuman or Degrading Treatment or Punishment

1

Setting the Stage

Why 'Reading' Brains Raises Fundamental Legal Questions for European Human Rights Law

1.1 INTRODUCTION

Traditionally, the majority of human rights pertain to physical actions and visible objects in the outside world. To a far lesser degree, they protect our *internal* lives, such as emotions, thoughts, and other mental states. Because our internal, mental lives have been conceived as being inaccessible to the outside world, their normative protection may have seemed unnecessary.[1]

However, in recent years, we have seen considerable progress in neurotechnologies. Some of these technologies make it possible to analyse the brain, yielding individualised brain information. Such developments help us to better understand the human brain in health and disease. For example, neurotechnologies appear useful in diagnosing brain disorders, such as epilepsy and certain forms of dementia, and specific brain features appear to correlate with aggressive behaviour. Interestingly, brain-derived data have also enabled researchers to make inferences about individual mental states, such as the identification of *recognition* and the detection of *lying*. As a result of these neurotechnological advancements, the private sphere of our minds is no longer inaccessible to others the way it used to be.

These scientific developments have raised normative questions, in particular regarding human rights.[2] In a recent Strategic Action Plan on Human Rights and Technologies in Biomedicine (2020–2025), the Committee on Bioethics of the Council of Europe draws attention to advances in neurotechnologies, which raise the prospect of increased understanding, monitoring, and controlling of the human brain. Such scientific advances will evoke novel legal questions relating to autonomy, privacy, and freedom of thought.[3] As the Committee points out, considerations

[1] Bublitz & Merkel 2014, p. 61; Alegre 2017, p. 224; Vermeulen & Roosmalen 2018, p. 738. Cf. Schabas 2013, p. 1768.

[2] Ienca 2021; UN Special Rapporteur on Freedom of Religion or Belief 2021.

[3] Committee on Bioethics of the Council of Europe 2019, § 14, 21–22 (accessible via www.coe.int).

of human rights often come into play at the end of the process when the technology has already been established and the technological pathways are irreversible. As this is often too late for robust modifications, there is a pressing need of *embedding* human rights input in the development phase of new technologies. In this way, the technology can be tailored to protecting fundamental rights and freedoms.[4]

In the same vein, the Grand Chamber of the European Court of Human Rights (ECtHR) accepts that, today, modern scientific technologies play an important role in the fight against crime. At the same time, it stresses that any State claiming a pioneer role in developing such technologies bears special responsibility. Those member States must strike the right balance between fundamental human rights on the one hand and the interests of introducing modern technology in criminal justice on the other.[5]

In line with these considerations, legal scholars are currently discussing the responsible use of a variety of emerging technologies that are entering criminal justice – or may soon do so. This debate includes digital technologies,[6] virtual reality systems,[7] and brain alternation through invasive and non-invasive techniques.[8] A particular area of research, central to this book, concerns forensic use of neurotechnologies that *analyse the brain* with the aim of obtaining information about brain features and mental properties.[9] Because, in a way, researchers in this context are 'reading' an individual's brain, these neurotechnologies are sometimes referred to as neurotechnological 'brain-reading'.[10] In what follows, I will use this term, without the quotation marks but keeping in mind that it is figurative.

Different technologies can be used to examine people's brains. Examples are magnetic resonance imaging (MRI), functional magnetic resonance imaging (fMRI), computed tomography (CT), electroencephalography (EEG), and positron emission tomography (PET).[11] These technologies are often referred to as 'neuroimaging'. Many scholars have underlined the (near-future) potential of neuroimaging for criminal law.[12] Much empirical research has been done on forensic use of

4 Ibid., § 15.

5 ECtHR (GC) 4 December 2008, appl. nos. 30562/04 and 30566/04 (*S. & Marper/UK*), § 105, 110. Cf. ECtHR 13 February 2020, appl. no. 45245/15 (*Gaughran/UK*), § 86: 'the Court recalls the importance of examining compliance with the principles of Article 8 where the powers vested in the state are obscure, creating a risk of arbitrariness especially where the technology available is continually becoming more sophisticated'.

6 Kooijmans & Mevis 2013; Ligthart, Meynen & Douglas 2022.

7 Lemley & Volokh 2018; Ligthart et al. 2021a.

8 Bublitz & Merkel 2014; Kirchmair 2019; Ligthart et al. 2021b.

9 Rusconi & Mitchener-Nissen 2013; Moratti & Patterson 2016; Claydon 2017; Meynen 2017; Van Toor 2017; Ligthart et al. 2020.

10 Mecacci & Haselager 2019, p. 444.

11 I will discuss these technologies in more detail in Chapter 2.

12 For example, Greely & Wagner 2011; Nadelhoffer & Sinnott-Armstrong 2012; Nadelhoffer et al. 2012; Simpson 2012; Morse & Roskies 2013; Jones, Schall & Shen 2014; Shen 2016; Meynen 2020.

neuroimaging, such as brain-based lie and memory detection[13] and neuroimaging to diagnose brain anomalies and to predict future dangerousness.[14] Moreover, some applications have already been used in criminal proceedings in many countries,[15] including European legal systems such as in England and Wales, the Netherlands, Italy, and Slovenia.[16] This kind of brain-reading has contributed to the determination of guilt, the imposition of sanctions, and, most prominently, to the assessment of legal responsibility (i.e. in the context of the insanity defence).[17]

In medicine, patients normally *consent* to neuroimaging, for example to diagnose traumatic brain injury or to identify a brain tumour. In criminal law, however, defendants and convicted offenders may well be reluctant to cooperate in brain-reading technology, since it could jeopardise their interests. At the same time, these technologies could be particularly valuable with respect to uncooperative defendants and offenders who are unwilling to share information. This raises the question of whether it could be legally permissible to apply brain-reading *coercively* – that is, against the will of the individual.[18] Coercive brain-reading in criminal law creates fundamental legal questions with respect to a variety of human rights. As follows from the literature, particularly relevant are the prohibition of ill-treatment, the right to respect for private life, the right to freedom of thought, the right to freedom of expression, and the privilege against self-incrimination.[19]

Recently, researchers from different disciplines have stressed the urgency of human rights concerns regarding emerging neurotechnologies. Their message is clear: it is time for the law to act.[20] To date, the permissibility of coercive brain-reading has mostly been discussed regarding the US legal context.[21] Meanwhile, there is a lack of well-developed European research on the possibilities and limitations of coercive brain-reading in criminal law.[22] The present book aims to fill this gap as far as it concerns a lack of *legal* scholarship. It provides a systematic analysis of the overarching legal framework for coercive forensic brain-reading in light of European human rights law.

13 Verschuere, Ben-Shakhar & Meijer 2011; Farah et al. 2014; Rosenfeld 2018.

14 Simpson 2012; Aharoni et al. 2013; Glenn & Raine 2014; Delfin et al. 2019.

15 Chandler 2015; Farahany 2015; Alimardani & Chin 2019.

16 Catley & Claydon 2015; De Kogel & Westgeest 2015; Hafner 2019; Ferrua 2020.

17 Ibid.

18 Farahany 2012a; Nugent 2012b; Shen 2013; Van Toor 2017; Ligthart et al. 2020.

19 For the European context, see, for example, Rusconi & Mitchener-Nissen 2013; Bublitz 2014; Encinas de Muñagorri & Saas 2016; Van Toor 2017; Ligthart 2019a; Ligthart et al. 2020.

20 Ienca & Andorno 2017; Yuste et al. 2017; Goering et al. 2021.

21 See, for example, Thompson 2005; Stoller & Wolpe 2007; Fox 2008; Meegan 2008; Holley 2009; Greely & Wagner 2011; Farahany 2012a, 2012b; Nugent 2012b; Shen 2013; Pardo & Patterson 2015; Blitz 2017.

22 A few examples: Rusconi & Mitchener-Nissen 2013; Bublitz 2014; Van Toor 2017; Ligthart et al. 2020.

1.2 COERCIVE BRAIN-READING IN CRIMINAL LAW: FOCUS ON EUROPE

Neuroimaging technologies enable us to examine brains and their activities. In general, two types of technologies can be distinguished: structural and functional neuroimaging.[23] *Structural* neuroimaging, like CT and MRI, shows the structure of a person's brain. It visualises brain anatomy and sometimes pathophysiological changes. By contrast, *functional* neuroimaging, such as fMRI, EEG, and PET, detects brain activity. These techniques yield information about brain functioning, sometimes allowing us to draw inferences about mental states.[24]

From various perspectives, research has been done on potential *forensic* applications of these neuroimaging technologies.[25] This book addresses four different types of brain-reading that have received much scholarly attention as they could contribute to answering central questions in criminal law:

1. brain-based lie detection,[26]
2. brain-based detection of recognition ('concealed information test' or 'guilty knowledge test'),[27]
3. brain-based diagnostics of mental and neural disorders,[28] and
4. brain-based prediction of future dangerousness ('neuroprediction').[29]

These four brain-reading applications are further discussed in Chapter 2, where their potential to assist in the determination of central notions of criminal law will be considered. For now, it suffices to note that it has been argued that these technologies could, each in their own way, assist in the determination of guilt, legal responsibility, and recidivism risks.[30]

As mentioned, some types of brain-reading have already been used in criminal justice.[31] Others, such as brain-based lie detection and concealed information tests, are in need of further research. Nevertheless, it is important to anticipate upcoming developments and to consider potential legal implications of coercive brain-reading in criminal law – before the technology actually arrives in court.[32] This is particularly

[23] Richmond 2012, p. 3.
[24] Roskies 2013a, 2013b.
[25] For example, Simpson 2012; Morse & Roskies 2013; Pardo & Patterson 2015; Moratti & Patterson 2016.
[26] Farah et al. 2014.
[27] Meijer et al. 2014.
[28] Simpson 2012.
[29] Glenn & Raine 2014.
[30] See, for example, Greely & Wagner 2011; Meixner & Rosenfeld 2011; Nadelhoffer et al. 2012; De Kogel & Westgeest 2015; Farahany 2015; Pardo & Patterson 2015, p. 108; Poldrack et al. 2018; Noyon et al. 2019; Meynen 2020.
[31] Catley & Claydon 2015; Chandler 2015; De Kogel & Westgeest 2015; Farahany 2015; Alimardani & Chin 2019; Hafner 2019; Ferrua 2020.
[32] Greely 2009, p. 53; Nadelhoffer & Sinnott-Armstrong 2012, p. 634.

important in view of the ambition that human rights considerations should already be embedded in the development phase of new (neuro)technologies.[33]

Human rights set boundaries to the permissible range of investigative powers in criminal law. Coercive use of brain-reading raises principal questions regarding fundamental rights, enshrined in the European Convention for the Protection of Human Rights and Fundamental Freedoms (ECHR) and in the Charter of Fundamental Rights (CFR) of the European Union (EU). More specifically, the question arises whether and, if so, under which conditions coercive brain-reading in criminal law could be permissible under:

A. the prohibition of torture, inhuman, and degrading treatment (Article 3 ECHR/Article 4 CFR),[34]
B. the right to respect for private life (Article 8 ECHR/Articles 7 and 8 CFR),[35]
C. the right to freedom of thought (Article 9 ECHR/Article 10 CFR),[36]
D. the right to freedom of expression (Article 10 ECHR/Article 11 CFR),[37] and
E. the privilege against self-incrimination (Article 6 ECHR/Articles 47 and 48 CFR[38]).[39]

Insofar the CFR contains rights that correspond to rights and freedoms guaranteed by the ECHR, Article 52(3) CFR holds that the meaning and scope of those rights shall be the same as of those guaranteed under the ECHR. Besides, the provisions of the Charter are addressed to the institutions and bodies of the EU and to national authorities when implementing EU law (Article 51 CFR). Accordingly, its relevance to the application of neurotechnology in national criminal cases is limited. Therefore, this book focusses on the well-developed and more nuanced case-law and doctrine on the ECHR.[40] Below, we will briefly consider the relevance of the above-mentioned human rights for coercive brain-reading in criminal law.

The five fundamental rights and freedoms mentioned here establish crucial legal conditions and boundaries with respect to coercive brain-reading. In addition, the right to a fair trial (Article 6 ECHR) could require procedural guarantees when forensic brain-reading has violated the Convention in the determination of a

33 As has been expressed by the Committee on Bioethics of the Council of Europe 2019, § 14–15, 21–22.
34 Ligthart 2019a. Cf. Thompson 2005.
35 Rusconi & Mitchener-Nissen 2013; Ligthart 2019b.
36 Rusconi & Mitchener-Nissen 2013; Bublitz 2014.
37 Ligthart 2020b.
38 See also Directive (EU) 2016/343.
39 Rusconi & Mitchener-Nissen 2013; Ligthart et al. 2020.
40 In developing a European legal framework for coercive forensic brain-reading, other European legal instruments may be relevant as well. Examples are the Convention on Human Rights and Biomedicine (Oviedo Convention), and Directive (EU) 2016/680 (on the protection of natural persons with regard to the processing of personal data by competent authorities for the purposes of the prevention, investigation, detection, or prosecution of criminal offences or the execution of criminal penalties).

criminal charge. The aim of this book is to identify and analyse these substantive conditions, boundaries, and procedural guarantees.

Such a systematic study is important for – at least – three reasons. First, brain-reading technologies have already entered criminal justice systems within Europe.[41] Meanwhile, an overarching legal analysis of their use has been lacking. Coercive brain-reading raises questions under different human rights enshrined in the European Convention on Human Rights. Article 1 of the Convention prescribes that these human rights should be secured by all member States to everyone within their jurisdictions. By analysing the legal implications of coercive brain-reading, this study informs and facilitates member States in the protection of fundamental rights when introducing brain-reading into criminal law.

Second, to date, the permissibility of coercive brain-reading has mostly been discussed regarding the US legal context. While US legal scholarship on coercive brain-reading provides helpful insights and directions, it cannot be transferred directly into European jurisdictions. The legal systems are fundamentally different (US Constitution v. ECHR). The unique European legal context requires its own debate, tailored to the system of European human rights law.[42] As yet, in-depth legal research on the relation between coercive brain-reading and human rights in Europe is scarce.[43]

Third, advances in neurotechnology have given rise to a fundamental debate about the sustainability of the present framework of human rights in Europe. In this debate, emerging technologies function as a lens on the law and its persuasives. In order to offer adequate human rights protection to our inner mental states and to protect citizens against different types of brain-reading, it has been argued to *reconsider* existing human rights.[44] Moreover, for this purpose, some authors argue that we should introduce *novel* human rights – 'neurorights' – such as a *right to mental privacy* 'which aims to protect any bit or set of brain information about an individual recorded by a neurodevice'.[45] Some scholars even advocate the development of a Universal Declaration of Human Neuro-Rights.[46] Meanwhile, others contend that existing human rights are well equipped to protect our minds and to regulate novel neurotechnologies. We should just interpret and specify these rights in light of neurotechnological developments.[47]

The debate about the sustainability of human rights in view of neurotechnology is not only a matter of scholarly deliberation. Legislators and policy-makers, including

41 Catley & Claydon 2015; De Kogel & Westgeest 2015; Hafner 2019; Ferrua 2020.

42 Cf. Meynen 2016a, p. 162; 2016b, p. 120.

43 A few examples: Van Toor 2017; Ligthart et al. 2020.

44 Bublitz 2014; McCarthy-Jones 2019; Bublitz 2021.

45 Ienca & Andorno 2017, p. 15. See also Bublitz & Merkel 2014; Lavazza 2018; Yuste, Genser & Herman 2021.

46 Sommaggio et al. 2017; Sommaggio & Mazzocca 2020.

47 Alegre 2017; Ligthart et al. 2020; Michalowski 2020; Bublitz 2022.

the Committee on Bioethics of the Council of Europe, are now collaborating with neuroscientists, ethicists, and lawyers with the aim of developing sustainable laws to protect brains and minds.[48] To anticipate the legal intricacies novel neurotechnologies raise, the Committee on Bioethics has considered that:

> It therefore needs to be assessed whether these issues can be sufficiently addressed by the existing human rights framework or whether new human rights pertaining to cognitive liberty, mental privacy, and mental integrity and psychological continuity, need to be entertained in order to govern neurotechnologies. Alternatively, other flexible forms of good governance may be better suited for regulating neurotechnologies.[49]

Recently, Chile has made progress in incorporating explicit neurorights into its constitution.[50] And Spain has presented a first version of a Digital Rights Charter that should also protect from neurotechnologies, therefore including a right to 'mental privacy'.[51] Meanwhile, the level and scope of human rights protection against brain-reading technologies in Europe are still unclear. Do we actually need explicit 'neurorights' in Europe? Prior to altering or introducing human rights intended to protect against brain-reading in criminal law, the precise scope of *existing* human rights should be determined.[52] Assessing the established scope of human rights protection against forensic brain-reading is the central aim of this book, facilitating the broader debate on the introduction of neurorights.

In conclusion, we should only develop and apply brain-reading technologies in a way that respects human rights.[53] The member States of the ECHR bear special responsibility for protecting fundamental rights and freedoms when introducing brain-reading in criminal justice.[54] Therefore, it is essential to systematically examine coercive forensic brain-reading in light of European human rights law. The upcoming chapters provides such an examination.

To date, no case-law of the ECtHR exists on coercive brain-reading in criminal law.[55] To overcome this lack of research material, this study follows a methodology that has also been used in previous publications.[56] It compares 'coercive forensic

48 Ienca 2021; UN Special Rapporteur on Freedom of Religion and Belief 2021; Report of the International Bioethics Committee of UNESCO, Ethical Issues of Neurotechnology, SHS/BIO/IBC28/2021/3Rev. (15 December 2021).

49 Committee on Bioethics of the Council of Europe 2019, p. 9.

50 Muñoz 2019; Yuste, Genser & Herrmann 2021.

51 Nadal 2020.

52 Cf. Ligthart et al. 2020; Michalowski 2020; Susi 2020; Ligthart, Kooijmans & Meynen 2021b.

53 As stressed in the Strategic Action Plan on Human Rights and Technologies in Biomedicine (2020–2025) of the Committee on Bioethics of the Council of Europe.

54 As emphasised by the Grand Chamber: ECtHR (GC) 4 December 2008, appl. nos. 30562/04 and 30566/04 (S. & *Marper*/UK), § 110.

55 Ienca & Andorno 2017; Ligthart et al. 2020.

56 Ligthart 2018, 2019a, 2019b, 2020b; Ligthart et al. 2020.

brain-reading' with other means of data-acquisition, about which case-law does already exist, such as mandatory DNA testing, obligatory witness testimonies, and coercive employment of X-ray (e.g. in prison). The legal implications of such 'comparable' means of investigation will be determined. From case-law on those comparable means, this study deduces legal boundaries that will be relevant with respect to coercive brain-reading under the ECHR. In that process of deduction, I will take account of both relevant similarities and important differences.

In addition, when drawing analogies, it is important to take into consideration the context of the analogy. For example, regarding the prohibition of ill-treatment, different aspects of brain-reading are relevant compared with the right to freedom of thought. Under Article 3 ECHR, the level of physical or mental suffering caused by coercive brain-reading is essential. Meanwhile, Article 9 ECHR is rather concerned with whether brain-reading identifies 'thoughts' in the meaning of Article 9(1) ECHR. Therefore, this book draws distinctive analogies in light of each specific right and freedom.

2

Brain-Reading Technologies

Their Legally Relevant Features

2.1 INTRODUCTION

This chapter discusses five brain-reading applications that can yield information from a person's brain and could therefore, potentially, contribute to answering central questions in criminal law. It considers the state of the art of brain-reading technology and identifies current possibilities and limitations in the context of criminal law. Consecutively, the following applications are discussed: (1) brain-based lie detection, (2) brain-based detection of recognition, (3) brain-based diagnostics of mental and neural disorders, and (4) brain-based prediction of future dangerousness.[1] This chapter also briefly signals another, relatively novel emerging brain-reading application: (5) the neural representation of real-time thoughts.

In order to examine how established human rights should respond to emerging brain-reading neurotechnologies, it is essential to understand the technologies and the kind of information they could disclose. Based on empirical studies,[2] this chapter prepares the ground for the normative analysis by examining the following descriptive features of each brain-reading application: (1) the precise information it yields, (2) how that information could contribute to answering central questions in criminal law, (3) what it means, *de facto*, for an individual to be subjected to the brain-reading application (from a medical point of view, like whether it is physically invasive and/or poses health risks), and (4) whether the brain-reading application

[1] Some of these tests, like lie detection and the CIT, can also be applied with other techniques, such as measuring changes of the autonomic nervous system (ANS) with a polygraph. Since the present study focusses on *brain*-reading, those techniques exceed the scope of this chapter.

[2] In this regard, Pardo & Patterson 2015, p. 42 warn that 'empirical claims about neuroscience and its relationship to the mind will presuppose some conception of the mind (and the phenomena picked out by the concept of mind). Whether this conception makes sense will affect the cogency of the claims.' Although an examination of the neuroscientific underpinnings and the philosophical conceptions of the mind as underlying the empirical studies could, indeed, be meaningful, such an examination is, however, beyond the scope of the present *legal* analyses from the human rights perspective.

requires active, passive,[3] or no participation of the subject. As this book is on the legal implications of *coercive* brain-reading, this chapter also considers the concept of coercion, focussing on two general types that could enable the enforcement of different brain-reading applications.

From here, this chapter proceeds as follows. The next sections consecutively discuss the characteristics and forensic possibilities of brain-based lie detection, the concealed information test (CIT), brain-based diagnostics, neuroprediction, and the neural representation of real-time thoughts. Next, Section 2.7 discusses two types of coercion that can be employed when enforcing different types of brain-reading. Section 2.8 draws conclusions.

2.2 BRAIN-BASED LIE DETECTION

2.2.1 *Type of Information and Legal Relevance*

One area of neuroscientific research that is relevant to criminal law concerns the detection of lying. How 'lying' should exactly be defined in this context is open to debate. Here, we use a concept that is used in both empirical studies and normative analyses: deliberately making false statements in a context where the norm is telling the truth.[4]

Brain-based lie detection aims to measure neural changes that correlate with the deliberate provision of deceptive information.[5] As Pardo and Patterson note:

> As with traditional polygraphs, the neuroscience research is looking for a correlation between lies, deceptive behavior or knowledge, on the one hand, and something else going on with the subject's body, on the other. With polygraphs it is increased heart rates, breathing, and perspiring; with neuroscience it is increased blood flow to certain regions of the brain or electrical activity.[6]

Clearly, accurate lie detection would be invaluable to criminal justice. It could be helpful in the context of police investigations and during the execution of criminal sanctions. Lie detection could contribute to verifying statements of defendants and convicted offenders, for example, as to whether the defendant was present at the crime scene at the time of the offence, or whether an offender has complied with the conditions of parole.[7]

3 'Passive participation' may sound contradictory. Here, this term is used to refer to those brain-reading applications that require participation in the sense that the person has to be willing to subject herself to the neuroimaging technology and lie still. The required participation mainly consists in the person not resisting or manipulating the measurements. See Meynen 2017, p. 320.

4 See, for example, Lisofsky et al. 2014, p. 113; Pardo & Patterson 2015, pp. 81, 100 and 108–110.

5 See, for example, Meijer & Verschuere 2018, pp. 219–220; Brown & Murphy 2010, p. 1138; Greely 2009, p. 47.

6 Pardo & Patterson 2015, p. 106.

7 Cf. Pardo & Patterson 2015, p. 79.

Brain-based lie detection might also contribute to diagnosing particular mental disorders, for example, in the context of the insanity defence.[8] In diagnosing mental disorders, the forensic psychiatrist often has to rely to a great extent on the patient's own account about his subjective mental states. Especially in the context of criminal law, patients, defendants, and convicted offenders might have reasons not to tell the truth or to malinger and fake certain symptoms of a mental disease, for example, in order to be acquitted by reason of insanity or to reduce time in prison.[9] Brain-based lie detection could be a helpful tool to verify statements about symptoms of mental illness, for instance when a defendant claims to have heard commanding voices at the time of the offence, forcing her to kill the victim.[10]

2.2.2 *Technological Features*

Lie detection with functional neuroimaging works through (indirect) measurements of brain activity while the subject answers a specific set of questions. The general assumption is that lying is a complex cognitive process, requiring suppression of the truth, communication of a coherent falsehood, and modifications of behaviour to convince the other of the provided false statements. The mental process of telling a lie is thought to activate specific brain areas, which can be detected with functional neuroimaging.[11]

In 2001, Spence et al. tested this assumption and they found that particular parts of the brain were indeed associated with lying.[12] Subsequent studies confirmed this assumption of brain-based lie detection as well.[13] There seems considerable agreement across studies on the brain areas that are more active during instructed lying than during truth telling.[14]

Most studies on brain-based lie detection focus on the use of fMRI.[15] This technology identifies changes in a magnetic field, caused by an increased amount of oxygen in blood flow in the brain ('hemodynamic response').[16] Although fMRI

8 Langleben, Willard & Moriarty 2017, 2019, 2020. Cf. Linden 2012.

9 Meynen 2016b, pp. 51–52.

10 Meynen 2017; Langleben, Willard & Moriarty 2012. Cf. Linden 2012, pp. 131–133.

11 Spence et al. 2001; Kozel et al. 2005, 2009.

12 Spence et al. 2001.

13 Farah et al. 2014; Gamer 2014; Lisofsky et al. 2014; Christ et al. 2009.

14 Farah et al. 2014, p. 124; Ganis 2018, pp. 150–152.

15 Farah et al. 2014; Gamer 2014; Lisofsky et al. 2014.

16 It works more or less as follows. Thinking, doing, feeling, seeing – it all requires activity in different brain areas. In order to be activated, the brain needs energy, provided through blood flow carrying oxygen from the lungs ('hemodynamic responses'). If the oxygen is released to an organ, such as the brain, a particular protein in our blood ('hemoglobin') becomes paramagnetic, and will therefore *disturb* the magnetic field inside an fMRI-scanner. If a brain area increases in activity, the blood flow will supply more oxygen than the activated brain area actually demands. As a consequence, the increase in blood flow in that brain area is not accompanied with the same increase in oxygen consumption by that area. Therefore, the oxygen content in the blood increases, *restoring* the magnetic field in an fMRI. This results in an increased imaging signal ('blood oxygen level dependent (BOLD) signal'). See Raichle 2009, 2010; Roskies 2013a, pp. 41–70.

produces noise, which may be unpleasant for the person in question,[17] it is generally considered safe. But not anyone can undergo fMRI. There are certain contraindications (conditions that make use of fMRI impossible):

> Contraindications include any metal in the body, pacemakers, and other devices. Even nonobvious metal, such as tiny fragments embedded in the eyes of metalworkers that otherwise may go undetected, could lead to serious burning. Also, the donut-shaped core of the machine is quite a small space. Individuals who are claustrophobic or who have a particularly large body frame may not be able to participate in fMRI research.[18]

Besides fMRI-based lie detection, researchers have also experimented with PET, single-photon emission computed tomography (SPECT), and EEG.[19] PET and SPECT work through localising radioactive contrast agent in the blood of the subject's brain.[20] For example, fluorine-18 can be injected and traced with a PET and SPECT-scan, visualising the fluorine-18 in the blood flow in the brain. Injection of radioactive chemicals is, however, physically invasive. Moreover, it exposes the subject to a certain dose of radiation and could entail a variety of side effects, such as fever, nausea, difficulty with breathing or swallowing, and unusual tiredness or weakness.[21] Exposure to radiation might even increase the risk of developing cancer. Rushing, Pryma & Langleben write:

> Doses of radiation below 1 Sv [=1000 mSv] are unlikely to produce any immediate detectable changes in humans, though they have risk of inducing mutations which may lead or predispose to cancer formation at a later time.[22]

According to the Dutch National Institute for Public Health and the Environment, a PET and SPECT of the brain exposes the subject to doses of radiation of, respectively, 1 and 6.9 millisievert (mSv). In general, it is assumed that an effective dose of 1 mSv increases the risk of developing cancer and die from it with 0.005 per cent.[23]

EEG detects electrical activity. Electrodes on the skull of the subject record different voltages of brain electricity. Those electrical charges reflect brain activity.[24] In clinical practice, EEG is routinely used by neurologists when diagnosing epilepsy.[25]

17 Shen 2013, p. 701.
18 Brown & Murphy 2010, p. 1138.
19 Meijer et al. 2016; Farah et al. 2014; Gamer 2014; Lisofsky et al. 2014.
20 Rushing, Pryma & Langleben 2012.
21 See, for example, www.mayoclinic.org (searched for 'Fludeoxyglucose F 18 (Intravenous Route)', visited on 26 June 2020).
22 Rushing, Pryma & Langleben 2012, p. 7.
23 www.rivm.nl, searched for 'Blootstelling aan straling in de gezondheidszorg' (visited on 15 April 2021).
24 Ganis & Rosenfeld 2011, p. 103; Haron-Jones & Peterson 2009, p. 170; Bartholow & Amodio 2009, p. 199.
25 Pillai & Sperling 2006.

In sum, brain-based lie detection has been applied with fMRI, PET, SPECT, and EEG. Most research focusses on fMRI. fMRI lie detection is based on the *differentiation of deception* (DoD) paradigm.[26] The basic idea of this paradigm is as follows. While an fMRI-scan measures brain activity, the subject answers a set of presented[27] questions by pressing a yes-or-no-button.[28] Whereas some questions relate to the crime ('did you steal the ring?'), others do not ('is Rome the capital of Italy?'). Each question must be answered twice: once truthfully and once deceptively.[29] According to the hypothesis, the brain areas that are involved in lying will show more activation during the deceptive responses compared with the truthful answers.[30] Hence, if the subject lies about having stolen the ring, the brain areas associated with lying will be more active compared with the truthful response to the question of whether Rome is the capital of Italy.

Using an fMRI differentiation of deception paradigm, Kozel et al. were able to identify 90 per cent of the lying subjects ('sensitivity').[31] Similar studies showed sensitivity levels between 71 per cent and 100 per cent.[32] But high sensitivity not always means that the test is accurate. It is also essential to know how many honest subjects were wrongfully qualified as a liar ('specificity'). For example, in 2009, Kozel et al. identified 100 per cent of the lying subjects. Meanwhile, they also accused no less than 67 per cent of the truthful subjects of being deceptive.[33] This meant that the specificity of the test was only 33 per cent. Improving the accuracy of lie detection is still an important scientific challenge.

This challenge closely relates to the issue of ecological validity. Can we equate lying in a laboratorial setting with lying in real life, such as in court? Telling a lie in court – 'I did not kill the victim' – may elicit different emotional arousal, for instance.[34] Meanwhile, fMRI lie detection with the differentiation of deception paradigm has only been tested in laboratorial settings. An important current challenge is to determine the accuracy of this test in real-life cases.

Another scientific concern about brain-based lie detection pertains to its sensitivity to 'countermeasures'.[35] These are deliberate physical or mental strategies employed by the subject aiming to *manipulate* or otherwise *distort* the test results.[36] As Kanwisher writes:

[26] Meijer et al. 2016, p. 595. This is different from the control question test paradigm, used in the context of the well-known polygraph test.
[27] Either visually or aurally: Pardo & Patterson 2015, p. 82, footnote 12.
[28] Kozel et al. 2005, p. 506.
[29] Meijer et al. 2016, p. 595.
[30] Spence 2008, p. 309.
[31] Kozel et al. 2005.
[32] Gamer 2014, p. 177.
[33] Kozel et al. 2009.
[34] Meijer et al. 2016, p. 599.
[35] Wagner et al. 2016; Ganis et al. 2011.
[36] Cf. Ben-Shakhar 2011, p. 200; Labkosky & Rosenfeld 2012, p. 1.

> Functional MRI data are useless if the subject is moving more than a few millimeters. (…) This is not just a matter of moving your head – you can completely mess up the imaging data just by moving your tongue in your mouth, or by closing your eyes and not being able to read the questions. Of course, these things will be detectable, so the experimenter would know that the subject was using countermeasures. But there are also countermeasures subjects could use that would not be detectable, like performing mental arithmetic. You can probably activate all of those putative lie regions just by subtracting seven iteratively in your head.[37]

As a consequence, to be successful, brain-based lie detection requires not only that the subject *observes* the presented questions and that he *answers* them by *pressing* a yes-or-no-button, it also requires the subject to *refrain* from using countermeasures. Accordingly, this brain-reading application requires *active participation* of the subject.

Due to present scientific limitations, more research is required before brain-based lie detection should be applied in real-life criminal cases.[38] Yet, despite current constrains, fMRI-based lie detection has already been offered on the commercial market.[39] It has even been introduced, though as yet rejected, as evidenced in criminal procedures in the USA.[40] These developments urge the law to anticipate future scientific developments in brain-based lie detection. As Greely notes: 'Should we develop effective lie detection, we will need to decide how, and under what circumstances, we want it to be usable'.[41]

2.3 BRAIN-BASED DETECTION OF RECOGNITION: THE P300-BASED CIT

2.3.1 *Type of Information and Legal Relevance*

The CIT is also known as the guilty knowledge test.[42] This test enables the detection of *recognition* of particular information, such as central aspects of a crime.[43] The CIT detects a brain signal that is related to salience – that is, to the importance of particular stimuli to an individual. In practice, things are usually salient to us because we *recognise* them. As Lykken, the founding father of the CIT, put it:

37 Kanwisher 2009, p. 12. Cf. Mecacci & Haselager 2019, p. 455.

38 For example, Wagner et al. 2016, p. 4; Farah et al. 2014, pp. 125–127; Gamer 2014, p. 180. Cf. Meijer & Verschuere 2017.

39 By companies such as NoLieMRI Inc. and Cephos Corporation. See also Greely 2009, p. 53.

40 For example, United States v. Semrau, 693 G.3d 510 (6th Cir. 2012). See for a discussion Farah et al. 2014, pp. 127–128; Jones, Schall & Shen 2014, p. 473; Pardo & Patterson 2015, pp. 86–88; Miller 2010.

41 Greely 2009, p. 53.

42 Lykken 1959, 1981.

43 See, for instance, Meijer et al. 2016, pp. 596–598; Rosenfeld et al. 2013, p. 118; Verschuere & Meijer 2014, p. 168; Meijer et al. 2014, p. 879; Farwell, Richardson & Richardson 2013, p. 268.

> Use of physiological measurements to detect not lying, but the presence of 'guilty knowledge' requires only the more reasonable assumption that a guilty person will show some involuntary physiological response (…) to stimuli related to remembered details of his crime.[44]

Such information – about whether the subject recognises particular crime-related stimuli – could contribute to legal decision-making, particularly in the determination of guilt or in reopening criminal cases.[45] For example, a CIT could determine whether a suspect recognises the murder weapon,[46] the stolen ring,[47] the crime scene,[48] the victim,[49] the location where the victim's body or murder weapon has been hidden,[50] or the password used to hack a computer system.[51]

Obviously, the mere recognition of an object related to a crime does not imply involvement or guilt. But it is certainly a finding that could be relevant to law enforcement, for example, to continue criminal investigations with respect to a particular person.[52]

In Japan, the CIT (applied with a polygraph) has already been used on a regular basis in criminal justice.[53] In the USA, the results of a brain-based recognition test similar to the CIT ('brain fingerprinting') have been used in a few criminal procedures as well.[54] Other types of memory detection have been introduced in criminal cases in Italy (Implicit Association Test)[55] and India (Brain Electrical Oscillation Signature Profiling).[56]

Apart from investigating crimes committed in the past, the CIT could also assist in identifying knowledge of a *future* criminal offence. Think, for example, of preventing terrorism.[57] As Meixner and Rosenfeld state, the 'concealed information test could be highly effective in detecting an individual's knowledge of a planned terrorist attack'.[58] Similarly, Meijer et al. concluded that the CIT could be helpful

44 Lykken 1959, p. 385.
45 For example, Verschuere & Meijer 2014, p. 166; Farwell 2012, pp. 131–132; Van Toor 2017, pp. 101–105. In Japan, the CIT also contributes to preventing false accusations: Osugi 2011, p. 258.
46 Lukács et al. 2016, p. 57.
47 Rosenfeld et al. 2013, p. 127.
48 Iacono 2011, p. 14.
49 Meijer et al. 2007, p. 235.
50 Osugi 2011, pp. 261–264; Meijer & Van Koppen 2008, p. 44.
51 Verschuere & Meijer 2014, p. 166
52 Iacono 2011, pp. 16–17. Cf. Verschuere & Meijer 2014, p. 168; Farwell, Richardson & Richardson 2013, p. 266.
53 Matsuda, Ogawa & Tsuneoka 2019; Osugi 2011; Iacono 2011.
54 Farwell 2012, pp. 132–133; Farwell & Makeig 2005. This test, and the way it has been presented, has received serious scientific critique: for example, Rosenfeld 2005; Meijer et al. 2013a.
55 Ferrua 2020, pp. 410–411.
56 Gaudet 2011.
57 Meixner & Rosenfeld 2011; Ben-Shakhar 2012, p. 7; Rosenfeld 2011, p. 83; Verschuere & Meijer 2014, pp. 166–167.
58 Meixner & Rosenfeld 2011, p. 153.

to unveil plans about a terrorist attack by detecting whether a person recognises the target, location, and date of the upcoming assault.[59]

Perhaps, CITs could also assist in identifying the preparation of other serious crimes, such as murder, rape, and robbery. At the same time, preparing such crimes often consists in collecting everyday tools, such as tie wraps, sport bags, a scooter, or a mobile phone. There can be many reasons why people recognise such objects (which have not been used in a crime yet). Hence, when applying CITs, it may be difficult to include enough relevant items in order to identify the preparation of, say, a robbery.

Finally, it has been argued that the CIT could contribute to forensic diagnostics.[60] Faking and malingering are central concerns in forensic mental evaluations.[61] Therefore, in some cases, CITs might be helpful to verifying claims of a defendant, for example, that he suffers from amnesia.[62]

2.3.2 *Technological Features*

To date, brain-based CITs have mainly been examined with EEG and fMRI.[63] Most studies used EEG.[64] Therefore, this section focusses on EEG-based CITs. Applying EEG will also be much easier and cheaper compared with fMRI, for example, at the police station or in prison.

Using EEG, the CIT measures a specific event-related potential (ERP): P300.[65] This positive electrical voltage in the brain occurs automatically between 300 and 800 milliseconds after observing a stimulus. It increases when the stimulus is significant to the subject.[66] As Rosenfeld writes:

> The P300 is a special ERP component that results whenever a *meaningful* piece of information is *rarely* presented among a random series of more frequently presented, non-meaningful stimuli often of the same category as the meaningful stimulus.[67]

Observing a meaningful stimulus provokes a larger P300-amplitude compared with non-meaningful stimuli. In general, this indicates that the subject *recognises* the stimulus.[68] The P300-CIT has a multiple-choice format with one relevant and multiple irrelevant

59 Meijer et al. 2013b.
60 Verschuere & Meijer 2014, p. 166; Meynen 2017.
61 Cf. Section 2.2.1.
62 Rosenfeld 2020, p. 4; Huntjes, Verschuere & McNally 2012; Ellwanger et al. 1996.
63 Meijer et al. 2016. Initially, the CIT was applied with measurements of the ANS, such as respiration, heart rate, and blood pressure: Lykken 1981; Ambach & Gamer 2018.
64 Meijer et al. 2016, p. 598.
65 For a recent review, see Rosenfeld 2020.
66 Sutton et al. 1965, p. 1187; Meijer et al. 2014, p. 881; Verschuere & Meijer 2014, p. 164.
67 Rosenfeld 2011, p. 64.
68 Verschuere & Meijer 2014, p. 164; Farwell 2012, p. 118.

but conceivable options. The options are selected in a way that they are equally plausible and indistinguishable for someone without intimate knowledge of the crime.[69]

For example, imagine that a defendant, suspected of having murdered a young white woman with dark hair, is subjected to a P300-based CIT. Five pictures are presented to the defendant: four pictures of a random young white women with brown hair (the 'irrelevants'); one of the actual victim (the 'probe'). If the defendant's P300-amplitude is significantly larger when observing the picture of the victim compared with the other pictures, that suggests that he *recognises* the victim.[70]

Clearly, this does not imply guilt. But if our suspect also recognises the murder weapon, the crime scene, the getaway car, and the clothes the victim wore when she was killed, the likelihood that the suspect somehow was involved in the crime will grow. Importantly, increasing the number of items will make the test more powerful. Presenting four questions, each with five possible answers (i.e. four irrelevants and one probe), means that the chance of an 'innocent' subject recognising all crime-related probes is limited to 0.16 per cent.[71]

Different protocols exist for the application of the P300-based CIT.[72] In general, they all consist in (1) EEG measurement of an ERP (P300), while (2) the subject attentively observes the presented stimuli (usually pictures). In order to measure P300, three electrodes are placed on the subject's scalp.[73] During the test, it is important that the subject pays full attention to observing the presented stimuli. The P300 wave will only occur when the subject is actively engaged.[74] Such *attentive* participation can be stimulated by requiring the subject to press a button if she perceives particular stimuli ('targets').[75] Whereas stimuli can be presented either auditory or visually,[76] the latter has been considered most accurate.[77]

69 Meijer & Van Toor 2021, pp. 103–104.

70 Cf. Meijer et al. 2007.

71 Rosenfeld et al. 2013, p. 119:

> For each question, if there are five choices, as above, the probability that a non-knowledgeable (i.e., innocent) subject will respond by chance with the largest physiological response to the probe item (a false positive outcome) is 1/5 = .2. If one can come up with as many as four independent questions about four independent items of information, the chance hit probability for all four is reduced to .2 to the 4th power = .0016. Researchers appreciate this feature of the CIT: the fact that by adding independent questions, the false positive probability can be reduced to whatever specifiable low value is required by a given agency or institution, thereby offering good protection to innocent suspects from mistaken decisions regarding their knowledge of crime-relevant information.

72 For example, Rosenfeld 2008; Labkovsky & Rosenfeld 2012; Hu et al. 2012; Farwell, Richardson & Richardson 2013.

73 Rosenfeld 2011, p. 64; Rosenfeld et al. 2008, p. 908; Farwell, Richardson & Richardson 2013, p. 270.

74 Picton 1992, p. 456.

75 Meixner & Rosenfeld 2014, p. 1997; Rosenfeld et al. 2013, p. 120; Farwell, Richardson & Richardson 2013, p. 293.

76 Rosenfeld et al. 2008, p. 906; Meixner & Rosenfeld 2014, p. 1997.

77 Rosenfeld et al. 2015a; Van der Cruyssen et al. 2021. See also Rosenfeld et al. 2015b; Ambach et al. 2010, p. 266.

Researchers have considered the P300 CIT a valid and accurate paradigm for identifying recognition, researched in over a thousand peer-reviewed publications.[78] The test has been qualified as 'highly accurate' in differentiating between knowledgeable and unknowledgeable subjects.[79] Meanwhile, there are important limitations. For example, the P300-CIT can be manipulated by using *countermeasures*.[80] According to Lukács et al., most effective are concealed responses such as small physical movements or recalling a person's name, performed when the *irrelevant* items appear.[81] For instance, if a guilty subject wants to manipulate the test, she could recall emotional memories during the presentation of random guns (irrelevants), but not when she observes the actual murder weapon (probe). Such concealed countermeasures assigned to irrelevant items aim to enlarge the P300 responses with respect to those stimuli, obstructing the identification of (significant) differences between P300-responses to irrelevants and probes.[82] Some countermeasures can be detected,[83] and valuable research has been done on how to limit the impact of manipulative responses.[84] Still, to date, the CIT's susceptibility to countermeasures is an important limitation.[85] Altogether, a successful P300-CIT requires the subject to *attentively observe* the presented stimuli and to *refrain* from using countermeasures. Therefore, the CIT requires *active participation*.[86]

In real life, the accuracy of a CIT can be threatened by exposing 'innocent' subjects to relevant information, for example, through the media or police investigation.[87] Meijer et al. write that once relevant items are leaked to an innocent suspect, the central rationale of the CIT will be jeopardised.[88] When a murder weapon has been repeatedly shown on TV, potentially many people could recognise it. This risk of leakage relates to the issue of ecological validity.[89] In order to limit this risk, a CIT should be performed as soon as possible after a suspect has been identified.[90] In addition, Meijer et al. emphasise that in real life, crimes are often committed under time constraints and stress, which might affect the perpetrator's perception of crime-related details. Moreover, criminal procedures often take place months or even years after a crime. As a consequence, perpetrators

78 Meijer et al. 2013a, pp. 157–158. Cf. Meixner Jr. 2018, p. 411; Meijer et al. 2016, p. 598; Meixner 2012, p. 1459.

79 Meijer et al. 2014, p. 881; Meixner & Rosenfeld 2014, pp. 1994–1995.

80 Rosenfeld et al. 2004; Mertens & Allen 2008; Ben-Shakhar 2011; Lukács et al. 2016.

81 Lukács et al. 2016, p. 57.

82 Rosenfeld et al. 2004.

83 Rosenfeld et al. 2013, pp. 120–121 and 124.

84 Rosenfeld 2008; Labkovsky & Rosenfeld 2012; Hu et al. 2012; Lukács et al. 2016.

85 Rosenfeld 2020.

86 Kraphol 2011, p. 160. Cf. Verschuere & Meijer 2014, p. 166.

87 Bradley et al. 2011.

88 Meijer et al. 2014, p. 897.

89 Meijer et al. 2016, p. 599; Murphy & Rissman 2020, pp. 14–19.

90 Van Toor 2017, pp. 84–89.

could simply forget certain crime-related items.[91] To improve the CIT's ecological validity, more field research is desirable.

2.4 BRAIN-BASED DIAGNOSTICS

2.4.1 *Type of Information and Legal Relevance*

Much research has been done on neuroimaging in mental diseases, like schizophrenia and depression. To date, the correlates found are not robust enough to be used in clinical or forensic psychiatric diagnostics.[92] But neuroimaging is not completely irrelevant in this context.[93] First, technologies such as MRI and CT can contribute to diagnosing particular types of dementia.[94] And as previously mentioned, EEG is used in identifying epilepsy.[95] Second, neuroimaging can be helpful to exclude or confirm somatic causes of mental disturbances, such as a brain tumour or traumatic brain injury.[96]

In some cases, the presence of such brain anomalies can help us to understand or clarify particular behaviour. Famous cases in this regard are those of Phineas Gage (traumatic brain injury)[97] and Michael Oft (brain tumour).[98] To illustrate how the existence of a brain abnormality could contribute to understanding and approaching criminal behaviour in individual cases, the case of Michael Oft is discussed below.[99]

Michael Oft was a healthy, forty-year-old schoolteacher, who at a certain moment in time developed a strong interest in pornography. In the year 2000, he had collected an expanding number of pornographic materials, much involving children and adolescents. Although he felt that his activities were inappropriate, therefore concealing them, he continued to act on his sexual impulses. He also started to make 'subtle sexual advances' towards his prepubescent stepdaughter, which he could conceal from his wife for several weeks. However, when his stepdaughter revealed Michael's secret, he was legally removed from their home. Paedophilia was diagnosed, and he

91 Meijer et al. 2016, p. 599.

92 See, for example, Rodrigues-Amorim et al. 2017; Mohnke et al. 2014; Kelly 2012, p. 114; Farah & Gillihan 2012, p. 465; Michael et al. 2012. Nonetheless, neuroimaging has actually been used to diagnose various types of mental disorders: Kelly 2012, p. 114; Farah & Gillihan 2012, p. 466. Companies such as the Amen Clinics offer brain-based diagnostics of, *inter alia*, depression, anxiety disorders, autism, addiction, ADHD, and PTSS: www.amenclinics.com; www.cerescan.com (visited on 21 October 2019).

93 See, for example, Edersheim, Brendel & Price 2012; Simpson 2012; Moratti & Patterson 2016.

94 Staffaroni et al. 2017; Health Quality Ontario 2014, p. 33; Lamar et al. 2012.

95 Pillai & Sperling 2006.

96 Meynen 2016b, p. 142; Kelly 2012, p. 114; Granacher 2012.

97 See, for example, O'Driscoll & Leach 1998.

98 Burns & Swerdlow 2003; Glenn & Raine 2014.

99 The case details are derived from Burns & Swerdlow 2003 and Glenn & Raine 2014, whose descriptions I follow closely.

was convicted for child molestation. In the context of his conviction, Michael had to choose between imprisonment or participating in a twelve-step treatment programme for sexual addiction. Of course, he chose the latter, but was expelled after soliciting sexual favours from female staff members and other clients at the rehabilitation centre. As a consequence, he had to serve his sentence after all. However, the night before he was due to be transported to prison, he complained about a severe headache. A neurologist ordered an MRI-scan, revealing a large tumour growing in Michael's brain. After the tumour was resected, Michael's behaviour returned to normal. He successfully participated in a treatment programme and was reunited with his wife and stepdaughter. After some months of normal behaviour, his wife discovered child pornography again. Michael was re-examined and it appeared that the tumour had regrown. After a second resection, Michael's behaviour returned to normal again.[100]

According to Glenn and Raine, this case 'comes almost as close as one can get to a causal connection between (…) brain pathology and deviant behaviour'.[101] Indeed, the chronological order of events is suggestive for a causal relation between the brain tumour and criminal behaviour. Meanwhile, the exact *normative* relevance of this relation is open to debate, especially with regard to central legal questions (e.g. was Michael legally insane?).[102]

What is clear though, is that the MRI-scan provided some objectivity to the mental evaluation in this case. Whereas Mr Oft could have had good reasons to *fake* his headache the night before he was to be brought to prison, the MRI-scan made any such suspicion disappear.[103] As previously mentioned, faking, malingering, and not cooperating with forensic evaluations are important limitations of forensic diagnostics. By employing such strategies, defendants sometimes try to reduce sentences or avoid involuntary admission to a forensic hospital. As the case of Michael Oft illustrates, neuroimaging can be a helpful tool in confirming or excluding the presence of brain anomalies. In that way, it provides a certain context to the other findings and observations.[104]

This is also illustrated by a Dutch criminal case. A seventy-one-year-old defendant, suspected of attempted extortion, had been evaluated by several behavioural experts and was subjected to both MRI and PET. The experts concluded that the defendant was suffering from frontotemporal dementia. As a result, he hardly had any moral sense of his actions. He lacked a sense of empathy for his victims and did not appreciate the consequences of his actions. Referring to the MRI- and PET-scans, the experts in this case concluded that it was highly unlikely that the suspect

[100] Burns & Swerdlow 2003; Glenn & Raine 2014.
[101] Glenn & Raine 2014, p. 57.
[102] Meynen 2016b, pp. 134–138. Cf. Burns & Swerdlow 2003.
[103] Meynen 2016b, p. 137.
[104] Linden 2012; Meynen 2020.

could have faked the symptoms of the diagnosed brain disorder.[105] The defendant's responsibility was considered diminished. A reduced sentence was imposed.

In sum, neuroimaging can contribute to forensic diagnostics by assisting in confirming or excluding brain abnormalities, such as a brain tumour, traumatic brain injury, some forms of dementia, and epilepsy. In some cases, such abnormalities can be legally relevant, particularly in the context of the insanity defence.[106] In fact, the results of different neuroimaging technologies, such as MRI, PET, and EEG, have already been used in assessing legal insanity in individual criminal cases.[107] Korponay and Koenings highlight that brain-reading data can function best as suggestive evidence, complementary and secondary to traditional forms of behavioural evidence that are presently used to assess legal insanity.[108]

Meanwhile, some scholars are rather sceptical about the potential contribution of brain-reading to forensic diagnostics. For example, Morse argues that '[o]ffenders do not wear portable scanners, at least not yet. The question will always be whether a present day scan is a valid indication of the defendant's retrospective mental state. (…) in many, and perhaps in most, cases we will not be sure'.[109]

While this might be a valid concern,[110] it is not a limitation that typically pertains to brain-reading technologies. The issue of retrospectivity is central to judging claims of legal insanity more generally,[111] irrespective of whether we use traditional behavioural tests or neuroimaging technologies.[112] Psychiatrists and psychologists aim to assess whether a defendant suffered from a disturbed mind *during the time of the offence*. To some extent, neuroimaging appears able to contribute to these assessments by providing another piece of relevant, objective information.[113]

2.4.2 *Technological Features*

Depending on the specific mental or neural anomaly that will be examined, both structural and functional neuroimaging can be used. For instance, whereas functional

105 *Rb.* Midden-Nederland 2 July 2015, ECLI:NL:RBMNE:2015:4866.

106 Meynen 2020; Pardo & Patterson 2015, p. 140. On the relation of dementia, epilepsy, and brain injury with criminal behaviour, see, for example, Baird, Kennett & Schier 2020; Mendez 2010; Fazel et al. 2011; Timonen et al. 2002; Liljegren et al. 2015.

107 See, for example, Hafner 2019; De Kogel & Westgeest 2015; Catley & Claydon 2015; Farahany 2015.

108 Korponay & Koenings 2016, p. 33. Cf. Bottalico & Santosuosso 2016, p. 134; Meynen 2016b, pp. 127–128; Noyon et al. 2019.

109 Morse 2012, p. 166. Cf. Nugent 2012a, p. 268.

110 The possibility that patients with a particular mental disorder will, in the future, wear portable scanners can, however, not be excluded: Gilbert 2015; Ligthart et al. 2021b. Moreover, wearable neuroimaging devices, like wearable EEGs, are already out on the consumer market: Ienca, Haselager & Emanuel 2018.

111 Bijlsma et al. 2019; Meynen 2016b, pp. 44–46.

112 Vincent 2011, p. 42.

113 Cf. Meynen 2016b, pp. 126, 128.

neuroimaging can contribute to diagnose epilepsy (EEG), structural neuroimaging such as MRI and CT can assist in localising a brain tumour and identifying traumatic brain injury. Sometimes, *functional* neuroimaging can also be employed to identify *structural* brain features, such as a PET-scan to identify a brain tumour or symptoms of dementia.[114] Below, two features of brain-reading technology will be discussed that are relevant from a normative perspective: harm and cooperation.

The first concern is potential *harm*. As discussed,[115] PET and SPECT expose the subject to certain doses of *radiation* and can entail various side effects. The same is true for a CT-scan (making an X-ray of the brain).[116] On average, a CT of the brain exposes the subject to an effective dose of radiation of 2.3 mSv.[117] Radiation exposure has been associated with an increased risk of developing cancer, both for the subject and for an unborn foetus when carried by the subject.[118]

(f)MRI uses a strong magnetic field. Therefore, the presence of any metal objects in or on the body is a contraindication for applying this technology.[119] To improve the visibility of MRI or CT, contrast agent should sometimes be injected into the subject's blood. Such injections are physically invasive and may cause side effects, ranging from nausea to cardiac arrest.[120]

Regarding the level of required *cooperation*, structural neuroimaging (aiming to image the subject's brain anatomy) does, usually, not require active participation of the subject. She just has to lie in the scanner, without making any movements that distort the test. In fact, this can be achieved without any participation whatsoever. If necessary, the subject could be sedated or brought in a state of general anaesthesia. Receiving general anaesthesia entails health risks. Apart from general side effects such as headaches, muscular pain, and nausea, it can cause chronic respiratory complications, as well as brain damage due to oxygen deficiency.[121]

Functional neuroimaging can be applied in order to examine either the brain in a state of rest (functional resting-state neuroimaging) or in a state of action (functional task-based neuroimaging).[122] Recent studies used resting-state fMRI in the examination of depression and schizophrenia.[123] Such a resting-state examination does not require *active* participation of the subject – there is no task to be performed. Yet, it does require *passive* participation: the subject has to lie in the scanner very quietly,

114 Treglia et al. 2019; Risacher & Saykin 2019; Zukotynsk et al. 2018.
115 Section 2.2.2.
116 Rushing, Pryma & Langleben 2012, p. 8.
117 www.rivm.nl, searched for 'Gemiddelde effectieve dosis per type CT-onderzoek' (visited on 19 December 2019).
118 Brenner & Hall 2007; Rushing, Pryma & Langleben 2012, p. 8.
119 See Section 2.2.2.
120 www.radiologyinfo.org (searched for 'Contrast Materials', visited on 26 June 2020).
121 Karcz & Papadakos 2013, pp. 21–23; Maity et al. 2012, p. 34; Curry, Viernes & Sharma 2011, pp. 21–28.
122 Roskies 2013a; Roskies 2013b.
123 Drysdale et al. 2017; Woodward & Cascio 2017.

keeping his brain in a state of rest, and refraining from mental or physical actions that will disrupt the imaging results.[124] In fact, this is also some kind of task.

When functional neuroimaging aims to examine how specific brain areas react to particular stimuli, cooperation will normally be required: the subject should perform a task that elicits brain activity (functional task-based neuroimaging). Clearly, this requires active participation.[125] When functional neuroimaging aims to identify structural brain features, such as a PET-scan in diagnosing a brain tumour, no participation of the subject will be required.

2.5 NEUROPREDICTION

2.5.1 *Type of Information and Legal Relevance*

Traditional risk assessment tools predict the risk of future offending based on all kind of risk factors that correlate with committing crimes. Think of a history of violence, childhood abuse, failure to form relationships, and addiction to alcohol or drugs.[126] Along the same lines, neuroprediction uses *neurobiological features* that, according to empirical studies, correlate with particular forms of criminal behaviour. Many neurobiological features have been studied, such as genetics, hormones, neurotransmitters, brain structures, and reduced or increased activity in particular brain regions.[127] Since this book focusses on brain-reading technologies, this section confines the discussion to risk factors that can be identified through neuroimaging – that is, risk factors relating to brain anatomy and brain activity.

Empirical research on neuropredictive brain-reading mainly focusses on aggression.[128] Studies have shown that reduction in both the anatomy and activity in the frontal lobe – a brain region that is involved in decision-making, impulse control, and social behaviour – correlates with antisocial behaviour of impulsivity and poor behavioural control.[129] Glenn and Raine even consider reduced functioning in this

124 Roskies 2013a, p. 47; Korponay & Koenigs 2016, p. 16. Experimental studies have examined protocols for functional resting-state neuroimaging while the subject is in a state of general anaesthesia. See, for example, Paasonen et al. 2018; Mhuircheartaigh et al. 2010.

125 Roskies 2013a, pp. 46–47; Korponay & Koenigs 2016, p. 16.

126 Bedard 2017, p. 279; Nadelhoffer et al. 2012, p. 79.

127 Glenn & Raine 2014; Rosell & Siever 2015; Nadelhoffer et al. 2012, pp. 80–85; Bedard 2017.

128 In this respect, two general types of aggression are often distinguished: impulsive (or active) and instrumental (or proactive) aggression. Whereas impulsive aggression constitutes in an abrupt, 'hot-headed' response to a (perceived) threat or provocation, instrumental aggression is premeditated, goal-oriented, and 'cold-blooded' (typical for, e.g., psychopaths). Both types of aggression are assumed to be intercorrelated. Together they contribute to an individual's 'total level' of aggression. Meanwhile, the results of a specific neuroprediction test could sometimes suggest an increased risk to one specific subtype of aggressive behaviour: Rosell & Siever 2015; Blair 2010.

129 For reviews, see Glenn & Raine 2014; Rosell & Siever 2015; Poldrack et al. 2018. See also Delfin et al. 2019; Kiehl et al. 2018.

part of the brain the best-replicated neuroimaging correlate of antisocial and violent behaviour.[130]

A well-known study on brain activity and prediction of antisocial behaviour was performed by Aharoni et al.[131] The researchers measured activity in a specific part of the frontal lobe of 96 adult offenders.[132] While in the fMRI scanner, the subjects performed an inhibition task. The researchers then related the neuroimaging data and other risk factors to the rearrest rate four years after release and found that '[t]he odds that an offender with relatively low anterior cingulate activity would be rearrested were approximately double that of an offender with high activity in this region, holding constant other observed risk factors'.[133] The authors emphasise that neurobiological markers of criminal behaviour are unlikely to outperform existing tools of risk assessment. Yet, they could potentially improve overall risk estimates together with traditional risk factors.[134]

Another part of the brain that receives attention in the literature on neuroprediction concerns the amygdala.[135] This is a brain region that plays an important role in processing emotions like fear and anger.[136] Research suggests that an overactive amygdala, as well as an inactive one, correlates respectively with impulsive and instrumental aggression.[137] Besides the *activity* of the amygdala, *anatomic* anomalies in this part of the brain appear to correlate with aggressive behaviour as well. For instance, research shows that lower amygdala volume is associated with a longstanding history of aggression, psychopathic features, and with increased risks for future violence.[138] For example, lower amygdala volume appears a significant risk factor for future violent behaviour.[139]

In view of the empirical data, it has been argued that neuroimaging data could be very helpful in predicting future dangerousness. For example, Glenn, Focquaert, and Raine expect that it would be possible in the future to identify with 80 per cent certainty that a child or young adult will develop persistent violent behaviour, by either neuroimaging, genetic tests, or other biological examinations.[140] If neuroprediction will indeed fulfil these expectations, it could add much to existing risk assessment tools.[141]

130 Glenn & Raine 2014, p. 56.
131 Aharoni et al. 2013. See also Aharoni et al. 2014.
132 More specifically, brain activity in the anterior cingulate cortex.
133 Aharoni et al. 2013, p. 6223.
134 Aharoni et al. 2013, p. 6224. See also Delfin et al. 2019; Kiehl et al. 2018.
135 Haller 2018; Pardini et al. 2014; Glenn & Raine 2014; Rosell & Siever 2015; Poldrack et al. 2018.
136 Raine 2013, p. 106; Yang et al. 2009, p. 986.
137 Blair 2010; Blair 2016.
138 Pardini et al. 2014; Bobes et al. 2013; Matthies et al. 2012.
139 Pardini et al. 2014, p. 79.
140 Glenn, Focquaert & Raine 2015, p. 1695.
141 Nadelhoffer et al. 2012; Nadelhoffer & Sinnott-Armstrong 2012; Witzel 2012; Meynen 2013, p. 97; Bottalico & Santosuosso 2016, pp. 132 and 134; Bedard 2017, pp. 310–313; Claydon 2017, p. 597.

But there are limitations. Perhaps most important is that studies on (neuro)biological risk factors represent average differences between groups. Many individuals *with* risk factors will not commit a crime. Some individuals *without* risk factors do offend.[142] Just like most other risk assessment tools, neuroprediction does not establish a causal link between risk factors and criminal behaviour.[143]

However, although neuroprediction has limitations, its contribution to criminal law could be very valuable. Predicting risks of recidivism is a central aspect of criminal justice, especially in the imposition and execution of criminal sanctions.[144] Meanwhile, whereas predicting risks is central to criminal law, existing risk assessment tools are far from perfect.[145] Including more reliable data is desirable.[146] Adding another piece of personalised, brain-derived information to current risk assessment tools will provide additional information to legal decision-makers.[147]

Importantly, neuroprediction need not *replace* existing tools of risk assessment. Instead, it could be *integrated* into the present range of tools, aiming to provide a best-informed risk of recidivism.[148] An interesting example of such an integrative approach is a recent study of Delfin et al., who performed a long-term follow-up study on the prediction of recidivism of forensic psychiatric patients. The researchers used both traditional risk assessment tools and data from resting-state SPECT-scans of the brain. One of the 'incremental effects of neuroimaging data' they reported concerned the increase of accuracy from 64 per cent to 82 per cent.[149] Although some studies show promising results, the responsible introduction of neuropredictive data into actual legal decision-making requires more research.[150]

2.5.2 *Technological Features*

Similar to the use of neuroimaging for diagnostics, neuroprediction can be applied with different structural and functional neuroimaging technologies. For instance, whereas low amygdala *volume* can be identified with MRI, its *activity* can be measured with a task-based fMRI.[151] And as the study of Delfin et al. shows, resting-state SPECT of certain brain regions can improve risk assessment as well.[152] As a consequence, the precise technology to be used and the accompanied invasiveness, health risks, and

[142] Glenn, Focquaert & Raine 2015, p. 1690.
[143] Encinas de Muñagorri & Saas 2016, p. 106; Glenn, Focquaert & Raine 2015, p. 1690.
[144] Bedard 2017, p. 274 et seq.; Nadelhoffer & Sinnott-Armstrong 2012, p. 634.
[145] Jeandarme et al. 2017a, 2017b.
[146] Douglas et al. 2017.
[147] Cf. Nadelhoffer et al. 2012, p. 86. Gkotsi & Gasser 2016, p. 65; Korponay & Koenigs 2016, p. 33; Bedard 2017, pp. 309–310; Aharoni et al. 2013, p. 6224.
[148] Witzel 2012, p. 195; Noyon et al. 2019, pp. 288–289; Tortora et al. 2020.
[149] Delfin et al. 2019. Cf. Zijlmans et al. 2021; Kiehl et al. 2018.
[150] Poldrack et al. 2018.
[151] Pardini et al. 2014; Bobes et al. 2013.
[152] Delfin et al. 2019.

TABLE 2.1 *Neuroimaging technologies, their measurements, and (legally) relevant features.*

	Measurements	Relevant features
Magnetic resonance imaging (MRI)	Magnetic response of brain tissue	Contraindications: metal objects in or on the body and claustrophobia; Injection of contrast agent could be required, which may entail side effects, otherwise safe
Computed tomography (CT)	X-ray of the brain	Radiation exposure; Injection of contrast agent could be required, which may entail side effects
Functional magnetic resonance imaging (fMRI)	Magnetic response of oxygen content in blood in the brain (hemodynamic responses)	Contraindications: metal objects in or on the body and claustrophobia; Injection of contrast agent could be required, which may entail side effects, otherwise safe
Electroencephalography (EEG), in particular P300 (CIT)	Electrical charges caused by brain activity	Relatively easy to apply, cheap, no dangers for the subject
Positron emission tomography (PET)	Radioactive contrast agent in blood in the brain	Radiation exposure; Injection of radioactive contrast agent is required, which could entail side effects
Single-photon emission computed tomography (SPECT)	Radioactive contrast agent in blood in the brain	Radiation exposure; Injection of radioactive contrast agent is required, which could entail side effects

level of required participation will depend on the specific brain feature that is evaluated.[153] As discussed in the previous sections, different neuroimaging techniques work via different measurements and have their own typical features (see Table 1).

2.6 NEURAL REPRESENTATION OF REAL-TIME THOUGHTS

A relatively novel, emerging type of brain-reading concerns the neural representation of real-time thoughts.[154] Combining functional neuroimaging with machine-learning algorithms, the possibility of identifying real-time thoughts based on someone's brain activity has been examined.[155] Lie detection and CITs require external input, such as the presentation of questions or pictures. The identification of real-time thoughts aims to identify what the subject is thinking at the moment of the examination, with no such external input required.[156]

153 See also Section 2.4.2.
154 See, for example, Haynes 2011.
155 Bauer & Just 2019.
156 Cf. Meynen 2017, pp. 315–318.

Using different methodologies, researchers are trying to decode the human brain.[157] Studies have focussed on the identification of emotions[158] and of thoughts about abstract physics concepts,[159] thoughts about suicide,[160] about particular past events,[161] political orientation,[162] and on the identification of hidden intentions.[163] Some publications showed high accuracy levels, such as detecting suicidal ideation with 91 per cent accuracy.[164] Still, this brain-reading application is in its infant stage.

Clearly, if neural identification of real-time thoughts will evolve, enabling us to identify what people think or believe at a particular moment, it may well become a powerful tool in criminal justice. For example, it could assist in determining what a person knows about a particular crime or an upcoming terrorist attack.

2.7 COERCION: PHYSICAL AND VOLITIONAL

2.7.1 *Introduction*

Thus far, we considered different brain-reading applications, their technological features, and their (potential) relevance for criminal justice. As this book is on *coercive* brain-reading, this section takes a closer look at the concept of coercion. It discusses two generic types of coercion that could enable the enforcement of brain-reading in criminal justice.

Different means and levels of pressure can be used in getting people to act as you wish, such as persuasion, leverage, making offers, exploitation, making threats, and employing physical force.[165] Yet not all of such means attain to 'coercion'.[166] The relevance of identifying what constitutes coercion and what does not lies in the generally accepted claim that coercion is incompatible with valid consent.[167] In general, for consent to be valid, it requires (1) the disclosure of appropriate information (2) to a competent person (3) who is permitted to make a voluntary choice.[168] Since coercion is considered to impair *voluntariness*, it is conceived to invalidate consent.[169]

The legal relevance of the concept of consent is not merely confined to domestic laws on clinical practice, research trials, contract law, and a variety of criminal

[157] For example, Nishimoto et al. 2011.
[158] Kassam et al. 2013.
[159] Mason & Just 2016.
[160] Just et al. 2017.
[161] Wang, Cherkassky & Just 2017; Just, Wang & Cherkassky 2017; Wang et al. 2016.
[162] Leshinskaya et al. 2017.
[163] Haynes et al. 2007.
[164] Just et al. 2017. For a critical reflection, see Dukhart et al. 2021; Just, Cherkassky & Brent 2021.
[165] Feinberg 1989, p. 189; Szmukler & Appelbaum 2008.
[166] Nelson et al. 2011.
[167] Kiener 2020, sect. 5; Eyal 2019, sect. 5.1; Feinberg 1989; Faden, Beauchamp & King 1986, Chs. 7 and 10.
[168] Eyal 2019, sect. 1; Appelbaum 2007, p. 1834; Faden, Beauchamp & King 1986, Chs. 8–10; Berg et al. 2001.
[169] Eyal 2019, sect. 5.1; Anderson 2021, sect. 3.3; Nelson et al. 2011; Faden, Beauchamp & King 1986, Chs. 7 and 10.

offences (e.g. burglary, assault, and rape).[170] It extends to European human rights law as well. Valid consent can prevent infringements of human rights in the context of a surgery (Articles 3 and 8 ECHR),[171] in sports and games, like in boxing and Escape Rooms (Articles 3, 8, and 5 ECHR), as well as in the course of executing police powers, such as searching cars and homes (Article 8 ECHR).

Discussions about consent and human rights often relate to medical interventions in criminal law,[172] such as forced feeding in prison.[173] Other examples concern surgical castration of sex offenders[174] and gynaecological examination of female prisoners.[175] When valid consent exists to such medical procedures, no issue will normally arise under the Convention.[176] For example, in the case of *Bogumil/Portugal*, a swallowed pellet of cocaine had been surgically removed from the applicant's stomach. The ECtHR considered that if there would have been informed consent to this medical procedure, no issue would have arisen under Article 3 ECHR.[177]

The next section discusses the concept of coercion and explains how different approaches of this concept could affect our normative analysis of coercive brain-reading in light of the ECHR. Although 'coercion' is arguably considered a characteristic aspect of the law in general[178] and essential to various concrete legal concepts,[179] in-depth debates on the theoretical understanding of coercion seem no central concern in common legal scholarship.[180] Under the ECHR, no generic legal doctrine on coercion has been developed yet.[181] In philosophy, however, the concept of coercion has received much attention.[182] Therefore, the discussion in the present section mainly focusses on the philosophical conceptualisation of coercion. This section will not take a position in the philosophical debate. Rather, it intends to provide a conceptual framework that can help us better understanding the position of the ECtHR in this matter. The ECtHR position is examined in the upcoming chapters.

170 See, for example, Berg et al. 2001; Appelbaum, Lidz & Klitzman 2009; Szmukler & Appelbaum 2008; Wertheimer 1987, Chs. 2, 4, 6, and 7.

171 See also Harris et al. 2018, p. 238; Vermeulen & Battjes 2018, p. 396.

172 Buelens, Herijgers & Illegems 2016; Richardson 2008.

173 Jacobs 2012, pp. 68–72.

174 CPT/Inf (2012)6, point 145.

175 ECtHR 13 May 2008, appl.no. 52515/99 (*Juhnke/Turkey*); ECtHR 22 July 2003, appl.no. 24209/94 (*Y.F./Turkey*). For a discussion, see Chapter 3, Section 3.3.4, factor 3.

176 ECtHR 6 November 2014, appl.no. 12927/13 (*Dvořáček/Czech Republic*).

177 ECtHR 3 October 2008, appl.no. 35228/03 (*Bogumil/Portugal*), § 71. Cf. European Commission of Human Rights 2 March 1983, appl.no. 9974/82 (*X./Denmark*), p. 284.

178 Hudges 2013; Lamond 2000; MacCormick 1984, Ch. 12.

179 For example, rape, extortion, and duress.

180 Some examples: Lamond 2000; Hughes 2013. Cf. Wertheimer 1987, who's approach has been developed and defended in US legal reasoning, *inter alia* regarding contract law and criminal responsibility: Anderson 2021, sect. 2.3.

181 Richardson 2008; Buelens, Herijgers & Illegems 2016.

182 For an overview see Kiener 2020; Anderson 2021.

2.7.2 Coercion: Threats, Baselines, and (Coercive) Offers

According to Kiener, coercion comes in two types: physical and volitional coercion.[183] *Physical* coercion works through employing force, determining a person's movements. Think of pushing another person against the wall, or imprisoning someone. In criminal law, physical force can sometimes be employed in order to arrest a suspect by handcuffing him, or in order to obtain a DNA sample, like a hair, while restraining the defendant.[184] Other examples are mechanical fixation of psychiatric patients and the use of chemical restraint – that is, the forcible administration of pharmaceuticals for the purpose of controlling a patient's behaviour.[185]

However, physical coercion will be ineffective to enforce brain-reading applications that require active or passive *cooperation* of the subject. After all, employing physical force to make someone observe stimuli attentively or to press a yes-or-no button after each question is hard to imagine. The same holds true for bringing a person's brain in a state of rest or preventing her from using countermeasures through the use of physical force.

Unlike physical coercion, *volitional* coercion usually works through making threats and arranging a person's situation so that she is compelled to perform a certain act to avoid harm.[186] The paradigmatic example is the robber's threat 'Your money or your life'. This threat arranges the situation of another person in a way that she has to hand over the money to avoid being killed. Other examples are the police officer threatening with a longer prison sentence if the suspect refrains from giving testimony, the law threatening the car driver with punishment for rejecting cooperation with a breathalyser test,[187] and the law threatening a witness with criminal sanctions for giving false testimony.[188] In this study, such threats, coming from the *law*, are referred to as 'legal threats'.[189]

As mentioned, physical coercion can be employed through a variety of means, such as pushing, handcuffing, imprisoning, and chemical restraint. The accepted means of volitional coercion are less clear. There is a debate about *threats* versus *offers*. Some theorists argue that only *threats* coerce,[190] while others accept that, in

183 Kiener 2020, sect. 1; Anderson 2021, sect. 2.1.1.

184 For the Dutch legal context, see, for example, Article 151b(3) Dutch Code of Criminal Procedure; *Kamerstukken II* 1999/00, 26271, 9, p. 17.

185 CPT/Inf(2017)6, p. 2.

186 Kiener 2020, sect. 1; Anderson 2021, sect. 2.2; Feinberg 1989.

187 For the Dutch legal context, see, for example, Articles 163(2) and 176(4) Dutch Road Traffic Law 1994.

188 For the Dutch legal context, see, for example, Article 207 Dutch Criminal Code. See also Article 294 Dutch Code of Criminal Procedure, threatening with custody if the witness refuses to answer the judge's questions.

189 Whether the law is or can actually be coercive is open to debate: Hudges 2013; Lamond 2000; Reidy & Riker 2008; MacCormick 1984, Ch. 12.

190 Nozick 1969; Wertheimer 1987; Berman 2002; Wertheimer & Miller 2014.

some cases, *offers* can be coercive too.[191] In short, the distinction between threats and offers is that threats make recipients worse off, while offers make them better off.[192] The above-mentioned robber's proposal – 'Hand over your money, or I will kill you' – typically qualifies as a threat, not as an offer, as the robber creates a situation in which one suddenly has to choose between losing money and losing life. An offer could be 'If you pay me, I will repair your car', because now the option of a car reparation is suddenly created, which makes a person better off. Unlike threats, offers will not normally restrict the recipient's freedom and are thus not considered coercive.

Determining whether a proposal makes someone worse off, qualifying as a threat, requires a certain baseline – that is, a hypothetical situation to compare with the situation after the proposer's intervention.[193] Two baselines are to be distinguished: a statistical baseline (i.e. the normally expected course of events) and a moral baseline (i.e. the morally required course of events). As Kiener notes, often, both baselines coincide.[194] For example, it is normally expected and morally required that people shall not be killed if they refuse to hand over money on demand. Compared with either the statistical or the moral baseline, the robber's proposal 'Your money or your life' makes the recipient worse off. Therefore, the proposal constitutes a threat and is coercive.

However, the statistical and moral baseline may sometimes diverge, as is the case in a famous example of Nozick:

> Suppose that usually a slave owner beats his slave each morning, for no reason connected with the slave's behavior. Today he says to his slave, 'Tomorrow I will not beat you if and only if you now do A'.[195]

Compared to what normally happens – the slave being beaten every morning (statistical baseline) – the slave owner's proposal makes the slave better off, qualifying as an offer.[196] Meanwhile, compared with the morally required course of events – not being beating at all, nor being a slave in the first place (moral baseline) – the proposal makes the slave worse off, qualifying as a threat. In order to determine whether the proposal is either a threat or an offer, one should decide which baseline to pick – an issue that has elicited considerable debate.[197]

191 Lyons 1975; Zimmerman 1981; Feinberg 1989; McGregor 2008; McMillan 2014.

192 Kiener 2020, sect. 2; Anderson 2021, sect. 2.2.

193 Wetheimer 1993, p. 244; Nozick 1969. As Feinberg 1989, p. 221 put it: 'Threats are projected consequences which are unwelcome compared to the consequences that would have resulted "otherwise", or "in the normal course of events", or "what might normally have been expected", whereas offers are projected consequences which are welcome when seen against that same background or measured from that same baseline'.

194 Kiener 2020, sect. 2.

195 Nozick 1969, p. 450.

196 Under the statistic approach, a variety of baselines will be conceivable: Feinberg 1989, pp. 224–226.

197 Feinberg 1989, pp. 221–228. See also, with further references Anderson 2021, sect. 2.3; Kiener 2020, sect. 2.

To illustrate the relevance of this distinction regarding legal threats, consider a free citizen, who is summoned by a judge as a witness to testify in a criminal trial, on pain of custody. In other words, the judge proposes 'Testify in court, or you will be taken into custody'. The *statistical* baseline, one could argue, renders this legal proposal a threat. After all, then, the proposal makes the witness worse off compared with the normal course of events: in normal life, the free citizen is not obliged to speak or testify (since no such opportunity exists), neither will he be taken into custody.[198] In contrast, following a *moral* baseline, the judge's proposal does not make the free citizen worse off: in the morally expected course of events, citizens are obliged to give testimony in criminal cases,[199] and the judge has a right to enforce this obligation through custody.[200] Accordingly, by adopting this moral standard, the free citizen is not worse off, so there would be no threat. As this example illustrates, in cases of legal threats, the statistical and moral baselines could diverge. Hence, whether the law and its institutions coerce may depend on whether one follows a moral[201] or statistical[202] view of coercion.[203]

Apart from threats, proposals could arguably coerce by being a 'coercive offer'. As noted above, some theorists reject that offers can coerce,[204] while others accept the idea of coercive offers.[205] An illustrative example of such an arguable coercive offer comes from Feinberg:

> Suppose opportunistic A holds out to unfortunate *B* the prospect of rescue or cure—but for a price. *B* is in an otherwise hopeless condition from which A can rescue her if she gives him what he wants. He will pay for the expensive surgery that alone can save her child's life provided that she becomes for a period his mistress. A thus uses his superior advantages to manipulate *B*'s options so that she has no more choice than she would have if a gunman pointed his pistol at her healthy child's head, and threatened to shoot unless she agreed to become his mistress.[206]

As Feinberg argues, offers like these appear coercive in that they rearrange a person's options in such a way that one has no choice but to comply, or else suffer an unacceptable consequence.[207]

198 Moreover, one has a fundamental right not to be obliged to express oneself (Article 10 ECHR) and not to be deprived of one's liberty (Article 5 ECHR).
199 Cf. ECtHR 22 November 2007, appl.no. 64752/01 (*Voskuil/The Netherlands*), § 86.
200 Cf. Wertheimer 1987, Ch. 7; Wertheimer & Miller 2014.
201 For example, Wertheimer 1987.
202 For example, Feinberg 1989.
203 See Anderson 2010 for an alternative approach, putting emphasis on 'enforcement'.
204 Nozick 1969; Wertheimer 1987; Berman 2002; Wertheimer & Miller 2014.
205 Lyons 1975; Zimmerman 1981; Feinberg 1989; McGregor 2008; McMillan 2014.
206 Feinberg 1989, p. 229.
207 Ibid., p. 230.

When and why an offer is actually coercive is under debate across theorists that accept the idea of coercive offers. Discussing these views would exceed the scope of this book. To illustrate how *prima facie* genuine offers may appear coercive in different contexts for different reasons, two examples are provided below. The first comes from Zimmerman:

> If *P* throws *Q* into the water and then offers to save *Q* (where he can do so at relatively little cost to himself) only if *Q* promises to give him his life savings afterwards, the offer is coercive and the promise void. If *P* just happens upon the scene, sees *Q* drowning, and offers to rescue him on exactly the same terms, *Q*'s promise is probably just as void, morally speaking anyway, since *P*'s offer is so grossly exploitive. But it does not follow from just this that *P* has coerced *Q*.[208]

In considering whether offers are coercive, Zimmerman argues to take into account whether the proposer *controls or arranges* the original baseline situation of the recipient, preventing the latter from moving from the actual pre-proposal situation to some alternative, more preferable pre-proposal situation.[209] Since *P* has arranged the baseline situation of *Q* by throwing him into the water, the subsequent offer to save *Q* in return for his life savings is coercive. The same goes for the offer in the slave-example mentioned above: the slave owner controls the baseline situation by preventing the slave from being a free individual, not having to choose between being beaten or performing some disagreeable task.[210]

The second example comes from McGregor:

> Getting the Congolese prisoner who is fed only twice a week by the warden to participate in a nontherapeutic and risky medical trial does not require the threat of harm if he fails to participate. The offer of four meals a week in exchange to agreeing to participate would suffice. People in miserable, vulnerable situations can be influenced, induced, 'forced' with minor offers, to do all kinds of things. Would it be a fully voluntary choice to participate in research in the Congolese prisoner example?[211]

According to McGregor, offers can coerce if they are in fact the only eligible option to the recipient in a miserable, *vulnerable* situation. Offers make their recipients 'better off' than the normal course of events. However, if the recipient finds herself

[208] Zimmerman 1981, pp. 134–135.

[209] Ibid., pp. 132–133:

> an offer is coercive only if Q would prefer to move from the normally expected pre-proposal situation to the proposal situation, but he would strongly prefer even more to move from the actual pre-proposal situation to some alternative pre-proposal situation. (…) it is all-important how Q came to be in such a vulnerable position. I would claim that for P's offer to be genuinely coercive it must be the case that he actively prevents Q from being in the alternative pre-proposal situation Q strongly prefers. (Cf. Pugh 2020, Ch. 4)

[210] Zimmerman 1981, pp. 132, 136.

[211] McGregor 2008, p. 52.

in miserable circumstances with no other options left and the proposer takes advantage of that situation, offers can have similar effects as threats.[212]

As McGregor stresses, the more miserable a person's situation is, the easier it is to 'offer' a better situation and get that person to do what you want. If only threats were coercive, the most worse off and vulnerable people would be the hardest to coerce, since it is difficult to make them worse off than they already are. Meanwhile, we should consider vulnerable populations more susceptible to coercion, not less so.[213] In McGregor's view, for an offer to be coercive, it is relevant whether the weaker party is dependent in some way on the stronger party and the stronger party has influence over whether some significant evil occurs to the weaker party. If the stronger party takes advantage of these conditions by offering a worse deal than he would do otherwise, the offer will be coercive.[214]

Some of the most discussed offers in practical ethics concern early release from prison by convicted sex offenders if they consent to surgical or chemical castration.[215] Other examples are offers to convicted offenders to reduce sentences if they consent to a neurointervention that aim to reduce their risk of recidivism, such as deep brain stimulation, transcranial magnetic stimulation, or pharmaceuticals.[216] Are these offers coercive?

Similarly, brain-reading could be offered to defendants in return for bail or probation, or to convicted offenders in return for parole. As Meynen notes, due to the *vulnerability* of defendants and convicted offenders – following from the very nature of criminal justice – such offers could sometimes constitute 'an offer you cannot refuse'.[217]

The next chapters discuss which account on coercion the ECtHR appears to follow. The relevance of this issue directly touches upon the level of human rights protection from brain-reading in criminal law. If the Court would only consider *threats* coercive, States may possibly circumvent human rights restrictions to forensic brain-reading by *offering* it to defendants and convicted offenders. After all, if such offers

212 Ibid.

213 Ibid.

214 Ibid., p. 54. This approach comes close to the distinctive concept of 'exploitation'. For example, from a legal perspective, Weatherburn 2019 has suggested to conceptualise labour exploitation as 'A knowingly taking unfair advantage of *B*'s position of vulnerability by means of the exercise of control showing a lack of respect for *B*'s human dignity, in order to gain a benefit' (p. 316). Cf. Feinberg 1989, p. 245 et seq.

215 Pugh 2020, Ch. 4; McMillan 2014; Wertheimer & Miller 2014; Shaw 2014; Douglas et al. 2013; Ryberg 2012.

216 Focquaert, Van Assche & Sterckx 2020; Knack, Chandler & Fedoroff 2020; Ryberg 2020, Ch. 2; Pugh 2018; Bomann-Larsen 2013.

217 Meynen 2017; Meynen 2020. Cf. Beecher 1962, p. 145: 'the prospect of an award of extreme benefit to the subject such as a great reduction in time of imprisonment or parole on pardon could constitute a bribe greater than the human spirit could be expected to support, with clear violation of the necessary requirements of the principle of consent'.

do not coerce, they will not therefore impair the subject's voluntariness and invalidate consenting decisions to brain-reading. This is an important matter because, as noted, valid consent can prevent State liability under European human rights.

2.8 CONCLUSION

This chapter provided a descriptive account of four central brain-reading applications, their technology, and their (potential) contribution to criminal law. Some brain-reading applications have already been used in criminal proceedings. Other techniques have merely been studied in research settings and discussed in the literature. From a normative point of view, two characteristics of neurotechnologies are of particular importance: potential harm and whether cooperation is required. Important current limitations of neuroimaging techniques concern accuracy, countermeasures, and ecological validity. Finally, the concept of coercion has been considered. Valid consent could prevent infringements of human rights, while coercion could nullify consent. From this perspective, it is important whether an offer could in fact be coercive. Scholarly opinions, however, diverge on this matter. Altogether, this chapter prepared the ground for the legal analyses in the upcoming chapters.

3

Coercive Brain-Reading and the Prohibition of Ill-Treatment

Article 3 ECHR

3.1 INTRODUCTION

A fundamental right that sets absolute normative boundaries to means of criminal investigation is the prohibition of torture, inhuman, and degrading treatment. As the member States have agreed on, and many other countries and legal systems endorse, we must proscribe any such levels of force in criminal proceedings.

When enforcing brain-reading in criminal law, different *means* of coercion are conceivable.[1] Especially when *physical* coercion will be used, such as mechanical or chemical restraint, coercive brain-reading might cause physical and/or mental harm. In addition, some brain-reading applications are by themselves physically intrusive, involve radiation exposure, or entail health risks. Accordingly, in some cases, coercive brain-reading might interfere with the subject's physical and/or mental integrity.[2] This could raise an issue under the prohibition of ill-treatment pursuant to Article 3 ECHR.[3]

The present chapter examines whether and under which conditions coercive brain-reading in criminal law could be permissible in light of Article 3 ECHR. Given the nature of the prohibition of ill-treatment, this chapter is mainly concerned with the question of whether coercive brain-reading would adversely affect people's physical or mental conditions, capable of violating Article 3 ECHR. Section 3.2 discusses the meaning and scope of the prohibition of ill-treatment. Section 3.3 considers the legal implications of Article 3 ECHR for coercive brain-reading. Section 3.4 draws conclusions.

1 See Chapter 2, Section 2.7.

2 In the context of Article 3 ECHR, 'mental integrity' is narrowly defined. Basically, it refers to mental pain and suffering.

3 Van Toor 2017, pp. 161–209, 433–434; Ligthart 2019a, 2020a. Cf. Rusconi & Mitchener-Nissen 2013, p. 8; Thompson 2005.

3.2 THE PROHIBITION OF ILL-TREATMENT (ARTICLE 3 ECHR)

According to Article 3 ECHR:

> No one shall be subjected to torture or to inhuman or degrading treatment or punishment.

This is an *absolute* prohibition.[4] Derogation can never be justified, irrespective of the victim's conduct, neither in times of war or public emergency (article 15(2) ECHR) nor for the purpose of fighting terrorism, countering organised crime, or saving lives.[5] Although some member States have argued to allow the balancing of competing interests, such as in cases on the expulsion of terrorists,[6] the European Court of Human Rights (ECtHR/the Court) refuses to revise its absolute approach:

> The philosophical basis underpinning the absolute nature of the right under Article 3 does not allow for any exceptions or justifying factors or balancing of interests, irrespective of the conduct of the person concerned and the nature of the offence at issue.[7]

Accordingly, any treatment that comes within the ambit of the prohibition of ill-treatment will therefore violate Article 3 ECHR.

Notwithstanding the absolute nature, contextual considerations can sometimes be taken into account. For example, Harris et al. signal that conditions of detention that would normally be incompatible with Article 3 ECHR shall not necessarily entail a violation when employed to prevent escape or suicide.[8] And whereas judicial corporal punishment is degrading contrary to Article 3 ECHR, imprisonment under 'normal' prison conditions, which may be just as or even more degrading, will not typically violate the prohibition of ill-treatment.[9] In general, whether a treatment elicits absolute protection under Article 3 ECHR depends on the level of suffering and/or humiliation that is involved.[10] That level must go beyond the

4 For discussion, see Separate opinion Judge Sir Gerald Fitzmaurice, under ECtHR 25 April 1978, appl.no. 5856/72 (*Tyrer/UK*), § 3–4; Greer 2015; Vorhaus 2002, pp. 382–385; Addo & Grief 1998; Duffy 1983, pp. 321–322; Vermeulen & Battjes 2018, p. 384; Mavronicola 2021.

5 ECtHR (GC) 1 June 2010, appl.no. 22978/05 (*Gäfgen/Germany*), § 107; ECtHR (GC) 11 July 2006, appl.no. 54810/00 (*Jalloh/Germany*), § 99; ECtHR 5 February 2020, appl.no. 31454/10 (*Ćwik/Poland*), § 68.

6 ECtHR (GC) 15 November 1996, appl.no. 22414/93 (*Chahal/UK*), § 75–76; ECtHR 5 May 2008, appl. no. 25424/05 (*Ramzy/The Netherlands*), § 125–130.

7 ECtHR (GC) 1 June 2010, appl.no. 22978/05 (*Gäfgen/Germany*), § 107.

8 Harris et al. 2018, p. 238.

9 Ibid.

10 ECtHR (GC) 11 July 2006, appl.no. 54810/00 (*Jalloh/Germany*), § 68; ECtHR (GC) 26 October 2000, appl.no. 30210/96 (*Kudła/Poland*), § 92; ECtHR 18 January 1978, appl.no. 5310/71 (*Ireland/UK*), § 163.

inevitable element of suffering or humiliation connected with a given form of legitimate treatment.[11]

In order to violate Article 3 ECHR, a treatment must attain a *minimum level of severity*.[12] Whereas the prohibition ill-treatment is absolute, the *threshold* is relative:

> The assessment of this minimum is, in the nature of things, relative; it depends on all the circumstances of the case, such as the nature and context of the treatment, the manner and method of its execution, its duration, its physical or mental effects and, in some instances, the sex, age and state of health of the victim.[13]

Other factors include the purpose for which a treatment has been inflicted, together with the intention and motivation of it.[14] The disproportionate nature of a treatment can be a relevant factor as well.[15]

Since the Court approaches the Convention as a living instrument that must be interpreted in light of present-day conditions,[16] the threshold of a minimum level of severity is not static. It can change over time.[17] In fact, the minimum level of severity has been reduced in recent years, broadening the scope of Article 3 ECHR.[18]

When a treatment breaches Article 3 ECHR, it qualifies as either degrading, inhuman, or torture.[19] Degradation is conceived as the least harmful treatment. Torture qualifies as most severe, with the distinguishing criteria being the intensity and severity of the suffering involved.[20] According to the Grand Chamber:

11 ECtHR (GC) 17 July 2014, appl.nos. 32541/08 and 43441/08 (*Svinarenko and Slyadnev/Russia*), § 116.

12 ECtHR (GC) 1 June 2010, appl.no. 22978/05 (*Gäfgen/Germany*), § 101; ECtHR (GC) 26 October 2000, appl.no. 30210/96 (*Kudła/Poland*), § 91; ECtHR 18 January 1978, appl.no. 5310/71 (*Ireland/UK*), § 163.

13 ECtHR (GC) 26 October 2000, appl.no. 30210/96 (*Kudła/Poland*), § 91. See also ECtHR (GC) 17 July 2014, appl.nos. 32541/08 and 43441/08 (*Svinarenko and Slyadnev/Russia*), § 114. Cf. Separate opinion Judge Sir Gerald Fitzmaurice to ECtHR 25 April 1978, appl.no. 5856/72 (*Tyrer/UK*), § 3–4; Vorhaus 2002, pp. 382–385; Addo & Grief 1998; Duffy 1983, pp. 321–322; Mavronicola 2021.

14 ECtHR (GC) 1 June 2010, appl.no. 22978/05 (*Gäfgen/Germany*), § 88; ECtHR 19 February 2015, appl. no. 75450/12 (*M.S./Croatia (No. 2)*), § 95; ECtHR 24 July 2014, appl.no. 28761/11(*Al Nashiri/Poland*), § 508; ECtHR 27 November 2003, appl.no. 65436/01 (*Hénaf/France*), § 47–60.

15 ECtHR 24 January 2006, appl.no. 39437/98 (*Ülke/Turkey*), § 62; ECtHR 5 April 2005, appl.no. 54825/00 (*Nevmerzhitsky/Ukraine*), § 94–98; ECtHR 4 February 2003, appl.no. 52750/99 (*Lorsé and others/The Netherlands*), § 71–74.

16 ECtHR (GC) 19 February 2013, appl.no. 19010/07 (*X and others/Austria*), § 139; ECtHR 25 April 1978, appl.no. 5856/72 (*Tyrer/UK*), § 31.

17 ECtHR (GC) 26 July 1999, appl.no. 25803/94 (*Selmouni/France*), § 100–101; ECtHR 27 November 2003, appl.no. 65436/01 (*Hénaf/France*), § 55.

18 Harris et al. 2018, p. 237.

19 The precise qualification can be relevant regarding the issue of compensation and for the state's reputation: Harris et al. 2018, p. 239; Addo & Grief 1998, pp. 511–512.

20 ECtHR 18 January 1978, appl.no. 5310/71 (*Ireland/UK*), § 167; Evans & Morgan 1998, p. 77. See also 2013, p. 259.

> Treatment is considered to be 'degrading' within the meaning of Article 3 when it humiliates or debases an individual, showing a lack of respect for, or diminishing, his or her human dignity, or when it arouses feelings of fear, anguish or inferiority capable of breaking an individual's moral and physical resistance.[21]

The qualification of 'degrading treatment' does not require any severe or long-lasting physical or mental effects.[22] Yet, the minimum level of severity must be attained. The public nature of a treatment and the intention to humiliate or debase can be relevant factors in assessing whether a treatment is degrading.[23] Meanwhile, absence of those factors will not necessarily prevent a treatment from falling within this category.[24] Instead, 'it may well suffice that the victim is humiliated in his own eyes, even if not in the eyes of others'.[25] This subjective approach does not apply without limitation.[26] As Duffy argues, views and reactions of the victim are important considerations. However, States should not be liable for actions that a victim finds degrading 'merely because of his own unreasonable attitudes or exceptionally sensitive nature'.[27]

The distinction between degrading and inhuman treatment is not always clear-cut.[28] Sometimes, one single treatment qualifies as both inhuman and degrading.[29] Still, inhuman treatment has its own descriptive definition:

> The Court has considered treatment to be 'inhuman' because, inter alia, it was premeditated, was applied for hours at a stretch and caused either actual bodily injury or intense physical or mental suffering.[30]

21 ECtHR (GC) 17 July 2014, appl.nos. 32541/08 and 43441/08 (*Svinarenko and Slyadnev/Russia*), § 115. See also ECtHR (GC) 1 June 2010, appl.no. 22978/05 (*Gäfgen/Germany*), § 89. Cf. ECtHR 18 January 1978, appl.no. 5310/71 (*Ireland/UK*), § 167.

22 ECtHR 25 March 1993, appl.no. 13134/87 (*Costello-Roberts/UK*), § 32; ECtHR 25 April 1978, appl.no. 5856/72 (*Tyrer/UK*), § 33.

23 ECtHR 6 March 2007, appl.no. 27473/02 (*Erdoğan Yağiz/Turkey*), 40–48; ECtHR 16 December 1997, appl.no. 20972/92 (*Raninen/Finland*), § 58.

24 ECtHR (GC) 17 July 2014, appl.nos. 32541/08 and 43441/08 (*Svinarenko and Slyadnev/Russia*), § 114; ECtHR (GC) 11 july 2006, appl.no. 54810/00 (*Jalloh/Germany*), § 68; ECtHR 16 December 1997, appl.no. 20972/92 (*Raninen/Finland*), § 55.

25 ECtHR 16 December 1997, appl.no. 20972/92 (*Raninen/Finland*), § 55; ECtHR 25 April 1978, appl. no. 5856/72 (*Tyrer/UK*), § 32.

26 See, for example, ECtHR 16 December 1997, appl.no. 20972/92 (*Raninen/Finland*), § 58; ECtHR 25 April 1978, appl.no. 5856/72 (*Tyrer/UK*), § 30.

27 Duffy 1983, p. 319.

28 Harris et al. 2018, p. 260; Vermeulen & Battjes 2018, p. 399.

29 For example, ECtHR (GC) 11 July 2006, appl.no. 54810/00 (*Jalloh/Germany*), § 82; ECtHR 18 October 2012, appl.no. 37679/08 (*Bureš/Czech Republic*), § 106. See also Harris et al. 2018, p. 260; Vermeulen & Battjes 2018, p. 391.

30 ECtHR (GC) 26 October 2000, appl.no. 30210/96 (*Kudła/Poland*), § 92. See also ECtHR (GC) 1 June 2010, appl.no. 22978/05 (*Gäfgen/Germany*), § 89.

Unlike degradation, inhuman treatment requires actual bodily injury or intense mental or physical suffering.[31] The suffering and humiliation involved must go beyond the inevitable element of suffering or humiliation connected with a given form of legitimate treatment.[32] In assessing whether the suffering and/or humiliation are severe enough to qualify as 'inhuman', the Court pays attention to the circumstances of the individual case. Relevant factors concern the age, sex, and state of health of the victim and the mental effects caused by the treatment.[33] The intention of causing suffering and inflicting inhuman treatment is a relevant factor, but not necessarily required.[34]

Finally, the most severe treatment prohibited by Article 3 ECHR – torture – is defined as 'deliberate inhuman treatment causing very serious and cruel suffering'.[35] As follows from the 'deliberate-requirement', the very serious and cruel suffering must be inflicted intentionally and for a certain purpose,[36] for example, as punishment, intimidation, or as a means of obtaining evidence.[37] Whether a treatment involves 'serious and cruel suffering' depends on all circumstances of the individual case.[38]

3.3 COERCIVE BRAIN-READING UNDER THE PROHIBITION OF ILL-TREATMENT

3.3.1 *Introduction*

Could coercive brain-reading be permissible under Article 3 ECHR? And, if so, under which legal conditions? This section delves into these questions. Section 3.3.2 draws an analogy between coercive brain-reading and existing methods of investigation about which Strasbourg case-law is currently available. Next, case-law on those existing methods will be analysed in Section 3.3.3. From this analysis, Section 3.3.4 deduces central limitations for coercive brain-reading in criminal law.

31 Vermeulen & Battjes 2018, p. 399.

32 ECtHR(GC) 26 October 2000, appl.no. 30210/96 (*Kudła/Poland*), § 92; ECtHR 7 July 1989, appl.no. 14038/88 (*Soering/UK*), § 100.

33 See, for example, ECtHR 27 November 2003, appl.no. 65436/01 (*Hénaf/France*), § 56.

34 ECtHR (GC) 17 July 2014, appl.nos. 32541/08 and 43441/08 (*Svinarenko and Slyadnev/Russia*), § 114; ECtHR (GC) 11 July 2006, appl.no. 54810/00 (*Jalloh/Germany*), § 82.

35 ECtHR (GC) 13 December 2012, appl.no. 39630/09 (*El-Masri/Former Yugoslav Republic of Macedonia*), § 197; ECtHR (GC) 1 June 2010, appl.no. 22978/05 (*Gäfgen/Germany*), § 90.

36 Vermeulen & Battjes 2018, p. 390.

37 Harris et al. 2018, p. 240. See, for example, ECtHR 30 September 2004, appl.no. 50222/99 (*Krastanov/Bulgaria*), § 53; ECtHR (GC) 27 June 2000, appl.no. 21986/93 (*Salman/Turkey*), § 114; ECtHR (GC) 26 July 1999, appl.no. 25803/94 (*Selmouni/France*) § 98–105.

38 ECtHR (GC) 26 July 1999, appl.no. 25803/94 (*Selmouni/France*) § 100; ECtHR (GC) 25 September 1997, appl.no. 23178/94 (*Aydin/Turkey*), § 84–86; ECtHR 9 March 2006, appl.no. 59261/00 (*Menesheva/Russia*), § 61–62.

3.3.2 *Coercive Forensic Brain-Reading: An Analogy with Forcible Medical Procedures to Obtain Evidence*

To date, no ECtHR case-law exits on coercive brain-reading in light of Article 3 ECHR. In order to enable the deduction of legal boundaries from Strasbourg case-law, this section compares coercive brain-reading with other means of criminal investigation.

In drawing analogies, we must take account of the context within we do so: here, we must focus on those aspects of coercive brain-reading that are relevant in light of Article 3 ECHR. In assessing the minimum level of severity and qualifying a particular treatment as degrading, inhuman or torture, the Court pays attention to the specific circumstances of an individual case. Some of these circumstances concern *the applicant*, that is, age, sex, and state of health. Others concern the *treatment* – that is the method, manner of execution, and purpose.[39] These three aspects of a treatment appear to be of particular importance in light of Article 3 ECHR. Therefore, they are central to the analogy below.

As will be argued, both the method and purpose of coercive brain-reading display *general similarities* with 'forcible medical procedures to obtain evidence of a crime'. The ECtHR defines such medical procedures as:

> a medical procedure in defiance of the will of a suspect in order to obtain from him or her evidence of his or her involvement in the commission of a criminal offence.[40]

According to this descriptive account, the *method* and *purpose* of this type of treatment consist in a *medical procedure in defiance of the person's will* in order to *obtain evidence from that person*. For example, in *Salikhov/Russia*, clipping the applicant's fingernails and the attempt to take a blood sample by force were intended to secure evidence of rape.[41] In *Jalloh/Germany*, emetics had been administered with force, in order to retrieve evidence of a drugs offence.[42] The complaint in *R.S./Hungary* concerned the non-consensual acquisition of a urine sample through catheterisation, with a view of determining whether the applicant had been involved in a traffic offence (alcohol- or drug-impaired driving).[43] The Court has qualified these methods as forcible medical procedures to retrieve evidence from inside a person's body.

39 ECtHR (GC) 26 October 2000, appl.no. 30210/96 (*Kudła/Poland*), § 91; ECtHR (GC) 1 June 2010, appl.no. 22978/05 (*Gäfgen/Germany*), § 88; ECtHR 24 July 2014, appl.no. 28761/11 (*Al Nashiri/Poland*), § 508.

40 ECtHR 2 July 2019, appl.no. 65290/14 (*R.S./Hungary*), § 57. See also ECtHR (GC) 11 July 2006, appl. no. 54810/00 (*Jalloh/Germany*), § 70; ECtHR 3 May 2012, appl.no. 23880/05 (*Salikhov/Russia*), § 73; ECtHR 13 May 2008, appl.no. 52515/99 (*Juhnke/Turkey*), § 71.

41 ECtHR 3 May 2012, appl.no. 23880/05 (*Salikhov/Russia*), § 75.

42 ECtHR (GC) 11 July 2006, appl.no. 54810/00 (*Jalloh/Germany*), § 75.

43 ECtHR 2 July 2019, appl.no. 65290/14 (*R.S./Hungary*), § 68.

The *method* of forensic brain-reading consists in the use of neuroimaging technologies, such as (f)MRI, EEG, and CT. These are in fact medical procedures. In essence, neuroimaging is developed and commonly employed for medical purposes, such as diagnosing epilepsy (EEG), a tumour, or traumatic brain injury (MRI, PET, CT).[44] Applying these technologies with coercion qualifies as a *medical procedure in defiance of the person's will*.

The *purpose* of forensic brain-reading is to yield information from the person's brain in order to determine guilt, legal responsibility, or a risk of recidivism. This objective relates closely to 'obtaining evidence from a person about his involvement in the commission of a criminal offence'.

Both method and purpose of coercive brain-reading are in a relevant way similar to the method and purpose of a forcible medical procedure to obtain evidence. Therefore, case-law on the latter could be useful in deducing a legal framework for coercive brain-reading under Article 3 ECHR. Clearly, apart from these general similarities, significant differences exist as well, especially in individual cases (e.g. clipping fingernails versus fMRI). We must take account of these differences too.

The third relevant characteristic of treatments in light of Article 3 ECHR concerns *the manner of execution*. Regarding coercive brain-reading, two central manners are conceivable: either using physical or volitional coercion.[45] Both types of coercion have been implicitly considered in Strasbourg case-law on Article 3 ECHR. For example, regarding physical coercion, the Court has dealt with the use of security beds and sedative drugs in order to prevent individuals from causing damage, absconding, or suppressing evidence.[46] An example of volitional coercion concerns mandatory drug testing in prison, requesting prisoners to provide urine samples on pain of penitentiary sanctions.[47] Existing case-law that deals with physical and volitional coercion under Article 3 ECHR could provide helpful insights in determining the legal boundaries of *coercive* brain-reading in criminal law.

3.3.3 *Forcible Medical Procedures to Obtain Evidence in Light of Article 3 ECHR*

Medical procedures that are necessary in view of established principles of medicine will not normally violate Article 3 ECHR.[48] The Court refers to the example of

44 Mecacci & Haselager 2019, p. 444; Greely & Wagner 2011, pp. 763–765, 768 and 772. See also Gross 1962.

45 See Chapter 2, Section 2.7.

46 ECtHR 31 May 2016, appl.no. 29106/13 (*Coman/Romania*), § 14, 38–40; ECtHR 29 September 2005, appl.no. 24919/03 (*Mathew/The Netherlands*), § 180; ECtHR 24 September 1992, appl.no. 10533/83 (*Herczegfalvy/Austria*), § 81.

47 ECtHR 11 October 2005, appl.no. 60682/00 (*Young/UK*). Cf. European Commission of Human Rights (EComHR) 6 April 1994, appl.no. 21132/93 (*Peters/The Netherlands*).

48 ECtHR (GC) 11 July 2006, appl.no. 54810/00 (*Jalloh/Germany*), § 69.

forced-feeding, aiming to save the life of a prisoner who refuses to eat.[49] In such cases, the Court must determine whether the medical necessity has convincingly been shown and whether sufficient procedural guarantees exist and are complied with.[50]

Forcible medical procedures *to obtain evidence*, such as taking blood, saliva, or urine samples, as well as forensic brain-reading, are not applied for reasons of therapeutic necessity. Rather, they serve to answering criminal *legal* questions.[51] Still, Article 3 ECHR does not as such prohibit recourse to a non-consensual medical procedure in order to obtain evidence of someone's involvement in the commission of a criminal offence.[52] As the Grand Chamber holds:

> any recourse to a forcible medical intervention in order to obtain evidence of a crime must be convincingly justified on the facts of a particular case. This is especially true where the procedure is intended to retrieve from inside the individual's body real evidence of the very crime of which he is suspected. The particularly intrusive nature of such an act requires a strict scrutiny of all the surrounding circumstances.[53]

For this strict scrutiny, the Court pays particular attention to the following framework of factors:

(1) the extent to which the forcible medical procedure was necessary to obtain the evidence,
(2) the health risks for the suspect,
(3) the manner in which the procedure was carried out and the physical pain and mental suffering it caused,
(4) the level of medical supervision available, and
(5) the actual effects of the procedure on the suspect's health.[54]

49 See also ECtHR 5 April 2005, appl.no. 54825/00 (*Nevmerzhitsky/Ukraine*), § 94; ECtHR19 June 2007, appl.no. 12066/02 (*Ciorap/Moldova*), § 77.

50 ECtHR (GC) 11 July 2006, appl.no. 54810/00 (*Jalloh/Germany*), § 69; ECtHR 19 February 2015, appl. no. 75450/12 (*M.S./Croatia (No. 2)*), § 98; ECtHR 18 October 2012, appl.no. 37679/08 (*Bureš/Czech Republic*), § 87; ECtHR 13 May 2008, appl.no. 52515/99 (*Juhnke/Turkey*), § 71; ECtHR 24 September 1992, appl.no. 10533/83 (*Herczegfalvy/Austria*), § 82.

51 Regarding forensic brain-reading, sometimes, its use may contribute to answering both legal and medical questions. For example, the results of neuroprediction can inform both the judge in the context of a parole request and the psychiatrist in choosing the best treatment.

52 ECtHR (GC) 11 July 2006, appl.no. 54810/00 (*Jalloh/Germany*), § 70; ECtHR 2 July 2019, appl.no. 65290/14 (*R.S./Hungary*), § 57; ECtHR 3 May 2012, appl.no. 23880/05 (*Salikhov/Russia*), § 74; ECtHR 13 May 2008, appl.no. 52515/99 (*Juhnke/Turkey*), § 72.

53 ECtHR (GC) 11 July 2006, appl.no. 54810/00 (*Jalloh/Germany*), § 71. See also ECtHR 2 July 2019, appl.no. 65290/14 (*R.S./Hungary*), § 57; ECtHR 3 May 2012, appl.no. 23880/05 (*Salikhov/Russia*), § 73–74; ECtHR 13 May 2008, appl.no. 52515/99 (*Juhnke/Turkey*), § 72.

54 ECtHR (GC) 11 July 2006, appl.no. 54810/00 (*Jalloh/Germany*), § 76; ECtHR 2 July 2019, appl.no. 65290/14 (*R.S./Hungary*), § 58; ECtHR 3 May 2012, appl.no. 23880/05 (*Salikhov/Russia*), § 75; ECtHR 3 October 2008, appl.no. 35228/03 (*Bogumil/Portugal*), § 70; Vermeulen & Battjes 2018, p. 394; Jacobs 2012, p. 124.

In light of all circumstances of the individual case, the medical procedure must not attain a minimum level of severity.[55] Below, these five factors are first considered in general, followed by a discussion tailored to forensic brain-reading.

Factor 1. Necessity: Proportionality and Subsidiarity

In determining whether a forcible medical procedure was necessary to obtain evidence, the Court takes into account both principles of proportionality and subsidiarity. Proportionality refers to the relationship between a medical procedure and its purpose in an individual case. Subsidiarity pertains to the relationship between the medical procedure and other possible means of obtaining the information that is sought.

Regarding *proportionality*, due regard must be had to the seriousness of the offence at issue.[56] For example, in *Jalloh/Germany*, a street dealer was arrested for selling drugs. At the time of his arrest, the dealer swallowed a pellet of cocaine. In order to obtain this piece of evidence, a doctor forcibly administered emetics to the dealer, both via a tube introduced through his nose into his stomach and by injection. As a result, the dealer regurgitated the swallowed pellet, containing almost 0.22 grams of cocaine.[57] Regarding the necessity of this forcible medical procedure to obtain evidence, the Grand Chamber considered that drug trafficking is a serious offence. However, in this case, it was clear that the dealer upon whom the medical procedure was imposed 'had been storing the drugs in his mouth and could not, therefore, have been offering drugs for sale on a large scale'.[58] This was also reflected in the sentence – six-month imprisonment, suspended on probation – which was at the lower end of the range of criminal sentences.

Another example is the case of *Salikhov/Russia*. In order to obtain evidence of rape, the police used force when clipping the applicant's fingernails. As a result, the applicant's fingers started to bleed. Also, the authorities attempted to take a blood sample by force. Regarding the necessity, the Court emphasised that rape is a serious criminal offence. Based on Article 3 and 8 ECHR, States have a positive obligation to enact legislation that provides effective punishment of rape and to apply them in practice through effective investigation and prosecution.[59] However, since the applicant had initially been willing to cooperate with the police demands, the forcible medical intervention was not considered essential (it did not meet the requirement of subsidiarity).

55 ECtHR (GC) 11 July 2006, appl.no. 54810/00 (*Jalloh/Germany*), § 76; ECtHR 3 May 2012, appl.no. 23880/05 (*Salikhov/Russia*), § 75.

56 ECtHR (GC) 11 July 2006, appl.no. 54810/00 (*Jalloh/Germany*), § 71; ECtHR 3 May 2012, appl.no. 23880/05 (*Salikhov/Russia*), § 73.

57 ECtHR (GC) 11 July 2006, appl.no. 54810/00 (*Jalloh/Germany*), § 13.

58 Ibid., § 77.

59 ECtHR 3 May 2012, appl.no. 23880/05 (*Salikhov/Russia*), § 76.

There is debate on whether proportionality and the severity of an offence should indeed be relevant factors in determining whether medical procedures to yield evidence violate Article 3 ECHR. In their dissenting opinion in *Jalloh/Germany*, Judges Wildhaber and Caflisch state that the majority of judges relied on a claim from proportionality by considering that the applicant had been selling drugs only on a small scale. Wildhaber and Caflisch think this is a strange line of argument, as it values the health of large dealers less than the health of small dealers. The more important the dealer, the more licit the use of emetics.[60]

Similarly, Judge Bratza could not accept that the seriousness of an offence should be a relevant factor in determining whether a treatment violates Article 3 ECHR.[61] Bratza recalls that the Court has repeatedly emphasised that Article 3 ECHR prohibits in absolute terms the use of torture, inhuman, and degrading treatment. This prohibition applies irrespective of the victim's conduct and without the balancing of competing public interests. In light of this absolute nature, Bratza argues that 'the threshold [of Article 3 ECHR] cannot change according to the gravity of the suspected offence or the urgency of the need to obtain evidence of the offence'.[62]

Indeed, it would be incompatible with the absolute nature to argue that although a treatment *prima facie* attains a minimum level of severity, it will not violate Article 3 ECHR because the treatment can be considered proportionate to the offence at issue. However, in *Jalloh/Germany*, no such reasoning was developed. As Van Kempen argues, the reasoning of the Grand Chamber in *Jalloh* rather indicates a 'one-way-approach' of *dis*proportionality.[63] Some forcible procedures to obtain evidence are by themselves *not* severe enough to attain a minimum level of severity. Still, the *dis*proportionate relation to the criminal offence can 'push' the treatment within the scope of Article 3 ECHR. Meanwhile, if a forcible medical procedure by itself already attains a minimum level of severity, the seriousness of the offence cannot prevent that treatment from violating Article 3 ECHR. Thus, considerations of proportionality have the ability to 'push' a treatment into the spheres of Article 3 ECHR, but cannot 'pull them out' of the zone of absolutely prohibited State conduct.

Unlike the interpretation of Judge Bratza, Van Kempen's 'one-way-approach' is compatible with the absolute nature of the prohibition of ill-treatment – that is, any treatment attaining a minimum level of severity violates Article 3 ECHR, 'irrespective of the conduct of the person concerned and the nature of the offence at issue'.[64]

60 Dissenting opinion of Judges Wildhaber and Caflisch under ECtHR (GC) 11 July 2006, appl.no. 54810/00 (*Jalloh/Germany*), point 4.

61 Concurring opinion of Judge Bratza under ECtHR (GC) 11 July 2006, appl.no. 54810/00 (*Jalloh/Germany*).

62 Ibid.

63 Van Kempen, comment to ECtHR (GC) 11 July 2006, appl.no. 54810/00 (*Jalloh/Germany*), *NJCM-Bulletin* 2007(3), pp. 365–366.

64 ECtHR (GC) 1 June 2010, appl.no. 22978/05 (*Gäfgen/Germany*), § 107.

According to the principle of *subsidiarity*, the authorities must demonstrate that they took into consideration alternative methods for recovering the evidence they sought to obtain.[65] For example, in *Jalloh/Germany*, the Grand Chamber accepted that it was vital to the police to determine the exact amount and quality of the drugs the applicant had been selling. However, it was not satisfied that the forcible administration of emetics was indispensable to obtain the evidence: 'The prosecuting authorities could simply have waited for the drugs to pass through his system naturally'.[66] In this case, the Court considered it significant that many member States of the Council of Europe did not use the forcible administration of emetics to investigate drug offences. The German police could equally have obtained the evidence by less intrusive methods. This finding had an important role in determining a violation of Article 3 ECHR.[67]

Similarly, in *R.S./Hungary*, the Court accepted that it was necessary to identify the blood alcohol level of the applicant. This was vital to determine whether he had used alcohol or drugs while driving a car. However, the Court considered recourse to catheterisation unnecessary, since the police also proceeded with taking a blood sample for the same purposes.[68]

In assessing whether the authorities should have favoured less intrusive means or methods, the nature of the information sought can be a relevant factor. As the Court considers in *Salikhov/Russia*:

> The purpose of the medical intervention was the collection of biological samples which could be later examined for traces of the victim's blood or epithelial cells. Such traces being by their nature fragile and perishable, time was of the essence and the procedures had to be carried out urgently.[69]

Apparently, in some cases, when the evidence is fragile and perishable by nature, urgent collection might be required. Potentially, such urgent need may, in specific cases, justify the use of more intrusive, but less time-consuming procedures to obtain the evidence.

Yet, although the evidence in *Salikhov/Russia* required urgent collection, the Court was not satisfied with the necessity of using force when clipping the applicant's fingernails.[70] The applicant had initially demonstrated willingness to cooperate with the police demands. Therefore, the Court sees no explanation as to why the police favoured the use of force instead. Notwithstanding the applicant's initial

65 ECtHR (GC) 11 July 2006, appl.no. 54810/00 (*Jalloh/Germany*), § 71; ECtHR 3 May 2012, appl.no. 23880/05 (*Salikhov/Russia*), § 73.

66 ECtHR (GC) 11 July 2006, appl.no. 54810/00 (*Jalloh/Germany*), § 77.

67 Ibid., § 82. Cf. Van Kempen, comment to ECtHR (GC) 11 July 2006, appl.no. 54810/00 (*Jalloh/Germany*), *NJCM-Bulletin* 2007(3), p. 365.

68 ECtHR 2 July 2019, appl.no. 65290/14 (*R.S./Hungary*), § 70.

69 ECtHR 3 May 2012, appl.no. 23880/05 (*Salikhov/Russia*), § 76.

70 Ibid., § 77.

willingness to cooperate, he 'was not invited to submit voluntarily to the clipping of his nails but rather was overpowered and pinned down by force against the table during the procedure'.[71] In these circumstances, the Court considered that the police violence was 'gratuitous'. The use of brute force did not appear necessary to obtaining the evidence.[72] Accordingly, when an individual is *willing* to submit evidence *voluntarily*, convincing arguments are required to explain and, possibly, justify the use of physical coercion instead.

Factor 2. Health Risks

A forcible medical procedure to obtain evidence 'must not entail any risk of lasting detriment to the person's health'.[73] In *Jalloh/Germany*, the Grand Chamber was unsatisfied that the forcible administration of emetics – which had previously resulted in the deaths of two people – entailed 'merely negligible health risks'.[74] In *Salikhov/Russia*, the Court seems to suggest that when determining the health risks of medical procedures, their deviation from the established 'best practice' could be taken into account:

> Discussion of the health risks associated with forcible medical intervention appears superfluous in the circumstances of the present case. Nevertheless, the Court cannot but note the applicant's submission that the clipping of his nails so close to the skin that his fingers started bleeding must have been painful. The procedure was carried out by an investigator, without appropriate supervision by a medical specialist, *and deviated from the established best practice in the field of forensic medicine in that it did not appear to have represented the least intrusive method of retrieving required samples of material from under his fingernails*.[75]

Unfortunately, the Court refrains from defining 'best practice' in this context. The consideration lends itself for at least two interpretations. First, the Court could have meant that, ideally, any medical procedure used in a forensic context should *in general* attain to best practice – taking into account all aspects of the procedure, such as its validity, accuracy, efficiency, side effects, and level of intrusion. Following this interpretation, the Court has formulated some kind of rule of evidence, such as the *Daubert* standard in the USA.[76] Second, the Court could have meant to express that, ideally, any medical procedure used in a forensic context should attain to

[71] Ibid.

[72] Cf. ECtHR19 June 2007, appl.no. 12066/02 (*Ciorap/Moldova*), § 87.

[73] ECtHR (GC) 11 July 2006, appl.no. 54810/00 (*Jalloh/Germany*), § 71; ECtHR 3 May 2012, appl.no. 23880/05 (*Salikhov/Russia*), § 73. Cf. ECtHR 5 January 2006, appl.no. 32352/02 (*Schmidt/Germany*), p. 4.

[74] ECtHR (GC) 11 July 2006, appl.no. 54810/00 (*Jalloh/Germany*), § 78.

[75] ECtHR 3 May 2012, appl.no. 23880/05 (*Salikhov/Russia*), § 79 (emphasis added).

[76] *Daubert* v. *Merrell Dow Pharmaceuticals, Inc.* (1993) 509 U.S. 579, 589.

best practice *in terms of the involved health risks*. In other words, States should only employ least intrusive procedures.

The considerations on best practice in *Salikhov/Russia* are part of a paragraph concerning the health risks associated with clipping fingernails. This suggests that the second interpretation is likely to align best with the intentions of the Court. Deliberations on issues such as validity, accuracy, and efficiency do not typically fit within the prohibition of ill-treatment. Article 3 ECHR is basically concerned with the level of physical and mental suffering that a treatment causes, not with the reliability of evidence.

Moreover, even under Article 6 ECHR – the right to a fair trial – the Court refrains from providing specific rules of evidence that relate to the validity, accuracy, and efficiency of means of evidence gathering.[77] The Court considers that the Convention 'does not lay down any rules on the admissibility of evidence as such, which is therefore primarily a matter for regulation under national law'.[78] Since the Court refrains from providing specific rules of evidence under Article 6 ECHR, it is unlikely that it would formulate such rules under the head of Article 3 ECHR.

Thus, the second interpretation is most convincing: in assessing the health risks of a forcible medical procedure to obtain evidence, it is relevant whether the procedure attains to a best practice in terms of the health risks involved. Put differently: it is relevant whether the procedure is least intrusive to obtain the evidence that is sought.

Meanwhile, it remains unclear why the Court refers to the firm standard of 'best practice' and not to less stringent qualifications such as 'standard of care', 'state of art', or 'general acceptance'. Also unclear is which domestic authority should assess whether a procedure attains to best practice or not. A medical specialist? A police officer? A judge? Regarding common medical procedures such as clipping fingernails, a police officer and judge will likely be able to determine which way of execution involves the lowest risk of causing harm. However, regarding more complicated procedures, such as injecting emetics or applying brain-reading, a medical specialist's view might be necessary.[79]

Factor 3. Manner of Execution, Physical Pain, and Mental Suffering

The manner in which a forcible medical procedure to obtain evidence is executed, must not attain a minimum level of severity. The level of physical pain and/or mental suffering caused by the procedure is essential in this regard.[80]

77 See Chapter 7.

78 ECtHR (GC) 17 October 2019, appl.nos. 1874/13 and 8567/13 (*López Ribalda and Others/Spain*), § 149–150; ECtHR 12 July 1988, appl.no. 10862/84 (*Schenk/Switzerland*), § 46.

79 Cf. ECtHR (GC) 11 July 2006, appl.no. 54810/00 (*Jalloh/Germany*), § 80; ECtHR 2 July 2019, appl.no. 65290/14 (*R.S./Hungary*), § 71.

80 ECtHR (GC) 11 July 2006, appl.no. 54810/00 (*Jalloh/Germany*), § 72; ECtHR 2 July 2019, appl.no. 65290/14 (*R.S./Hungary*), § 72; ECtHR 3 May 2012, appl.no. 23880/05 (*Salikhov/Russia*), § 73. Cf. ECtHR19 June 2007, appl.no. 12066/02 (*Ciorap/Moldova*), § 84–87.

In *Jalloh/Germany*, the Court considered that pinning down the applicant and feeding him emetics via a tube through his nose must have caused him pain and anxiety. And the *injection* of another emetic constituted a further bodily intrusion against the applicant's will.[81] Furthermore, the Court took account of the applicant's *mental* suffering while he waited for the emetics to take effect: 'During this time he was restrained and kept under observation by police officers and a doctor. Being forced to regurgitate under these conditions must have been humiliating for him'.[82]

In *Salikhov/Russia*, the police restrained the applicant as well. They pushed him against a table when clipping his fingernails and pinned him to the floor when trying to obtain a blood sample, using their weight on his limbs and head for restraint.[83] Both before and during these medical procedures, the applicant was repeatedly beaten with a rubber truncheon. He was pushed around and injured his head against a desktop computer. In line with its central approach, the Court stressed that:

> any recourse to physical force in respect of a person deprived of his liberty which has not been made strictly necessary by his own conduct diminishes human dignity and is in principle an infringement of the right set forth in Article 3 of the Convention.[84]

In *Salikhov*, the use of physical coercion was unnecessary and could not be conducive to facilitating the collection of forensic evidence. Rather, it was intended to arouse feelings of fear and inferiority, debasing the applicant, breaking his psychological resistance, and forced him into submission.[85]

In *R.S./Hungary*, the Court argued that given the intrusive nature of the employed catheterisation, this case had to be distinguished from interventions that are of 'minor importance' (such as taking saliva with a buccal swab[86]). Although the procedure was carried out by a doctor in a medical emergency service, the police officers restrained the applicant and handcuffed him throughout the medical procedure.[87] The manner in which the procedure had been carried out was 'liable to arouse in the applicant feelings of insecurity, anguish and stress that were capable of humiliating and debasing him'.[88]

In all three examples – *Jalloh*, *Salikhov*, *R.S.* – it was the accumulation of restraining the applicant, enforcing the medical procedure, and employing additional

[81] ECtHR (GC) 11 July 2006, appl.no. 54810/00 (*Jalloh/Germany*), § 79. See also § 82. Cf. ECtHR19 June 2007, appl.no. 12066/02 (*Ciorap/Moldova*), § 84–87; ECtHR 5 April 2005, appl.no. 54825/00 (*Nevmerzhitsky/Ukraine*), § 97.

[82] ECtHR (GC) 11 July 2006, appl.no. 54810/00 (*Jalloh/Germany*), § 79.

[83] ECtHR 3 May 2012, appl.no. 23880/05 (*Salikhov/Russia*), § 77–78.

[84] Ibid., § 78.

[85] Ibid.

[86] ECtHR 15 May 2018, appl.no. 41079/16 (*Caruana/Malta*), § 41.

[87] ECtHR 2 July 2019, appl.no. 65290/14 (*R.S./Hungary*), § 69.

[88] Ibid., § 72.

violence that together resulted in a manner of execution in breach of Article 3 ECHR. Meanwhile, sometimes, the 'mere' restraining of a person can by itself raise an issue under the prohibition of ill-treatment. For instance, in *Bureš/Czech*, the applicant had been restrained to his bed in a sobering-up centre for almost two hours, merely because of his 'restlessness'. Strapping the applicant resulted in severe bilateral paresis of his elbow nerves. Restraining the applicant in this way caused him great distress and physical suffering, constituting an inhuman and degrading treatment in breach of Article 3 ECHR.[89]

However, measures of mechanical and chemical restraint[90] are not *in principle* prohibited under Article 3 ECHR.[91] Imposing such measures on *patients* in psychiatric hospitals can be permissible based on medical standards in psychiatry. Those standards could allow recourse to restraint when no other measures can calm down an agitated individual and prevent him from harming himself or others.[92] Restrained patients must be under close supervision.[93] In order to convincingly show that these requirements are satisfied with, the Court underlines the importance of properly recording every use of restraint.[94]

Apart from restraining *patients*, employing measures of restraint in a *criminal legal* context, such as handcuffing, will not necessarily raise an issue under Article 3 ECHR either, provided that:

> the measure has been imposed in connection with lawful arrest or detention and does not entail use of force, or public exposure, exceeding what is reasonably considered necessary in the circumstances. In this regard, it is of importance for instance whether there is reason to believe that the person concerned would resist arrest or abscond, cause injury or damage or suppress evidence.[95]

Thus, confining prisoners to a restraint bed without medical necessity will not, as a rule, give rise to a breach of Article 3 ECHR.[96] In light of all circumstances of the

89 ECtHR 18 October 2012, appl.no. 37679/08 (*Bureš/Czech Republic*), § 88–90. Cf. ECtHR 29 May 2012, appl.nos. 16563/08, 40841/08, 8192/10 and 18656/10 (*Julin/Estonia*), § 127; ECtHR 19 February 2015, appl.no. 75450/12 (*M.S./Croatia (No. 2)*), § 102; ECtHR 31 March 2009, appl.no. 14612/02 (*Wiktorko/Poland*), § 55–57.

90 The latter consists in the forcible administration of pharmaceuticals for the purpose of controlling: CPT/Inf(2017)6.

91 See, for example, ECtHR 31 May 2016, appl.no. 29106/13 (*Coman/Romania*), § 38–43; ECtHR 24 September 1992, appl.no. 10533/83 (*Herczegfalvy/Austria*), § 79–84.

92 ECtHR 19 February 2015, appl.no. 75450/12 (*M.S./Croatia (No. 2)*), § 104. See on this: ECtHR 18 October 2012, appl.no. 37679/08 (*Bureš/Czech Republic*), § 95–96; ECtHR 19 February 2015, appl.no. 75450/12 (*M.S./Croatia (No. 2)*), § 105.

93 ECtHR 18 October 2012, appl.no. 37679/08 (*Bureš/Czech Republic*), § 102.

94 Ibid., § 103.

95 ECtHR (GC) 17 July 2014, appl.nos. 32541/08 and 43441/08 (*Svinarenko and Slyadnev/Russia*), § 117. Also: ECtHR 29 September 2005, appl.no. 24919/03 (*Mathew/The Netherlands*), § 180; ECtHR 27 November 2003, appl.no. 65436/01 (*Hénaf/France*), § 48.

96 ECtHR 29 May 2012, appl.nos. 16563/08, 40841/08, 8192/10, and 18656/10 (*Julin/Estonia*), § 124. See also ECtHR 13 February 2014, appl.no. 66393/10 (*Tali/Estonia*), § 58, 79–82.

individual case,[97] the means of restraint must not be disproportionate to the aims pursued.[98] For instance, in *Hénaf/France*, restraining a seventy-five-year-old prisoner to a hospital bed to prevent absconding was considered disproportionate.[99] In reaching this conclusion, the Court took into account the applicant's age, state of health, the absence of any previous conduct indicating a serious security risk, and the fact that two police officers were guarding the applicant's room.[100]

In *Julin/Estonia*, the applicant had been confined to a restraint bed for almost nine hours in a row because of aggressive behaviour towards prison officers. The Court considered that even if the initial confinement was justified, there were no convincing reasons for continuing the measure of restraint up to nearly nine hours.[101] The Court held that:

> Confinement to a restraint bed, without medical reasons – which have not been shown to have existed in the present case – should rarely need to be applied for more than a few hours.[102]

After six hours, the authorities in *Julin/Estonia* decided to continue the applicant's confinement twice because his 'behaviour' was 'abnormal' although he was 'silent'. In view of the great distress and physical discomfort the prolonged confinement must have caused, these reasons were 'wholly insufficient' to justify the physical restraint.[103] Article 3 ECHR had been violated.[104]

Factors 4 and 5. Level of Medical Supervision and Actual Health Effects

Also of particular importance is the level of medical supervision in respect of a forcible medical procedure to obtain evidence.[105] As the Grand Chamber holds in *Jalloh/Germany*: 'Another material consideration in such cases is whether the forcible medical procedure was ordered and administered by medical doctors and whether the person concerned was placed under constant medical supervision'.[106]

[97] ECtHR 20 January 2011, appl.no. 891/05 (*Kashavelov/Bulgaria*), § 38.

[98] ECtHR 27 November 2003, appl.no. 65436/01 (*Hénaf/France*), § 56; ECtHR 20 January 2011, appl. no. 891/05 (*Kashavelov/Bulgaria*), § 39. Cf. ECtHR 18 October 2012, appl.no. 37679/08 (*Bureš/Czech Republic*), 96, 100; ECtHR 19 February 2015, appl.no. 75450/12 (*M.S./Croatia (No. 2)*), § 105.

[99] ECtHR 27 November 2003, appl.no. 65436/01 (*Hénaf/France*), § 56.

[100] Ibid.

[101] ECtHR 29 May 2012, appl.nos. 16563/08, 40841/08, 8192/10, and 18656/10 (*Julin/Estonia*), § 127.

[102] Ibid.

[103] Ibid.

[104] Cf. ECtHR 13 February 2014, appl.no. 66393/10 (*Tali/Estonia*), § 81–82.

[105] ECtHR (GC) 11 July 2006, appl.no. 54810/00 (*Jalloh/Germany*), § 76; ECtHR 3 May 2012, appl.no. 23880/05 (*Salikhov/Russia*), § 75.

[106] ECtHR (GC) 11 July 2006, appl.no. 54810/00 (*Jalloh/Germany*), § 73. See also ECtHR 3 May 2012, appl.no. 23880/05 (*Salikhov/Russia*), § 73; ECtHR 3 October 2008, appl.no. 35228/03 (*Bogumil/Portugal*), § 70. Cf. ECtHR 29 May 2012, appl.nos. 16563/08, 40841/08, 8192/10, and 18656/10 (*Julin/Estonia*), § 125; ECtHR 18 October 2012, appl.no. 37679/08 (*Bureš/Czech Republic*), § 86, 104.

In *Salikhov/Russia*, the Court was unsatisfied that clipping the applicant's fingernails was carried out by an investigator without appropriate supervision by a medical specialist.[107] The required supervision should entail both the assessment of the individual's health risks *prior* to the procedure and constant medical supervision *during* the procedure.[108]

A final central factor is whether the medical procedure has actually affected the subject's health and whether it entails lasting adverse health effects.[109] In this regard, the Court must assess whether a causal link exists between the forcible medical procedure and the detrimental health effects on the person concerned.[110]

In conclusion, forcible medical procedures to obtain evidence about the subject's involvement in a crime are not as such prohibited by Article 3 ECHR. In assessing whether such procedures attain a minimum level of severity, a strict scrutiny of all relevant circumstances is required. A framework of five factors is of particular importance: (1) the necessity of the forcible medical procedure to obtain the evidence, (2) the health risks to the suspect, (3) the manner in which the procedure was carried out and the physical pain and mental suffering it caused, (4) the level of medical supervision, and (5) the actual effects of the procedure on the suspect's health. The next section considers how these factors, deduced from Strasbourg case-law, could be extrapolated to coercive brain-reading in criminal justice.

3.3.4 *Coercive Forensic Brain-Reading under the Prohibition of Ill-Treatment*

Within the context of Article 3 ECHR, coercive brain-reading displays relevant similarities with what the Court defines as 'a medical procedure in defiance of the will of the person in order to obtain from him evidence of his involvement in committing a crime'.[111] Such medical procedures are not *ipso facto* prohibited by Article 3 ECHR. Similarly, it might be possible that some forms of coercive brain-reading could be allowed. However, as discussed, any recourse to forcible medical procedures in the acquisition of evidence must be convincingly justified in light of the facts of the case. As previously cited:

> This is especially true where the procedure is intended to retrieve from inside the individual's body real evidence of the very crime of which he is suspected. The particularly intrusive nature of such an act requires a strict scrutiny of all the surrounding circumstances.[112]

107 ECtHR 3 May 2012, appl.no. 23880/05 (*Salikhov/Russia*), § 79.
108 ECtHR (GC) 11 July 2006, appl.no. 54810/00 (*Jalloh/Germany*), § 80.
109 ECtHR (GC) 11 July 2006, appl.no. 54810/00 (*Jalloh/Germany*), § 74; ECtHR 3 May 2012, appl.no. 23880/05 (*Salikhov/Russia*),§ 73; ECtHR 3 October 2008, appl.no. 35228/03 (*Bogumil/Portugal*), § 70.
110 Cf. ECtHR (GC) 11 July 2006, appl.no. 54810/00 (*Jalloh/Germany*), § 81.
111 See Section 3.3.2.
112 ECtHR (GC) 11 July 2006, appl.no. 54810/00 (*Jalloh/Germany*), § 71–76. Also ECtHR 2 July 2019, appl. no. 65290/14 (*R.S./Hungary*), § 57; ECtHR 3 May 2012, appl.no. 23880/05 (*Salikhov/Russia*), § 73–74.

The strict review should particularly focus on the framework of five factors discussed in the previous section. One may argue, however, that unlike taking blood for retrieving DNA or recovering a swallowed pellet of cocaine through administering emetics (both constituting a forcible medical procedure to obtain evidence[113]), brain-reading does not yield *real*, that is, *tangible evidence* about a specific crime. Instead, it 'merely' acquires *data* about a person's brain structure or its activity in response to a particular action or stimuli, which enables the examiner to drawing inferences about certain brain or mental states. Thus, in view of the quotation above, one could argue that since brain-reading is not intended to retrieve *real evidence* from inside the individual's body, there is no reason to assume that the framework of five factors is essential to coercive brain-reading.

However, the fact that brain-reading does not yield real evidence need not be decisive in the normative analysis under Article 3 ECHR. It is not the acquisition of real evidence that requires a strict scrutiny of all five factors, but rather the *particularly intrusive nature* of such procedures.[114]

Indeed, in the course of brain-reading, the level of *physical* intrusion clearly differs from the forcible admission of emetics (*Jalloh*) or compelled catheterisation (*R.S.*). Still, coercive brain-reading does interfere with the subject's physical integrity. A CT-scan exposes the subject to radiation. PET and SPECT require the injection of radioactive contrast agent into the person's blood. Sometimes, CT and (f)MRI require similar injections. With EEG, electrodes are placed on the subject's skull. And, although minor, (f)MRI affects the magnetic nuclei of atoms in the brain. Clearly, when physical coercion is used, additional interferences with the subject's body will arise.

Admittedly, just like (properly) clipping fingernails and taking a blood sample,[115] the bodily intrusions caused by brain-reading technology are minor and relatively slight. Meanwhile, the Court qualifies clipping fingernails and taking blood as forcible medical procedures that require a strict scrutiny of all five factors.[116] Therefore, it is not unreasonable to expect that the Court would follow a similar approach regarding coercive brain-reading. Moreover, apart from its physical invasiveness, coercive brain-reading will also intrude certain mental aspects of life.[117] As Brownsword argues, '[w]ith the development of powerful new brain-imaging technologies (...) researchers have a window into the brains and, possibly, into a deeper understanding of the mental lives of their participants'.[118]

[113] ECtHR 3 May 2012, appl.no. 23880/05 (*Salikhov/Russia*); ECtHR (GC) 11 July 2006, appl.no. 54810/00 (*Jalloh/Germany*). Cf. ECtHR 2 July 2019, appl.no. 65290/14 (*R.S./Hungary*), § 68.

[114] See also Jacobs 2012, p. 124.

[115] See, for example, ECtHR 15 May 2018, appl.no. 41079/16 (*Caruana/Malta*), § 41; ECtHR 20 January 2009, appl.no. 20689/08 (*W./The Netherlands*), p. 8; ECtHR 7 December 2006, appl.no. 29514/05 (*Van der Velden/The Netherlands*), p. 9.

[116] ECtHR 3 May 2012, appl.no. 23880/05 (*Salikhov/Russia*), § 75–81.

[117] Cf. Van Toor 2017, pp. 205–206.

[118] Brownsword 2012, p. 223; McCarthy-Jones 2019.

Altogether, coercive brain-reading intends to retrieve information from inside the subject's brain, invading her physical integrity and intruding her mental live. Therefore, we can safely argue that the framework of five factors formulated in respect of forcible medical procedures will be equally relevant to coercive brain-reading. Let us take a closer look at these factors.

Factor 1. Necessity: Proportionality and Subsidiarity

The more intrusive coercive brain-reading is, the more severe the related crime should be to avoid disproportionality. If a brain-reading test is by itself not severe enough to attain a minimum level of severity, the disproportionate relation to the offence could still raise an issue under Article 3 ECHR. Meanwhile, following a one-way-approach of proportionality, if coercive brain-reading does already attain a minimum level of severity by itself, the seriousness of the offence cannot prevent a violation of Article 3 ECHR.

The intrusiveness of brain-reading depends on a variety of factors. First, the involved level of *physical* intrusion is relevant. This level will depend on the precise brain-reading technology that is used. In general, brain-reading entails only minor physical intrusions.[119] Examining an individual's brain with neuroimaging is not likely to attain such a level of physical invasiveness that it would be disproportionate to most criminal offences.[120]

Second, brain-reading is also *mentally* intrusive. It enables the authorities to draw inferences about a person's mental states without consent. In respect of brain-reading applications like the CIT, Van Toor argues that such technologies bypass the person's will not to disclose personal information 'stored' in the brain. Therefore, he argues, the person is no longer treated as a human being, but rather as an *object* for retrieving information.[121] According to Van Toor, such use of brain-reading constitutes an 'inferior, excluding and degrading treatment', which he considers 'inhuman' as well.[122] In making this argument, Van Toor refers to Bublitz and Merkel,[123] who state:

119 Cf. ECtHR 7 December 2006, appl.no. 29514/05 (*Van der Velden/The Netherlands*), p. 9; ECtHR 5 January 2006, appl.no. 32352/02 (*Schmidt/Germany*), pp. 4–5; ECtHR 15 May 2018, appl.no. 41079/16 (*Caruana/Malta*), § 36, 41.

120 Cf. the use of X-Ray without valid consent: EComHR 10 December 1984, appl.no. 10435/83 (*Acmanne and others/Belgium*).

121 Van Toor 2017, pp. 205–206.

122 Ibid., p. 206: '*Mijns inziens is het omzeilen van de wil van een persoon omtrent het delen van persoonlijke herinneringen een inferieure, uitsluitende en (daardoor) vernederende handeling. (…) Daarnaast kan hij geen zelfstandige en persoonlijke beslissingen nemen met betrekking tot het delen van zijn, niet-anders geopenbaarde, verhaal. Dat is mensonwaardig*'.

123 Ibid., p. 205.

> It is the sinister side of neuroscientific techniques to bypass the first-person perspective and to treat the other as a physical object, reducing them to an object of nature, treating them according to natural laws and negating their control over their own minds. This heteronomous access to the inner realm of others may amount to mental programming, conditioning, brainwashing, and objectification. And this is what respect for human dignity forbids. Respect for persons as subjects entails respect for their first-person perspective and implies prohibitions on direct interventions.[124]

These are interesting thoughts. However, in my view, Van Toor's argument is not persuasive in respect of brain-reading technology. First, the quotation of Bublitz and Merkel relates to their discussion of the legal implications of non-consensual *neurointerventions*. These interventions aim to *alter* or *manipulate* the brain. Examples are deep brain stimulation, pharmaceuticals, and transcranial magnetic stimulation. Whereas brain-reading aims to obtain *information* about the brain, neurointerventions aim to *intervene* in the brain and actually change mental states and behaviour. Both techniques are fundamentally different, also from a normative (legal and ethical) perspective.[125]

Indeed, regarding *neurointerventions*, it may be arguable that coercively *changing* the brain and neural correlates of mental states 'reduces people to an object of nature', raising an issue concerning human dignity and physical or mental integrity under Article 3 ECHR.[126] In *Tyrer/UK*, a case concerning the infliction of corporal punishment by the police, the Court considered that *treating a person as an object* can indeed diminish human dignity:

> The very nature of judicial corporal punishment is that it involves one human being inflicting physical violence on another human being. Furthermore, it is institutionalised violence that is in the present case violence permitted by the law, ordered by the judicial authorities of the State and carried out by the police authorities of the State. (…) Thus, although the applicant did not suffer any severe or long-lasting physical effects, his punishment - *whereby he was treated as an object in the power of the authorities* - constituted an assault on precisely that which it is one of the main purposes of [Article 3] to protect, namely a person's dignity and physical integrity.[127]

However, whether the ECtHR would be inclined to extrapolate this reasoning to coercive *brain-reading* is not clear at all. Methods of data-acquisition that approach a defendant or detainee as an object of investigation, rather than a subject, are quite common in criminal law (especially in inquisitorial legal systems). When forcibly

[124] Bublitz & Merkel 2014, p. 73.
[125] For example, Birks & Douglas 2018; Vincent, Nadelhoffer & McCay 2020; Forsberg 2021.
[126] Cf. Kirchmair 2019.
[127] ECtHR 25 April 1978, appl.no. 5856/72 (*Tyrer/UK*), § 33 (emphasis added). See also ECtHR (GC) 28 September 2015, appl.no. 23380/09 (*Bouyid/Belgium*), § 90.

taking blood for a blood alcohol test, or pulling out a hair for a DNA analysis, the individual can hardly be considered anything else than an object of investigation. Typically, these methods of criminal investigation are not conceived as to diminish human dignity and violate Article 3 ECHR. Moreover, even regarding the forcible means of retrieving evidence in the cases of *Jalloh*, *Salikhov* and *R.S.*, the Court has not referred to the issue of objectification at all.[128]

One could respond that obtaining information about a defendant's memories and other mental states through coercive brain-reading differs from taking blood and hair: whereas the latter acquires *biological material*, brain-reading yields *cognitive information*.[129] According to Van Toor, this distinction is relevant here. Unlike biological material, cognitive information can only be disclosed via *rational means* of the person himself. That is, only when the individual *decides* to disclose such information. Van Toor argues that eliminating the individual's rationality through brain-reading – bypassing the subject's will not to reveal cognitive information – impairs the person in being human and violates his intrinsic honour.[130]

Whether this argument is compelling regarding present brain-reading applications is debatable. First, brain-reading technologies do not *directly* yield any *cognitive information*. Rather, they obtain rough *data* about *biological features and responses*. These data enable the examiner to draw inferences about certain mental states and cognitive functions. In the same vein: taking blood for DNA analysis does not in itself reveal whether the suspect had sexual intercourse with the victim on the day of the offence. Drawing such conclusions requires more evidence and logical steps.

Second, current brain-reading applications, such as CITs and lie detection, do not have the ability to completely circumvent the individual's rationality by 'downloading' her thoughts or memories directly from the brain. Subjects will remain able to prevent their memories and lies from being identified. One can *decide* not to press a yes-or-no-button in the context of lie detection. One can *refuse* to observe the presented stimuli attentively during a CIT. And one can *choose* to distort the procedure and test results by using countermeasures. The acquisition of brain data with present forms of brain-reading will always involve at least some rational process of the subject.

Perhaps, futuristic brain-reading such as the neural representation of real-time thoughts may one day enable us to significantly restrict or circumvent the person's rationality in disclosing mental states. However, since only moving one's tongue could already distort present-day neuroimaging assessments,[131] it is unclear whether

[128] ECtHR (GC) 11 July 2006, appl.no. 54810/00 (*Jalloh/Germany*); ECtHR 3 May 2012, appl.no. 23880/05 (*Salikhov/Russia*); ECtHR 2 July 2019, appl.no. 65290/14 (*R.S./Hungary*).

[129] Cf. Van Toor 2017, p. 206.

[130] Ibid., p. 206: '*Kortom, zijn rationaliteit volledig uitschakelen is een aantasting van het mens-zijn en een schending van intrinsieke eer die elke mens in gelijke mate toekomt*'.

[131] Kanwisher 2009, p. 12; Mecacci & Haselager 2019, p. 455.

such innovative forms of brain-reading will be able to 'completely eliminate' rationality. But let us – for the sake of the argument – assume they could. Then still, it remains unclear whether and why bypassing a person's rationality by measuring brain activity would arouse such levels of pain, suffering, fear, anguish, or feelings of inferiority that this will raise an issue under Article 3 ECHR.

Of note, making arguments from rationality will inevitably touch upon conceptual ambiguities. At present, it is unclear how to understand 'rationality', which mental processes exactly qualify as such, and how they are relevant in a normative way.[132] Prior to determining the potential implications of bypassing rationality in light of Article 3 ECHR, it would be valuable to get a clearer understanding of the concept of rationality more generally.

Regarding *subsidiarity*, less intrusive methods should prevail over coercive brain-reading. For example, suppose that law enforcement authorities intend to examine whether an uncooperative defendant suffered from dementia at the time of the offence. Recently, a neurological examination on dementia has been performed in a hospital. In such cases, it would prevail to request the existing brain-derived data over coercing the suspect into another brain scan.[133] In addition, coercion should only be used if it is clear that the subject is not willing to cooperate in a brain-reading test. Physical coercion is only allowed when strictly necessary in view of the subject's own behaviour.[134]

In some cases, the fragile and perishable nature of the information sought could require urgent collection.[135] Hence, when time is of essence, coercive brain-reading could potentially be acceptable even though a less intrusive, but more time-consuming method for acquiring the information is available. However, regarding brain-based diagnostics, neuroprediction, and lie detection, the information need not qualify as 'fragile and perishable'.[136] When a defendant suffered from a neural anomaly during the time of the offence, that anomaly could be detectable with neuroimaging a day, a week, as well as a month after the offence (such as a brain tumour).[137] Similarly, the underlying assumption of lie detection – that the complex

[132] Ligthart, Meynen & Douglas 2022.

[133] Moreover, in some cases, it may be arguable that a physically non-invasive brain-reading application, such as a short lie detection test, could be less 'intrusive' than traditional methods of criminal investigation, like incarnation and all-day interrogations. Cf. Van Toor 2017, p. 200.

[134] Cf. ECtHR 3 May 2012, appl.no. 23880/05 (*Salikhov/Russia*), § 77–78.

[135] Discussed in Section 3.3.3.

[136] Yet, we cannot exclude the possibility that sometimes the nature of the information does require urgent collection. In such cases, the need for urgent collection should convincingly be shown to exist.

[137] Particular neural pathologies, like a brain tumour and certain forms of dementia, may develop in different rates. See, for example, Dagogo & Shaw 2018. In addition, medical reasons may require urgent neuroimaging, for example, if there are reasons to believe that a defendant or detainee suffers from acute cerebral bleed.

process of lying activates particular brain regions more than others – is also insensitive to time. Whether one lies today, next week, or next month, the same process of lying will be engaged in terms of activating the same brain areas. Admittedly, after a period of time, one could forget certain aspects of a particular event. But determining whether someone remembers things correctly is different from assessing whether one is lying, that is, whether one *deliberately* makes false statements.

Sometimes, the information sought with a CIT *could* qualify as 'fragile and perishable', therefore requiring urgent collection. First, if the subject *forgets* particular aspects of a past event due to time delay, detecting *recognition* of those aspects will be difficult or impossible.[138] For instance, research has shown that when a CIT is conducted with a time delay of one until two weeks,[139] the detection ability tends to be decreased compared with a similar test conducted immediately after a mock crime.[140] Time delay appears to exert a stronger effect on peripheral details that do not directly relate to the crime (like a picture on the wall). Recognition of central aspects appears less sensitive to time delay.[141] Hu and Rosenfeld found that employing a P300-CIT one month after a mock crime 'seemed about equally sensitive when compared with the immediately tested guilty participants (…). This is probably due to the fact that the item used in the present P300-CIT was the most central detail of the crime: the item that was stolen'.[142] Sometimes, urgent application of a CIT could also be desirable to limit the risk of leaking relevant items to the public, which can affect the test's reliability.[143] Altogether, in some cases, the urgent need of collecting information about a person's recognition can be a relevant factor in determining the necessity of applying a coercive CIT.

Factor 2. Health Risks

Forcible medical procedures to obtain evidence should not entail any risks of lasting detriment to the person's health. Merely negligible health effects could be acceptable.[144] In this regard, a medical expert's view can be valuable but is not necessarily decisive.[145] In addition, it is relevant whether the medical procedure attains to best practice in terms of health risks.

138 Meijer et al. 2016, p. 599; Van Toor 2017, p. 79.

139 This research mainly focussed on the CIT with measurements of the autonomic nervous system.

140 Rosenfled et al. 2013, p. 123; Hu & Rosenfeld 2012, p. 1097; Peth, Vossel & Gamer 2012, p. 381; Nahari & Ben-Shakhar 2011, p. 733; Gamer, Kosiol & Vossel 2010. 105.

141 Rosenfeld et al. 2013, p. 123; Hu & Rosenfeld 2012, p. 1091.

142 Hu & Rosenfeld 2012, p. 1097.

143 Van Toor 2017, p. 88. See Chapter 2, Section 2.3.2.

144 Discussed in Section 3.3.3.

145 Cf. ECtHR (GC) 11 July 2006, appl.no. 54810/00 (*Jalloh/Germany*), § 79; ECtHR 2 July 2019, appl.no. 65290/14 (*R.S./Hungary*), § 71.

Health risks differ across neuroimaging technologies. Generally, (f)MRI and EEG are considered safe.[146] CT, PET, and SPECT expose the subject to radiation, which could potentially increase the risk of developing cancer. Rushing, Pryma, and Langleben write that:

> With an increasing number of scans in a single patient, an increase in cancer risk can be expected and should be included in risk/benefit ratio considerations. While the risk of cancer induction from ionizing radiation from diagnostic imaging studies is real (and unnecessary exposures should be avoided), it is impossible to accurately estimate the risk from a given scan, though the risk is certainly very low.[147]

The exact individualised risk will depend on the precise part of the body to be scanned, together with the person's sex and age, which are both relevant factors in the Courts determination under Article 3 ECHR.[148] Whether the health risks involved with CT, PET and SPECT will either qualify as merely negligible or rather unacceptable, calls for an expert's view and political consideration. Interestingly, Dutch criminal law permits the use of X-ray (±0.2 mSv) to search a person's body, but rules out the use of CT (±2.3 mSv) because the radiation doses of the latter have been considered too high.[149]

Coercive brain-reading should probably only be employed if it attains to best practice in terms of health risks. The authorities should use the safest method to yield the information that is sought. For example, when the results of a recently employed PET-scan are available, it would probably not attain to best practice to order another PET-scan, which would again expose the subject to certain doses of radiation. Similarly, if the information sought could be obtained through both an MRI and CT, using MRI would, in general, qualify as best practice since this technology does not involve radiation exposure, unlike CT. Such an approach of the Court's considerations on best practices aligns with the requirement of subsidiarity, discussed above under factor 1. Ultimately, which technology should qualify as the safest shall depend on all circumstances of the individual case. For this judgement, a medical expert's view will be valuable.

Factor 3. Manner of Execution, Physical Pain, and Mental Suffering

Coercive brain-reading must not attain a minimum level of severity. The involved level of physical and/or mental suffering is essential in this regard.[150] As argued

[146] Though contraindications could exist for (f)MRI, such as the presence of metal objects in the body or being claustrophobic. See Chapter 2, Section 2.2.2.

[147] Rushing, Pryma & Langleben 2012, pp. 7–8.

[148] Smith-Bindman et al. 2009, p. 2079; Brenner & Hall 2009, p. 2281; Rushing, Pryma & Langleben 2012, p. 7. See also Section 3.2.

[149] Articles 56 and 195 of the Dutch Code of Criminal Procedure and *Kamerstukken II* 1999/00, 26983, 3, p. 18. See also *Kamerstukken II* 1994/95, 24263, 3, p. 52; *Kamerstukken II* 1993/94, 23445, 3, p. 36.

[150] Cf. ECtHR (GC) 11 July 2006, appl.no. 54810/00 (*Jalloh/Germany*), § 72, 79; ECtHR 3 May 2012, appl.no. 23880/05 (*Salikhov/Russia*), § 73; ECtHR19 June 2007, appl.no. 12066/02 (*Ciorap/Moldova*), § 84–87. Discussed in Section 3.3.3

under factor 1, brain-reading will not normally involve serious physical pain and/or mental suffering. However, although the technology itself is considered generally safe, different *means of coercion* could increase the risk of causing physical pain and/or mental suffering. Below, brain-reading with both volitional and physical coercion is considered.

VOLITIONAL COERCION. Clearly, making threats or offers will not typically involve additional interferences with the subject's physical or mental integrity. As long as the neuroimaging technology does not cause serious physical pain and/or mental suffering, volitionally coerced brain-reading is unlikely to attain a minimum level of severity.[151]

Meanwhile, regarding CITs, the use of volitional coercion could possibly increase the risk of arousing feelings of fear, anguish, or inferiority. These tests require the subject to observe the presented stimuli attentively.[152] This test of recognition appears most accurate when the observation is visual.[153] The mental impact of being coerced into a visual CIT will depend on the content of the images the subject has to look at. Think of images of a dead body at the crime scene. Observing such stimuli can elicit strong emotional reactions and may have profound mental effects on the observer. The precise effects of watching such images could depend on personal circumstances. For example, if the subject has a relative who has been murdered, it is possible that the images of a corpse at a crime scene have considerable mental impact. A CIT may then arouse higher levels of fear, anguish, and/or inferiority compared with a subject who has not been a victim of such crimes.

One could reject this argument by contending that mental effects like these are unlikely to exceed the mental impact of confronting a defendant with crime-related images during a regular police interrogation.[154] In both cases, the individual observes pictures of a crime. In general, presenting cruel crime-related images in the context of police interrogations will not attain a minimum level of severity.

The case of *Jager/The Netherlands* provides an illustration. The applicant complained about the fact that during police interrogations photographs of his wife and children were displayed among pictures of the nine-year-old victim's partially undressed dead body (the so-called *Zaanse verhoormethode*). The idea of this interrogation method is that by unconsciously observing the photographs, a guilty suspect will remember facts of the crime insofar he has been responsible for them. Such unconscious recognition can be detected through body language.[155] Regarding the level of mental suffering this method caused, the ECtHR considered that:

151 Cf. Thompson 2005, p. 1626; Van Toor 2017, pp. 199–200.
152 Chapter 2, Section 2.3.2.
153 Van der Cruyssen et al. 2021; Rosenfeld et al. 2015a; Rosenfeld 2015b; Ambach et al. 2010, p. 266.
154 Cf. Van Toor 2017, pp. 199–200.
155 ECtHR 14 March 2000, appl.no. 39195/98 (*Jager/The Netherlands*).

> The Court does not find it established that the use of this method has resulted in mental pain and suffering for the applicant to such an extent that it amounts to inhuman treatment within the meaning of Article 3 of the Convention. The Court therefore cannot find that this interrogation method, as such, or the manner in which it has been applied in the present case attains the minimum level of severity required under Article 3 of the Convention.[156]

Whether a similar line of reasoning should apply to coercive CITs is not immediately clear. At least, a relevant distinction exists between displaying pictures during a regular police interrogation and during a volitionally *coerced* CIT. In the context of regular interrogations, defendants are legally free not to look at the images. They can close their eyes or look the other way without being subjected to official legal threats. Meanwhile, in the course of a *coerced* CIT, the subject has less discretion in (not) observing the presented stimuli. The employed coercion – either volitional or physical – will impair the voluntariness of the subject's decision to observe the presented pictures.[157] When the law, for example, threatens non-cooperation in brain-reading with punishment or extended custody, the subject may no longer have a voluntary choice: he *must* cooperate and observe each image attentively in order to avoid the negative consequences. Therefore, perhaps, the level of mental suffering caused by a coercive CIT may sometimes exceed the level of suffering connected with a legitimate form of displaying crime-related images in the context of a regular interrogation. Whether the involved level of suffering could possibly attain a minimum level of severity is as yet unclear from Strasbourg case-law.

In some cases, the question may be raised whether a person is actually *coerced* into brain-reading or cooperates out of *free will*. A relevant feature of volitionally coerced brain-reading is that the subject gives her consent to it. To avoid negative consequences, she *chooses* to cooperate with the brain-reading test. Sometimes, informed consent could negate state liability under Article 3 ECHR.[158] As previously mentioned,[159] in *Bogumil/Portugal*, a swallowed pellet of cocaine was surgically removed from the applicant's stomach with the aim of avoiding serious health risks. The Court considered that if there were informed consent to this medical procedure, no question would have arisen under Article 3 ECHR.[160] In the case of *V.C./Slovakia*, the Court put it as follows:

[156] Ibid., § 3.

[157] See Chapter 2, Section 2.7.

[158] Harris et al. 2018, p. 238; Vermeulen & Battjes 2018, p. 396; Buelens, Herijgers & Illegems 2016, pp. 503, 508, and 509.

[159] See Chapter 2, Section 2.7.

[160] ECtHR 3 October 2008, appl.no. 35228/03 (*Bogumil/Portugal*), § 71: '*Si en effet il y a eu consentement éclairé, comme l'allègue le Gouvernement, aucune question ne se pose sous l'angle de l'article 3 de la Convention*'. See also EComHR 2 March 1983, appl.no. 9974/82 (*X./Denmark*), p. 284.

> the Court reiterates that the very essence of the Convention is respect for human dignity and human freedom. It has held that in the sphere of medical assistance, even where the refusal to accept a particular treatment might lead to a fatal outcome, the imposition of medical treatment *without the consent of a mentally competent adult* patient would interfere with his or her right to physical integrity.[161]

The only exception concerns emergencies where medical treatment cannot be delayed and consent can therefore not be obtained.[162]

It is generally accepted that valid informed consent requires (1) disclosure of appropriate information (2) to a competent patient (3) who is permitted to make a voluntary choice.[163] The ECtHR endorses these requirements.[164] In some cases, concerning 'vulnerable patients', the Court also requires *explicit* consent.[165]

Regarding the validity of informed consent to forensic brain-reading, the key question will be whether the subject's consent can be considered *voluntary*.[166] A generally accepted claim in philosophy is that *threats* are coercive, negating voluntariness and therefore invalidate consent.[167] Hence, *threatening* a person to cooperate with brain-reading – for example: 'If you do not cooperate with a lie detection test, your pre-trial detention will be extended' – clearly constitutes coercion and invalidates consent.[168]

Less clear is whether *offers* could be coercive too and negate consent as well. In the course of forensic brain-reading, an offer could read as follows: 'If you cooperate with this neuroprediction test, we might approve your request for parole'. As discussed in Chapter 2, two central approaches exist on the coerciveness of offers: (1) offers can never be coercive[169] and (2) offers can be coercive sometimes – for example, in cases of vulnerability and power asymmetry, when no other options exist but

161 ECtHR 8 November 2011, appl.no. 18968/07 (*V.C./Slovakia*), § 105 (emphasis added). Cf. ECtHR 12 June 2012 appl.no. 29518/10 (*N.B./Slovakia*), § 74–75. Similarly, it is clear from generally recognised standards such as the Convention on Human Rights and Biomedicine that medical procedures may only be carried out with valid informed consent of the person involved. The Convention on Human Rights and Biomedicine is relevant when interpreting the ECHR, regardless of whether the State at issue has ratified it. See, for example, ECtHR 23 July 2015, appl.no. 10060/07 (*Bataliny/Russia*), § 55; ECtHR 21 February 2006, appl.no. 28602/95 (*Tüm Haber Sen and Çınar/Turkey*), § 39.

162 ECtHR 8 November 2011, appl.no. 18968/07 (*V.C./Slovakia*), § 108. See also Article 3(2) of the Charter of Fundamental Rights of the European Union.

163 Eyal 2019, sect. 5.1; Anderson 20121, sect. 3.3. See also Chapter 2, Section 2.7.

164 Buelens, Herijgers & Illegems 2016.

165 Ibid.

166 Cf. Knack, Chandler & Fedoroff 2020; Pugh 2018. Regarding the provision of appropriate information to enable valid informed consent to brain-reading, see *inter alia* Brownsword 2012, p. 233; Edwards 2012, pp. 250–252; Ford & Aggarwal 2012, pp. 333–334; Farah et al. 2014, p. 124.

167 Chapter 2, Section 2.7.

168 Cf. cases on mandatory urine tests in prison, where consent to provide a urine sample does not prevent from infringements: ECtHR 11 October 2005, appl.no. 60682/00 (*Young/UK*); EComHR 6 April 1994, appl.no. 21132/93 (*Peters/The Netherlands*).

169 For example, Nozick 1969; Wertheimer 1987.

to consent, or when the proposer controls or arranges the recipient's pre-proposal baseline situation.[170] Regarding medical procedures in a criminal legal context, the limited amount of Strasbourg case-law on Articles 3 and 8 ECHR suggests, with caution, sympathy for the second approach: sometimes, offers could coerce.

For example, in *Juhnke/Turkey*, the applicant complained that Articles 3 and 8 ECHR had been violated because she had been subjected to a gynaecological examination without valid consent during her time of imprisonment.[171] According to the Turkish government, the examination pursued the aim of protecting the prison guards from false allegations of rape. The government argued that the applicant had given consent to the examination.[172] Regarding the voluntariness of consent, the Court held that:

> in certain circumstances, a person in detention cannot be expected to continue to resist submitting to a gynaecological examination, given her *vulnerability at the hands of the authorities*, who exercise *complete control* over her throughout her detention.[173]

The Court addressed the applicant's complaint under the right to respect for private life and found a violation of Article 8 ECHR.[174]

Similarly, in *Y.F./Turkey*, the applicant complained that the forced gynaecological examination of his wife violated her right to respect for private life.[175] The government contended that performing such an examination would not have been possible without the woman's consent. She could have objected the examination when she was taken to the doctor. The Court disagreed: 'the applicant's wife could not have been expected to resist submitting to such an examination in view of her vulnerability at the hands of the authorities who exercised complete control over her throughout her detention'.[176] Article 8 ECHR had been violated. Following a similar reasoning in *Yazgül Yılmaz/Turkey*,[177] the Court considered the gynaecological examination of a minor female detainee to violate Article 3 ECHR.[178]

Considering these cases, Buelens, Herijgers, and Illegems emphasise the difficulty of getting *free* consent of detainees. Because of their vulnerability and the imbalance of power, people in prison cannot be expected to continue resisting

[170] McGregor 2008; Feinberg 1989; Zimmerman 1981.
[171] ECtHR 13 May 2008, appl.no. 52515/99 (*Juhnke/Turkey*).
[172] Ibid., § 60.
[173] Ibid., § 76 (emphasis added).
[174] Ibid., § 79–82.
[175] ECtHR 22 July 2003, appl.no. 24209/94 (*Y.F./Turkey*).
[176] Ibid., § 34.
[177] ECtHR 1 February 2011, appl.no. 36369/06 (*Yazgül Yılmaz/Turkey*), § 45: '*En outre, l'on ne pouvait s'attendre à ce que Mlle Yılmaz résistât à un tel examen, eu égard à sa vulnérabilité alors qu'elle se trouvait aux mains des autorités, qui ont exercé un contrôle total sur elle tout au long de sa garde à vue*'.
[178] Ibid., § 47–54.

medical examinations offered by the prison authorities. Therefore, these authors conclude that there seems a factual presumption that detainees cannot give their voluntary consent to medical procedures initiated by prison authorities.[179]

Recently, the Court adopted a similar argument in respect of an *arrested suspect*. The applicant in *R.S./Hungary* complained under Article 3 ECHR about being catheterised under control of police officers, in order to determine whether he was under influence of alcohol or drugs as he was a road user. Concerning the validity of the applicant's consent, the Court considered to have 'doubts as to whether the applicant, being in the hands of the authorities and in their complete control, had any option in practice but to undergo the impugned procedure'.[180]

Similarly, regarding the use of surgical castration in the context of treating sexual offenders, such as in prison or in a psychiatric hospital, the Committee for the Prevention of Torture (CPT) warns that in individual cases, consent to these interventions may not actually be voluntary:

> given the context in which the intervention is offered, it is questionable whether consent to the option of surgical castration will always be truly free and informed. A situation can easily arise whereby patients or prisoners acquiesce rather than consent, believing that it is the only available option to them to avoid indefinite confinement.[181]

In conclusion, valid informed consent can negate state liability under Article 3 ECHR. The Court does not explicitly accept or reject that 'coercive offers' invalidate consent just like threats. Yet, the case-law shows that in particular situations, especially where the proposer has strong authority over the vulnerable recipient, like in prison settings and in criminal proceedings,[182] a close examination of the voluntariness of consent is at least required.[183]

PHYSICAL COERCION. When a defendant or convicted offender refuses to cooperate in brain-reading, it would, at least in theory, be conceivable to secure him in a way that enables a brain-reading test.[184] Physical coercion can only be effective in

179 Buelens, Herijgers & Illegems 2016, p. 506.

180 ECtHR 2 July 2019, appl.no. 65290/14 (*R.S./Hungary*), § 65. Cf. ECtHR 8 November 2011, appl.no. 18968/07 (*V.C./Slovakia*), where a patient's consent to sterilisation had been requested in such circumstances that the Court did not consider her decision to be free. The Court held that: 'The way in which the hospital staff acted was paternalistic, since, in practice, the applicant *was not offered any option but to agree to the procedure* which the doctors considered appropriate in view of her situation'. (§ 114, emphasis added).

181 CPT/Inf (2012)6, point 145.

182 ECtHR 11 December 2008, appl.no. 4268/04 (*Panovits/Cyprus*), § 68.

183 See also Buelens, Herijgers & Illegems 2016, pp. 484–485.

184 Van Toor 2017, p. 113.

respect of brain-reading applications that do not require cooperation by the subject. Examples are CT and MRI to examine whether the person suffers from a tumour or traumatic brain injury.

Employing measures of restraint in the course of criminal justice is not as such prohibited under Article 3 ECHR.[185] To be permissible, such measures must be imposed in connection with a lawful arrest or detention. They should not entail additional force nor public exposure exceeding what is reasonably necessary in the given circumstances.[186] In this regard, the Court takes into account whether there is reason to believe that the individual would resist arrest, abscond, cause injury, or *suppress evidence*.[187]

With respect to forensic brain-reading, it is arguable that by refusing, resisting, or manipulating the test, the defendant or convicted offender aims to suppress evidence or to conceal important information in the context of a penal procedure. Whether restraining the subject will exceed what is reasonably necessary shall depend on the facts of the individual case.[188] At least, it is clear that confining individuals to a restraint bed without medical reasons should rarely last any longer than a few hours.[189] This requirement is not likely to raise fundamental issues in cases of brain-reading. Brain-reading applications that are eligible for physical coercion will normally not take much more than twenty (CT) to forty-five (MRI) minutes.[190]

What may give rise to serious concerns though, is that the employed *means* of restraint must not cause a level of physical pain and/or mental suffering that attains a minimum level of severity. Movements of almost any part of the body – even one's tongue – can distort the imaging results.[191] Thus, if the subject resists, a successful neuroimaging assessment will require *complete* restraint.[192] Generally, two types of restraint are conceivable in this respect: mechanical and chemical restraint.

Concerning *mechanical restraint*, the subject's body, arms, and legs could be secured by using straps and a restraint bed.[193] Depending on the circumstances of

185 Here, we focus on restraining non-patients.

186 Discussed in Section 3.3.3

187 ECtHR (GC) 17 July 2014, appl.nos. 32541/08 and 43441/08 (*Svinarenko and Slyadnev/Russia*), § 117; ECtHR 17 June 2014, appl.no. 70719/10 (*Zamfirachi/Romania*), § 46; ECtHR 29 September 2005, appl.no. 24919/03 (*Mathew/The Netherlands*), § 180; ECtHR 27 November 2003, appl.no. 65436/01 (*Hénaf/France*), § 48; ECtHR 16 December 1997, appl.no. 20972/92 (*Raninen/Finland*), § 56.

188 ECtHR 20 January 2011, appl.no. 891/05 (*Kashavelov/Bulgaria*), § 38.

189 ECtHR 29 May 2012, appl.nos. 16563/08, 40841/08, 8192/10, and 18656/10 (*Julin/Estonia*), § 127.

190 See, for example, www.brainstrust.org.uk, searched for 'Brain tumour symptoms and diagnosis' (visited on 9 January 2020). Recent developments in MR-STAT could possibly reduce the (f)MRI scanning time to less than ten minutes: Sbrizzi et al. 2018; Van der Heide et al. 2020; www.nwo.nl, searched for 'MR-STAT: unlocking MRI's full quantification potential' (visited on 8 July 2020).

191 For example, Kanwisher 2009, p. 12; Mecacci & Haselager 2019, p. 455.

192 Cf. Van Toor 2017, p. 113.

193 See, for example, CPT/Inf(2017)6.

a specific case, such means of restraint can cause great distress, physical suffering, and 'physical discomfort', which could raise an issue under Article 3 ECHR.[194]

Apart from securing the subject's body, her head should be secured as well. In theory, this could be achieved by using means such as a vacuum fixation mouthpiece. In medicine, this technique is used for neuroimaging to fixate a patient's head.[195] However, regarding a resisting subject in a criminal justice context, measures like these could cause serious levels of physical pain, feelings of fear, anguish, and inferiority. Together with strapping the subject's body, arms, and legs, restraining a person's head bears a serious risk of attaining a minimum level of severity.

Noteworthy is a statement of the CPT regarding the use of mechanical restraint in respect of psychiatric patients, stressing that 'vital functions of the patient, such as respiration and the ability to communicate, must not be hampered'.[196] Using means of restraint such as a vacuum mouthpiece will impair the subject's ability to communicate and adversely affect respiration.

Regarding *chemical restraint*,[197] structural neuroimaging could, again at least in theory, be employed while the subject is in a state of general anaesthesia. However, receiving general anaesthesia entails serious health risks.[198] These range from regular side effects such as headaches, muscular pain, and nausea, to rare respiratory complications and brain damage due to oxygen deficiency.[199] Moreover, it is plausible to argue that coercively bringing an individual in a state of unconsciousness in order to perform a forensic brain-reading test could arouse feelings of fear, anguish, and inferiority in a way that attains a minimum level of severity. Meanwhile, it follows from Strasbourg case-law that in some exceptional cases, for example, when a person responds extremely aggressively, forcible injection of sedatives could be permissible.[200]

In conclusion, using both mechanical and chemical restraint to enable brain-reading entails serious risks of causing a level of physical discomfort, pain, great distress, and/or mental suffering that could attain a minimum level of severity, able of violating Article 3 ECHR. To avoid this risk, States could favour the use of *volitional* rather than *physical* coercion.

[194] ECtHR 18 October 2012, appl.no. 37679/08 (*Bureš/Czech Republic*), § 90; ECtHR 19 February 2015, appl.no. 75450/12 (*M.S./Croatia (No. 2)*), § 102; ECtHR 29 May 2012, appl.nos. 16563/08, 40841/08, 8192/10 and 18656/10 (*Julin/Estonia*), § 127; ECtHR 13 February 2014, appl.no. 66393/10 (*Tali/Estonia*), § 81–82.

[195] Russo et al. 2016 (including a clear image); Sweeney et al. 2003.

[196] CPT/Inf(2017)6, Section 3.3.

[197] The forcible administration of pharmaceuticals for the purpose of controlling the individual's behaviour, see CPT/Inf(2017)6, p. 2.

[198] Chapter 2, Section 2.4.2.

[199] Karcz & Papadakos 2013, pp. 21–23; Maity et al. 2012, p. 34; Curry, Viernes & Sharma 2011, pp. 21–28.

[200] For example, ECtHR 24 September 1992, appl.no. 10533/83 (*Herczegfalvy/Austria*), § 81–84. Cf. Forsberg 2021.

Factors 4 and 5. Level of Medical Supervision and Actual Health Effects

When employing medical procedures in the acquisition of evidence, the authorities should assess the individualised health risks *prior* to the procedure. Also, they should ensure medical supervision *during* the procedure.[201] Regarding neuroimaging, such as (f)MRI, contraindications can exist.[202] Therefore, a medical assessment of the subject's health risks will be essential prior to forensic brain-reading. In addition, since even clipping a suspect's fingernails should be accompanied with 'appropriate medical supervision',[203] the Court is likely to require such supervision during the more complicated employment of coercive brain-reading as well.

A final factor of importance is whether the forcible medical procedure has actually affected the person's state of health or resulted in lasting adverse health effects. Regarding coercive brain-reading, health effects of both the neuroimaging technology and the employed means of coercion should be assessed. In this regard, the potential effects of radiation exposure will be relevant. However, determining the required causal link between a forensic brain scan and subsequent health issues,[204] such as the development of cancer, shall often be hardly feasible.

Since the adverse health effects of neuroimaging often tend to be minimal, in practice, the health effects of the *restraining methods* shall be most important. As the case of *Bureš/Czech Republic* illustrates, assessing a causal link between means of restraint and emerged health issues appears feasible. In that case, experts had concluded that 'the applicant had suffered very severe bilateral paresis of the elbow nerves caused by the compression of nerves and blood vessels, that this injury still limited his ability to play the violoncello and that it would have a long-lasting effect which was unlikely to be permanent'.[205] Accordingly, the Court held that the means of restraint had caused great distress and physical suffering. Article 3 ECHR had been violated.

Synthesis: Attaining a Minimum Level of Severity?

Coercive brain-reading could but need not attain a minimum level of severity. We cannot be sure which reasoning the Court would be inclined to adopt in individual cases on specific brain-reading technologies. But the use of *physically coerced* brain-reading is likely to entail serious risks of causing physical discomfort, pain, great distress, and/or mental suffering, able of attaining a minimum level of severity and violating Article 3 ECHR. Meanwhile, applying brain-reading with *volitional coercion*, without additional physical force, shall not typically debase the individual or cause physical pain or mental suffering capable of violating Article 3 ECHR.

[201] Discussed in Section 3.3.3.
[202] Brown & Murphy 2010, p. 1138.
[203] ECtHR 3 May 2012, appl.no. 23880/05 (*Salikhov/Russia*), § 79.
[204] ECtHR (GC) 11 July 2006, appl.no. 54810/00 (*Jalloh/Germany*), § 81.
[205] ECtHR 18 October 2012, appl.no. 37679/08 (*Bureš/Czech Republic*), § 89.

3.4 CONCLUSION

Until the Court develops an approach tailored to coercive forensic brain-reading in light of Article 3 ECHR, the precise legal implications in this regard remain unclear. Within the context of Article 3 ECHR, relevant similarities exist between coercive brain-reading on the one hand and forcible medical procedures to obtain evidence from defendants on the other hand. Based on this analogy, this chapter identified a framework of five factors that should be of particular importance regarding coercive brain-reading in criminal justice: (1) the extent to which coercive brain-reading is necessary to obtain the information, (2) the health risks for the subject, (3) the manner in which the procedure was carried out and the physical pain and mental suffering it caused, (4) the level of medical supervision available, and (5) the actual effects of the procedure on the subject's health.

Considering these factors leads to the conclusion that coercive brain-reading is not as such prohibited by Article 3 ECHR. Employing brain-reading with *volitional* coercion will not typically cause any physical pain or mental suffering that attains a minimum level of severity. Meanwhile, enforcing brain-reading with *physical* coercion is likely to cause physical discomfort, pain, distress, and/or mental suffering capable of attaining the threshold of Article 3 ECHR. Ultimately, to avoid a violation of Article 3 ECHR in individual cases, States should at least take account of the five factors discussed in this chapter.

4

Coercive Brain-Reading and the Right to Respect for Private Life

Article 8 ECHR

4.1 INTRODUCTION

Much of our thoughts, emotions, memories, and opinions are conceived as private matters. Many such private matters we think should receive human rights protection. Accordingly, Article 8 ECHR guarantees the right to respect for private life. This right includes the protection of our personal data. It also prescribes to respect our physical, psychological, and moral integrity. Clearly, reading people's brains and identifying personal mental states without consent raises questions regarding Article 8 ECHR.[1] These questions are central to the present chapter. It examines whether and under which conditions coercive brain-reading in criminal justice could be permissible in view of the right to respect for private life as guaranteed by Article 8 ECHR.

The outline of this chapter is as follows. Section 4.2 briefly discusses the meaning and scope of the right to respect for private life pursuant to Article 8 ECHR. Section 4.3 examines the legal implications of coercive brain-reading in criminal law under Article 8 ECHR. Section 4.4 draws conclusions.

4.2 THE RIGHT TO RESPECT FOR PRIVATE LIFE (ARTICLE 8 ECHR)

4.2.1 *Introduction*

Article 8 ECHR reads as follows:

> 1. Everyone has the right to respect for his private and family life, his home and his correspondence.
>
> 2. There shall be no interference by a public authority with the exercise of this right except such as is in accordance with the law and is necessary in a democratic

[1] Rusconi & Mitchener-Nissen 2013; Van Toor 2017; Ligthart 2019b; Ligthart et al. 2020.

> society in the interests of national security, public safety or the economic well-being of the country, for the prevention of disorder or crime, for the protection of health or morals, or for the protection of the rights and freedoms of others.

In essence, the first paragraph of this provision aims to protect individuals against arbitrary interferences with their private and family life, home, and correspondence.[2] Yet, not any such interference will necessarily *violate* Article 8 ECHR. Instead, infringements can be justified via Article 8(2) ECHR when they are in accordance with the law, serve a legitimate aim, and are necessary in a democratic society.

In examining complaints about Article 8 ECHR, the Court normally begins with determining whether this provision is applicable to the individual case and whether the issue at stake constitutes an infringement. Next, it examines whether the infringement is justified or whether it constitutes a violation.[3] Accordingly, in what follows, first, the meaning and scope of the right to respect for private life will be considered, followed by a discussion of the justification clause of Article 8(2) ECHR.

4.2.2 *Article 8(1) ECHR: The Right to Respect for Private Life*

The first paragraph of Article 8 ECHR prescribes to respect four distinctive privacy interests of each individual: one's private life, family life, home, and correspondence. In particular, coercive brain-reading raises questions regarding the right to respect for *private life*. The present chapter focusses on this part of Article 8(1) ECHR.

When interpreting the rights guaranteed by Article 8 ECHR, the notion of personal autonomy is an important principle.[4] Meanwhile, the Court holds that:

> it would be too restrictive to limit the notion of 'private life' to an 'inner circle' in which the individual may live his or her own personal life as he or she chooses, thus excluding entirely the outside world not encompassed within that circle. Article 8 thus guarantees a right to 'private life' in the broad sense, including the right to lead a 'private social life', that is, the possibility for the individual to develop his or her social identity.[5]

2 ECtHR (GC) 29 March 2016, appl.no. 56925/08 (*Bédat/Switzerland*), § 73; ECtHR(GC) 12 November 2013, appl.no. 5786/08 (*Söderman/Sweden*), § 78; ECtHR (GC) 15 March 2012, appl.nos. 4149/04 and 41029/04 (*Aksu/Turkey*), § 59; ECtHR (GC) 13 December 2012, appl.no. 39630/09 (*El-Masri/Former Yugoslav republic of Macedonia*), § 248.

3 Harris et al. 2018, pp. 502–503. For example, ECtHR (GC) 19 February 1998, appl.nos. 116/1996/735/932 (*Guerra and others/Italy*), § 57; ECtHR (GC) 4 December 2008, appl.nos. 30562/04 and 30566/04 (*S. & Marper/UK*), § 59–126.

4 ECtHR (GC) 5 September 2017, appl.no. 61496/08 (*Bărbulescu/Romania*), § 70; ECtHR (GC) 15 March 2012, appl.nos. 4149/04 and 41029/04 (*Aksu/Turkey*), § 58; ECtHR (GC) 10 April 2007, appl.no. 6339/05 (*Evans/UK*), § 71; ECtHR 29 April 2002, appl.no. 2346/02 (*Pretty/UK*), § 61.

5 ECtHR(GC) 5 September 2017, appl.no. 61496/08 (*Bărbulescu/Romania*), § 70; ECtHR(GC) 4 December 2008, appl.nos. 30562/04 and 30566/04 (*S. & Marper/UK*), § 66. See also ECtHR 16 December 1992, appl.no. 13710/88 (*Niemietz/Germany*), § 29.

The Grand Chamber of the ECtHR has repeatedly reiterated that the notion of 'private life' within the meaning of Article 8 ECHR is a broad concept, which does not lend itself for an exhaustive definition.[6] This aligns with the Court's central approach of the Convention, considering it a *living instrument* that should be interpreted in light of the present-day conditions.[7] The meaning and scope of 'private life' are continuously evolving, sensitive to technological, social, and ethical developments within society.[8] Nonetheless, it is clear that 'private life' covers the individual's (I) personal data,[9] (II) physical integrity,[10] and (III) moral, psychological, and mental integrity.[11] These three sub-dimensions of the right to respect for private life are discussed below.

I Personal Data

The right to respect for private life covers the protection of 'personal data'. Referring to Article 2 of the Data Protection Convention, the Court defines personal data as 'any information that relates to an identified or identifiable individual'.[12] According to Article 4 of the General Data Protection Regulation (GDPR), 'personal data' means 'any information relating to an identified or identifiable natural person ("data subject"); an identifiable natural person is one who can be identified, directly or indirectly, in particular by reference to an identifier such as a name, an identification number, location data, an online identifier or to one or more factors specific to the physical, physiological, genetic, mental, economic, cultural or social identity of that natural person'.

In the Court's view, protecting personal data is of fundamental importance to the enjoyment of the right to respect for private life. Article 8 ECHR comprises 'the right to a form of informational self-determination, allowing individuals to rely on their right to privacy as regards data which, albeit neutral, are collected, processed and disseminated collectively and in such a form or manner that their Article 8 rights may be engaged'.[13]

6 For example, ECtHR (GC) 25 September 2018, 76639/11 (*Denisov/Ukraine*), § 95; ECtHR (GC) 24 January 2017, appl.no. 25358/12 (*Paradiso and Campanelli/Italy*), § 159.

7 ECtHR (GC) 19 February 2013, appl.no. 19010/07 (*X and others/Austria*), § 139; ECtHR 25 April 1978, appl.no. 5856/72 (*Tyrer/UK*), § 31; Council of Europe 2020b, p. 7.

8 Cf. Concurring opinion Judge Sicilianos, joined by Judge Raimondi under ECtHR (GC) 19 February 2013, appl.no. 19010/07 (*X and others/Austria*), § 3; Michalowski 2020, p. 406.

9 ECtHR (GC) 8 November 2016, appl.no. 18030/11 (*Magyar Helsinki Bizottság/Hungary*), § 191; ECtHR (GC) 4 December 2008, appl.nos. 30562/04 and 30566/04 (*S. & Marper/UK*), § 66–67.

10 ECtHR (GC) 25 September 2018, appl.no. 76639/11 (*Denisov/Ukraine*), § 95; ECtHR (GC) 24 January 2017, appl.no. 25358/12 (*Paradiso and Campanelli/Italy*), § 159; ECtHR (GC) 29 March 2016, appl.no. 56925/08 (*Bédat/Switserland*), § 72.

11 Ibid. See also ECtHR (GC) 12 September 2012, appl.no. 10593/08 (*Nada/Switzerland*), § 151; ECtHR 24 July 2014, appl.no. 7446/12 (*Remetin/Croatia (No. 2)*), § 70.

12 ECtHR (GC) 8 November 2016, appl.no. 18030/11 (*Magyar Helsinki Bizottság/Hungary*), § 192.

13 ECtHR (GC) 27 June 2017, appl.no. 931/13 (*Satakunnan Markkinapörssi Oy and Satamedia Oy/Finland*), § 137.

In considering whether personal information relates to someone's 'private life' in the meaning of Article 8 ECHR,[14] and whether the collection, storage, or use of information infringes this right,[15] the Court has due regard to:

(1) the nature of the records,
(2) the results that may be obtained,
(3) the specific context in which the information has been recorded and retained, and
(4) the way in which these records are used and processed.[16]

As an illustration, the Court has applied these factors to the taking and retaining of a photograph on arrest. It argued that since the 'applicant's custody photograph was taken on his arrest and will be held indefinitely on a local database for use by the police and that the police may also apply facial recognition and facial mapping techniques to the photograph, the Court has no doubt that the taking and retention of the applicant's photograph amounts to an interference with his right to private life within the meaning of Article 8 § 1'.[17]

Other examples of infringements under the head of protecting personal data concern the *collection* of personal information through an obligatory census form, via a GPS tracking system, through secret video recordings, and by taking cellular samples for DNA analysis.[18] Apart from *collecting* personal data, the mere *storing* of such information infringes Article 8 ECHR as well, regardless the subsequent use of the stored data.[19] Furthermore, the Grand Chamber holds that the *disclosure* of information 'relating to an individual's private life' will also infringe the right to respect for private life.[20]

II Physical Integrity

The Court considers a person's body 'the most intimate aspect of private life'.[21] The right to respect for private life protects against the infliction of sufficiently adverse

14 ECtHR (GC) 4 December 2008, appl.nos. 30562/04 and 30566/04 (*S. & Marper/UK*), § 67; ECtHR 4 November 2014, appl.nos. 11809/12 and 35284/13 (*Straka and others/Slovakia*), § 79.
15 ECtHR 13 February 2020, appl.no. 45245/15 (*Gaughran/UK*), § 70.
16 See also De Vries 2018, p. 673.
17 ECtHR 13 February 2020, appl.no. 45245/15 (*Gaughran/UK*), § 70.
18 European Commission of Human Rights (EComHR) 10 March 1981, appl.no. 8741/79 (*X/Germany*); ECtHR 2 September 2010, appl.no. 35623/05 (*Uzun/Germany*); ECtHR 5 October 2010, appl.no. 420/07 (*Köpke/Germany*); ECtHR 14 April 2020, appl.no. 75229/10 (*Dragan Petrović/Serbia*), § 69, 79; ECtHR 13 February 2020, appl.no. 45245/15 (*Gaughran/UK*), § 63.
19 ECtHR (GC) 4 December 2008, appl.nos. 30562/04 and 30566/04 (*S. & Marper/UK*), § 66; ECtHR (GC) 16 February 2000, appl.no. 27798/95 (*Amann/Switzerland*), § 69; ECtHR 13 February 2020, appl.no. 45245/15 (*Gaughran/UK*), § 70.
20 ECtHR (GC) 8 November 2016, appl.no. 18030/11 (*Magyar Helsinki Bizottság/Hungary*), § 191. See also ECtHR 26 May 2020, appl.no. 1122/12 (*P.T./the Republic of Moldova*), § 28.
21 ECtHR 22 July 2003, appl.no. 24209/94 (*Y.F./Turkey*), § 33.

effects on the individual's physical integrity.[22] Not just any act interfering with a person's body necessarily infringes Article 8 ECHR.[23] Still, the right to respect for private life encompasses a broad scope of physical intrusions.[24] These range from minor non-consensual medical interventions such as taking saliva,[25] blood,[26] urine,[27] and obliging an X-ray,[28] to physical searches by the police,[29] gynaecological examination in prison,[30] and rape.[31]

Some of these interferences with bodily integrity have the ability of infringing the prohibition of ill-treatment pursuant to Article 3 ECHR as well. While the legal protection under Article 3 ECHR is stronger – because it is absolute – the threshold to attract that protection is higher. Unlike Article 8, Article 3 ECHR *only* protects against interferences with people's bodies that attain 'a minimum level of severity'.[32] When a measure is not severe enough to attain the threshold of Article 3 ECHR, Article 8 ECHR provides additional protection to our physical and mental integrity: 'where a measure falls short of Article 3 treatment, it may fall foul of Article 8 of the Convention which, *inter alia*, provides for the protection of physical and moral integrity under'. the head of respect for the individual's private life."[33]

III Moral, Psychological, and Mental Integrity

Whereas much Strasbourg case-law exists on the protection of personal data and physical integrity, the meaning, scope, and theoretical rationales of the right to moral, psychological, and mental integrity are less clear.[34] Case-law suggests that 'moral' and 'psychological' integrity are interchangeable terms.[35] Incidentally, the

[22] ECtHR 6 February 2001, appl.no. 44599/98 (*Bensaid/UK*), § 46; ECtHR 17 January 2017, appl.no. 10851/13 (*Dömötör/Hungary*), § 40; ECtHR 25 March 1993, appl.no. 13134/87 (*Costello-Roberts/UK*), § 36. See also De Vries 2018, p. 691.

[23] ECtHR (GC) 26 June 2019, appl.no. 41720/13 (*Nicolae Virgiliu Tănase/Romania*), § 128; ECtHR 25 March 1993, appl.no. 13134/87 (*Costello-Roberts/UK*), § 36.

[24] For overviews, see Marshall 2009, pp. 168–201; Rainy, McCormick & Ovey 2021, pp. 411–414; De Vries 2018, pp. 690–697; Harris et al. 2018, pp. 519–522.

[25] ECtHR 14 April 2020, appl.no. 75229/10 (*Dragan Petrović/Serbia*); ECtHR 15 May 2018, appl.no. 41079/16 (*Caruana/Malta*).

[26] ECtHR 5 January 2006, appl.no. 32352/02 (*Schmidt/Germany*).

[27] EComHR 6 April 1994, appl.no. 21132/93 (*Peters/The Netherlands*).

[28] EComHR 10 December 1984, appl.no. 10435/83 (*Acmanne and others/Belgium*).

[29] ECtHR 12 January 2010, appl.no. 4158/05 (*Gillan and Quinton/UK*).

[30] ECtHR 13 May 2008, appl.no. 52515/99 (*Juhnke/Turkey*).

[31] ECtHR 4 December 2003, appl.no. 39272/98 (*M.C./Bulgaria*).

[32] See Chapter 3, Section 3.2.

[33] ECtHR 1 June 2017, appl.no. 9635/13 (*Dejnek/Poland*), § 70. For example, ECtHR 13 May 2008, appl. no. 52515/99 (*Juhnke/Turkey*), § 71, 75–82.

[34] Bublitz 2020; Michalowski 2020, p. 406; Douglas & Forsberg 2021; Bublitz 2018, p. 303.

[35] De Vries 2018, p. 690.

Court also refers to 'mental' integrity in this regard.[36] However, it has yet refrained from providing a precise definition of these notions.[37] At least it is clear that the Court considers mental health as a crucial part of private life, associated with moral integrity.[38] Some authors assume that the right to respect for moral, psychological, and mental integrity is merely confined to a right to mental health.[39]

However, narrow interpretations like these may be too restrictive.[40] The individual's moral and psychological integrity also embrace complaints about bullying at school,[41] well-founded fear for physical abuse,[42] and loss of honour and reputation.[43,44] Furthermore, secretly taking footage of a minor when she was about to take a shower constituted a violation of the girl's 'personal integrity'.[45] In addition, the Grand Chamber has repeatedly considered that together with the notion of physical integrity, a person's psychological integrity embraces multiple aspects of a person's identity such as gender identification, sexual orientation, name, and elements relating to a person's right to image.[46] Thus, confining the notions of moral, psychological, and mental integrity to only a right to mental health is not convincing.[47]

In view of emerging neurotechnologies that may disclose and/or alter human mental states, some authors have suggested to understand the right to mental integrity more broadly, as a right to 'mental self-determination'.[48] That is, a right to control over the content of our own mental lives.

It is plausible that a broader understanding like this will indeed receive increased support in the near future.[49] The Committee on Bioethics of the Council of

36 For example, ECtHR 12 October 2006, appl.no. 13178/03 (*Mayeka and Kaniki Mitunga/Belgium*), § 83. This term appears interchangeable with 'psychological' integrity as well. For example, in ECtHR 14 January 2020, appl.no. 41288/15 (*Beizaras and Levickas/Lithuania*), § 128 the Court uses the term 'mental' integrity, referring to another case on the same subject matter, where it used the term 'psychological' integrity (ECtHR 7 May 2019, appl.no. 12509/13 (*Panayotova and Others/Bulgaria*), § 58–59).

37 De Vries 2018, p. 690; Bublitz 2020; Michalowski 2020.

38 ECtHR 26 November 2009, appl.no. 25282/06 (*Dolenec/Croatia*), § 165; ECtHR 6 February 2001, appl.no. 44599/98 (*Bensaid/UK*), § 47.

39 Ienca & Andorno 2017, p. 18; Bubltiz 2013, p. 248.

40 Ligthart, Douglas & Meynen 2021.

41 ECtHR 24 July 2012, appl.no. 41526/10 (*Đorđević/Croatia*), § 97–98.

42 ECtHR 30 November 2010, appl.no. 2660/03 (*Hajduová/Slovakia*), § 49.

43 ECtHR 28 October 2014, appl.no. 20531/06 (*Ion Cârstea/Romania*) § 38; ECtHR 21 November 2013, appl. no. 16882/03 (*Putistin/Ukraine*), § 32.

44 See also Michalowski 2020.

45 ECtHR (GC) 12 November 2013, appl.no. 5786/08 (*Söderman/Sweden*), § 86.

46 ECtHR (GC) 29 March 2016, appl.no. 56925/08 (*Bédat/Switzerland*), § 72; ECtHR (GC) 25 September 2018, appl.no; 76639/11 (*Denisov/Ukraine*), § 95.

47 Cf. Marshall 2009, p. 168, who suggests a broader interpretation of these notions, including the protection of personal data.

48 Bublitz 2020; Ienca & Andorno 2017; Bublitz & Merkel 2014. Cf. Sententia 2004.

49 Ligthart et al. 2021a, pp. 8–9.

Europe writes in its Strategic Action Plan on Human Rights and Technologies in Biomedicine (2020–2025):

> Technological developments in the field of biomedicine create new possibilities for intervention in individual behaviour. For instance, certain technologies raise the prospect of increased understanding, monitoring, and control of the human brain, while other developments allow for the permanent health monitoring of individuals. These developments raise novel questions relating to autonomy, privacy, and even freedom of thought. (…) In the light of these developments, the third pillar of the Strategic Action Plan addresses concerns for physical and mental integrity. Guaranteeing respect for a person's integrity in the sphere of biomedicine is one of the central tenets of the Oviedo Convention. *This is understood as the ability of individuals to exercise control over what happens to them with regard to, inter alia, their body, their mental state, and the related personal data.*[50]

According to the Committee on Bioethics, the notion of 'mental integrity' embraces the ability to control our own mental states. Within that approach, the right to mental integrity guarantees individuals to exercise control over what happens to their mental states. In other words, the right then comprises a right to mental self-determination.

Whether the Court would be inclined to adopt a similar interpretation of the right to moral, psychological, and mental integrity is an open question. To date, it has accepted 'private life' to comprise a general right to self-determination[51] as well as a more specified right to informational self-determination.[52] The recognition of a specific right to *mental* self-determination may well fit within the Court's current understanding of the right to respect for private life pursuant to Article 8 ECHR.[53]

Some aspects of our life, such as our home, body, and personal identity, we conceive as so private that they *ipso facto* fall within a person's private domain covered by Article 8 ECHR. Meanwhile, sometimes, the right to resect for private life could offer legal protection even beyond such private areas. Even when the private nature of, for instance, particular information is not crystal clear, the ECtHR is willing to accept private life protection in certain circumstances:

> There are a number of elements relevant to a consideration of whether a person's private life is concerned by measures effected outside a person's home or private premises. Since there are occasions when people knowingly or intentionally

[50] Committee on Bioethics of the Council of Europe 2019, § 21–22 (emphasis added).

[51] ECtHR (GC) 27 August 2015, appl.no. 46470/11 (*Parrillo/Italy*), § 153.

[52] ECtHR (GC) 27 June 2017, appl.no. 931/13 (*Satakunnan Markkinapörssi Oy and Satamedia Oy/Finland*), § 137.

[53] Cf. Michalowski 2020.

> involve themselves in activities which are or may be recorded or reported in a public manner, a person's reasonable expectations as to privacy may be a significant, although not necessarily conclusive, factor.[54]

Through applying this reasonable-expectation-of-privacy-test, the Court has *broadened* the scope of the right to respect for private life. Among others, it has afforded private life protection against the secretly taking of footage of a defendant at the police station for the purposes of video identification because the defendant did not have any expectation of such footage being taken.[55] Other examples are the secretly monitoring of communication of employees by the employer[56] and the disclosure of closed-circuit television (CCTV) material, displaying footage of an attempted suicide in public space.[57]

The Court, meanwhile, is not willing to broaden the privacy protection afforded by Article 8(1) ECHR to just any kind of information that can be obtained about an individual:

> A person walking along the street will inevitably be visible to any member of the public who is also present. Monitoring by technological means of the same public scene (for example, a security guard viewing through closed-circuit television) is of a similar character.[58]

The idea of connecting privacy protection to people's subjective expectations – their reasonable expectations of privacy – has been criticised.[59] The central objection is that expectations can be managed and modified, for example, by the law and novel technologies that make traditional aspects of private life more transparent, such as the Internet, smartphones, and GPS tracking systems. Apart from these well-known technologies, brain-reading might change traditional boundaries of the private (mental) domain as well, altering our reasonable expectations of privacy.[60]

Will developments in emerging technology indeed be able to reduce the scope of current private life protection? Probably not. The Court does not typically employ the reasonable-expectation-of-privacy-test in order to *limit* privacy protection, but

54 ECtHR 2 September 2010, appl.no. 35623/05 (*Uzun/Germany*), § 44. See also ECtHR (GC) 10 November 2015, appl.no. 40454/07 (*Couderc and Hachette Filipacchi Associés/France*), § 84; ECtHR 26 July 2007, appl.no. 64209/01 (*Peev/Bulgaria*), § 38–39. Other relevant factors include whether public information is systematically collected and stored in files held by the authorities: ECtHR (GC) 4 May 2000, appl.no. 28341/95 (*Rotaru/Romania*), § 43; ECtHR 2 September 2010, appl.no. 35623/05 (*Uzun/Germany*), § 45; ECtHR 25 September 2001, appl.no. 44787/98 (*P.G. and J.H./UK*), § 57.

55 ECtHR 17 July 2003, appl.no. 63737/00 (*Perry/UK*), § 40–41.

56 ECtHR (GC) 5 September 2017, appl.no. 61496/08 (*Bărbulescu/Romania*), § 16–21 and 80–81.

57 ECtHR 28 January 2003, appl.no. 44647/98 (*Peck/UK*), § 60–62.

58 ECtHR 2 September 2010, appl.no. 35623/05 (*Uzun/Germany*), § 44. See also ECtHR 25 September 2001, appl.no. 44787/98 (*P.G. and J.H./UK*), § 57.

59 Purshouse 2016; Nouwt 2008, pp. 395–396; Van Toor 2017, pp. 283–286.

60 Cf. Edwards 2012, p. 257; McCarthy-Jones 2019; Alegre 2017.

rather to *extend* the scope of Article 8 ECHR. To date, the use of technologies that have made life more transparent, such as GPS and CCTV, are still covered by the right to respect for private life.[61] Hence, it is not likely that the Court would be inclined to *restrict* the level of privacy protection because technologies diminish our expectations of privacy. And as it appears, managing privacy expectations through restrictive regulation cannot nullify privacy protection under Article 8 ECHR:

> It is open to question whether – and if so, to what extent – the employer's restrictive regulations left the applicant with a reasonable expectation of privacy. Be that as it may, an employer's instructions cannot reduce private social life in the workplace to zero. Respect for private life and for the privacy of correspondence continues to exist, even if these may be restricted in so far as necessary.[62]

Altogether, the right to respect for private life covers a wide range of aspects of our personal lives. It even protects some of our personal interests beyond typical private areas such as our body, home, and personal identity. Meanwhile, as will be discussed in the next section, not every State interference with people's private lives will violate Article 8 ECHR.

4.2.3 *Article 8(2) ECHR: Justifying Infringements*

According to Article 8(2) ECHR, infringements of the right to respect for private life can be justified if they (I) are in accordance with the law, (II) serve one or more of the legitimate aims referred to in Article 8(2) ECHR, and (III) are necessary in a democratic society in order to achieve any such aim.[63] These three requirements are discussed below.[64]

I In Accordance with the Law

To be justified, infringements of Article 8(1) ECHR must have some basis in domestic law, which can be either statutory or judge-made law.[65] That legal basis must be adequately accessible and formulated with sufficient precision to enable citizens to regulate their behaviour. Citizens should be able – if needed with appropriate advice – to reasonably foresee the potential legal consequences of their actions.[66] To meet

61 For example, ECtHR 2 September 2010, appl.no. 35623/05 (*Uzun/Germany*), § 49–53; ECtHR 28 January 2003, appl.no. 44647/98 (*Peck/UK*), § 58–63; ECtHR 17 July 2003, appl.no. 63737/00 (*Perry/UK*), § 51.

62 ECtHR (GC) 5 September 2017, appl.no. 61496/08 (*Bărbulescu/Romania*), § 80.

63 See, for example, ECtHR (GC) 4 December 2015, appl.no. 47143/06 (*Roman Zakharov/Russia*), § 227.

64 For a more detailed discussion, see Lavrysen 2018; Harris et al. 2018, p. 514 *et seq*; Gerards 2013.

65 ECtHR (GC) 14 September 2010, appl.no. 38224/03 (*Sanoma Uitgevers B.V./The Netherlands*), § 83.

66 ECtHR (GC) 24 January 2017, appl.no. 25358/12 (*Paradiso and Campanelli/Italy*), § 169; ECtHR (GC) 15 November 2016, appl.nos. 28859/11 and 28473/12 (*Dubská and Krejzová/Czech Republic*), § 167; ECtHR (GC) 4 December 2015, appl.no. 47143/06 (*Roman Zakharov/Russia*), § 227.

these requirements and comply with the rule of law, the domestic law must provide adequate legal protection against arbitrariness. It should indicate with sufficient clarity the scope of discretion of the competent authorities.[67] The level of required precision will largely depend on the content of the instrument in question, the field it is designed to cover, and the number and status of those to whom it is addressed.[68]

II Legitimate Aim

Article 8(2) ECHR accepts the following legitimate aims to interfere with people's private lives: national security, public safety or the economic well-being of the country, the prevention of disorder or crime, the protection of health or morals, and the protection of the rights and freedoms of others. This exhaustive enumeration somewhat delimits the number of legitimate purposes. Yet, as Lavrysen notes, the Court's practice is to easily accept that an infringement pursues one of these legitimate interests.[69]

III Necessary in a Democratic Society

To be necessary in a democratic society, an infringement of Article 8(1) ECHR must correspond to a pressing social need and the means employed should be proportionate to the aims pursued.[70] The 'pressing-social-need-standard' relates to the weight and importance of the pursued aims. Apart from being legitimate, the aims should be 'pressing' as well.[71] Meanwhile, the Court has refrained from defining the notion of a 'pressing social need'. Therefore, some authors have considered this requirement 'highly confusing'.[72]

To be proportionate, the adduced reasons to justify an infringement must be relevant and sufficient.[73] The provided reasons should be linked to the invoked legitimate aim and outweigh the harm inflicted on the right to respect for private life.[74] A fair balance must be struck between the relevant competing interests at stake.[75]

67 ECtHR (GC) 4 December 2008, appl.nos. 30562/04 and 30566/04 (*S. & Marper/UK*), § 95; ECtHR (GC) 26 October 2000, appl.no. 30985/96 (*Hasan and Chaush/Bulgaria*), § 84; ECtHR 24 September 1992, appl.no. 10533/83 (*Herczegfalvy/Austria*), § 89.

68 ECtHR (GC) 4 December 2008, appl.nos. 30562/04 and 30566/04 (*S. & Marper/UK*), § 96; ECtHR (GC) 26 October 2000, appl.no. 30985/96 (*Hasan and Chaush/Bulgaria*), § 84. ECtHR 24 September 1992, appl.no. 10533/83 (*Herczegfalvy/Austria*), § 89.

69 Lavrysen 2018, p. 314.

70 ECtHR (GC) 9 October 2003, appl.no. 48321/99 (*Slivenko/Latvia*), § 113; ECtHR (GC) 18 October 2006, appl.no. 46410/99 (*Üner/The Netherlands*), § 54; ECtHR 26 April 1979, appl.no. 6538/74 (*The Sunday Times/UK (No. 1)*), § 59.

71 Gerards 2013, p. 467; Lavrysen 2018, p. 317.

72 Lavrysen 2018, p. 317. Cf. Gerards 2013, p. 467.

73 ECtHR (GC) 24 January 2017, appl.no. 25358/12 (*Paradiso and Campanelli/Italy*), § 179; EHCtHR (GC) 4 December 2008, appl.nos. 30562/04 and 30566/04 (*S. & Marper/UK*), § 101.

74 Lavrysen 2018, pp. 317–318; Gerards 2013, p. 467.

75 ECtHR (GC) 24 January 2017, appl.no. 25358/12 (*Paradiso and Campanelli/Italy*), § 181; ECtHR (GC) 15 November 2016, appl.nos. 28859/11 and 28473/12 (*Dubská and Krejzová/Czech Republic*), § 176 and 180; ECtHR (GC) 4 December 2008, appl.nos. 30562/04 and 30566/04 (*S. & Marper/UK*), § 118 and 125.

In determining whether an infringement is necessary, the national authorities enjoy a margin of appreciation.[76] States are allowed either a 'wide', a 'certain', or a 'narrow' margin.[77] The broader this margin, the more discretion States enjoy in finding a 'fair balance' between the competing interests at stake.[78]

The breadth of the margin of appreciation varies among individual cases and depends on a number of relevant factors, such as the nature of the right at issue and the nature and purpose of the infringement.[79] If the right at stake is crucial to the individual's effective enjoyment of intimate or key rights, such as the right to personal autonomy, identity, and human dignity,[80] the margin tends to be narrower. If a particularly important facet of an individual's existence or identity is at stake, the margin of appreciation will normally be restricted as well.[81] Meanwhile, if no consensus exists across the member States of the Council of Europe, either as to the relative importance of the interest at issue or as to the best way of protecting it, the margin will be wider. This especially holds true when the case raises sensitive moral or ethical questions.[82]

4.2.4 *Conclusion*

Article 8(1) ECHR guarantees the right to respect for private life. The notion of private life is broad. No exhaustive definition can be provided. Yet, it is clear that it embraces the protection of personal data and the protection of our physical, moral, psychological, and mental integrity. Whereas relatively much case-law exists on the right to respect for *physical* integrity, the meaning and scope of *moral*, *psychological*, and *mental* integrity are less clear. At least, the limited case-law suggests that confining these notions to merely a right to mental health would be too restrictive.

When States interfere with the private lives of their citizens, Article 8(1) ECHR need not be violated. Infringements could be justified under Article 8(2) ECHR when they are in accordance with the law, serve a legitimate interest, and are necessary in a democratic society. In determining the necessity, States enjoy a margin of appreciation. The breadth of this margin depends on the circumstances of the

76 ECtHR (GC) 24 January 2017, appl.no. 25358/12 (*Paradiso and Campanelli/Italy*), § 181; ECtHR (GC) 4 December 2008, appl.nos. 30562/04 and 30566/04 (*S. & Marper/UK*), § 102.

77 Lavrysen 2018, p. 328.

78 Gerards 2011, pp. 105–107.

79 ECtHR (GC) 4 December 2008, appl.nos. 30562/04 and 30566/04 (*S. & Marper/UK*), § 102; ECtHR 13 February 2020, appl.no. 45245/15 (*Gaughran/UK*), § 77.

80 Gerards 2011, pp. 112–113.

81 Ibid. See, for example, ECtHR (GC) 4 December 2007, appl.no. 44362/04 (*Dickson/UK*), § 78; ECtHR (GC) 11 July 2002, appl.no. 28957/95 (*Christine Goodwin/UK*), § 90.

82 ECtHR (GC) 24 January 2017, appl.no. 25358/12 (*Paradiso and Campanelli/Italy*), § 182; ECtHR (GC) 4 December 2008, appl.nos. 30562/04 and 30566/04 (*S. & Marper/UK*), § 102; ECtHR 13 February 2020, appl.no. 45245/15 (*Gaughran/UK*), § 77 and 84.

individual case. The following section examines coercive brain-reading in light of the right to respect for private life.

4.3 COERCIVE FORENSIC BRAIN-READING UNDER THE RIGHT TO RESPECT FOR PRIVATE LIFE

4.3.1 *Introduction*

This section examines whether and under which legal conditions coercive brain-reading in criminal law would be permissible in light of the right to respect for private life pursuant to Article 8 ECHR. First, we draw an analogy between coercive brain-reading and other methods of data-acquisition about which case-law on the right to respect for private life is currently available (Section 4.3.2). In Section 4.3.3, the Court's approach to those existing methods will be analysed. From this analysis, legal boundaries will be deduced in respect of coercive brain-reading in criminal law (Section 4.3.4).

4.3.2 *Coercive Forensic Brain-Reading: An Analogy with Forensic DNA Testing*

In determining whether the acquisition and storage of personal information come within the scope of the right to respect for private life, the Court has due regard to the following four factors:

I. the nature of the records,
II. the results that may be obtained,
III. the specific context in which the information has been recorded and retained, and
IV. the way in which these records are used and processed.[83]

In light of these factors, an analogy with forensic DNA testing comes to the fore.[84] I will explain the relevant similarities between DNA testing and brain-reading below.

I and II Nature of the Information and Potential Results

Regarding the nature of DNA samples, the Grand Chamber stresses that they contain *unique* data about an individual that allows for identification.[85] Because the

83 See Section 4.2.2; ECtHR (GC) 4 December 2008, appl.nos. 30562/04 and 30566/04 (*S. & Marper/UK*), § 66; ECtHR 13 February 2020, appl.no. 45245/15 (*Gaughran/UK*), § 70; ECtHR 4 November 2014, appl.nos. 11809/12 and 35284/13 (*Straka and others/Slovakia*), § 79; De Vries 2018, p. 673.

84 Ligthart et al. 2020; Ligthart 2019b.

85 ECtHR (GC) 4 December 2008, appl.nos. 30562/04 and 30566/04 (*S. & Marper/UK*), § 72, 75, 84. Also ECtHR 22 June 2017, appl.no. 8806/12 (*Aycaguer/France*), § 33.

information enshrined in DNA relates to an *identified or identifiable individual*, it qualifies as personal data.[86]

Forensic brain-reading will be applied to a specific, identified individual. Think of a particular defendant or convicted offender. Clearly, in such cases, the yielded information 'relates directly to the identified individual'. Just like DNA, brain-reading data constitute *personal data*.[87]

Similar to DNA, the information obtained by structural brain-reading is to be considered *unique* as well. The structure of each brain is different. Even the brains of monozygotic twins are not identical.[88] Recent research suggests that particular brain structures ('brain prints') could enable the biometric identification of individuals.[89] Similarly, each individual's brain activity (more specifically: brain connectivity[90]) appears unique too, allowing for accurate biometric identification.[91] As Finn et al. put in *Nature Neuroscience*:

> Here we show that an individual's functional brain connectivity profile is both unique and reliable, similarly to a fingerprint. We demonstrate that it is possible, with near-perfect accuracy in many cases, to identify an individual from a large group of subjects solely on the basis of his or her connectivity matrix.[92]

Thus, like DNA, the results of both structural and functional brain-reading qualify as unique personal data. They could even enable biometric identification.[93]

Furthermore, DNA testing and forensic brain-reading are analogous in the sense that the data they produce relate to biological features of the individual. They yield information about the structure of someone's DNA, the structure of one's brain, DNA in saliva or blood, haemodynamics in blood, and brain electricity.

There are important differences as well. Unlike brain-reading, DNA analyses will not disclose mental states. And although theoretically possible, brain-reading shall not typically be used as a means of biometric identification. Furthermore, while DNA testing enables the identification of ethnicity and familial relationships, forensic brain-reading will not. Still, although the data yielded through brain-reading and DNA testing are not identical, their nature and, to some extent, the potential results are analogous in a relevant way under Article 8 ECHR.[94]

86 ECtHR (GC) 4 December 2008, appl.nos. 30562/04 and 30566/04 (*S. & Marper/UK*), § 68.

87 Rainey et al. 2020; Ienca 2021, p. 39; Ligthart 2019b.

88 Mohr et al. 2004; Biondi et al. 1996, p. 1366.

89 See, for example, Aloui, Nait-Ali & Naceur 2018, who correctly 'recognised' 99.6 per cent of the individuals (n = 220) with MRI, based on their brain anatomy.

90 The statistical relationship between brain activity in different brain areas.

91 Ienca & Andorno 2017, p. 14; Farahany 2012a, pp. 380–381; Farahany 2012b, p. 1281.

92 Finn et al. 2015, p. 1669. See also Jalbrzikowski et al. 2020; Waller et al. 2017; Ruiz-Blondet, Jin & Laszlo 2016.

93 An important distinction: unlike DNA databases, to date, no central 'brain databases' exist that would enable identification based on brain features.

94 See also Ligthart et al. 2020, pp. 5–8.

III. and IV The Context and Possible Use of the Information

DNA testing and forensic brain-reading aim to assist in answering central questions in criminal law. Regarding DNA samples, the Court has noted that individuals may also reap a certain benefit from DNA analyses and from retaining their personal information in a database: the information allows 'for a rapid elimination of the applicant as a possible suspect of a particular crime in the investigation of which material containing DNA had been found'.[95]

This is, *mutatis mutandis*, also true for brain-reading in criminal law. Brain-reading can contribute to the determination of a defendant's guilt, legal responsibility, and risk of recidivism.[96] Meanwhile, the defendant or convicted offender may also *request* brain-reading in order to strengthen his claim of not knowing anything about the crime he is suspected of, to support his defence of legal insanity, or to assist in one's claim of having a low risk to reoffend.[97]

Whether brain-reading data will actually be useful in an individual case will depend on whether the subject engages in countermeasures that manipulate the test results. Such countermeasures will prevent the authorities from obtaining useful information. Are DNA analyses sensitive to countermeasures as well? In fact, they are. Indeed, when the authorities have decided to take a hair or a blood sample by force, the suspect can no longer prevent the acquisition of his DNA profile by the authorities. Meanwhile, obtaining a DNA profile from a suspect will not necessarily result in 'useful' evidence. As Verschuere and Meijer stress, many accepted forms of evidence like fingerprints and DNA are vulnerable to simple means of manipulation, such as wearing gloves.[98] In the same vein, Iacono argues:

> Just as the case may be for [concealed information tests], a crime scene that does not turn up a 'hit' in the form of incriminating fingerprints does not necessarily exonerate a suspect. There are various reasons why fingerprints may not be present, including the application of 'countermeasures' like wearing gloves of wiping the scene clean.[99]

Regarding brain-reading, countermeasures are typically employed *during* the test. Regarding DNA testing, countermeasures are normally employed *prior* to the test. In both cases, the means of manipulation aim to conceal personal (biological) information that could adversely affect the subject's position in a criminal or penal procedure. Both DNA and brain-reading data can contribute to answering central question in criminal law. Both have the potential of exonerating the subject, and both are sensitive to manipulation by the subject.

95 ECtHR 20 January 2009, appl.no. 20689/08 (*W./The Netherlands*), p. 8. Also: ECtHR 7 December 2006, appl.no. 29514/05 (*Van der Velden/The Netherlands*), p. 9.
96 See Chapter 2.
97 Cf. Meynen 2018, p. 3.
98 Verschuere & Meijer 2014, p. 168.
99 Iacono 2011, pp. 16–17. Cf. Farwell, Richardson & Richardson 2013, p. 266.

In the course of criminal-legal procedures, the yielded brain-reading data will likely be stored, for example, as part of the (digital) case files and on the computers involved in the brain-reading assessment. In case-law on DNA testing, the Court has developed a legal framework tailored to storing personal data in the interest of the detection, prosecution, and prevention of crime.[100] This framework has also been applied to the storage of fingerprints, photographs, and data about previous suspicions.[101] Similarly, this framework could provide direction regarding the regulation of retaining the results of forensic brain-reading.

In conclusion, in light of the four factors the Court takes into account when determining whether the collection and use of personal data infringes Article 8 ECHR, coercive forensic brain-reading is in a relevant way analogous to taking, analysing, and retaining personal data in the context of DNA testing. Although DNA testing and brain-reading are not identical, case-law on DNA can be helpful in determining the legal boundaries of brain-reading in criminal law.[102]

4.3.3 *Forensic Collection and Storage of DNA in Light of Article 8 ECHR*

4.3.3.1 Introduction

This section considers the Court's approach on the non-consensual collection and storage of DNA under the right to respect for private life. First, it is determined whether and how the forensic collection and storage of DNA infringes the right to respect for private life. Next, the justification clause of Article 8(2) ECHR will be considered. The analysis in this section discusses general rules and principles pertaining to DNA, which will be considered with respect to brain-reading in Section 4.3.4.

4.3.3.2 Article 8(1) ECHR

The right to respect for private life comprises the protection of physical integrity. The Court considers our body the most intimate aspect of private life.[103] The acquisition of information through any compulsory medical intervention interferes

[100] ECtHR (GC) 4 December 2008, appl.nos. 30562/04 and 30566/04 (*S. & Marper/UK*); ECtHR 13 February 2020, appl.nos. 53205/13 and 63320/13 (*Trajkovski and Chipovski/North Macedonia*); ECtHR 4 June 2013, appl.nos. 7841/08 and 57900/12 (*Peruzzo/Germany and Martens/Germany*); ECtHR 20 January 2009, appl.no. 20689/08 (*W./The Netherlands*); ECtHR 7 December 2006, appl.no. 29514/05 (*Van der Velden/The Netherlands*).

[101] For example, ECtHR 18 April 2013, appl.no. 19522/09 (*M.K./France*); ECtHR 13 February 2020, appl. no. 45245/15 (*Gaughran/UK*); ECtHR 18 September 2014, appl.no. 21010/10 (*Brunet/France*).

[102] See also Ligthart et al. 2020; Ligthart 2019b.

[103] ECtHR 19 December 2013, appl.no. 45872/06 (*Yuriy Volkov/Ukrain*), § 84; ECtHR 15 March 2012, appl.no. 24429/03 (*Solomakhin/Ukraine*), § 33; ECtHR 22 July 2003, appl.no. 24209/94 (*Y.F./Turkey*), § 33; ECtHR 16 September 2014, appl.no. 50131/08 (*Atudorei/Romania*), § 160.

with the right to respect for private life, even when the intervention is 'of minor importance'.[104]

Taking blood or saliva to extract and examine DNA, which the Court qualifies as 'medical testing',[105] interferes with the individual's *physical integrity* and thus with the right to respect for private life.[106] Other examples of relatively minor interferences with a person's body that infringe the right to physical integrity concern mandatory drug testing in prison through urine samples[107] and the obligation to undergo an X-ray in the context of tuberculosis screening.[108]

Apart from physical integrity, the notion of private life comprises the protection of *personal data*. According to Harris et al., the collection, storage, and disclosure of personal data by the State infringe the right to respect for private life.[109] As mentioned before,[110] the systematic collection and storage of personal data through GPS surveillance infringe Article 8(1) ECHR,[111] as does the taking and storing of a police photograph on arrest.[112] Also, storing information about individuals by security services infringes the right to respect for private life, regardless of whether the information has been obtained through covert surveillance methods.[113] In addition, disclosing personal information, such as the disclosure of medical data during a criminal or civil trial, interferes with personal data as well, infringing the right to respect for private life.[114]

The Grand Chamber considers DNA profiles and cellular samples to constitute personal data as they relate to identified or identifiable individuals.[115] Considering

104 ECtHR 19 December 2013, appl.no. 45872/06 (*Yuriy Volkov/Ukrain*), § 84; ECtHR 15 March 2012, appl.no. 24429/03 (*Solomakhin/Ukraine*), § 33; ECtHR 22 July 2003, appl.no. 24209/94 (*Y.F./Turkey*), § 33; ECtHR 13 May 2008, appl.no. 52515/99 (*Juhnke/Turkey*), § 71 and 76.

105 ECtHR 13 July 2006, appl.no. 58757/00 (*Jäggi/Switserland*), § 38; ECtHR 7 February 2002, appl. no. 53176/99 (*Mikulić/Croatia*), § 64. See also ECtHR 5 January 2006, appl.no. 2352/02 (*Schmidt/ Germany*), p. 4.

106 ECtHR 14 April 2020, appl.no. 75229/10 (*Dragan Petrović/Serbia*), § 69, 79; ECtHR 15 May 2018, appl.no. 41079/16 (*Caruana/Malta*), § 26; ECtHR 20 January 2009, appl.no. 20689/08 (*W./The Netherlands*), p. 7; ECtHR 7 December 2006, appl.no. 29514/05 (*Van der Velden/The Netherlands*), p. 8; ECtHR 5 January 2006, appl.no. 2352/02 (*Schmidt/Germany*), p. 4.

107 EComHR 9 September 1998, appl.no. 34199/96 (*Galloway/UK*); EComHR 6 April 1994, appl.no. 21132/93 (*Peters/The Netherlands*); ECtHR 27 September 2005, appl.no. 56745/00 (*Black/UK*), p. 4.

108 EComHR 10 December 1984, appl.no. 10435/83 (*Acmanne and others/Belgium*), p. 255.

109 Harris et al., 2018, p. 538.

110 Section 4.2.2.

111 ECtHR 2 September 2010, appl.no. 35623/05 (*Uzun/Germany*), § 49–52.

112 ECtHR 13 February 2020, appl.no. 45245/15 (*Gaughran/UK*), § 70.

113 For example, ECtHR (GC) 16 February 2000, appl.no. 27798/95 (*Amann/Switzerland*), § 70; ECtHR (GC) 4 May 2000, appl.no. 28341/95 (*Rotaru/Romania*), § 44–46. Cf. ECtHR 13 February 2020, appl. no. 45245/15 (*Gaughran/UK*), § 70.

114 ECtHR 25 February 1997, appl.no. 22009/93 (*Z./Finland*), § 62–71; ECtHR 10 October 2006, appl. no. 7508/02 (*L.L./France*), § 33–34. Cf. ECtHR 26 May 2020, appl.no. 1122/12 (*P.T./the Republic of Moldova*), § 28. Cf. ECtHR 28 January 2003, appl.no. 44647/98 (*Peck/UK*); ECtHR 30 March 2021, appl.no. 51220/13 (*M.C./UK*).

115 ECtHR (GC) 4 December 2008, appl.nos. 30562/04 and 30566/04 (*S. & Marper/UK*), § 68. See also ECtHR 13 February 2020, appl.nos. 53205/13 and 63320/13 (*Trajkovski and Chipovski/North Macedonia*), § 43; ECtHR 13 February 2020, appl.no. 45245/15 (*Gaughran/UK*), § 63.

the four relevant factors – the nature of the records, potential results, specific context, and the way the records are used and processed – the Court holds that DNA profiles and cellular samples obtained in the course of criminal proceedings carry data pertaining to a person's private life in the meaning of Article 8 ECHR. Collecting such personal information without consent infringes the right to respect for private life,[116] as does their non-consensual retention.[117]

In sum, the non-consensual collection and storage of cellular samples and DNA profiles infringe the right to respect for private life in various ways. The forensic *collection* of these biological features constitutes an infringement via the notions of *physical integrity* and *personal data* as embraced by the concept of 'private life'. Furthermore, *storing* such personal information entails an additional infringement, again via the notion of *personal data*. The following section discusses how the Court approaches these infringements under Article 8(2) ECHR. Could they be justified or will they violate Article 8 ECHR?

4.3.3.3 Article 8(2) ECHR

The *collection* of personal data through a coercive medical procedure, such as DNA testing, can be justified when it is in accordance with the law, serves a legitimate interest, and is necessary in a democratic society. Regarding the law-test, Strasbourg case-law on forensic DNA testing and on other coercive medical procedures to acquire information hardly indicates any specific requirements. Both the Court and Commission are rather brief about this issue. Often, they confine their considerations to verifying whether the procedure has some accessible basis in domestic law, whether it was executed in accordance with that legal basis, and whether the impugned measure was foreseeable.[118]

Yet, in the recent case of *Dragan Petrović/Serbia*, the Court seems to suggest that the law should at least limit the circle of persons from whom a cellular sample

[116] ECtHR 4 June 2013, appl.nos. 7841/08 and 57900/12 (*Peruzzo/Germany and Martens/Germany*), § 28, 32–33, 42–49; ECtHR 13 February 2020, appl.nos. 53205/13 and 63320/13 (*Trajkovski and Chipovski/North Macedonia*), § 37, 40, 43, 46–47. See also Harris et al. 2018, pp. 538–539.

[117] ECtHR (GC) 4 December 2008, appl.nos. 30562/04 and 30566/04 (*S. & Marper/UK*), § 67, 70–77; ECtHR 13 February 2020, appl.no. 45245/15 (*Gaughran/UK*), § 63.

[118] ECtHR 15 May 2018, appl.no. 41079/16 (*Caruana/Malta*), § 33–37; ECtHR 4 June 2013, appl.nos. 7841/08 and 57900/12 (*Peruzzo/Germany and Martens/Germany*), § 36–38; ECtHR 19 December 2013, appl.no. 45872/06 (*Yuriy Volkov/Ukrain*), § 88–89; ECtHR 5 January 2006, appl.no. 2352/02 (*Schmidt/Germany*), p. 4; ECtHR 20 January 2009, appl.no. 20689/08 (*W./The Netherlands*), p. 8; ECtHR 7 December 2006, appl.no. 29514/05 (*Van der Velden/The Netherlands*), p. 8. Cf. EComHR 10 December 1984, appl.no. 10435/83 (*Acmanne and others/Belgium*), p. 256; EComHR 6 April 1994, appl.no. 21132/93 (*Peters/The Netherlands*); EComHR 9 September 1998, appl.no. 34199/96 (*Galloway/UK*); ECtHR 27 September 2005, appl.no. 56745/00 (*Black/UK*), p. 5; ECtHR 5 July 1999, appl.no. 31534/96 (*Matter/Slovakia*), § 65; ECtHR 3 October 2008, appl.no. 35228/03 (*Bogumil/Portugal*), § 87–88.

may be taken.[119] In this case, the applicant complained that taking a DNA sample from him violated his right to respect for private life. According to the domestic legal basis, taking blood and employing other 'medical procedures' were allowed in respect of any given person when such were deemed medically necessary in order to establish 'facts of importance' to a criminal investigation. The Court held that this provision allowed such procedures in respect of a potentially very large group of persons. Such an unrestricted legal basis entails the risk of arbitrariness, while in fact citizens should be able to reasonably foresee the potential legal consequences of their actions. In the Court's view, the interference with the applicants' private life was therefore not 'in accordance with the law'. Article 8 ECHR had been violated.[120]

As to the second requirement – serving a legitimate interest – the Court has considered that:

> Article 8 of the Convention does not as such prohibit recourse to a medical procedure in defiance of the will of a suspect in order to obtain from him evidence of his involvement in the commission of a criminal offence.[121]

The Court accepts that the non-consensual collection of blood and saliva for DNA testing serves the legitimate interest of preventing crime, which includes the securing of evidence for the purpose of detecting and prosecuting criminal offences.[122]

Whether the non-consensual collection of cellular samples for DNA testing meets the third requirement – is it necessary in a democratic society? – will depend on the circumstances of the individual case. Within a 'certain' margin of appreciation,[123] the medical procedure should be proportionate to the aims pursued. Both the severity of the interference and the gravity of the criminal offence are relevant factors. With respect to taking a saliva sample in the investigation of a murder, for instance, the Court in *Caruana/Malta* considered that:

[119] ECtHR 14 April 2020, appl.no. 75229/10 (*Dragan Petrović/Serbia*).

[120] Ibid., § 83–84. Cf. Chapter 3, Section 3.3.3; ECtHR (GC) 11 July 2006, appl.no. 54810/00 (*Jalloh/Germany*), § 70: 'Even where it is not motivated by reasons of medical necessity, Articles 3 and 8 of the Convention do not as such prohibit recourse to a medical procedure in defiance of the will of a suspect in order to obtain from him evidence of his involvement in the commission of a criminal offence'.

[121] ECtHR 15 May 2018, appl.no. 41079/16 (*Caruana/Malta*), § 31. See also ECtHR (GC) 11 July 2006, appl.no. 54810/00 (*Jalloh/Germany*), § 70; ECtHR 3 May 2012, appl.no. 23880/05 (*Salikhov/Russia*), § 73. Cf. Chapter 3, Section 3.3.3.

[122] Ibid., § 38. Also ECtHR 4 June 2013, appl.nos. 7841/08 and 57900/12 (*Peruzzo/Germany and Martens/Germany*), § 40; ECtHR 20 January 2009, appl.no. 20689/08 (*W./The Netherlands*), p. 8; ECtHR 5 January 2006, appl.no. 2352/02 (*Schmidt/Germany*), p. 4; ECtHR 7 December 2006, appl.no. 29514/05 (*Van der Velden/The Netherlands*), p. 9. See also ECtHR (GC) 4 December 2008, appl. nos. 30562/04 and 30566/04 (*S. & Marper/UK*), § 100; ECtHR 13 February 2020, appl.nos. 53205/13 and 63320/13 (*Trajkovski and Chipovski/North Macedonia*), § 49; ECtHR 13 February 2020, appl.no. 45245/15 (*Gaughran/UK*), § 75.

[123] ECtHR 15 May 2018, appl.no. 41079/16 (*Caruana/Malta*), § 39; ECtHR 5 January 2006, appl.no. 2352/02 (*Schmidt/Germany*), p. 5.

> the taking of a buccal swab is an act of a very short duration, it usually causes no bodily injury or any physical or mental suffering, and thus is of minor importance. (…) In the present case, the applicant was a witness present on the scene of the murder. Moreover, according to the authorities, her sample was necessary to determine the accused's motive for the murder. Murder constitutes a serious offence, in respect of which the State has obligations arising under Article 2 of the Convention vis-à-vis the victims of such crime and their relatives. It was thus both reasonable and necessary to gather as much evidence as possible. Taking all these considerations into account as well as the important public interest in the prosecution of serious crime and the fact that Contracting States enjoy a certain margin of appreciation in this matter, the Court cannot find that the measure in question was disproportionate.[124]

Similarly, in *Schmidt/Germany*, the Court held that, in general, taking a blood sample, when employed *lege artis* by a medical doctor, is of very short duration, causes only minor bodily injury, and cannot be said to cause intense physical or mental suffering.[125] Whereas such a compulsory measure is of 'minor importance', the information obtained was necessary to determine the applicant's authorship of a letter which amounted to a criminal offence of 'particular gravity' (it concerned the accusation of a third person to have killed five people in a right-wing extremist attack). Taking account of all relevant circumstances, the forcible acquisition of the applicant's cellular samples for DNA testing was not disproportionate to the legitimate aims pursued.[126]

Apart from *collecting* cellular samples and DNA profiles, *storing* such personal data infringes the right to respect for private life as well. Again, such infringements could be justified under Article 8(2) ECHR when in accordance with the law, pursuing a legitimate interest, and being necessary in a democratic society. The landmark case on this matter is the case of *S. & Marper/UK*.[127] The applicants had been charged with attempted robbery respectively with harassment. Their fingerprints and DNA samples were taken and subsequently stored. Although, ultimately, the applicants had not been convicted, the police refused to destroy their fingerprints and DNA. The Grand Chamber provides a deliberation on the blanket and indiscriminate storage of cellular samples, DNA profiles, and fingerprints of nonconvicted former defendants in a national database.

124 ECtHR 15 May 2018, appl.no. 41079/16 (*Caruana/Malta*), § 41.

125 Cf. ECtHR 20 January 2009, appl.no. 20689/08 (*W./The Netherlands*), p. 8; ECtHR 7 December 2006, appl.no. 29514/05 (*Van der Velden/The Netherlands*), p. 9, in which cases the Court qualified the interferences made by the compilation and retention of cellular samples for DNA testing as 'relatively slight'.

126 ECtHR 5 January 2006, appl.no. 2352/02 (*Schmidt/Germany*), pp. 4–5.

127 ECtHR (GC) 4 December 2008, appl.nos. 30562/04 and 30566/04 (*S. & Marper/UK*).

Regarding the law-test, the Grand Chamber reiterates that for storing cellular samples, DNA profiles, and fingerprints, it is as essential as in telephone tapping, covert intelligence-gathering, and secret surveillance to have:

> clear, detailed rules governing the scope and application of measures, as well as minimum safeguards concerning, *inter alia*, duration, storage, usage, access of third parties, procedures for preserving the integrity and confidentiality of data and procedures for its destruction, thus providing sufficient guarantees against the risk of abuse and arbitrariness.[128]

In *S. & Marper/UK*, the retention of DNA records and fingerprints had a clear basis in domestic law. However, the law did not spell out precisely the required conditions and arrangements for storing and using this kind of personal data. It basically provided that 'retained samples and fingerprints must not be used by any person except for purposes related to the prevention or detection of crime, the investigation of an offence or the conduct of a prosecution'.[129] In this regard, the Grand Chamber held that 'the prevention or detection of crime' is formulated in rather general terms. Therefore, it could give rise to an extensive interpretation.[130] Meanwhile, since these questions about the law were closely related to the broader issue of whether the infringement was necessary in a democratic society, the Court did not decide on whether the legal basis complied with the 'quality-of-law-requirement' within the meaning of Article 8(2) ECHR.[131] It addressed these issues in respect of the requirement of necessity.

Regarding the legitimate aim of retaining DNA records and fingerprints, the Court accepts that such measures pursue the interest of detecting and therefore preventing crime. The initial collection of the data serves the aim of linking a particular person to the crime of which one is suspected. Their retention pursues the broader purpose of assisting in the identification of future offenders.[132]

Regarding the necessity, the Grand Chamber starts with outlining some general principles concerning the protection of personal data. Such protection is of fundamental importance to a person's enjoyment of the right to respect for private life. Therefore, domestic laws should guarantee appropriate safeguards to prevent any

[128] Ibid., § 99. See also ECtHR 22 June 2017, appl.no. 8806/12 (*Aycaguer/France*), § 43–45.

[129] ECtHR (GC) 4 December 2008, appl.nos. 30562/04 and 30566/04 (*S. & Marper/UK*), § 97–98.

[130] Ibid., § 99.

[131] Ibid. Cf. ECtHR 13 February 2020, appl.no. 45245/15 (*Gaughran/UK*), § 73; ECtHR 13 February 2020, appl.nos. 53205/13 and 63320/13 (*Trajkovski and Chipovski/North Macedonia*), § 48; ECtHR 4 June 2013, appl.nos. 7841/08 and 57900/12 (*Peruzzo/Germany and Martens/Germany*), § 39.

[132] ECtHR (GC) 4 December 2008, appl.nos. 30562/04 and 30566/04 (*S. & Marper/UK*), § 100. Also ECtHR 13 February 2020, appl.no. 45245/15 (*Gaughran/UK*), § 75; ECtHR 13 February 2020, appl. nos. 53205/13 and 63320/13 (*Trajkovski and Chipovski/North Macedonia*), § 49; ECtHR 4 June 2013, appl.nos. 7841/08 and 57900/12 (*Peruzzo/Germany and Martens/Germany*), § 40; ECtHR 20 January 2009, appl.no. 20689/08 (*W./The Netherlands*), p. 8; ECtHR 7 December 2006, appl.no. 29514/05 (*Van der Velden/The Netherlands*), p. 9.

such use of personal data as may be inconsistent with Article 8 ECHR – especially when the data are processed automatically and used for police purposes.[133] More specifically, the law must ensure that the retained information is relevant and not excessive in relation to the purposes for which it has been stored. Preserving data in a way that enables the identification of individuals should not last any longer than necessary for the aims of retention. Importantly, the law must adequately guarantee that retained personal data are efficiently protected from misuse and abuse.[134] These considerations are of particular significance regarding the protection of specific categories of sensitive data such as DNA information, containing the individual's genetic make-up that is of great personal value to both the person concerned and to his relatives.[135]

Meanwhile, the interests of the individual and the community as a whole in protecting personal data – including DNA and fingerprints – could sometimes be outweighed by the legitimate interest of crime prevention. But the intrinsic private nature of this information calls for careful scrutiny of any State measure concerning the non-consensual retention and use of personal data.[136]

Regarding the margin of appreciation, the Court holds that the core principles of data protection – retention should be proportionate to the purpose of collection and must be limited in time – have been consistently applied by most member States. Moreover, most member States only allow cellular samples to be taken in criminal proceedings from individuals suspected of having committed a criminal offence of a certain gravity. After acquittals or discharges, samples and DNA profiles are normally to be removed or destroyed. Against the backdrop of these considerations, the Court stresses that England, Wales, and Northern Ireland appear the only jurisdictions that allow the indefinite retention of DNA material and fingerprints of *any* person, of *any* age, suspected of *any* recordable offence.[137] The strong consensus across the member States about storing DNA and fingerprints narrows the margin of appreciation.[138] Moreover, any State pioneering in developing novel forensic technologies, such as in DNA testing, holds special responsibility in striking a right balance between the competing interests at stake.[139] As the Grand Chamber argues:

[133] ECtHR (GC) 4 December 2008, appl.nos. 30562/04 and 30566/04 (*S. & Marper/UK*), § 103. See also ECtHR 4 June 2013, appl.nos. 7841/08 and 57900/12 (*Peruzzo/Germany and Martens/Germany*), § 42; ECtHR 22 June 2017, appl.no. 8806/12 (*Aycaguer/France*), § 38. Cf. ECtHR 18 April 2013, appl.no. 19522/09 (*M.K./France*), § 35; ECtHR 18 September 2014, appl.no. 21010/10 (*Brunet/France*), § 35.

[134] Ibid.

[135] ECtHR (GC) 4 December 2008, appl.nos. 30562/04 and 30566/04 (*S. & Marper/UK*), § 103; ECtHR 4 June 2013, appl.nos. 7841/08 and 57900/12 (*Peruzzo/Germany and Martens/Germany*), § 42.

[136] ECtHR (GC) 4 December 2008, appl.nos. 30562/04 and 30566/04 (*S. & Marper/UK*), § 104.

[137] Ibid., § 107–110.

[138] Ibid. See also ECtHR 13 February 2020, appl.no. 45245/15 (*Gaughran/UK*), § 80–84.

[139] ECtHR (GC) 4 December 2008, appl.nos. 30562/04 and 30566/04 (*S. & Marper/UK*), § 112.

> the protection afforded by Article 8 of the Convention would be unacceptably weakened if the use of modern scientific techniques in the criminal-justice system were allowed at any cost and without carefully balancing the potential benefits of the extensive use of such techniques against important private-life interests.[140]

Ultimately, the Court was unsatisfied about the blanket and indiscriminate nature of the domestic laws. The retention of DNA records and fingerprints was allowed irrespectively of the nature or gravity of the offence at issue. The authorities were permitted to take and retain DNA and fingerprints from a person of any age, arrested in connection with a recordable crime, including minor and non-imprisonable offences. Moreover, the retention was not limited by time: the material could be retained indefinably, regardless the nature and severity of the offence concerned. In addition, only limited possibilities were available for an acquitted individual to have the data removed from the national database or to have his DNA material destroyed. No provision enabled an independent review of the justification of retention according to defined criteria, such as the severity of the offence, previous arrests, the strength of the suspicion against the person, and any other special circumstances.[141]

These blanket and indiscriminate powers of retention failed to strike a fair balance between the competing public and private interests at stake. The UK overstepped any acceptable margin of appreciation. Therefore, the retention of personal data in *S. & Marper/UK* constituted a disproportionate infringement of the right to respect for private life. Article 8 ECHR had been violated.[142]

Apart from the 'general principles' provided in *S. & Marper/UK*, the Court's specific critique on the law of the England, Wales, and Northern Ireland does not provide a general legal framework for the storage of DNA under Article 8 ECHR. Meanwhile, from the list of limiting factors that were *not* properly addressed in domestic law,[143] we might conversely deduce that when domestic law *does* take all these factors into account properly, storing DNA data may well satisfy the requirement of being 'necessary in a democratic society', passing the test of Article 8(2) ECHR.[144]

The Court seems to confirm this view in the cases of *Peruzzo/Germany* and *Martens/Germany*. Although these cases concerned the collection and storage of DNA of *convicted* offenders, the Court explicitly addressed those factors that were

[140] Ibid.

[141] Ibid., § 119.

[142] Ibid., § 120–126. See also ECtHR 13 February 2020, appl.no. 45245/15 (*Gaughran/UK*), § 94–98; ECtHR 13 February 2020, appl.nos. 53205/13 and 63320/13 (*Trajkovski and Chipovski/North Macedonia*), § 52–55; ECtHR 18 April 2013, appl.no. 19522/09 (*M.K./France*), § 39–47; ECtHR 18 September 2014, appl.no. 21010/10 (*Brunet/France*), § 38–45.

[143] That is, the nature and gravity of the offence, the age of the individual, a limitation in time, and the possibility for acquitted persons to have their data removed.

[144] Koops 2009, Section 5.

not adequately incorporated in the law in *S. & Marper/UK*.[145] Since German law *did* limit the storage of DNA material according to these factors, the infringements of private life were considered proportionate and necessary in a democratic society.

In contrast, in *Trajkovski and Chipovski/North Macedonia*, the domestic law did not limit the retention of DNA in accordance with the factors discussed in *S. & Marper*, therefore violating Article 8 ECHR.[146] The relevance of these factors is not limited to DNA and fingerprints. They also apply to other types of personal data, such as storing photographs of convicted offenders and retaining information about previous suspicions.[147]

4.3.3.4 Conclusion

The non-consensual taking and storage of cellular samples and DNA profiles in the context of criminal law infringe the right to respect for private life. More specifically, the collection of such material, for example, through taking saliva or a blood sample, interferes with the notions of physical integrity and personal data as are comprised by the right to respect for private life. The subsequent storage of the acquired information entails another infringement, again via the notion of personal data. Taking into account a variety of relevant factors, the collection and storage of DNA material in individual cases can, however, be justified for the detection, prosecution, and prevention of crime.

4.3.4 *Coercive Forensic Brain-Reading under the Right to Respect for Private Life*

4.3.4.1 Introduction

Could coercive brain-reading be permissible in view of the right to respect for private life pursuant to Article 8 ECHR? Based on relevant similarities and important differences, the following sections deduce general views from Strasbourg case-law on forensic DNA testing that provide helpful guidance in regulating coercive brain-reading in criminal law. First, we will examine whether and, if so, how different types of coercive brain-reading infringe the right to respect for private life (Section 4.3.4.2). Next, we consider whether and under which legal conditions coercive forensic brain-reading could be justified (Section 4.3.4.3).

145 ECtHR 4 June 2013, appl.nos. 7841/08 and 57900/12 (*Peruzzo/Germany and Martens/Germany*), § 43–49.

146 ECtHR 13 February 2020, appl.nos. 53205/13 and 63320/13 (*Trajkovski and Chipovski/North Macedonia*), § 50–54.

147 ECtHR 13 February 2020, appl.no. 45245/15 (*Gaughran/UK*), § 87–97; ECtHR 18 September 2014, appl.no. 21010/10 (*Brunet/France*).

4.3.4.2 Infringing Article 8 ECHR?

Brain-reading in criminal procedures will involve the *collection* and *storage* of brain data. In some cases, the acquired and stored information might also be *disclosed*, for example, through the public hearing of an expert or by publishing the legal verdict. Does the collection, storage, and disclosure of brain-reading data infringe the right to respect for private life?

In considering whether coercive brain-reading infringes Article 8(1) ECHR, Van Toor applies the reasonable-expectation-of-privacy-test.[148] He uses this criterion since 'no other test or criterion has been given a prominent place in the case-law of the Court'.[149] The analysis in this chapter will not use the reasonable-expectations-of-privacy-test. In my view, Strasbourg case-law provides clearer criteria to determine whether coercive brain-reading infringes the right to respect for private life. It is clear that this right protects our personal data, physical integrity, and moral, psychological, and mental integrity. These aspects of our lives we conceive so private that they are *ipso facto* covered by Article 8(1) ECHR. In protecting these private interests, the reasonable-expectation-of-privacy-test is superfluous. Below, the protected notions of personal data, physical integrity, and moral, psychological, and mental integrity are discussed in respect of coercive brain-reading.

PERSONAL DATA. The Court has not yet considered to what extent forensic brain-reading data enjoy protection under Article 8(1) ECHR. But it is clear that given the evident private nature of such data, which relate directly to the identified subject, they qualify as 'personal data'.[150] The non-consensual collection, storage, and disclosure of such data in the context of criminal justice is likely to infringe the right to respect for private life.[151]

In respect of cellular samples, DNA profiles, and fingerprints, the Court draws distinctions concerning the level of privacy *sensitivity* of these categories of personal data.[152] These differences in privacy sensitivity are relevant in determining

[148] Van Toor focusses on the CIT.

[149] Van Toor 2017, 283: 'Omdat geen andere test of criterium een prominente plaats heeft bemachtigd in de rechtspraktijk van het Hof, wordt de redelijke verwachting van privacy door mij gebruikt om de inbreuk op een van de vier facetten van privacy mee te beoordelen'. Regarding the US legal context, the reasonable-expectation-of-privacy-test has been used to examine whether different types of coercive brain-reading fall within the scope of the Fourth Amendment of the Bill of Rights. Unlike Article 8 ECHR, the Fourth Amendment protects from unreasonable searches and seizures *only* when the individual has a reasonable subjective expectation of privacy. See Meixner Jr. 2018, p. 423; Blitz 2017, pp. 81–83; Pardo & Patterson 2015, pp. 153–154; Kilbride & Iuliano 2015, p. 192; Shen 2013, p. 699; Pustilnik 2012, pp. 14–15; Holley 2009, pp. 12–13.

[150] Ienca 2021, p. 39; Rainey et al. 2020; Ienca & Andorno 2017, p. 13. Cf. Harris et al. 2018, p. 540.

[151] Cf. ECtHR 13 February 2020, appl.no. 45245/15 (*Gaughran/UK*), § 70; ECtHR (GC) 4 December 2008, appl.nos. 30562/04 and 30566/04 (*S. & Marper/UK*), § 70–86.

[152] ECtHR (GC) 4 December 2008, appl.nos. 30562/04 and 30566/04 (*S. & Marper/UK*), § 86 and 120; ECtHR 13 February 2020, appl.no. 45245/15 (*Gaughran/UK*), § 80–81.

the severity of an infringement of the right to respect for private life, which is in turn essential when examining the requirement of proportionality under Article 8(2) ECHR.[153]

Regarding DNA material in general, the Court stresses that

> bearing in mind the rapid pace of developments in the field of genetics and information technology, the Court cannot discount the possibility that in the future the private-life interests bound up with genetic information may be adversely affected in novel ways or in a manner which cannot be anticipated with precision today.[154]

More specifically, focussing on *cellular samples*, the Court holds that in addition to their 'highly personal nature', they contain much sensitive information about the individual, including information about the person's health. They also contain a unique genetic code of great relevance to both the individual and her relatives.[155] As the Court argues:

> Given the nature and the amount of personal information contained in cellular samples, their retention per se must be regarded as interfering with the right to respect for the private lives of the individuals concerned. That only a limited part of this information is actually extracted or used by the authorities through DNA profiling and that no immediate detriment is caused in a particular case does not change this conclusion.[156]

Because cellular samples are rich in genetic and health information, their retention is to be considered 'particularly intrusive'.[157]

Regarding *DNA profiles*, the Court argues that they carry a more limited amount of personal information, extracted from cellular samples in a coded form. Still, they do contain substantial amounts of unique personal data. Although the information is 'objective and irrefutable', their processing through automated means allows for going well beyond neutral identification. Among others, DNA profiles enable the identification of genetic relationships between individuals.[158] In *S. & Marper/UK*, the Court held that the DNA profiles' capacity of identifying genetic relationships is sufficient to conclude that their retention infringes the right to the private life. This conclusion will not be affected by the fact that the information is encoded, only comprehensible with the use of computer technology, and can only be interpreted by a limited number of persons. The Court also stressed that the processing of DNA profiles allows the authorities to assess the likely ethnic origin of the

[153] See Section 4.3.4.3.

[154] ECtHR (GC) 4 December 2008, appl.nos. 30562/04 and 30566/04 (*S. & Marper/UK*), § 71. Cf. ECtHR 13 February 2020, appl.no. 45245/15 (*Gaughran/UK*), § 80 (developments in facial recognition).

[155] ECtHR (GC) 4 December 2008, appl.nos. 30562/04 and 30566/04 (*S. & Marper/UK*), § 72.

[156] Ibid., § 73.

[157] Ibid., § 120.

[158] Ibid., § 74–76.

donor.[159] Recently, the Court held that the use of DNA profiles for familial searching is of 'highly sensitive nature' and in need of very strict control.[160]

Regarding *fingerprints*, the Court argues that they do not carry as much information as cellular samples and DNA profiles. Still, they contain unique objective information about an individual, allowing for identification with precision in a wide range of circumstances.[161]

Let us now consider the sensitivity of different types of brain-reading data.

Diagnostics. Employing brain-reading in the context of diagnosing a mental or brain disorder will yield data about the individual's mental health. Such information constitutes by its very nature 'highly sensitive personal data regardless of whether it was indicative of a particular medical diagnosis'.[162] Moreover, if the data entail information about the subject's sexual interests, for instance in the context of a paraphilic disorder, the sensitivity of the acquired information might increase. Our sexual preferences are conceived as a most intimate aspect of private life.[163] Similarly, the Data Protection Convention as well as the GDPR qualify personal data about health and sexual life as 'special' data (Article 6 of the Convention and Article 9 GDPR).

Importantly, brain-reading for other purposes than diagnostics – such as neuroprediction or lie detection – may yield 'medical data' as well. First, such non-medical use of brain-reading could incidentally reveal information about the subject's health.[164] For instance, fMRI-based lie detection could unexpectedly indicate the presence of a brain tumour.[165] Second, although non-medical neuroimaging does not aim to obtain medically relevant brain data, brain scans could still do so. Examining the brain with fMRI in the course of lie detection will also yield other, additional brain information not relevant to lying. Such an fMRI yields *collateral data*. Subjecting these data to decoding systems and/or analytical methods other than those employed for lie detection could possibly provide additional information about the subject's mental health.[166]

Neuroprediction. The results of neuroprediction are sensitive as well. They reveal information about the person's emotional and behavioural traits, indicating a

[159] Ibid., § 75–76.

[160] ECtHR 13 February 2020, appl.no. 45245/15 (*Gaughran/UK*), § 81.

[161] ECtHR (GC) 4 December 2008, appl.nos. 30562/04 and 30566/04 (*S. & Marper/UK*), § 78–86; ECtHR 13 February 2020, appl.no. 45245/15 (*Gaughran/UK*), § 80.

[162] ECtHR 26 January 2017, appl.no. 42788/06 (*Surikov/Ukraine*), § 75. See also ECtHR 27 February 2018, appl.no. 66490/09 (*Mockutė/Lithuania*), § 94; ECtHR 26 May 2020, appl.no. 1122/12 (*P.T./the Republic of Moldova*), § 26, 31.

[163] See, for example, ECtHR 22 October 1981, appl.no. 7525/76 (*Dudgeon/UK*), § 52; ECtHR 26 October 1988, appl.no. 10581/83 (*Norris/Ireland*), § 46; ECtHR 12 April 2012, appl.no. 43547/08 (*Stübing/Germany*), § 59.

[164] Edwards 2012, p. 251; Ford & Aggarwal 2012, pp. 333–334; Illes et al. 2002.

[165] Meynen 2018, p. 2.

[166] Cf. Claydon 2017, p. 5.

particular risk of future dangerousness. They closely relate to the subject's mental health. Think of brain-reading to identify the inactivity of the person's prefrontal cortex. The potential disclosure of neurobiological predispositions to antisocial behaviour, for example, through a legal verdict, can have far-reaching consequences for the individual's private life. Apart from the issue of stigmatisation, disclosing a person's risk of future dangerousness or even of future arrest could hamper job applications, mortgage requests, and insurance policies.[167] It could adversely affect the person's private life interests in a way that exceeds the scope of the legal procedure for which the neuroprediction was initially applied.

Lie detection and *concealed information tests.* In general, these applications are likely to yield the least sensitive data compared with information about mental health, sexual interests, and future dangerousness. The data recovered with forensic lie detection and CITs will normally not comprise a large or special sensitive area of the subject's private life. They merely relate to a particular past act or event, which is only relevant within the limited context of the criminal or penal procedure, such as whether one recognises a particular gun or sports bag, or whether one lies about an alibi.[168] The information to be obtained is limited to the specific brain reactions in response to the presented questions or stimuli (such as 'Did you have tea with that particular person, at that particular time, at that particular location?' And 'Do you recognise this particular gun?').[169] This argument of yielding only limited information holds especially true regarding the CIT employed with EEG, detecting only one specific brain reaction (P300) in response to the presented pictures.

In conclusion, the severity of an interference with people's personal data will depend on the privacy-sensitivity of the brain-reading data concerned. Information about mental health and sexual interests are considered highly sensitive. The results of brain-based lie detection and CITs are, in general, to be considered least sensitive in this regard. Meanwhile, we should not overlook the possibility that in the future private-life interests bound up with brain-reading may be adversely affected in novel ways or in a manner we cannot anticipate today. Subjecting *prima facie* limited amounts of brain-reading data to novel decoding algorithms might possibly reveal sensitive information about medical predispositions, emotional traits, sexual proclivities, or biometric identification.[170]

In light of the analogy between brain-reading and DNA testing, the question arises whether the results of brain-reading are, in general, more – or less – sensitive compared with the information yielded in the context of DNA testing. As discussed,

[167] Cf. Tortora et al. 2020, p. 5.

[168] By contrast, the data yielded in the context of brain-based diagnostics and neuroprediction can, just like DNA, also contribute to other (future) legal proceedings.

[169] As previously mentioned, neuroimaging in the course of lie and memory detection can yield 'collateral data'.

[170] Cf. Claydon 2017, p. 5.

with DNA testing, State authorities obtain personal information of 'highly sensitive nature', similar to personal data pertaining to people's mental health,[171] as are recovered through brain-based diagnostics. Considering the private character of brain-based memory detection, Meegan states:

> It would be difficult to argue that this type of evidence gathering [brain-based memory detection] is more invasive to one's privacy than other accepted types of evidence gathering (e.g., tissue samples for DNA-testing).[172]

Meegan may be right as far as *current* brain-reading is concerned. DNA carries an enormous amount of highly sensitive information, concerning health, ethnic origin, and genetic relationships.[173] Even though law enforcement only uses a fraction of the data enshrined in DNA, all other kinds of sensitive information are potentially out there.[174]

The extent to which present brain-reading applications involve an unfiltered collection of personal data depends on the particular test and its technology.[175] As discussed, a CIT employed with EEG yields only a limited amount of information: just P300-signals in response to specific pictures. Meanwhile, when neuroimaging shows the detailed structure or activity of the whole brain, such as CT and (f)MRI, the data could enable to draw much more inferences than the test was initially employed for (e.g. regarding mental health or biometrically identifying characteristics). Still, the sensitivity of forensic brain-reading data is not likely to exceed the level of sensitivity of DNA information. As Pardo and Patterson note:

> For example, we assume that many people would expect a greater privacy interest in the content of information about their blood (e.g., HIV status) or their genetic information (…) than in the content of their memories or evoked utterances on a variety of nonpersonal matters.[176]

Future developments in the neural representation of real-time thoughts might change this view. If it would be possible to detect real-time thoughts, the information that will be yielded may no longer be restricted by the purpose of the test, but rather by those things the subject (accidently) thinks about,[177] such as one's sexual

[171] ECtHR 26 January 2017, appl.no. 42788/06 (*Surikov/Ukraine*), § 75; ECtHR 27 February 2018, appl. no. 66490/09 (*Mockutė/Lithuania*), § 94.

[172] Meegan 2008, p. 16. See also Fox 2008, p. 2. Cf. Van Toor 2017, p. 288: 'De informatierijkheid van een DNA-profiel is dus vele mate hoger dan de informatie die wordt verkregen met (neuro) geheugendetectie'.

[173] ECtHR (GC) 4 December 2008, appl.nos. 30562/04 and 30566/04 (*S. & Marper/UK*), § 72–76; ECtHR 13 February 2020, appl.no. 45245/15 (*Gaughran/UK*), § 81.

[174] Cf. ECtHR (GC) 4 December 2008, appl.nos. 30562/04 and 30566/04 (*S. & Marper/UK*), § 72–73.

[175] Ligthart et al. 2020, p. 7.

[176] Cf. Pardo & Patterson 2015, p. 161.

[177] Cf. Meynen 2019, p. 8.

interests, political preferences, or adherence to a certain religion.[178] Ultimately, such a 'trawl-like' detection of mental states might yield *more, and more sensitive* information compared with DNA testing.

PHYSICAL INTEGRITY. Using medical procedures without consent interferes with the individual's physical integrity and infringes the right to respect for private life. This holds true regardless of whether the intervention is of 'minor importance', such as taking saliva or blood for DNA testing or acquiring urine samples in prison in the course of mandatory drug testing.[179] Similarly, obliging a chest X-ray in the context of tuberculosis screening constitutes a medical procedure against the subjects' will, infringing the right to respect for private life.[180]

Just like taking blood, saliva, urine samples, and X-ray, neuroimaging is basically a medical procedure. It has been developed for and is commonly employed in medicine, for instance to diagnose epilepsy (EEG), localise a tumour or assess traumatic brain injury (MRI, PET, CT).[181] Following the same line of reasoning as the Court: since coercive neuroimaging constitutes a medical procedure without consent, it interferes with the subject's physical integrity and infringes the right to respect for private life.[182]

Meanwhile, further developments in neuroimaging might, at some point, relativise the medical nature of the technology. Brain-reading may become available to consumers and law enforcement officials, being applied without any medical skills for non-medical purposes.[183] Furthermore, novel techniques might potentially enable the detection of brain data without any form of physical intrusion. Still, in such cases, coercive brain-reading infringes the right to respect for private life via the notion of personal data. Clearly, when brain-reading is used with physical coercion, an additional interference with physical integrity will arise.

MORAL, PSYCHOLOGICAL, AND MENTAL INTEGRITY. Finally, the question can be raised: would coercive brain-reading interfere with the individual's moral, psychological, and mental integrity?[184] Since the precise meaning and scope of these notions are

[178] This may even raise an issue under the right to freedom of thought, conscience, and religion (discussed in Chapter 5).

[179] ECtHR 15 May 2018, appl.no. 41079/16 (*Caruana/Malta*), § 26; ECtHR 20 January 2009, appl.no. 20689/08 (*W./The Netherlands*), p. 7; ECtHR 7 December 2006, appl.no. 29514/05 (*Van der Velden/The Netherlands*), p. 8; ECtHR 5 January 2006, appl.no. 2352/02 (*Schmidt/Germany*), p. 4; EComHR 9 September 1998, appl.no. 34199/96 (*Galloway/UK*); EComHR 6 April 1994, appl.no. 21132/93 (*Peters/The Netherlands*); ECtHR 27 September 2005, appl.no. 56745/00 (*Black/UK*), p. 4.

[180] EComHR 10 December 1984, appl.no. 10435/83 (*Acmanne and others/Belgium*).

[181] Mecacci & Haselager 2019, p. 444; Greely & Wagner 2011, pp. 763–765, 768 and 772.

[182] See also Chapter 3, Section 3.3.4.

[183] For example, Ienca, Haselager & Emanuel 2018.

[184] Cf. Lavazza 2018; Lavazza 2021.

unsure,[185] the exact implications of coercive brain-reading remain unclear as well. At least it is clear that the right to moral, psychological, and mental integrity protects against actions that affect or impede mental health, gender identification, and sexual orientation. This right also covers issues such as harassment, fear for physical abuse, and loss of honour and reputation.[186]

In general, brain-reading will not typically *affect* the brain or mental states. It will not normally diminish mental health, for instance, or obstruct a person's sexual orientation by changing brain states or neural processes. Although brain-reading is mentally intrusive, it will not actually *interfere* with the subject's brain or mental capacities. It only 'detects' the brain and its activity from outside.[187]

Yet, when physical coercion is used, for example by administering sedatives or general anaesthesia, the subject's mental capacities – and possibly his mental health – will be affected.[188] When volitional coercion is used, it is unlikely that forensic brain-reading will interfere with the subject's moral, psychological, or mental integrity. However, as previously discussed,[189] in very specific cases, volitionally coerced CITs could possibly arouse feelings of fear or somehow affect the subject's sense of honour. This could be the case if the subject is obliged to observe cruel pictures, which can have considerable mental impact. Meanwhile, as discussed, it is unclear from Strasbourg case-law whether obliging people to observe such cruel imagines will be able to arouse feelings of fear or inferiority in the meaning of Article 3 ECHR. Similarly, the limited amount of case-law on moral, psychological, and mental integrity does not indicate whether such obligations would be capable of infringing Article 8(1) ECHR.

Further debates about how to understand the right to moral, psychological, and mental integrity might give rise to different conclusions. If the Court appears inclined to understand this right as comprising the ability to control what happens with our mental states and with the related personal data,[190] coercive brain-reading will probably infringe this sub-dimension of the right to respect for private life as well.[191]

In conclusion, the forensic *collection*, *storage*, and *disclosure* of brain-reading data will infringe the right to respect for private life via the notion of personal data. Coercive brain-reading will also interfere with the subject's physical integrity and possibility with her moral, psychological, and/or mental integrity as are protected by Article 8 ECHR.

[185] Bublitz 2020; Michalowski 2020.

[186] See Section 4.2.2.

[187] By contrast, neurotechnologies that aim to *change* individual mental states, such as brain stimulation and pharmaceuticals, do elicit debates over a right to 'mental integrity'. See, for example, Bublitz & Merkel 2014; Focquaert & Schermer 2015; Craig 2016; Ligthart et al. 2021b.

[188] See Chapter 2, Section 2.4.2.

[189] Chapter 3, Section 3.3.4, factor 3.

[190] Cf. Committee on Bioethics of the Council of Europe 2019, § 22. See Section 4.2.2.

[191] Cf. Ligthart et al. 2021a, pp. 8–9.

However, no such infringements should arise if the subject *consents* to brain-reading. Similar to the previously discussed case-law about informed consent under Article 3 ECHR,[192] the Court has elaborated on the relevance of consent in light of Article 8 ECHR.[193]

Regarding medical interventions, the Court holds that '[a]ny medical intervention against the subject's will, or without the free, informed and express consent of the subject, constitutes an interference with his or her private life'.[194] Medical procedures that are employed *with* the subject's valid consent will not normally infringe Article 8 ECHR.[195] In the case of *Davut Cakicisoy and others/Cyprus*, the applicants complained under Article 8 ECHR that the authorities had taken blood samples for DNA analysis but had not informed them about the exact purposes for which those samples were used and retained.[196] When considering these complaints, the Court stressed that this case had to be distinguished from those cases where blood samples had been taken under *compulsory powers*, such as in *S. & Marper/UK*.[197] In the present case, the applicants *volunteered* their samples and *signed consent forms*, all aiming to identifying the remains of missing relatives. Against the backdrop of these considerations, the Court found:

> no indication that there has been an infringement of the applicants' right to respect for their private life in that the applicants consented to give the samples, were informed of the purpose of the samples and there is not the least indication that the samples have been used for any other purpose.[198]

Similarly, informed consent to forensic brain-reading will be able to prevent Article 8 ECHR from being infringed. The main question regarding the validity of informed consent in this regard will be whether consent is given voluntarily. More precisely, the criminal justice context might render a person 'vulnerable'. As a result, his consent could be unfree and thus invalid.[199]

In the context of Article 8 ECHR, the Strasbourg institutions have agreed that consensually participating in forensic medical procedures will not prevent infringements when the law threatens non-cooperation with adverse consequences. In *Acmanne and others/Belgium*, the Commission considered that the requirement to cooperate with a chest X-ray (non-compliance was punishable) infringed the right

[192] Chapter 3, Section 3.3.4, factor 3.
[193] See also Buelens, Herijgers & Illegems 2016.
[194] ECtHR 13 May 2008, appl.no. 52515/99 (*Juhnke/Turkey*), § 76. See also ECtHR 22 July 2003, appl. no. 24209/94 (*Y.F./Turkey*), § 43; ECtHR 29 April 2002, appl.no. 2346/02 (*Pretty/UK*), § 63; ECtHR 15 January 2013, appl.no. 8759/05 (*Csoma/Romania*), § 42, 48–50; ECtHR 16 September 2014, appl.no. 50131/08 (*Atudorei/Romania*), § 161–164. See also Harris et al. 2018, p. 522–523.
[195] Cf. ECtHR 5 October 2006, appl.no. 75725/01 (*Trocellier/France*); Buelens, Herijgers & Illegems 2016.
[196] ECtHR 23 September 2014, appl.no. 6523/12 (*Davut Cakicisoy and others/Cyprus*), § 49.
[197] See also ECtHR 5 January 2006, appl.no. 32352/02 (*Schmidt/Germany*).
[198] ECtHR 23 September 2014, appl.no. 6523/12 (*Davut Cakicisoy and others/Cyprus*), § 50.
[199] See Chapter 2, Section 2.7 and Chapter 3, Section 3.3.4.

to respect for private life.[200] Analogously, the obligation to provide a urine sample in prison for the purpose of drug testing (refusal was threatened with a disciplinary sanction or additional days of detention) infringes Article 8 ECHR.[201] The same is true for a blood alcohol test where non-cooperation is threatened by the law as constituting a criminal offence.[202] The actual realisation of a legal threat through a criminal conviction for refusing cooperation to provide cellular samples for DNA testing infringes the right to respect for private life as well.[203] Recently, the Court has explicitly accepted that legal threats invalidate consent under Article 8 ECHR:

> The Court considers that the taking of a DNA sample from the applicant amounted to an interference with his 'private life' within the meaning of Article 8 of the Convention. The fact that the applicant agreed to give a sample of his saliva to the police officers was, in this context, of no relevance, since he only did so under the threat that either a saliva sample or a blood sample would otherwise be taken from him by force.[204]

In light of these examples, we can safely conclude that informed consent to brain-reading, given under the pressure of a legal threat, will not normally prevent Article 8 ECHR from being infringed.

Case-law on Article 8 ECHR suggests that *offering* medical procedures in the context of criminal justice may sometimes invalidate consent as well.[205] At least, it indicates that in particular situations, such as when the State has strong authority over a vulnerable individual, like in prison settings and in criminal proceedings,[206] a close examination of the voluntariness of consent shall be required.[207]

4.3.4.3 Violating Article 8 ECHR?

As argued in the previous section, both the collection of brain-reading data as well as their subsequent storage and/or disclosure will infringe the right to respect for private life. This section examines whether these infringements are likely to *violate* Article 8 ECHR or whether they could possibly be justified. To be justified, they should meet the central requirements of (1) being in accordance with the law,

200 EComHR 10 December 1984, appl.no. 10435/83 (*Acmanne and others/Belgium*), p. 255.
201 EComHR 6 April 1994, appl.no. 21132/93 (*Peters/The Netherlands*); EComHR 9 September 1998, appl.no. 34199/96 (*Galloway/UK*); ECtHR 11 October 2005, appl.no. 60682/00 (*Young/UK*), pp. 3 and 12.
202 EComHR 4 December 1978, appl.no. 8239/78 (*X./The Netherlands*), pp. 187 and 189.
203 ECtHR 22 June 2017, appl.no. 8806/12 (*Aycaguer/France*), § 35.
204 ECtHR 14 April 2020, appl.no. 75229/10 (*Dragan Petrović/Serbia*), § 79.
205 See Chapter 3, Section 3.3.4, factor 3.
206 ECtHR 11 December 2008, appl.no. 4268/04 (*Panovits/Cyprus*), § 68.
207 ECtHR 13 May 2008, appl.no. 52515/99 (*Juhnke/Turkey*), § 76–82; ECtHR 22 July 2003, appl.no. 24209/94 (*Y.F./Turkey*), § 34. See also Buelens, Herijgers & Illegems 2016, pp. 484–485; De Vries 2018, p. 694.

(2) serving a legitimate interest, and (3) being necessary in a democratic society for the legitimate aim(s) pursued.

In principle, the first two requirements need not to be an obstacle to coercive brain-reading, as long as its use is regulated by sound – accessible and foreseeable – domestic law, allowing its employment in the legitimate interest of the detection, prosecution, and prevention of crime. Perhaps, member States should create new laws, setting out the precise criteria for coercive brain-reading in different stages of criminal law. They should provide adequate legal protection against arbitrariness and indicate with sufficient clarity the scope of discretion of the competent authorities. In addition, Strasbourg case-law indicates that domestic laws should ensure the assessment of foreseeable consequences of a planned medical procedure. Subjects must be informed about these consequences beforehand, in a way that enables them to give informed consent.[208] Although developing novel laws specified to brain-reading could raise legal and practical challenges, it will not raise any obstacles in-principle.[209]

Meanwhile, whether coercive brain-reading meets the third requirement – being necessary in a democratic society – may elicit more fundamental debates. To be necessary in a democratic society, an infringement of Article 8(1) ECHR must respond to a pressing social need and the means employed must be proportionate to the aims pursued. In considering these requirements, the Court takes into account that a margin of appreciation is left to the States. The breadth of this margin depends on a number of relevant factors. In what follows, the margin of appreciation for coercive forensic brain-reading is discussed. Next, the requirements of a pressing social need and proportionality will be considered.

MARGIN OF APPRECIATION FOR COERCIVE BRAIN-READING. In securing the detection and prevention of crime, States enjoy ‘a certain’ margin of appreciation. They have some discretion in deciding which measures they take, both in general and in individual cases.[210] The breadth of this margin will depend on the severity of the criminal offence in question.[211]

With respect to the use of coercive brain-reading in criminal law, no consensus exists across the member States of the Council of Europe. Neither concerning the relative importance of the interests at stake, nor as to the best way of protecting

[208] ECtHR 15 January 2013, appl.no. 8759/05 (*Csoma/Romania*), § 42; ECtHR 2 June 2009, appl.no. 31675/04 (*Codarcea/Romania*), § 105; ECtHR 5 October 2006, appl.no. 75725/01 (*Trocellier/France*), p. 9; Buelens, Herijgers & Illegems 2016, p. 485.

[209] Cf. Ligthart et al. 2020, p. 6.

[210] ECtHR (GC) 28 October 1994, appl.no. 14310/88 (*Murray/UK*), § 90; ECtHR 6 September 1978, appl.no. 5029/71 (*Klass and others/Germany*), § 49.

[211] ECtHR 8 July 2014, appl.no. 3910/13 (*M.P.E.V. and others/Switzerland*), § 58. Cf. ECtHR (GC) 28 October 1994, appl.no. 14310/88 (*Murray/UK*), § 90. See also Van Toor 2017, p. 299.

them. For example, recently, Spain has opened for public consultation a first draft of domestic rights that should regulate neurotechnologies, including a right to mental privacy.[212] In the Netherlands, both the policy-oriented and scholarly debate on how the law should approach emerging neurotechnologies such as brain-reading are still in a preliminary stage.[213] Meanwhile, the French Civil Code prescribes that neuroimaging shall only be used for medical purposes, scientific research, or in the context of judicial expert opinions (including criminal cases).[214]

These examples clearly illustrate that to date no consensus exists across the member States on how to regulate the use of brain-reading in criminal law. Apart from this legal ambiguousness, brain-reading raises sensitive *ethical* and *moral* questions, which are currently under debate.[215] Both the lack of legal consensus and the moral and ethical sensitivity of forensic brain-reading suggest to broaden the margin of appreciation.[216]

At the same time, as the Grand Chamber argued in *S. & Marper/UK*:

> the protection afforded by Article 8 of the Convention would be unacceptably weakened if the use of modern scientific techniques in the criminal-justice system were allowed at any cost and without carefully balancing the potential benefits of the extensive use of such techniques against important private-life interests. (…) The Court considers that any State claiming a pioneer role in the development of new technologies *bears special responsibility* for striking the right balance in this regard.[217]

Whereas the ethical and moral sensitivity and a lack of consensus *broaden* the margin of appreciation,[218] being a pioneer in introducing modern scientific technologies into criminal justice, such as coercive brain-reading,[219] *narrows* the margin. Introducing coercive brain-reading in criminal law imposes a 'special responsibility' upon pioneering States to strike a right balance between all competing interests.

212 Nadal 2020; First draft of the Spanish Carta de Derechos Digitales, Article XXIV(1c): 'Las condiciones, límites y garantías de implantación y empleo en las personas de las neurotecnologías serán reguladas por la ley con la finalidad de: (…) Asegurar la confidencialidad y seguridad de los datos obtenidos o relativos a sus procesos cerebrales y el pleno dominio y disposición sobre los mismos'.

213 Ligthart, Kooijmans & Meynen 2021b; Van Toor 2017.

214 Encinas de Muñagorri & Saas 2016, p. 81; Desmoulin-Canselier 2020, pp. 535–536.

215 For example, Meynen 2020; Mecacci & Haselager 2019; Lavazza 2018; Meynen 2017; Ienca & Andorno 2017; Ryberg 2017a; Roskies 2015, pp. 683–693; Ford & Aggarwal 2012; Vincent 2011.

216 Cf. ECtHR (GC) 16 December 2010, appl.no. 25579/05 (*A, B and C/Ireland*), § 233; ECtHR (GC) 10 April 2007, appl.no. 6339/05 (*Evans/UK*), § 81; Van Toor 2017, p. 297.

217 ECtHR (GC) 4 December 2008, appl.nos. 30562/04 and 30566/04 (*S. & Marper/UK*), § 112 (emphasis added).

218 ECtHR (GC) 24 January 2017, appl.no. 25358/12 (*Paradiso and Campanelli/Italy*), § 182; ECtHR (GC) 4 December 2008, appl.nos. 30562/04 and 30566/04 (*S. & Marper/UK*), § 102.

219 Although the results of different neuroimaging technologies have already been used in various criminal justice systems within Europe, deploying such technology *with coercion* is yet no common practice, rather reserved for pioneering States.

The breadth of the margin of appreciation further depends on the nature of the Convention right(s) at stake. If coercive brain-reading infringes the individual's effective enjoyment of intimate or key rights, or interferes with another particularly important facet of a person's existence or identity, the margin tends to be narrower.[220] As discussed, coercive brain-reading will interfere with the individual's personal data and physical integrity, infringing the right to respect for private life pursuant to Article 8 ECHR. Employing such means of data-acquisition – revealing particular brain anomalies, identifying a specific lie, or detecting the recognition of a particular crime-related stimulus – will, however, not typically infringe an intimate or key right, nor will it interfere with a particularly important facet of the individual's existence or identity.[221] Accordingly, the margin of appreciation should not be narrowed in this regard.

This is, however, an issue of scholarly debate. Focussing on the CIT, Van Toor argues that this technique *will* interfere with an important facet of the individual's identity and infringe a key right: the right to personal autonomy.[222] As Van Toor argues, memories are shielded from the outside world. As long as they are not disclosed by the individual herself, no one can ever know of them. Moreover, memories are central to human existence, forming a considerable part of our personal identity: 'what a person goes through in life, which relationships he enters into, maintains and loses, and how he continues or adjusts his behaviour based on his experiences, shape his personality'.[223] According to Van Toor, having control over the disclosure of our own memories is key to private life.[224] Interfering with a person's autonomy in this regard infringes an 'intrinsic component' of her personality.[225] When undisclosed personal information can no longer be shielded from the outside world, hardly anything will remain of the notion of private life.[226] Consequently, Van Toor

[220] ECtHR (GC) 4 December 2008, appl.nos. 30562/04 and 30566/04 (*S. & Marper/UK*), § 102; ECtHR (GC) 4 December 2007, appl.no. 44362/04 (*Dickson/UK*), § 78; ECtHR (GC) 11 July 2002, appl.no. 28957/95 (*Christine Goodwin/UK*), § 90.

[221] Cf. Ferrua 2020, p. 412.

[222] Van Toor 2017, pp. 298, 363–367. Cf. Lavazza 2018, p. 4; Ienca & Andorno 2017, p. 14.

[223] Van Toor 2017, p. 298.

[224] Ibid.: 'Herinneringen zijn van de buitenwereld afgeschermd en wel op zo'n manier dat, wanneer [zij] niet door de persoon zelf op enigerlei wijze worden geopenbaard, anderen nooit kennis ervan kunnen nemen. (…) Daarnaast maken zij deel uit van de kern van het menselijk bestaan. De mens is natuurlijk meer dan een optelsom van zijn herinneringen [en] ervaring, maar deze bepalen voor een belangrijk deel de persoonlijke identiteit. Wat een persoon meemaakt in zijn leven, welke relaties hij aangaat, onderhoudt en verliest en hoe hij vervolgens op basis van zijn ervaringen zijn gedrag continueert of aanpast, vormen zijn persoonlijkheid. De vrije beschikking over herinneringen is mijns inziens een kernonderdeel van het privéleven'.

[225] Ibid., p. 366: 'de aantasting van de autonomie met betrekking tot herinneringen maakt een inbreuk op een intrinsiek bestanddeel van de persoonlijkheid'.

[226] Ibid.: 'Als niet-geopenbaarde persoonlijke informatie niet meer af te zonderen is, is van een persoonlijke levenssfeer niet of maximaal in zeer geringe mate sprake'.

argues that coercive CITs adversely affect the core of Article 8 ECHR, therefore narrowing the margin of appreciation.[227]

This is an interesting thought.[228] And at first sight, the argument may sound appealing. Yet, in my view, it is not persuasive with respect to brain-reading in criminal law. Van Toor's argument seems to presuppose that the CIT enables to yield memories about *a range of personal experiences*, such as (all) personal relationships the subject had so far. This is, however, not very likely. Instead, the CIT employed with EEG, measuring P300-amplitudes, basically detects just one single brain reaction in response to the specific stimuli that are presented to the subject. Next, the collected data enable the examiner to draw inferences about whether the subject recognised the presented stimuli. Does she recognise a *particular* gun, *specific* victim, a *specific* crime scene, or a *particular* sports bag used during a robbery? Measurements like these are not likely to identify a range of memories and experiences central to people's identity and to their human existence.

Similarly, brain-based lie detection with fMRI only yields information about the truthfulness of *specific* statements about a *particular* event, such as a specific crime. For instance, was the defendant indeed drinking tea with her neighbour during the time of the offence? As Meynen puts it:

> Both [the P300-test and lie detection] are 'one trick ponies': lie detection can only detect deceit, while P300 can only detect salience/recognition. In both techniques, it is the response in combination with the external stimulus (statement or images) that provides information about relevant aspects of a subject's state of mind (assuming the technique works well). Without the statements or pictures, we know nothing about the subject's mind. In fact, this is a simple form of mind reading, basically detecting a specific mental attitude or response regarding a specific phenomenon. Whatever else may be going on in a person's mind remains undetected. This implies that the examiner has to know what he or she is looking for, e.g. the truthfulness of a particular statement or the salience of a particular object (or series of objects).[229]

Some brain-reading applications, such as lie detection and CITs, enable to draw inferences about particular *mental states* of an individual. However, in a forensic context, these tests will not normally disclose a wide range of personal memories or thoughts essential to a person's personality. Typically, they only yield information that is closely related to a particular event, such as a crime (gun, crime scene, *etc.*).

The same holds true, *mutatis mutandis*, for neuroprediction, measuring particular brain responses to specific stimuli. Brain-reading for this purpose has the ability

[227] Ibid., p. 298.
[228] Cf. Goering et al. 2021, p. 6.
[229] Meynen 2017, p. 317.

to identify a person's emotional reactions. But in the context of criminal law, the assessment of someone's risk to reoffend shall typically relate to a specific crime and emotional trait, such as aggression. Clearly, this reveals more about a person than the mere recognition of a sport bag or gun. Still, neuroprediction in the course of a criminal or penal procedure is not likely to disclose a broad range of traits and characteristics that are together essential to the individual's identity. Rather, the test will focus on particular proclivities, elicited by specific stimuli that are relevant to the crime concerned.

As discussed,[230] brain-reading might sometimes yield *intimate* information relating to the person's identity, for example regarding his mental health or sexual preferences. The 'intimate' nature of such information is certainly relevant to assessing the *sensitivity* of the collected personal data and for determining the *severity* of the infringement of private life. But the acquisition of sensitive data should not as a rule imply an infringement of an intimate or key right, narrowing the margin of appreciation accordingly. As an illustration, the Court conceives cellular material and DNA profiles to be highly sensitive (relating almost directly to a person's identity). Nonetheless, the non-consensual collection of DNA appears not to interfere with a particular important facet of the individual's identity, nor does it infringe an intimate or key right. The margin of appreciation is not restricted in such a way.[231]

The limited scope of brain-reading applications might change when novel methods enable the re-analysis of the data obtained by present-day brain-reading applications. Such future analyses could make it possible to drawing inferences about more and/or other mental states than the test initially identified.[232] Similarly, if further developments in neurotechnology would enable the identification of real-time thoughts, the data shall be less delimited by the specific purpose of the test. Rather, it might then be defined by those things the subject thinks about. Potentially, such brain-reading could reveal much about the person's preferences, memories, and personality.

In considering the margin of appreciation in respect of CITs, Van Toor also puts significant weight to the fact that brain-reading technologies such as CITs are to date the only methods that enable the *disclosure of yet undisclosed personal information*.[233] They are exceptional and restrict the individual's autonomy to disclose such information.[234]

However, in my view, brain-reading is not exceptional in the ability of disclosing yet undisclosed information.[235] This technology is not as 'disruptive' as it might seem

[230] Section 4.3.4.2.
[231] See Section 4.3.3.
[232] Cf. Rainey et al. 2020.
[233] Cf. Goering et al. 2021. p. 6.
[234] Van Toor 2017, p. 289. See also pp. 298, 363–367. Cf. Lavazza 2018, p. 4.
[235] Moreover, whether such forms of brain-reading indeed disclose *undisclosed* information is also open to debate. In fact, we express thoughts, moods, and emotions by the way we look, react, and behave as well: Ryberg 2017b, p. 209.

at first sight.[236] Other yet existing means of investigation can disclose undisclosed information as well. Imagine, for example, that a traffic police officer, by means of ordinary law enforcement without a criminal charge, asks a car driver whether and, if so, how many drinks he had during the time he was home alone prior to his driving. As long as the driver refuses to answer this question and refuses to cooperate with a breathalyser test, the information the police officer is looking for stays *undisclosed*. However, if the police officer legally coerces the driver to participate in a blood alcohol test, the *undisclosed* blood alcohol level will be *disclosed* after all. In that case, the police *bypasses the individual's choice not to reveal the personal information*.

Compulsory blood alcohol tests infringe the right to respect for private life. However, they can be justified to protect the rights and freedoms of others.[237] In determining the margin of appreciation, the Strasbourg institutions do not put special weight to the fact that such blood alcohol tests *disclose yet undisclosed information*, restricting personal autonomy in the meaning of Article 8 ECHR. Similarly, obliging prisoners to provide urine samples in the context of mandatory drug testing, *revealing yet unrevealed information* about drug use, appears not to infringe the prisoners' right to personal autonomy in a way that narrows the margin of appreciation.[238]

In fact, it is hardly surprising that the non-consensual collection of personal data through blood alcohol tests and mandatory drug testing does not typically infringe the right to personal autonomy. The Court defines this right as 'the right to make choices as to how to lead one's own life'.[239] In general, the mere disclosure of a limited amount of personal data, for example, about whether one has used alcohol or drugs, will not restrict the individual in choosing how to live his life.

Similarly, disclosing undisclosed brain-reading data infringes the right to respect for private life, both via the notions of physical integrity and personal data. However, the *detection* of certain physiological or neural parameters of specific mental states is unlikely to restrain the individual from leading his life as he wants to.[240] Such brain-reading will not infringe the key right to personal autonomy in the meaning of Article 8 ECHR. By contrast, cases where this key right had been at stake concerned issues on abortion, voluntary euthanasia, and the legal recognition of transsexuals.[241]

[236] Cf. Ienca 2021, p. 71.

[237] EComHR 4 December 1978, appl.no. 8239/78 (*X./The Netherlands*); ECtHR 15 June 1999, appl.no. 43486/98 (*Tirado Ortiz and Lozano Martin/Spain*).

[238] For example, EComHR 9 September 1998, appl.no. 34199/96 (*Galloway/UK*); EComHR 6 April 1994, appl.no. 21132/93 (*Peters/The Netherlands*); ECtHR 27 September 2005, appl.no. 56745/00 (*Black/UK*), p. 4.

[239] ECtHR 3 September 2015, appl.no. 10161/13 (*M. and M./Croatia*), § 171. Cf. ECtHR 29 April 2002, appl.no. 2346/02 (*Pretty/UK*), § 62; Koffeman 2010, p. 55.

[240] Cf. Ferrua 2020, p. 412.

[241] For example, ECtHR (GC) 16 December 2010, appl.no. 25579/05 (*A, B and C/Ireland*), § 216; ECtHR 24 June 2014, appl.no. 33011/08 (*A.K./Latvia*), § 63; ECtHR 29 April 2002, appl.no. 2346/02 (*Pretty/UK*), § 61–67; ECtHR 10 March 2015, appl.no. 14793/08 (*Y.Y. Turkey*), § 65–66; ECtHR 11 July 2002, appl.no. 25680/94 (*I./UK*), § 70–73.

In conclusion, concerning the detection and prevention of crime, States enjoy a 'certain' margin of appreciation in deciding which measures to take. Coercive brain-reading infringes the right to respect for private life. However, it will not as such interfere with the enjoyment of intimate or key rights, nor with other particular important aspects of the subject's identity or personality. Accordingly, there are no reasons to restrict the margin of appreciation in this respect. Meanwhile, there are factors that broaden the margin: the lack of consensus across the member States and the moral and ethical sensitivity of coercive brain-reading. At the same time, being a pioneer in introducing novel neurotechnologies into criminal justice imposes a special responsibility upon the State to strike the right balance. Altogether, these considerations justify a certain discretion for the member States in introducing and regulating coercive brain-reading in criminal law.

Pressing Social Need and Proportionality

To be justified, coercive brain-reading should correspond to a pressing social need. Apart from being legitimate, the aims must be of such weight and importance that they qualify as 'pressing'. As to using emerging technologies for the detection, prosecution, and prevention of crime, the Grand Chamber held in *S. & Marper/UK* that:

> The Court finds it to be beyond dispute that the fight against crime, and in particular against organised crime and terrorism, which is one of the challenges faced by today's European societies, depends to a great extent on the use of modern scientific techniques of investigation and identification.[242]

Employing brain-reading in the detection, prosecution, and prevention of crime is likely to correspond to a pressing social need, such as protecting (national) security and preventing (serious) crime and public disorder.[243] In view of the increasing emphasis on public security in many European societies,[244] the social need of fighting crime will probably only increase.

Finally, in order to comply with the requirements of Article 8(2) ECHR, coercive brain-reading should be *proportionate* to the legitimate aims it pursues. The adduced reasons must be relevant and sufficient to outweigh the personal interests of private life. As argued above, presumably, a certain margin of appreciation is left to the States. Whether a particular brain-reading test will be proportionate in an individual case shall depend on the circumstances of the case. Some general considerations with regard to the proportionality are provided below, distinguishing between (I) the collection, (II) storage, and (III) disclosure of brain-reading data.

[242] ECtHR (GC) 4 December 2008, appl.nos. 30562/04 and 30566/04 (*S. & Marper/UK*), § 105. Cf. ECtHR 13 February 2020, appl.nos. 53205/13 and 63320/13 (*Trajkovski and Chipovski/North Macedonia*), § 51.

[243] Cf. Van Toor 2017, pp. 301–302.

[244] Partially motivated by increased terrorist threats. See, for example, Drewer & Ellermann 2016.

I. Collection. In determining the proportionality of coercively collecting brain-reading data, the severity of the infringement is essential. Coercive brain-reading infringes the right to respect for private life in at least two ways: by interfering with the subject's (1) bodily integrity and (2) personal data. The use of physical coercion could possibly interfere with the subject's mental integrity as well.

In the context of DNA testing (taking a blood or saliva sample), the Court considers the interferences with *bodily integrity* to be of very short duration, not normally causing bodily injury nor physical or mental suffering. Therefore, such interferences are of 'minor importance' and 'relatively slight'.[245]

Completing a neuroimaging assessment usually takes more time than taking a blood or saliva sample.[246] But it will not typically cause injury or suffering – provided that no physical coercion is used. Indeed, sometimes, an injection of contrast agent might be required, such as for CT, PET, and SPECT. Such injections are physically invasive. Although the *injection* of contrast agent may be more invasive than the *collection* of a blood sample, both will not normally entail serious physical injury nor involve mental or physical suffering. Interfering with bodily integrity through coercive brain-reading is unlikely to qualify as a 'severe' infringement of the right to respect for private life. Rather, we should conceive such infringements as relatively slight and/or of minor importance, somewhat similar to DNA testing.

Regarding the interference with *personal data*, the severity will depend on the amount and sensitivity of the information that is obtained.[247] The amount and sensitivity of the results will vary across different types of brain-reading. Meanwhile, compared with DNA, we saw that both the sensitivity and amount of brain-reading data are somewhat delimited by the purpose of the test (such as recognising something specific). Present types of brain-reading are not likely to exceed the sensitivity of information obtained through DNA analysis,[248] which produces much and highly sensitive information about health, genetic relationships, and ethnic origin.

Crucially, in spite of the highly sensitive nature of DNA, the ECtHR has repeatedly ruled that the compulsory collection and subsequent examination of cellular material and DNA profiles for identification purposes was – with a certain discretion for the State – necessary and proportionate for the detection and prevention of crime.[249]

[245] ECtHR 15 May 2018, appl.no. 41079/16 (*Caruana/Malta*), § 41; ECtHR 20 January 2009, appl.no. 20689/08 (*W./The Netherlands*), p. 8; ECtHR 7 December 2006, appl.no. 29514/05 (*Van der Velden/The Netherlands*), p. 9.

[246] Note, that recent developments in MR-STAT could enable to reducing the (f)MRI scanning time to less than ten minutes: Sbrizzi et al. 2018; Van der Heide et al. 2020; www.nwo.nl, searched for 'MR-STAT: unlocking MRI's full quantification potential' (visited on 8 July 2020).

[247] Cf. ECtHR (GC) 4 December 2008, appl.nos. 30562/04 and 30566/04 (*S. & Marper/UK*), § 86, 120; ECtHR 13 February 2020, appl.no. 45245/15 (*Gaughran/UK*), § 81.

[248] See Section 4.3.4.2. Cf. Meegan 2008, p. 16; Fox 2008, p. 2; Van Toor 2017, p. 288.

[249] See, for example, ECtHR 15 May 2018, appl.no. 41079/16 (*Caruana/Malta*); ECtHR 4 June 2013, appl.nos. 7841/08 and 57900/12 (*Peruzzo/Germany and Martens/Germany*); ECtHR 20 January 2009,

In light of these considerations, and given the relevant similarities between forensic brain-reading and DNA testing, coercive brain-reading stands a good chance of being proportionate in individual cases in view of detecting, prosecuting, and preventing crime.

II. Storage. Whether the storage of personal data strikes a fair balance strongly depends on how such storage will be regulated by domestic law. The law should guarantee appropriate safeguards to prevent arbitrariness, excessiveness, and misuse and abuse of the stored data. This especially holds true if the data are processed automatically and used for police purposes.[250]

Regarding brain-reading data, it is as essential as in DNA testing, telephone tapping, covert intelligence-gathering, and secret surveillance,[251] to have clear, detailed rules governing the scope and application of powers of retention. Minimum safeguards will be required, concerning duration, storage, usage, access of third parties, preserving the integrity and confidentiality of the data, and for data destruction. Such minimum standards should provide sufficient guarantees against the risk of abuse and arbitrariness. For instance, the purpose for which brain-reading data are allowed to be stored must be defined and specified in law. As the Grand Chamber held in *S. & Marper/UK*, the purpose of 'the prevention or detection of crime' is formulated too broadly, giving rise to extensive interpretation.[252]

The law must also ensure that retained information is *relevant* and *not excessive* in relation to the purpose for which it is stored.[253] In the course of brain-reading, this requirement not only implies that the test should be accurate, but also that the test must be *valid*. It should measure what it is supposed to measure. Concerning the requirement of the data not being excessive to the purpose of the test, the law should only allow the storage of information that is essential to answering the legal question for which the test is employed: collateral information should not be retained.[254]

Stored brain-reading data should neither be excessive in relation to the nature and gravity of the offence at issue. In *S. & Marper/UK*, the Court criticised the

appl.no. 20689/08 (*W./The Netherlands*); ECtHR 7 December 2006, appl.no. 29514/05 (*Van der Velden/The Netherlands*); ECtHR 5 January 2006, appl.no. 2352/02 (*Schmidt/Germany*).

250 See Section 4.3.3.3.

251 ECtHR (GC) 4 December 2008, appl.nos. 30562/04 and 30566/04 (*S. & Marper/UK*), § 99; ECtHR 22 June 2017, appl.no. 8806/12 (*Aycaguer/France*), § 43–45.

252 ECtHR (GC) 4 December 2008, appl.nos. 30562/04 and 30566/04 (*S. & Marper/UK*), § 99. Cf. ECtHR 14 April 2020, appl.no. 75229/10 (*Dragan Petrović/Serbia*), § 83–84.

253 ECtHR (GC) 4 December 2008, appl.nos. 30562/04 and 30566/04 (*S. & Marper/UK*), § 103; ECtHR 4 June 2013, appl.nos. 7841/08 and 57900/12 (*Peruzzo/Germany and Martens/Germany*), § 42; ECtHR 22 June 2017, appl.no. 8806/12 (*Aycaguer/France*), § 38. Cf. ECtHR 18 April 2013, appl.no. 19522/09 (*M.K./France*), § 35; ECtHR 18 September 2014, appl.no. 21010/10 (*Brunet/France*), § 35.

254 Cf. ECtHR 4 June 2013, appl.nos. 7841/08 and 57900/12 (*Peruzzo/Germany and Martens/Germany*), § 45: 'The cellular material itself has to be destroyed without delay once it is no longer needed for the purpose of establishing the DNA profile'.

domestic law for allowing the retention of DNA information from a person of any age, arrested in connection with any recordable offence, including minor and non-imprisonable offences.[255] The law should also differentiate in storing personal data from convicted offenders on the one hand, and those who have not been convicted on the other hand:

> Of particular concern in the present context is the risk of stigmatisation, stemming from the fact that persons in the position of the applicants, who have not been convicted of any offence and are entitled to the presumption of innocence, are treated in the same way as convicted persons. (…) It is true that the retention of the applicants' private data cannot be equated with the voicing of suspicions. Nonetheless, their perception that they are not being treated as innocent is heightened by the fact that their data are retained indefinitely in the same way as the data of convicted persons, while the data of those who have never been suspected of an offence are required to be destroyed.[256]

Regarding the retention of brain-reading data, a risk of stigmatisation is particularly relevant with respect to neuroprediction. These tests label the individual with a certain risk of committing a crime. If such a risk has not yet been materialised, as we should assume in respect of *non-convicted* persons,[257] storing such data will be harder to justify compared with *convicted* offenders, whose risks of committing crimes have already been confirmed (because they have committed a crime).[258] The law should take into account this distinction, for example by requiring predictive brain-data to be destroyed when the subject has been acquitted.

In addition, storing personal data should not last any longer than necessary for the aims of storage. And the law must adequately guarantee that retained personal data are efficiently protected from misuse and abuse.[259] As in the context of DNA, storage of brain-reading data should be limited by time. The individual concerned must

[255] ECtHR (GC) 4 December 2008, appl.nos. 30562/04 and 30566/04 (*S. & Marper/UK*), § 119 (discussed in Section 4.3.3.3). See also ECtHR 13 February 2020, appl.no. 45245/15 (*Gaughran/UK*), § 94; ECtHR 13 February 2020, appl.nos. 53205/13 and 63320/13 (*Trajkovski and Chipovski/North Macedonia*), § 53.

[256] ECtHR (GC) 4 December 2008, appl.nos. 30562/04 and 30566/04 (*S. & Marper/UK*), § 122. See also ECtHR 18 April 2013, appl.no. 19522/09 (*M.K./France*), § 33; ECtHR 18 September 2014, appl.no. 21010/10 (*Brunet/France*), § 37. Regarding the retention of DNA information of convicted offenders, see ECtHR 4 June 2013, appl.nos. 7841/08 and 57900/12 (*Peruzzo/Germany and Martens/Germany*); ECtHR 13 February 2020, appl.no. 45245/15 (*Gaughran/UK*); ECtHR 13 February 2020, appl.nos. 53205/13 and 63320/13 (*Trajkovski and Chipovski/North Macedonia*).

[257] Ashworth & Zedner 2014.

[258] Walker 1997, p. 7.

[259] ECtHR (GC) 4 December 2008, appl.nos. 30562/04 and 30566/04 (*S. & Marper/UK*), § 103; ECtHR 13 February 2020, appl.nos. 53205/13 and 63320/13 (*Trajkovski and Chipovski/North Macedonia*), § 52; ECtHR 4 June 2013, appl.nos. 7841/08 and 57900/12 (*Peruzzo/Germany and Martens/Germany*), § 42; ECtHR 22 June 2017, appl.no. 8806/12 (*Aycaguer/France*), § 38.

be able to request for her data to be destroyed. The Court prefers an independent review of the justification of ongoing storage according to defined criteria, such as the severity of the offence, previous arrests, the strength of the suspicion against the person, and any other special circumstances.[260]

III. Disclosure. Concerning the disclosure of medical information through criminal legal proceedings, the Court holds that the interests of the individual and community as a whole 'in protecting the confidentiality of medical data may be outweighed by the interest in investigation and prosecution of crime and in the publicity of court proceedings'.[261] The Court notes that each criminal proceeding entails adverse consequences for the private life of the individual who committed a crime. Normally, such consequences are compatible with Article 8 ECHR, as long as they do not exceed the regular and inevitable consequences of such criminal proceedings.[262] The right to respect for private life does not protect against a loss of reputation or any other personal, social, psychological, or economic suffering that is a foreseeable consequence of one's own actions, such as the commission of a criminal offence or other misconduct entailing a measure of legal responsibility.[263] However, in disclosing (sensitive) personal data through legal proceedings, any additional interference with private life should be limited as far as possible to what is strictly necessary given the specific features of the procedure and the facts of the individual case.[264]

4.3.4.4 Synthesis

The collection, storage, and disclosure of brain-reading data in criminal justice infringe the right to respect for private life pursuant to Article 8 ECHR, both via the notions of physical integrity and personal data. The severity of infringements will vary across different brain-reading tests and technologies. Meanwhile, infringements caused by coercive brain-reading will not typically exceed the severity of infringements that arise in the course of forensic DNA testing (provided that no additional physical force is used). States will probably enjoy a 'certain' margin of appreciation in employing brain-reading for the detection, prosecution, and prevention of

[260] ECtHR (GC) 4 December 2008, appl.nos. 30562/04 and 30566/04 (*S. & Marper/UK*), § 119; ECtHR 13 February 2020, appl.nos. 53205/13 and 63320/13 (*Trajkovski and Chipovski/North Macedonia*), § 53; ECtHR 13 February 2020, appl.no. 45245/15 (*Gaughran/UK*), § 94; ECtHR 4 June 2013, appl.nos. 7841/08 and 57900/12 (*Peruzzo/Germany and Martens/Germany*), § 46–50.

[261] ECtHR 25 February 1997, appl.no. 22009/93 (*Z./Finland*), § 97. Cf. ECtHR (GC) 4 December 2008, appl.nos. 30562/04 and 30566/04 (*S. & Marper/UK*), § 104.

[262] ECtHR 27 June 2017, appl.no. 50446/09 (*Jankauskas/Lithuania (No. 2)*), § 76.

[263] ECtHR (GC) 25 September 2018, appl.no. 76639/11 (*Denisov/Ukraine*), § 98; ECtHR 27 July 2004, appl.nos. 55480/00 and 59330/00 (*Sidabras and Džiautas/Lithuania*), § 49.

[264] See ECtHR 10 October 2006, appl.no. 7508/02 (*L.L./France*), § 45. Cf. ECtHR 25 February 1997, appl. no. 22009/93 (*Z./Finland*), § 113; ECtHR 29 June 2006, appl.no. 11901/02 (*Panteleyenko/Ukraine*), § 61.

crime. This section emphasised that, despite the highly sensitive nature of DNA material, the ECtHR has repeatedly ruled that the compulsorily taking, examination, and retention of cellular material and DNA profiles for identification purposes was – with a certain discretion for the State – necessary and proportionate for the detection and prevention of crime and for the protection of the rights and freedoms of others. In light of these considerations, I conclude that, when provided with sufficient legal safeguards, Article 8 ECHR will not as such proscribe coercive brain-reading in criminal law.

4.4 CONCLUSION

The Court finds it beyond dispute that the fight against crime depends to a large extent on the use of modern scientific techniques of investigation. At the same time, the protection of Article 8 ECHR would be unacceptably weakened if the use of modern scientific techniques in criminal justice would be allowed at any cost and without carefully balancing their potential benefits against important private-life interests.

Article 8 ECHR will not as such prohibit coercive use of present types of brain-reading for the detection, prosecution, and prevention of crime. But it does require sufficient safeguards to protect from potential abuse and arbitrariness, on pain of violating the right to respect for private life. The precise guarantees that domestic laws should adopt are yet to be established. Case-law on DNA provides helpful directions in developing a private-life-approach tailored to coercive brain-reading in criminal law. Clearly, the casuistic case-law on DNA testing cannot be applied to forensic brain-reading directly. But it provides a valuable point of departure.

If novel neuroimaging technologies or analytical methods will enable to detect more, and more sensitive personal data, such as about people's political preferences or religious adherences, Article 8 ECHR will offer stronger legal protection. Such forms of brain-reading might raise additional issues under the right to freedom of thought, conscience, and religion, as guaranteed by Article 9 ECHR. The implications of coercive brain-reading in light of Article 9 ECHR will be discussed in Chapter 5.

5

Coercive Brain-Reading and the Rights to Freedom of Thought and to Freedom of Expression

Articles 9 and 10 ECHR

5.1 INTRODUCTION

Reading brains and identifying mental states has the potential of raising an issue under the right to freedom of thought as set out in Article 9 ECHR.[1] This provision reads as follows:

> 1. Everyone has the right to freedom of thought, conscience and religion; this right includes freedom to change his religion or belief and freedom, either alone or in community with others and in public or private, to manifest his religion or belief, in worship, teaching, practice and observance.
>
> 2. Freedom to manifest one's religion or beliefs shall be subject only to such limitations as are prescribed by law and are necessary in a democratic society in the interests of public safety, for the protection of public order, health or morals, or for the protection of the rights and freedoms of others.

The right prescribed in the first paragraph consists in an internal and external dimension: the *forum internum* and the *forum externum*.[2] The right to freedom of thought, conscience, and religion comprises the internal dimension. The right to manifest our religion and belief concerns the external dimension.[3] Infringements of the *forum externum* can sometimes be justified under Article 9(2) ECHR. Meanwhile, the *forum internum* is absolute. Any infringement automatically amounts to a violation.[4]

According to the *Human rights handbooks* of the Council of Europe, the internal dimension of Article 9 ECHR seeks at its most basic level 'to prevent state

[1] Cf. UN Special Rapporteur on Freedom of Religion or Belief 2021.

[2] See Roberts 2020.

[3] Harris et al. 2018, p. 573; Vermeulen & Roosmalen 2018, p. 738.

[4] Vermeulen & Roosmalen 2018, p. 738; Harris et al. 2018, p. 573. Article 9(1) ECHR is, however, not exempted from derogation in times of war or other public emergency threatening the life of the nation: Article 15(2) ECHR.

indoctrination of individuals by permitting the holding, development, and refinement and ultimately change of personal thought, conscience and religion'.[5] Other handbooks endorse this view. For example, Vermeulen and Roosmalen write that the internal dimension of Article 9 ECHR guarantees that States may never interfere with the most intimate and inner sphere of their citizens. They are not allowed to dictate what people have to believe, nor may they use coercion to make individuals change their beliefs, for instance through 'brainwashing'.[6]

Apart from prohibiting State interferences that *control* what people think and believe, Article 9(1) ECHR also protects against coercive measures that aim to *disclose* our thoughts, conscience, or religion.[7] According to Vermeulen and Roosmalen, the *forum internum* forbids *any form of compulsion to express thoughts* or to divulge a religion. It guarantees that States may never use inquisitorial methods to discover personal thoughts and convictions.[8]

This view leads back to the birth of Article 9 ECHR, where its 'founding fathers' considered that the right to freedom of thought, conscience, and religion intends to protect:

> not only from 'confessions' imposed for reasons of State, but also from those abominable methods of police enquiry or judicial process which rob the suspect or accused person of control of his intellectual faculties and of his conscience.[9]

A similar view is expressed in the General Comment on Article 18 of the International Covenant on Civil and Political Rights (ICCPR): 'No one can be compelled to reveal his thoughts or adherence to a religion or belief'.[10] According to the UN Special Rapporteur on Freedom of Religion or Belief, 'mental privacy' is a core attribute of freedom of thought.[11]

It is particularly this part of Article 9 ECHR that raises questions regarding coercive brain-reading. Could brain-reading be permitted in light of the right not to reveal thoughts, convictions, and religion?[12] Typically, forensic brain-reading will not yield

5 Murdoch 2012, p. 18.

6 Vermeulen & Roosmalen 2018, p. 738. Cf. Harris et al. 2018, pp. 573–575; Evans 1997, p. 294.

7 Harris et al. 2018, pp. 574–575; Murdoch 2012, p. 18; Taylor 2005, p. 120. See, for example, ECtHR 3 June 2010, appl.nos. 42837/06, 3237/07, 3269/07, 35793/07, and 6099/08 (*Dimitras and others/Greece*); ECtHR 2 May 2010, appl.no. 21924/05 (*Sinan Işik/Turkey*); ECtHR 21 February 2008, appl.no. 19516/06 (*Alexandridis/Greece*); ECtHR 18 February 1999, appl.no. 24645/94 (*Buscarini and Others/San Marino*).

8 Vermeulen & Roosmalen 2018, p. 738. Cf. Taylor 2005, p. 202; ECtHR 2 February 2010, appl.no. 21924/05 (*Sinan Işik/Turkey*), § 42: 'What is at stake is the right not to disclose one's religion or beliefs, which falls within the *forum internum* of each individual'.

9 European Commission of Human Rights, *Preparatory Work on Article 9 of the European Convention on Human Rights*, Strasbourg, 16 August 1959, pp. 3–4.

10 General Comment No. 22: The right to freedom of thought, conscience, and religion (Art. 18), CCPR/C/21/Rev.1/Add.4, para. 3.

11 UN Special Rapporteur on Freedom of Religion or Belief 2021, para. 26. The Rapporteur further notes that the right not to reveal one's thoughts against one's will could arguably include a right to remain silent.

12 Bublitz 2014, pp. 7–8; Rusconi & Mitchener-Nissen 2013, p. 8; Ligthart 2020b.

information about conscience or religion.[13] The key question is whether brain-reading in criminal law discloses a person's 'thoughts' in the meaning of Article 9 ECHR.

Interestingly, Article 9 ECHR covers the *manifestation* of religion and belief, but not of *thoughts*. Yet, thoughts can be 'manifested' through actions. Primarily via speech and expression covered by Article 10 ECHR.[14] Can we qualify the disclosure of information through brain-reading as an 'expression' in the meaning of Article 10 ECHR? And if so, how would the legal protection afforded by Article 9 and 10 ECHR coincide in respect of coercive brain-reading?

The central question of this chapter is twofold: will coercive brain-reading infringe the right to freedom of thought and will it be covered by the right to freedom of expression?[15] The outline is as follows. Section 5.2 examines the meaning and scope of the right to freedom of thought. Section 5.3 examines the legal implications of the freedom of thought for the use of coercive brain-reading in criminal law. Section 5.4 addresses the legal implications of coercive brain-reading in light of the freedom of expression. Section 5.5 draws conclusions.

5.2 THE RIGHT TO FREEDOM OF THOUGHT (ARTICLE 9 ECHR)

5.2.1 *Introduction*

Much case-law and scholarship exist on the right to freedom of *conscience* and *religion*.[16] But the precise meaning and scope of the notion of *thought* are still unclear.[17] Does the right to freedom of thought protect against the forcible disclosure of *any* mental property regardless its content? Or should we consider Article 9 ECHR as only comprising *particular* kinds of thoughts?[18] When interpreting the notion of thoughts, three central approaches are conceivable, respectively, putting emphasis on:

(1) religion: covering only thoughts and convictions that originate from religion;
(2) conscience: covering only thoughts and convictions (including religions) that have a major impact on the person's way of living;
(3) thought: covering practically any thought, without additional requirements.[19]

[13] However, when they do, they will therefore come within the scope of Article 9(1) ECHR.

[14] Evans 1997, p. 285; Loucaides 2012, pp. 84–85; Murdoch 2012, p. 16; Bublitz 2014, p. 2; Alegre 2017, p. 224. The legal implications of coercive brain-reading in light of Article 10 ECHR are discussed in Section 5.4.

[15] See also Ligthart 2020b; Ligthart et al. 2020.

[16] E.g. Council of Europe 2020a; Harris et al. 2018, Ch. 12; Vermeulen & Roosmalen 2018; Rainey, McCormick & Ovey 2021, Ch. 17; Murdoch 2012, pp. 16–21; Taylor 2005; Evans 2001; Evans 1997.

[17] Evans 2001, p. 52; Taylor 2005, p. 119; Bublitz 2018, pp. 300–301; McCarthy-Jones 2019, p. 2; Ligthart et al. 2020; Ligthart 2020b; UN Special Rapporteur on Freedom of Religion or Belief 2021; Bublitz 2021.

[18] Bublitz 2014, p. 2; Ligthart et al. 2020, pp. 3–4.

[19] De Jong 2000, p. 23. De Jong discusses these approaches in the context of Article 18 of the UDHR. The formulation of Article 9 ECHR has been based on Article 18 UDHR (see Section 5.2.2).

To determine which approach is – or ought to be – leading, Strasbourg case-law on freedom of *thought* can provide some helpful insights. However, case-law that explicitly deals with complaints about the notion of *thought* is scarce. To better understand the existing case-law and to determine what is meant by 'thought' in Article 9(1) ECHR, this section starts with an examination of the legal history of the right to freedom of thought. In light of these historical considerations, the Strasbourg case-law on freedom of thought will be discussed, together with the views from the literature.

5.2.2 *Legal History*

In August 1949, the founding fathers of the ECHR proposed that the convention should guarantee a list of fundamental rights and freedoms, including 'The Freedom of religious practice and teaching, as laid down in Article 18 of the Declaration of the United Nations'.[20] After an amendment of the UK, the Committee agreed on a text that included freedom of *thought*: the convention should guarantee 'freedom of thought, conscience and religion, as laid down in Article 18 of the Declaration of the United Nations'.[21]

As a result of this proposal, the preliminary draft of the ECHR provided a right that was identical to Article 18 of the Universal Declaration of Human Rights (UDHR): 'Everyone has the right to freedom of thought, conscience and religion; this right includes freedom to change his religion or belief, and freedom, either alone or in community with others and in public or private, to manifest his religion or belief in teaching, practice, worship and observance'.[22] After some minor textual changes, Article 9(1) ECHR, as we know it today, was born on 4 November 1950.[23]

The drafters of Article 9(1) ECHR did not spend much consideration on the exact meaning and scope of this right.[24] The formulation was basically derived from the then already existing Article 18 UDHR.[25] Therefore, the preparatory work on Article 9(1) ECHR is not very illuminating about the wordings used in this provision.[26] In order to understand these wordings – particularly the term 'thought' – we should examine why they had been chosen in the first place, during the codification process of Article 18 UDHR.[27] In addition, the legal history of Article 9 ECHR reveals

20 European Commission of Human Rights, *Preparatory Work on Article 9 of the European Convention on Human Rights*, Strasbourg, 16 August 1959, p. 2.

21 Ibid, p. 3.

22 Ibid, p. 8.

23 Ibid, pp. 17–18.

24 Cf. Loucaides 2012, p. 80.

25 See also Fawcett 1987, p. 236.

26 Evans 2001, p. 38 draws attention to the limitations of the *Travaux Préperatoires* of the ECHR, since they 'are neither complete nor particularly revealing as regards the reasons for the development of the various drafts of the convention'. Cf. Harris et al. 2018, p. 22.

27 Cf. Evans 2001, p. 50.

some affinities with Article 18 ICCPR.[28] Therefore, preparatory work on the latter might also provide helpful insights for the interpretation of 'thoughts' in the meaning of Article 9 ECHR.

The Draft Outline of the International Bill of Rights of 4 June 1947, which ultimately evolved into the UDHR, contained an Article 14, which read as follows: 'There shall be freedom of conscience and belief and of private and public religious worship'.[29] In line with preceding draft proposals,[30] no reference was made to freedom of 'thought'. The explicit protection of freedom of thought was proposed for the first time by France, suggesting the following Article 20 for the International Bill of Rights:

> The individual freedom of conscience, belief and thought is an absolute and sacred right. The practice of a private or public worship and the manifestations of opposite convictions can be subject only to such limitations as are necessary to protect public order, morals and the rights and freedoms of others.[31]

In response, Lebanon argued that this right should also guarantee the fundamental freedom to *change* opinions and beliefs. It suggested the following formulation: 'Individual freedom of thought and conscience, to hold or change beliefs, is an absolute and sacred right'.[32] This text was adopted by the Drafting Committee and renumbered into Article 16 of the Draft UDHR:

> 1. Individual freedom of thought and conscience, to hold and change beliefs, is an absolute and sacred right.
>
> 2. Every person has the right, either alone or in community with other persons of like mind and in public or private, to manifest his beliefs in worship, observance, teaching and practice.[33]

Discussing this draft Article 16, the chairman of the Drafting Committee noted that the proposed text only pertained to freedom of 'conscience and belief'.[34] If this were true, the word 'thought' in paragraph 1 would have been identical to 'belief'.[35] However, a subsequent discussion on the meaning and importance of the notion of

[28] European Commission of Human Rights, *Preparatory Work on Article 9 of the European Convention on Human Rights*, Strasbourg, 16 August 1959, p. 18. Article 18 ICCPR states: 'Everyone shall have the right to freedom of thought, conscience and religion. This right shall include freedom to have or to adopt a religion or belief of his choice, and freedom, either individually or in community with others and in public or private, to manifest his religion or belief in worship, observance, practice and teaching'.

[29] Schabas 2013, p. 283 (see also p. 755). See also the Plan of the Draft Outline of an International Bill of Rights at pp. 305–307.

[30] Schabas 2013, p. 118.

[31] Ibid, p. 792.

[32] Ibid, p. 863.

[33] Ibid, pp. 534, 1248, and 1391.

[34] Ibid, p. 1573.

[35] Cf. the preparatory work on Article 18 ICCPR as collected by Bossuyt 1987, p. 355: 'The question was raised whether the words "thought" and "belief" in this article were intended to be different concepts'. See also Evans 1997, p. 203.

'thought' arose when Lebanon submitted an amendment, aiming to change Article 16 of the Draft UDHR as follows:

> Everyone has the right (is entitled) to freedom of religion, conscience and belief; this right includes freedom to change his religion or belief, and freedom, either alone or in community with other persons of like mind and in public or private, to manifest his religion or belief in teaching, practice, worship and observance.[36]

According to the Lebanese representative, this amendment embodied all the essential elements of the original provision. It only added freedom of religion.[37] However, the Soviet Union objected that the amendment did not make any allusion to freedom of *thought*: 'Science had a right to protection on the same terms as religion. Out of respect for the heroes and martyrs of science, those words should not be deleted'.[38]

Lebanon replied that it left out freedom of thought simply because that right was also proposed under Articles 17 and 18 of the Draft UDHR, which should together guarantee a right to freedom of thought, expression, and opinion.[39] Yet, since Lebanon was also very keen on protecting freedom of thought, just like the Soviet Union, it agreed to reinclude 'thought' in its amendment.[40]

Besides the Soviet Union, France also objected to the removal of freedom of *thought* in Article 16 Draft UDHR. It argued that '[f]reedom of thought differed from freedom of expression in that the latter was subject to certain restrictions for the sake of public order. It might be asked why freedom of inner thought should have to be protected even before it was expressed. That was because the opposite of *inner* freedom of thought was the *outward* obligation to profess a belief which was not held. Freedom of thought thus required to be formally protected in view of the fact that it was possible to attack it indirectly'.[41]

Ultimately, Lebanon inserted freedom of thought in its amendment, proposing that 'Everyone has the right to freedom of religion, conscience, belief and thought, including freedom to change his religion or belief'.[42]

However, now China objected, because Article 16 should only protect freedom of *religion and belief*; freedom of thought was dealt with in Articles 17 and 18.[43] The UK agreed with China: in essence, Article 16 concerned the freedom of

36 Schabas 2013, p. 1766.
37 Also satisfying the wishes of the USA, UK, and Israel: Schabas 2013, pp. 1764–1766.
38 Schabas 2013, p. 1766.
39 Which eventually evolved into Article 19 UDHR: 'Everyone has the right to freedom of opinion and expression; this right includes freedom to hold opinions without interference and to seek, receive and impart information and ideas through any media and regardless of frontiers'.
40 Schabas 2013, p. 1766.
41 Ibid, pp. 1766–1767. Which argument was supported by the Soviet Union (p. 1768).
42 Ibid, p. 1767.
43 Ibid.

religion. It would be better not to include any other considerations.[44] In addition, if 'thought' was introduced in the first part of the sentence as proposed by Lebanon, it should also be included in the second part – freedom to *change* religion, belief, and thought – which the UK considered rather inappropriate in a Declaration on Human Rights.[45]

The Soviet Union disagreed. It argued that considering the proposed Article 16 as purely religious was unjustified, since atheists had the right to have their freedom of thought protected as well.[46] Uruguay noted that freedom of thought was the fundamental freedom from which freedom of religion and belief have been derived. Therefore, it suggested to guarantee freedom of thought (which was also proposed under Articles 17 and 18) prior to the provision on freedom of religion (Article 16).[47]

In response to this debate, the chairman of the Drafting Committee suggested to vote. Should freedom of thought also be guaranteed by the proposed Articles 17 and 18, on freedom of thought, expression, and opinions? Or would it be sufficient to guarantee this freedom only through the proposed Article 16, together with the freedom of conscience and religion?

France argued that freedom of thought had a metaphysical significance. Unlike the other rights of the proposed Articles 17 and 18, such as the freedom of expression and opinion, freedom of thought is an unconditional right. It cannot be subjected to any restrictions of public nature. Because of the great difference in degree between freedom of thought on the one hand and freedom to hold opinions on the other hand, France preferred to guarantee freedom of thought only under Article 16 of the Draft UDHR.[48]

The Philippines were also in favour of guaranteeing freedom of thought in Article 16.[49] China agreed with France as well. According to European ideas, freedom of thought was indeed the basis of freedom of belief. Although belief implied thought, freedom of thought had historically preceded freedom of belief. Therefore, China suggested to guarantee 'the right to freedom of thought, religion and belief'.[50]

Eventually, a subcommittee was appointed, composed of France, Lebanon, the UK, and Uruguay. This commission had to reconsider the drafts of Articles 16 and 17. They unanimously recommended the following text for Article 16:

44 Ibid, p. 1768. Cf. the view of the Philippines.

45 Ibid, p. 1768. Unfortunately, the UK did not substantiate this claim.

46 Ibid.

47 Ibid.

48 Ibid. The UK thought that metaphysical considerations were being pushed too far, that the proposed Article 17 contained elements without which freedom of thought could not exist, and that it would therefore be better to stick with the original wordings of both Article 16 and 17 of the Draft UDHR (p. 1769).

49 Ibid, p. 1768.

50 Ibid.

> Everyone has the right to freedom of thought, conscience and religion; this right includes freedom to change his religion or belief, and freedom, either alone or in community with others, in public or private, to manifest his religion or belief in teaching, practice, worship and observance.[51]

The Commission on Human Rights approved this text.[52] The altered Article 16 was included in the subsequent Draft UDHR of 18 June 1948.[53]

Many States were satisfied now. The text of Article 16 Draft UDHR was the result of a detailed study and lengthy debate, uniting the different views expressed.[54] Still, some objections were raised and amendments submitted.[55] Cuba argued that everyone has some kind of faith, even those who are not religious. But no distinction should be made between such different faiths. All of them are worth to respect. Therefore, Cuba proposed an alternative text for Article 16, which took into account the two essential aspects of human belief: philosophy and religion:[56]

> Every person has the right freely to profess a religious or philosophical belief, this right includes freedom to change his religion or belief, and freedom, either alone or in community with others, in public or private, to manifest his religion or belief in teaching, practice, worship and observance.[57]

Among others, the USA objected to the Cuban amendment, as it only mentioned freedom of religious and philosophical belief. Thereby, it would exclude the cultural, scientific, and political aspects of the freedom that Article 16 ought to guarantee.[58] In the same vein, the Soviet Union argued to put particular emphasis on freedom of *thought*. This notion should be guaranteed to promote the development of modern sciences. It takes into account the existence of free-thinkers whose reasoning had led them to discard all old-fashioned beliefs and religious fanaticism: 'The times when scientists were condemned to be burnt at the stake were past, and science occupied a most important place in human life'.[59] The Soviet Union proposed the following text:

> Everyone must be guaranteed freedom of thought and freedom to perform religious services in accordance with the laws of the country concerned and the requirements of public morality.[60]

51 Ibid, p. 1789. The subcommittee also recommended replacing the word 'thought' in Articles 17 and 18 by 'opinion', and that Article 16 should precede those articles.

52 Ibid, p. 1789.

53 Ibid, pp. 1940–1946. With the slightly different formulation of 'either alone or in community with others and in public or private'.

54 Ibid, pp. 2490–2502.

55 Ibid, pp. 2271–2272.

56 Ibid, p. 2502.

57 Ibid, p. 2271.

58 Ibid, p. 2490.

59 Ibid, p. 2489.

60 Ibid, p. 2271.

Uruguay agreed to extend freedom of thought to the realms of politics and science. It argued that Article 16 of the Draft UDHR put too much emphasis on the freedom of *religion*. Nonetheless, just like most other States,[61] Uruguay was unable to accept the amendment of the Soviet Union, because it allowed *domestic laws* to *control* the exercise of freedom of thought.[62] Furthermore, some States, like Belgium, Lebanon, and Guatemala, were worried about the fact that the Soviet Union's proposal did not explicitly recognise the freedom of religion.[63] The Soviet Union emphasised that, indeed, all forms of thought should be respected equally. Yet, it considered that 'freedom of thought' was broad enough: it includes scientific, philosophical but also religious thoughts.[64]

Just like Venezuela,[65] China agreed that freedom of thought includes freedom of conscience and religion. However, making this explicit should not be conceived problematic; the UDHR should never be criticised for being too explicit.[66] Ultimately, all amendments were rejected, except the one of France that replaced the word *croyance* in the France text by the less religious flavoured term *conviction*.[67] On 10 November 1948, the following Article 16 was adopted:

> Everyone has the right to freedom of thought, conscience and religion; this right includes freedom to change his religion or belief, and freedom, either alone or in community with others and in public or private, to manifest his religion or belief in teaching, practice, worship and observance.[68]

After a renumbering, this article resulted in Article 18 UDHR as we know it today – which inspired the authors of Article 9 ECHR.

This examination of the legal history of Article 18 UDHR reveals no clear definition of freedom of *thought*. Rather, it shows that controversy existed about the meaning and scope of this right and about its importance compared to freedom of religion and to the freedom to hold and express opinions and ideas.

Still, although some States disagreed about the best place in the Declaration to recognise freedom of thought, there seemed considerable agreement on the relation between thought, belief, and religion. While not all States explicitly agreed with France on the metaphysical significance of freedom of thought, many acknowledged that the freedom of *thought* was the fundamental freedom, from which freedom of religion and conscience had been derived.[69] In addition, as argued by the Soviet Union, Uruguay, the USA and Cuba, freedom of thought should not be

61 Ibid, p. 2489–2503.
62 Ibid, p. 2499.
63 Ibid, pp. 2492, 2498 and 2499.
64 Ibid, p. 2500.
65 Ibid, p. 2498.
66 Ibid, pp. 2495–2496.
67 Ibid, pp. 2495 and 2504.
68 Ibid, p. 2536.
69 Ibid, pp. 1768, 2495–2496, 2498, 2500 (Uruguay, China, Philippines, Venezuela, Soviet Union). Cf. Chile (chairman), suggesting that thought and belief are interchangeable terms in this context: p. 1573.

confined to religion and conscience only. Instead, it comprises science, philosophy, and politics as well.[70]

Let us now turn back to the three central approaches for the interpretation of the right to freedom of *thought*.[71] We can safely conclude that the first approach – covering only thoughts and convictions that originate from religion – should not apply in light of the discussed legal history of Articles 9 ECHR and 18 UDHR. The discussion on the importance of including the notion of thought in Article 18 UDHR clarifies that *not only* religious thoughts *but also* political, scientific, and philosophical thoughts enjoy legal protection.[72]

The authors of Article 18 UDHR did not confine the scope of the freedom of thought to religious thoughts only. Neither seemed they inclined to broaden this right to basically *any* kind of view or personal opinion. As France argued, there is a great difference in degree between the freedom to hold an opinion and the freedom of thought. Only the latter is unconditional. As De Jong states, if 'every thought is to be included, the distinction between the freedom of thought, conscience and religion on the one hand and freedom of expression and opinion on the other becomes blurred'.[73] Accordingly, the States agreed to guarantee freedom of thought only through the present Article 18 UDHR, not through Article 19 UDHR.[74]

A similar distinction has been made in the ECHR. Article 9 ECHR guarantees the right to freedom of thought, conscience, and religion. Article 10 ECHR recognises the right to freedom of expression, including the freedom to hold an opinion and to receive and impart information and ideas. Unlike the right to freedom of thought, the freedom of expression is not absolute. It may be subjected to formalities, conditions, restrictions, or penalties under Article 10(2) ECHR. In light of this systematic difference between the freedom of thought on the one hand and the freedom to hold opinions, receive, and impart ideas and information on the other hand, the third approach – covering practically any thought, without additional requirements – is not convincing.

Whereas the first and third approaches are not supported from a legal historical point of view, the second approach appears plausible – covering only thoughts and convictions (including religions) that have a major impact on the person's way of living.[75] After all, the only thoughts that were explicitly mentioned concerned philosophy, science, and politics.

70 Ibid, pp. 1766, 2490, 2489, 2500–2503. According to the USA, the freedoms guaranteed in Article 16 Draft UDHR should also comprise a cultural aspect (p. 2490). However, it is unclear whether the USA approached culture as an aspect of thoughts, of conscience, or of both. See also UN Special Rapporteur on Freedom of Religion and Belief 2021, para. 2–3.

71 See Section 5.2.1.

72 Cf. De Jong 2000, pp. 24–26.

73 De Jong 2000, p. 26.

74 Which prescribes that 'Everyone has the right to freedom of opinion and expression; this right includes freedom to hold opinions without interference and to seek, receive and impart information and ideas through any media and regardless of frontiers'.

75 Cf. De Jong 2000, p. 33.

Of note, according to the General Comment on Article 18 ICCPR, 'Article 18.1 is far-reaching and profound; it encompasses *freedom of thought on all matters*, personal conviction and the commitment to religion or belief'.[76] At first glance, this statement seems to suggest a broad scope of the freedom of thought.[77] However, it does not provide a clear definition of which thoughts enjoy protection.[78] It only states that the thoughts that *are* protected can concern any matter. At least two interpretations are conceivable: (1) *any* kind of thought is protected, including any idea, opinion, and memory, regardless their content and level of impact on a person's way of living and (2) only thoughts that have a *major impact* on a person's way of living are protected, regardless their precise matter, that is, they can concern religion, philosophy, science, politics, and alike.

The preparatory work of the General Comment on Article 18 ICCPR suggests that the latter interpretation aligns best with the intention of its creators.[79] Mr. Wennergren argued that freedom of thought, as a specific right, was a far-reaching concept and should embrace the absolute freedom of opinion as well.[80] In response, Mr. Sadi proposed that:

> in order to reflect Mr. Wennergren's suggestion about developing the concept of freedom of thought, the first sentence should say that the concept of freedom of thought, conscience, religion and belief encompassed a whole range of personal and collective convictions in the political, economic, social, scientific and intellectual spheres. The meaning of freedom of thought encompassed all those aspects.[81]

Next, Miss Chanet argued that in order to exercise freedom of *opinion* within the meaning of Article 19 ICCPR, people should first be able to exercise freedom of *thought* as guaranteed in Article 18 ICCPR. Although an overlap exists between both rights, the general Comment on Article 18 ICCPR should clarify what separates both provisions. In this context, Chanet argued that there was no need to state that the freedom of thought, conscience, religion, and belief is far-reaching. Instead, it would suffice to note that it encompasses the spheres of *personal convictions*.[82] To indicate that freedom of thought is not limited to the sphere of *religious* conviction only, Mrs. Higgins proposed a text that indicates that Article 18 ICCPR encompasses freedom of thought 'on all matters'.[83] Accordingly, paragraph 1 of the General Comment had been adopted.[84]

76 General Comment No. 22: The right to freedom of thought, conscience, and religion (Art. 18) CCPR/C/21/Rev.1/Add.4, para. 1 (emphasis added).

77 Cf. Alegre 2017, pp. 224–225.

78 Cf. Evans 1997, p. 213.

79 For recent developments, see UN Special Rapporteur on Freedom of Religion and Belief 2021.

80 CCPR/C/SR.1162, para. 14.

81 Ibid, para. 34.

82 Ibid, para. 36.

83 Ibid, para. 40. See also Mr. Dimitrijevic, para. 43. Cf. Harris et al. 2018, p. 571: 'The scope of Article 9 is wide, in that it covers forms of both religious *and* non-religious belief'. (emphasis added).

84 CCPR/C/SR.1162, paras. 50–52.

Whilst the General Comment on Article 18 ICCPR might *prima facie* suggest a broad scope of freedom of thought, including any idea, opinion, intention, or memory, the preparatory work indicates that Articles 18 and 19 ICCPR are two separate rights. The former requires at least a personal or collective conviction. Although Article 18 ICCPR has often been interpreted as only safeguarding personal convictions associated with religion,[85] the General Comment clarifies that the freedom of thought encompasses a whole range of personal convictions, *inter alia* in the political, economic, social, scientific, and intellectual spheres. Freedom of thought on all matters. Meanwhile, in a recent report, the UN Special Rapporteur on Freedom of Religion and Belief seems to hint at a broader understanding of the right to freedom of thought, taking account of neuroscientific definitions of 'thought' as well.[86]

The next section further explores the meaning and scope of the right to freedom of thought pursuant to Article 9 ECHR, by considering Strasbourg case-law together with the literature.

5.2.3 *Case-Law and Literature*

As Rainey, McCormick, and Ovey note, virtually every complaint before the Court about Article 9 ECHR concerns an alleged infringement of the freedom to *manifest* religion or belief.[87] Article 9(1) ECHR guarantees the freedom to manifest *religion* and *belief*. Yet, it does not cover the manifestation of *thought* and *conscience*.[88] Therefore, most case-law does not elaborate on 'thoughts' in the meaning of Article 9 ECHR. In addition, Rainey, McCormick, and Ovey warn that case-law on Article 9 ECHR can be inconsistent and loosely reasoned.[89] Despite these limitations, this section examines whether and, if so, which interpretation of 'thought' is expressed in Strasbourg case-law and decisions.

According to the Court, the scope of Article 9 ECHR is wide in the sense that it comprises both religious and non-religious thoughts, convictions, and beliefs.[90] Among others, it covers Buddhism, veganism, pacifism, and fascism.[91] In 1993, the European Commission on Human Rights (EComHR/Commission) considered in *F.P./Germany* that Article 9 ECHR 'is essentially destined to protect religions or theories on philosophical or ideological universal values'.[92] This suggests a somewhat

85 CCPR/C/SR.1162, para. 43.

86 UN Special Rapporteur on Freedom of Religion and Belief 2021, para. 11.

87 Rainey, McCormick & Ovey 2021, p. 462.

88 Evans 1997, p. 284; Harris et al. 2018, p. 573. Meanwhile, the expression of thoughts and conscience is covered by Article 10 ECHR: Evans 1997, p. 285; Bublitz 2014, p. 2; Murdoch 2012, p. 16.

89 Rainey, McCormick & Ovey 2021, p. 461. See also Roberts 2020, p. 31.

90 ECtHR 25 May 1993, appl.no. 14307/88 (*Kokkinakis/Greece*), § 31; Harris et al. 2018, p. 571.

91 ECtHR 7 December 2010, appl.no. 18429/06 (*Jakóbski/Poland*); EComHR 10 February 1993, appl. no. 18187/91 (*C.W./UK*); EComHR 16 May 1977, appl.no 7050/75 (*Arrowsmith/UK*); EComHR 21 May 1976, appl.no. 6741/74 (*X/Italy*). For more examples see Harris et al. 2018, p. 572; Council of Europe 2020a para. 17–19.

92 EComHR 23 March 1993, appl.no. 19459/92 (*F.P./Germany*).

restrictive interpretation. In the case of *F.P./Germany*, Article 9 ECHR could not be invoked regarding an imposed disciplinary sanction of dismissal from the military service for having made discriminatory remarks about Jewish people in the presence of other soldiers, which violated the duty of political loyalty. Those sanctions did, however, fall within the scope of Article 10 ECHR, but were 'necessary in a democratic society'.[93]

In line with this approach – that Article 9 ECHR does not protect just any opinion or utterance – the Commission in *Putz/Austria* considered that the imposition of penalties by the national court upon the applicant for stating that the judges used *Nazi und Ostblockmethoden* to prosecute him did 'not show any lack of respect for his freedom of thought under Article 9 of the Convention'.[94] In contrast, the applicants' complaint in *Hazar and Açik/Turkey*, arguing that their prison sentences for belonging to the Communist Party of Turkey violated the right to freedom of thought, was admissible under Article 9 ECHR.[95] These cases suggest a somewhat narrow approach to the *forum internum*.

Meanwhile, the case of *Salonen/Finland* rather suggests a broader understanding. In this case, the EComHR had to decide whether the applicants' wish to give their daughter a particular forename[96] was covered by the right to freedom of thought. As the Commission argued, '[t]aking into consideration the comprehensiveness of the concept of thought, this wish can be deemed as a thought in the sense of Article 9'.[97]

Unlike the decisions in *F.P*, *Putz*, and *Hazar and Açik*, in the case of *Salonen*, the Commission highlighted the *comprehensiveness* of the notion thought in the meaning of Article 9 ECHR. Among others, it encompasses a person's desire to give a child a particular name. How should we understand these casuistic differences?

As both the Commission and Court have previously considered, the holding of a *conviction* should amount to more than mere opinions or ideas. It must concern a weighty and substantial aspect of human life and behaviour. Similarly, a *belief* must attain a certain level of cogency, seriousness, cohesion, and importance to be protected under Article 9 ECHR.[98] As an illustration, applying this criterion to a non-religious critical opinion on vaccination, the Grand Chamber argued that such opinions constitute no *conviction* or *belief* of sufficient cogency, seriousness, cohesion, and importance as to elicit protection under Article 9 ECHR.[99]

93 Ibid.

94 EComHR 3 December 1993, appl.no. 18892/91 (*Putz/Austria*).

95 EComHR 11 October 1991, appl.nos. 16311/90, 16312/90, and 16313/90 (*Hazar and Açik/Turkey*).

96 Namely: Ainut Vain Marjaana (The One and Only Marjaana).

97 EComHR 2 July 1997, appl.no. 27868/95 (*Salonen/Finland*).

98 EComHR, 10 March 1981, appl.no. 8741/79 (*X/Germany*), p. 138; ECtHR 25 February 1982, appl.nos. 7511/76; 7743/76 (*Campbell and Cosans/UK*), § 36; ECtHR 29 April 2002, appl.no. 2346/02 (*Pretty/UK*), § 82; ECtHR 7 July 2011, appl.no. 23459/03 (*Bayatyan/Armenia*), § 110; ECtHR (GC) 29 June 2007, appl.no. 15472/02 (*Folgerø and Others/Norway*), § 84. See also Renucci 2005, pp. 12–14.

99 ECtHR (GC), 8 April 2021, appl.nos. nos. 47621/13 and 5 others (*Vavřička and Others/Czech Republic*), § 335.

Case-law concerning the freedom of *thought* is scarce. However, when outlining the general principles in cases on the freedom of conscience or religion, the Court seems to have extrapolated its somewhat restricted approach to all notions protected by Article 9(1) ECHR. That is, to conscience, religion, and thoughts:

> The right to freedom of thought, conscience and religion denotes views that attain a certain level of cogency, seriousness, cohesion and importance.[100]

In S.A.S./*France*, the Grand Chamber confirmed this view, adding that the right to freedom of thought, conscience, and religion denotes *only* those views that attain a certain level of cogency, seriousness, cohesion, and importance.[101] Although the complaints in these cases did not concern the freedom of *thought*, the 'general considerations' that the Court outlines do give insight in the scope of the *forum internum* of Article 9 ECHR, which includes the freedom of thought. When determining what kinds of mental states and content are covered by the freedom of thought, case-law on the sister freedoms of conscience and religion can provide valuable insights.[102] In line with the Court's consideration in S.A.S./*France*, a person's intention to vote for a political party is essentially a thought protected by *the forum internum*.[103]

In conclusion, the Strasbourg institutions appear reluctant to protect *religious thoughts only*.[104] They are neither willing to protect just *any mere opinion or idea* under Article 9 ECHR.[105] Instead, Strasbourg case-law suggests sympathy for the position that Article 9 ECHR is limited to thoughts and convictions that have *a major impact* on our way of living. It only covers thoughts that attain a certain level of cogency, seriousness, cohesion, and importance.

This approach is endorsed in the literature as well. Whereas the terms 'thought, conscience and religion' suggest a potentially wide scope of Article 9 ECHR, Murdoch argues that case-law indicates a somewhat narrow approach. Personal beliefs must attain certain thresholds to be protected.[106] Similarly, Rainey, McCormick, and Ovey write that although Article 9 ECHR extends to a wide range of religious and

100 ECtHR 15 January 2013, appl.nos. 48420/10, 59842/10, 51671/10 and 36516/10 (*Eweida and others/UK*), § 81. See also ECtHR 7 December 2010, appl.no. 18429/06 (*Jakóbski/Poland*), § 44; ECtHR 6 November 2008, appl.no. 58911/00 (*Leela Förderkreis E.V. and others/Germany*), § 80.

101 ECtHR (GC) 1 July 2014, appl.no. 43835/11 (S.A.S./*France*), § 55. See also ECtHR (GC) 26 April 2016, appl.no. 62649/10 (*İzzettin Doğan and others v. Turkey*), § 68.

102 Bublitz 2021, pp. 70–71.

103 ECtHR 8 July 2008, appl.no. 9103/04 (*Georgian Labour Party/Georgia*), § 120; ECtHR 11 January 2007, appl.nos. 55066/00 and 55638/00 (*Russian Conservative Party of Entrepreneurs and others/Russia*), § 76. Cf. Partsch 1981, p. 213.

104 ECtHR 7 December 2010, appl.no. 18429/06 (*Jakóbski/Poland*); EComHR 10 February 1993, appl. no. 18187/91 (*C.W./UK*); EComHR 16 May 1977, appl.no 7050/75 (*Arrowsmith/UK*); EComHR 21 May 1976, appl.no. 6741/74 (*X/Italy*). See also Harris et al. 2018, p. 572; Council of Europe 2020a, para. 14–23.

105 EComHR 23 March 1993, appl.no. 19459/92 (*F.P./Germany*); EComHR 3 December 1993, appl.no. 18892/91 (*Putz/Austria*).

106 Murdoch 2012, p. 16. Cf. Renucci 2005, pp. 12–13.

non-religious convictions and philosophies, the Court has confirmed that to be protected, thoughts, conscience, and religion must attain a certain level of cogency, seriousness, cohesion, and importance.[107]

As Carolyn Evans notes, Article 9(1) ECHR distinguishes between two complex and similar ideas. On the one hand, 'religion or belief', and on the other hand, 'thought and conscience'.[108] According to Evans, 'thought and conscience' comprise political, philosophical, ethical, and intellectual positions in human affairs.[109] Meanwhile, she argues that 'the words thought and conscience are – perhaps even to a greater extent than religion and belief – vague and difficult to convincingly define'.[110]

Similarly, Malcolm Evans distinguishes between patterns of 'thought and conscience' on the one hand, and 'religion or belief' on the other hand. He sees little reason to distinguish further between thought and conscience.[111] In addition, he argues that interpreting Article 9 ECHR as embracing any idea or view carries the danger that when taken in marginal cases, it might justify a lowering of the high level of protection accorded to the freedom of thought.[112] Since the right to freedom of thought is absolute, 'it might otherwise be argued that advertising, or any other means of changing people's opinions, might be covered'.[113]

According to Bublitz, the absolute nature of freedom of thought has indeed resulted in confining the scope of the right. In face of practical necessities and arguably ethical duties to interfere with the inner realm of citizens in some cases, as in the context of coerced psychiatry, freedom of thought is simply interpreted so narrowly that many interventions do not qualify as infringements.[114]

Regarding Article 18 ICCPR, Partsch also endorses that freedom of thought is not confined to religious thoughts only, nor that it embraces any mere opinion or idea:

> Although no definition of 'thought' or 'conscience' is provided, taken together with 'religion' they include all possible attitudes of the individual toward the world, society, and toward that which determines his fate and the destiny of the world, be it a divinity, some superior being or just reason and rationalism, or chance. 'Thought' includes political and social thought; 'conscience' includes all morality. 'Religion or belief' is not limited to a theistic belief but comprises equally nontheistic and even atheistic beliefs.[115]

107 Rainey, McCormick & Ovey 2021, p. 462.
108 Evans 2001, p. 52.
109 Ibid, p. 66.
110 Ibid, p. 52.
111 Evans 1997, p. 289.
112 Ibid, footnote 30.
113 Ibid, p. 295.
114 Bublitz 2015, p. 1317. See also Taylor 2005, pp. 159 and 199.
115 Partsch 1981, pp. 213–214.

Similarly, De Jong is inclined to conclude that when interpreting the right to freedom of *thought*, the primary emphasis should be on fundamental beliefs.[116]

In sum, there seems considerable consensus among scholars on the view that not just any opinion or idea falls within the ambit of the freedom of thought. A certain threshold is required. Meanwhile, in recent literature, broader interpretations have been advocated as well.[117] Referring to the exceptional case of *Salonen/Finland* (discussed above), Alegre argues that the concept of 'thought' is potentially broad. It includes emotional states, political opinions, and trivial thought processes.[118] As she writes:

> My decision on what colour socks to wear, how I feel about Monday mornings or my thoughts on capital punishment are all capable of coming within the scope of freedom of thought. It is, however, unclear what that means in practical terms for the obligation to protect my freedom to think about these things as opposed to my rights to act on or express those thoughts.[119]

In view of emerging technologies and changing societies in the twenty-first century, Alegre makes a case for novel guidance on the meaning of the freedom of thought in the modern context. She argues 'to put the right to freedom of thought firmly on the legal map before we lose it'.[120]

In the same vein, Bublitz has argued to *revalue and reconstruct* the fundamental freedom of thought.[121] The concept of thought in the meaning of freedom of thought is yet under-elaborated. This is probably because thoughts are conceived factually intangible and beyond the reach of controlling interventions.[122] People's inner thoughts are largely exercised inside an individual's heart and mind,[123] with which (State) interference has been deemed epistemologically impossible. Therefore, the limits of the notion of thoughts have yet simply not required in-depth debate.[124] However, Bublitz continues, whereas this premise of intangibility of thoughts may have been well-founded during the time in which the central principles of western democracies and modern constitutions were formulated, at present, neuroscience enables us to make reasonable assumptions about the content of people's mental states.[125] Today, our mental content is no longer shielded from the outside world. Therefore, we are in need of a clear definition of protected 'thoughts'.[126]

116 De Jong 2000, p. 33.
117 Bublitz 2014; Alegre 2017; McCarthy-Jones 2019.
118 Alegre 2017, p. 224. Cf. Bublitz 2021, p. 58.
119 Ibid. Cf. O'Callaghan & Shiner 2021, p. 140.
120 Alegre 2017, p. 232.
121 Bublitz 2014; Bublitz 2015; Bublitz 2020; Bublitz 2021.
122 Bublitz 2014, p. 3. Cf. Alegre 2017, p. 221; Vermeulen & Roosmalen 2018, p. 738.
123 Harris et al. 2018, p. 573; Gomien 2005, p. 95.
124 Bublitz 2014, p. 5; McCarthy-Jones 2019, p. 5; Alegre 2017, p. 221. Cf. Evans 2001, p. 68.
125 Bublitz 2014, p. 17. Cf. McCarthy-Jones 2019; Alegre 2017.
126 See also UN Special Rapporteur on Freedom of Religion and Belief 2021.

Against the backdrop of these considerations, Bublitz suggests to understand 'thoughts' as:

> mental states that have content, meaning, or as philosophers of mind say, that are intentional in the sense of referring to something beyond themselves (the 'object' one thinks, worries or dreams about). I wish to leave for further discussion distinctions between mental states such as thoughts and emotions and only note that psychology provides evidence that they are factually strongly interwoven entities. (…) At any rate, the scope of Art. 9 should not only entail thoughts as states but thinking as a process, and accordingly, the manifold mental processes which thinking involves. Moreover, it would be too narrow if it only captured fully rational, logical thinking. Associative and creative thinking, thinking with inner images, mental simulations, poetic and even surrealist thought should be comprised.[127]

In this interpretation, thoughts do not necessarily need to attain a certain level of cogency, seriousness, cohesion, and importance to enjoy protection from Article 9 ECHR. Instead, the freedom of thought would embrace *any thought about anything*. Such an unlimited understanding of 'thoughts' will considerably broaden the scope of the right to freedom of thought. It will unconditionally prohibit any interference with any mental property that has content or meaning. It will proscribe in absolute terms any form of coercion to divulge such mental properties.

However, according to Bublitz, sometimes, good reasons can exist to change or reveal certain mental states of an individual. Non-consensual psychiatric interventions that change particular mental states may sometimes be necessary for safety reasons.[128] And in ticking bomb scenarios, pressing State interests to reveal what a person *knows* are easy to conceive. Moreover, sometimes, individuals have legal duties to speak and reveal mental content, for example as a witness in court.[129] Therefore, Bublitz brings the absolute nature of the freedom of thought into question. He proposes to develop some narrow exceptions that could justify certain infringements of the right to freedom of thought.[130]

Another proposal to rethink and broaden the scope of the right to freedom of thought comes from McCarthy-Jones. Due to twenty-first century threats to freedom of thought that are posed by emerging technologies, the contours of this right need to be redefined, he argues.[131] McCarthy-Jones suggests placing core mental processes that enable *mental autonomy*, such as attentional and cognitive agency, at the centre of the right to freedom of thought. Furthermore, he suggests that:

[127] Bublitz 2014, p. 18. Cf. Bublitz 2021, pp. 58, 75; Bublitz 2013, pp. 245–246.
[128] Bublitz 2014, pp. 10, 19–20, 24; Bublitz 2015, pp. 1312, 1317.
[129] Bublitz 2014, p. 23. Cf. Harris et al. 2018, p. 575.
[130] Bublitz 2014, pp. 24–25; Bublitz 2015, pp. 1329–1331; Bublitz 2021, pp. 90–93.
[131] McCarthy-Jones 2019, 2021.

> we should expand the domain of the right to FoT [freedom of thought] to cover external actions that are arguably constitutive of thought. This includes reading, writing, and many forms of internet search behavior. Such 'thought' is currently not protected by the right to FoT and hence not sheltered by its absolute protection.[132]

Similar to Bublitz, McCarthy-Jones notes that society may sometimes wish certain infringements of freedom of thought to be permissible. Whereas today, warrants can be granted to search an individual's home, it is imaginable that a future judge grants a warrant for a 'mental search', using neuroimaging.[133] Therefore, McCarthy-Jones calls for a public debate on whether the right to freedom of thought should remain unconditional, or whether some exceptions should be allowed.[134]

5.2.4 *Conclusion*

It is clear that Article 9(1) ECHR not only covers State interferences that *control* peoples' thoughts. It also protects against coercive measures to *disclose* our thoughts. Less clear, though, is what the notion of 'thought' exactly means. Three central approaches are conceivable: the freedom of thought (1) protects religious thoughts only, (2) protects those thoughts that have a major impact on the individual's way of living, or (3) protects any thought, that is, any mental property regardless its content.

Since the text of Article 9 ECHR has been derived from Article 18 UDHR, the *travaux préparatoires* of Article 9 ECHR provide not much clarity about the meaning and scope of the notion of 'thought'. The preparatory work on Article 18 UDHR, meanwhile, reveals a discussion on the importance of explicitly recognising the right to freedom of *thought* next to conscience and religion and on the need of separating this right from the freedom of opinion and expression. Although this discussion does not provide a clear definition of 'thought', it carefully suggests the second approach: the freedom of thought protects thoughts that are significant to the individual's way of living, such as scientific, philosophical, and political thoughts.

Several commentators have endorsed this somewhat narrow understanding. As Carolyn Evans has argued, together with conscience, the notion of thought embraces political, philosophical, ethical, and intellectual positions in human affairs. At the same time, in view of emerging technologies that may enter, alter, and/or reveal mental states, some authors have argued to rethink the scope as well as the absolute nature of the right to freedom of thought.

When outlining the general principles under Article 9 ECHR, the Grand Chamber appears to have adopted a somewhat restrictive position too: the right to freedom of thought, conscience, and religion denotes only those views that attain a certain level of cogency, seriousness, cohesion, and importance.

132 McCarthy-Jones 2019, p. 11. Cf. Loucaides 2012, p. 86.
133 McCarthy-Jones 2019, p. 7; McCarthy-Jones 2021, pp. 39–41.
134 McCarthy-Jones 2019, pp. 12–13.

5.3 COERCIVE BRAIN-READING UNDER THE RIGHT TO FREEDOM OF THOUGHT

5.3.1 *Introduction*

This section examines the legal implications of the right to freedom of thought pursuant to Article 9 ECHR with respect to coercive brain-reading in criminal justice. In order to enable the deduction of legal boundaries from existing case-law, Section 5.3.2 draws an analogy between coercive forensic brain-reading on the one hand and existing means of criminal investigation on the other hand. Next, Section 5.3.3 considers whether the right to freedom of thought would protect against coercive brain-reading in criminal justice. Section 5.3.4 discusses whether reconsidering Article 9 ECHR would be necessary to offer adequate protection in respect of brain-reading, as has been proposed by Bublitz and McCarthy-Jones.

5.3.2 *Coercive Brain-Reading: An Analogy with Obligatory Witness Testimonies*

When drawing analogies, we should take account of the context within we do so. Here, we must focus on those aspects of coercive brain-reading that are relevant in light of the right to freedom of thought pursuant to Article 9 ECHR. Decisive in this context are the *mental properties and their content* as are identified through forensic brain-reading. Do they qualify as a thought in the meaning of Article 9 ECHR?

In light of the previous examination of the meaning and scope of freedom of thought, it is clear that brain-based *diagnostics* and *prediction* – revealing biological parameters of (neural) disorders, brain anomalies, and neural predispositions to particular behaviour – do not typically disclose any mental property that could possibly constitute a 'thought' in the meaning of Article 9 ECHR.[135] Indeed, sometimes, brain-reading for these purposes may reveal sexual proclivities or emotional traits, such as the tendency to behave aggressively. However, Article 9 ECHR does not typically pertain to such personal *characteristics*. The freedom of thought covers personal *views* that people may adopt, develop, change, and share, such as a political opinion and a scientific position. Personal information about emotions and sexual preferences is, however, covered by the right to respect for private life under Article 8 ECHR[136] and possibly by the freedom of expression pursuant to Article 10 ECHR.[137]

The analogy below and the subsequent analyses in this section focus on *brain-based lie detection* and the *concealed information test*. Unlike diagnostics and risk assessment, these types of brain-reading have at least the potential to detect a

[135] Ligthart et al. 2020, p. 4.

[136] See Chapter 4. See, for example, ECtHR 22 October 1981, appl.no. 7525/76 (*Dudgeon/UK*), § 52.

[137] See Section 5.4.

person's thoughts in the meaning of Article 9 ECHR. fMRI and EEG can be used in order to identify particular brain processes during the answering of questions and the observation of stimuli. Depending on the test design, these technologies can yield information about *lies*, *knowledge*, or *recognition*. Using these tests in criminal justice, a defendant or witness can be coerced to reveal, for example, whether or not she was present at the crime scene during the time of the offence (lie detection), or whether she recognises the victim and/or perpetrator of the assault (concealed information test).

Regarding witnesses, today, we can acquire similar information using existing methods of criminal investigation. That is, through obligatory witness testimony. For example, if a witness of an assault is summoned to testify in court under oath, the judge can ask her whether she was present at the crime scene during the offence. And does she recognise the victim and/or defendant? Whereas obligatory testimonies require witnesses to answer the questions truthfully, present forms of brain-reading require to perform a certain task in accordance with the instructions. Not giving evidence as a witness without a valid legal excuse, or answering the questions deceptively, can, in many jurisdictions, lead to custody or to the imposition of sanctions.[138] Indeed, in many cases, we cannot be sure whether a witness tells the truth or not. This is exactly one of the reasons why brain-reading could contribute to current methods of interrogation and to witness examinations: it yields *objective* information about subjective mental content.[139]

Clearly, relevant differences exist between reading brains of defendants and convicted offenders and giving testimony as a witness. Yet what is important in light of Article 9 ECHR is that by imposing some kind of behavioural duty upon the individual (performing a task v. answering a question), brain-based lie detection, concealed information tests, and obligatory witness testimonies disclose more or less similar mental properties with more or less similar mental content.[140] For example: Do you remember what you were doing during the time of the offence? Did you speak the truth when you told the police that you know who has committed the crime? Do you recognise the victim, perpetrator and/or murder weapon? Do you think the victim was an aggressive person? And did you have an argument with the victim about money, the night before she was killed? The central question is whether such mental content qualifies as a 'thought' in the meaning of Article 9 ECHR.[141] The following section delves into this question.

138 Cf. ECtHR 22 November 2007, appl.no. 64752/01 (*Voskuil/The Netherlands*), § 86: 'The Court observes that the duty to give evidence in criminal proceedings is ordinarily a normal civic duty in a democratic society governed by the rule of law'.

139 Pardo & Patterson 2015, p. 79.

140 Cf. Redmayne 2007, p. 233: 'It seems better to describe defendants who are placed under a duty to cooperate as being in a similar – though perhaps not quite so sympathetic – situation to witnesses who are required to incriminate an intimate'.

141 Ligthart et al. 2020, pp. 4–5.

5.3.3 *Would the Freedom of Thought Protect against Coercive Forensic Brain-Reading?*

We have seen that the right to freedom of thought, in its current understanding, prohibits the coercive disclosure of thoughts that attain a certain threshold. In addition, we discussed that brain-based lie detection, concealed information tests, and obligatory witness testimony reveal, in general, similar mental properties with similar mental content. The question is: are those mental properties and content covered by the right to freedom of 'thought'? In other words, will Article 9(1) ECHR offer absolute protection against coercive brain-reading in criminal law?

The *forum internum* of Article 9(1) ECHR comprises the right not to disclose our religion, convictions, and thoughts.[142] Whether the right to freedom of thought protects from coercive brain-reading depends on whether the yielded information qualifies as a *thought* in the meaning of Article 9(1) ECHR. Considering brain-based lie and memory detection in criminal cases, Bublitz states that it is 'hard to imagine a better paradigmatic case against which freedom of thought should provide protection'.[143] However, in light of the discussed legal history, case-law, and literature, it might be less clear whether the Court would indeed consider brain-based lie detection and concealed information tests in criminal law as disclosing 'thoughts' in the meaning of Article 9 ECHR.

To be protected, a thought should attain a certain level of cogency, seriousness, cohesion, and importance. Examples of such thoughts concern philosophical attitudes, political ideas, and scientific views. In respect of Article 18 ICCPR, the official documents refer to other personal and collective convictions, such as in the economic, social, and intellectual spheres.[144]

Admittedly, a specific lie during criminal proceedings (e.g. about one's alibi) and the fact that a suspect recognises the crime scene and the murder weapon will be quite 'important' to that individual. However, such mental content will not typically constitute a coherent, cogent and serious personal view tantamount to, for instance, political, philosophical, scientific, intellectual, or social positions.

Brain-based lie detection and concealed information tests reveal similar mental properties with similar content as obligatory witness testimonies. They are typically concerned with mental properties such as knowledge about the name of the perpetrator, recognising the victim, or remembering what one was doing during the time of the offence. Strasbourg case-law on mandatorily disclosing these kinds of mental states through obligatory witness testimonies suggests that the Court is reluctant to qualify such mental states as 'thoughts'. Rather, the Court approaches the disclosure

[142] Vermeulen & Roosmalen 2018, p. 738; ECtHR 2 February 2010, appl.no. 21924/05 (*Sinan Işik/Turkey*), § 42.

[143] Bublitz 2014, p. 8. See also Bublitz 2021, p. 79.

[144] CCPR/C/SR.1162, para. 34; Partsch 1981, pp. 213–214.

of such mental states as the *conveyance of information or ideas* or as the *expression of an opinion* – protected by Article 10 ECHR. I illustrate this below.

In *Wanner/Germany*,[145] the applicant had been summoned to appear before the investigating judge to be examined as a witness in the context of an assault. For that assault, he had previously been convicted irrevocably. The judge explained the applicant that he was a witness now. Therefore, he was required to tell the truth. Giving false testimony or refusing to give evidence was threatened with detention. Notwithstanding these notifications, the applicant maintained that he had not been present at the crime scene and could therefore not say anything about those who had taken part in the assault. Subsequently, he was convicted for giving false testimony and sentenced to six months imprisonment, suspended on probation.[146] The applicant complained before the Court about his conviction for giving false testimony. He argued that unlawful pressure had been exerted on him to confess about his accomplices in the assault.[147] The Court, 'being the master of characterisation to be given in law to the facts of the case', considered that this complaint was to be examined under the freedom of expression pursuant to Article 10 ECHR.[148]

In examining the admissibility of the complaint, the Court recalls that the Grand Chamber does not rule out that Article 10 ECHR also protects *a negative aspect* of the right to freedom of expression.[149] As the EComHR considered earlier: 'the right to freedom of expression by implication also guarantees a "negative right" not to be compelled to express oneself, i.e. to remain silent'.[150] Whether Article 10 ECHR did protect such a right in *Wanner/Germany* would have been determined if the applicant had complained about the coercion to testify. But his complaint rather focussed on the fact that he was found guilty of giving false testimony.[151] Nevertheless, assuming that Article 10 ECHR applies in these circumstances, the Court argued that the complaint would, in any event, be inadmissible because the infringement met the requirements of Article 10(2) ECHR.

The Court underlines that the duty to give evidence in criminal proceedings is ordinarily a normal civic duty in a democratic society governed by the rule of law.[152] The only thing the applicant had been asked was providing the names of his accomplices in the assault.[153] The domestic court's decision not to exempt the applicant from the legal obligation as a witness to give evidence in a criminal case was not

[145] ECtHR 23 October 2018, appl.no. 26892/12 (*Wanner/Germany*).

[146] Ibid, § 8–16.

[147] Referring to Articles 3, 6, 10, and 14 ECHR.

[148] ECtHR 23 October 2018, appl.no. 26892/12 (*Wanner/Germany*), § 37.

[149] Ibid, § 39. See ECtHR (GC) 3 April 2012, appl.no. 41723/06 (*Gillberg/Sweden*), § 86.

[150] EComHR 7 April 1994, appl.no. 20871/92 (*Strohal/Austria*). See also Harris et al. 2018, p. 595.

[151] ECtHR 23 October 2018, appl.no. 26892/12 (*Wanner/Germany*), § 39.

[152] ECtHR 22 November 2007, appl.no. 64752/01 (*Voskuil/The Netherlands*), § 86; ECtHR 23 October 2018, appl.no. 26892/12 (*Wanner/Germany*), § 42.

[153] ECtHR 23 October 2018, appl.no. 26892/12 (*Wanner/Germany*), § 42.

disproportionate to the aims of preventing crime and maintaining the authority of the judiciary.[154]

In this case, the obligation to recall and disclose a simple fact – the names of those who committed a crime – and the subsequent conviction for giving false testimony were considered under Article 10 ECHR. The Court – being the master of legal characterisation of the facts – made no allusion to Article 9 ECHR at all. Similarly, in earlier cases, such as *K./Austria* and *Strohal/Austria*, complaints about coercion to disclose mental states as a witness have been dealt with under Article 10 ECHR.[155] Not under Article 9 ECHR.

As these examples illustrate, obliging an individual to disclose simple facts in the context of a criminal procedure do not typically qualify as the disclosure of any 'thoughts' in the meaning of Article 9 ECHR. Rather, this is conceived as the conveyance of information as protected by Article 10 ECHR. Accordingly, revealing similar crime-related information through coercive brain-reading, such as lie detection and the concealed information test, is unlikely to qualify as the disclosure of 'thoughts' either. As a consequence, these brain-reading tests will not typically be covered by the right to freedom of thought.

Technological developments might change this view. Further developments in the neural representation of real-time thoughts could have significant implications in light of Article 9 ECHR.[156] For instance, think of a person subjected to brain-reading who unintentionally thinks about his political preference, religious adherence, or moral convictions. The non-consensual identification of such collateral information will interfere with the *forum internum*, violating Article 9 ECHR.

5.3.4 *Should the Right to Freedom of Thought Be Reconsidered?*

In view of recent neurotechnological developments that enable us to bypass traditional epistemic boundaries of people's mental states, both Bublitz and McCarthy-Jones have proposed to understand the right to freedom of thought more broadly. According to Bublitz, this right should encompass any kind of mental property with content or meaning. McCarthy-Jones argues that it should cover mental processes that enable mental autonomy. He also proposes to include external actions that are constitutive of thought, such as reading, writing, and Internet search behaviour.[157] At the same time, both authors suggest reconsidering the absolute nature of the *forum internum*, because in some cases good reasons could exist to reveal mental states of an individual.

[154] Ibid, § 43.

[155] EComHR 13 October 1992 appl.no. 16002/90 (*K./Austria*), § 45; EComHR 7 April 1994, appl.no. 20871/92 (*Strohal/Austria*).

[156] See also Chapter 4, Section 4.3.4.2.

[157] Both proposals have been discussed in Section 5.2.3. Cf. UN Special Rapporteur on Freedom of Religion and Belief 2021.

The idea of reconsidering the absolute nature of freedom of thought follows from the premise that the right not to reveal thoughts is completely enshrined in the *forum internum*. Because the inner part of the freedom of thought is absolute, interferences will always imply a rights violation, even when good reasons exist to reveal particular mental states.[158]

Vermeulen and Roosmalen endorse this premise. The *forum internum* encompasses the right not to disclose thoughts. They argue that the *inner part* of Article 9 ECHR guarantees that the State may never use inquisitorial methods to discover an individual's personal thoughts and convictions. It prohibits any form of compulsion to express thoughts or to divulge a religious or non-religious conviction.[159]

Indeed, in *Sinan Işik/Turkey*, the Court held explicitly that the right not to disclose *religion* and *belief* is covered by the *forum internum*:

> What is at stake is the right not to disclose one's religion or beliefs, which falls within the *forum internum* of each individual. This right is inherent in the notion of freedom of religion and conscience. To construe Article 9 as permitting every kind of compulsion with a view to the disclosure of religion or belief would strike at the very substance of the freedom it is designed to guarantee.[160]

Meanwhile, in the same case, the Court also recognised a right of non-disclosure under the *external* part of Article 9(1) ECHR. It deduced this right from the freedom to *manifest* a religion or belief:

> the right to manifest one's religion or beliefs also has a negative aspect, namely an individual's right not to be obliged to disclose his or her religion or beliefs and not to be obliged to act in such a way that it is possible to conclude that he or she holds – or does not hold – such beliefs. Consequently, State authorities are not entitled to intervene in the sphere of an individual's freedom of conscience and to seek to discover his or her religious beliefs or oblige him or her to disclose such beliefs.[161]

In earlier cases, the Court followed a similar approach under the *external* part of Article 9 ECHR. In *Dimitras and others/Greece*, the applicants complained about the legal procedure of taking an oath as a witness in criminal proceedings. Any witness who wished to make a solemn declaration had to reveal that she was not an Orthodox Christian. Sometimes, this requirement even involved the disclosure of being an atheist or an adherer of the Jewish faith. The Court considered that the right to *manifest* religious convictions also comprises a negative aspect. That is, the right not to be obliged to *reveal* one's religious denomination or convictions, and not to be compelled to adopt conduct from which it could be inferred that one has – or

[158] Bublitz 2014, pp. 8, 23–25; Bublitz 2021, pp. 90–93; McCarthy-Jones 2019, pp. 5 and 7.

[159] Vermeulen & Roosmalen 2018, pp. 738–739. See also Alegre 2017, p. 223.

[160] ECtHR 2 February 2010, appl.no. 21924/05 (*Sinan Işik/Turkey*), § 42.

[161] Ibid, § 41 (emphasis added). Cf. ECtHR 17 February 2011, appl.no. 12884/03 (*Wasmuth/Germany*), § 50 and 51.

does not have – such convictions.[162] Requiring a witness to disclose her religious adherence before an investigative judge infringes this negative right under Article 9(1) ECHR.[163] After an examination of Article 9(2) ECHR, the Court concluded that the infringement was not justified in principle nor proportionate to the interests pursued. Article 9 ECHR had been violated.[164]

Similarly, in *Alexandridis/Greece*, the applicant complained about the procedure of taking an oath to practise as a lawyer. This procedure assumed that a lawyer who appears before a court was an Orthodox Christian, wishing to take the religious oath. Any lawyer preferring a solemn declaration was obliged to declare either that she was an atheist or that her religion prohibits the taking of oaths. Again, the Court considered that the right to *manifest* religious convictions embraces a negative aspect *not to disclose* one's religious adherence.[165] State authorities should not inquire about an individual's religious beliefs. Neither should they oblige individuals to demonstrate such beliefs. The Court found a violation of Article 9 ECHR (without an explicit examination under Article 9(2) ECHR).

Thus, on the one hand, the Court recognises the right not to disclose our religion and belief under the *forum internum*. At the same time, it deduces this right from the freedom to manifest religion and belief under the *forum externum*. This reasoning seems inconsistent.[166] If the right not to disclose religion and belief is enshrined in the *forum internum*, it is absolute. In that case, interferences can never be justified. Meanwhile, when this right is deduced from the *forum externum*, infringements can be justified under Article 9(2) ECHR. Both possibilities cannot coincide. Rights are either absolute or qualified.[167]

Regardless this arguable inconsistency, the Court's reasoning in these cases could provide some direction in developing an approach on coercive brain-reading that aligns with the proposals of Bublitz and McCarthy-Jones: (1) covering the results of current and future brain-reading applications and (2) allowing for some exceptions.[168] Let us consider this below.

162 ECtHR 3 June 2010, appl.nos. 42837/06, 3237/07, 3269/07, 35793/07, and 6099/08 (*Dimitras and others/Greece*), § 78.

163 Ibid, § 80.

164 Ibid, § 88. Cf. ECtHR 17 February 2011, appl.no. 12884/03 (*Wasmuth/Germany*), § 51–54: the legal tax obligation upon the applicant to disclose his non-affiliation which the church was not disproportionate to the aims pursued. No violation of Article 9 ECHR.

165 ECtHR 21 February 2008, appl.no. 19516/06 (*Alexandridis/Greece*), § 38. See also ECtHR 15 June 2010, appl.no. 7710/02 (*Grzelak/Poland*), § 87; ECtHR 17 February 2011, appl.no. 12884/03 (*Wasmuth/Germany*), § 50.

166 Cf. Taylor 2005, pp. 127–135.

167 Cf. the prohibition of torture (Article 3 ECHR). Ill-treatment is prohibited in absolute terms (see Chapter 3). It would be inconsistent with this absolute nature to accept that, sometimes, this absolute right allows for infringements after all. See Mavronicola 2021.

168 See also Ligthart 2020b.

Regarding the right not to disclose religion and belief, the Court seems to struggle whether this is a right typically protected by the absolute *forum internum* or is rather part of the right to manifestation in the *forum externum*.[169] In line with this struggle, two general approaches are conceivable regarding coercive brain-reading.

First, the Court could consider a complaint about disclosing facts or memories through coercive brain-reading under the *forum internum*. Most likely, this approach will not offer much protection. After all, these applications do not typically yield any 'thoughts' in the specified meaning of Article 9(1) ECHR. Forensic brain-reading is unlikely to disclose any mental content that constitutes an important, coherent, cogent, and serious personal view similar to political, philosophical, scientific, intellectual, or social positions.[170]

Secondly, the Court could approach these complaints as concerning the negative aspect of the right to manifest thoughts (i.e. the right not to disclose them). However, while Article 9(1) ECHR guarantees the right to manifest religion and belief, it does not cover the *manifestation* of *thoughts*. Yet, thoughts can be 'manifested' through actions. Primarily via speech and expression, covered by Article 10 ECHR.[171] The Grand Chamber does not exclude the possibility that the right to freedom of expression pursuant to Article 10 ECHR comprises a negative aspect. That is, a right not to express or impart all kind of information, including everyday thoughts, opinions, ideas, and simple facts.[172] Following this approach, coercive brain-reading will be covered by the broader right to freedom of non-expression pursuant to Article 10 ECHR. Meanwhile, infringements of this right can sometimes be justified via Article 10(2) ECHR. This approach seems able to satisfy the central objectives of the proposals of Bublitz and McCarty-Jones: offering protection against current and future brain-reading applications, while allowing some forms of non-consensual disclosure of mental states and content.

As long as no complaints are lodged to the ECtHR about the use of coercive brain-reading, we can only make an informed guess which approach the Court would be inclined to follow. But there are good reasons to assume that the Court would prefer the second approach. The scope of the *forum internum* appears to be narrow.[173] The Court tends to avoid considering complaints in light of the inner part

[169] Cf. Taylor 2005, pp. 159, 199–202.

[170] See Section 5.3.3.

[171] As Evans 1997, p. 285 writes: 'a pattern of "thought" or "conscience" can only be "expressed". Therefore, there can be no question of manifesting or "actualizing" thought or conscience under Article 9. Expression of thought or conscience are the exclusive preserve or Article 10'. Cf. Loucaides 2012, pp. 84–85; Murdoch 2012, p. 16; Bublitz 2014, p. 2; Alegre 2017, p. 224.

[172] ECtHR (GC) 3 April 2012, appl.no. 41723/06 (*Gillberg/Sweden*), § 86; ECtHR 23 October 2018, appl. no. 26892/12 (*Wanner/Germany*), § 39. See also EComHR 7 April 1994, appl.no. 20871/92 (*Strohal/ Austria*).

[173] Discussed in Section 5.2. See also Harris et al. 2018, p. 573; Murdoch 2012, p. 16; Evans 1997, pp. 294–295; Bublitz 2015, p. 1317.

of Article 9(1) ECHR. Rather, it understands most complaints as concerning issues of *manifestation*.[174] Unlike Article 9 ECHR, Article 10 ECHR covers the right to 'manifest' all kinds of opinions, ideas, and information. This right includes a negative aspect. Regarding brain-reading, this negative aspect enables to protect against coercion to express or impart mental content. Such an approach would align with the Court's case-law on obligatory witness testimonies, revealing more or less similar mental properties with more or less similar content.

By considering coercive brain-reading under the right to freedom of expression (Article 10 ECHR), the need for broadening the scope of freedom of thought (Article 9 ECHR) will decrease, at least from the perspective of coercive brain-reading.[175] And since Article 10(2) ECHR allows for some exceptions, there is no need to reconsider the absolute nature of Article 9 ECHR.[176] Approaching brain-reading under the freedom of non-expression raises further questions regarding Article 10 ECHR. These questions are considered in Section 5.4.

5.3.5 *Conclusion*

Current forensic brain-reading techniques will not typically yield information about 'thoughts' in the meaning of Article 9(1) ECHR. The information these technologies normally reveal do not attain a certain level of cogency, coherence, seriousness, and importance tantamount to, for example, political opinions, philosophical ideas, social positions, and scientific views. Instead, the results of forensic brain-reading are more akin to mental states disclosed in the context of obligatory witness testimonies; they involve information directly related to a crime. Disclosing such mental content is unlikely to raise an issue under the freedom of thought as guaranteed by Article 9 ECHR. Complaints about revealing similar mental content through obligatory witness testimonies have been dealt with under the right to freedom of non-expression pursuant to Article 10 ECHR. By approaching the

174 See for an exhaustive elaboration on this issue Taylor 2005, pp. 116–202, who concludes: 'In short, the single most striking point that emerges in the discussion of the *forum internum* in this chapter is that the absolute, unimpugnable and fundamental nature of the *forum internum* has been undermined by European institutions through persistent avoidance of principles that permit the *forum internum* rights to be asserted by applicants'. See also Rainey, McCormick & Ovey 2021, p. 462; O'Callaghan & Shiner 2021, p. 132.

175 This book focusses on neurotechnological brain-reading in criminal justice. As noted in Chapter 1, discussions over human rights such as the freedom of thought are elicited by advances in other technologies too, such as neuroenhancement, closed-loop brain implants, virtual reality, and deep brain stimulation. Whether the present framework of human rights provides sufficient protection in view of other technologies than brain-reading is a question that exceeds the scope of this study.

176 This would respect the intentions of the drafters of Article 18 UDHR, who were reluctant to authorise domestic laws to control the inner part of the freedom of thought: Schabas 2013, pp. 2499, 2503.

obligation to convey brain-reading data under the freedom of non-expression, the need to reconsider the scope and absolute nature of the right to freedom of thought is likely to decrease.

5.4 COERCIVE BRAIN-READING AND THE RIGHT TO FREEDOM OF EXPRESSION

5.4.1 *Introduction*

According to Article 10 ECHR:

> 1. Everyone has the right to freedom of expression. This right shall include freedom to hold opinions and to receive and impart information and ideas without interference by public authority and regardless of frontiers. This Article shall not prevent States from requiring the licensing of broadcasting, television or cinema enterprises.
>
> 2. The exercise of these freedoms, since it carries with it duties and responsibilities, may be subject to such formalities, conditions, restrictions or penalties as are prescribed by law and are necessary in a democratic society, in the interests of national security, territorial integrity or public safety, for the prevention of disorder or crime, for the protection of health or morals, for the protection of the reputation or rights of others, for preventing the disclosure of information received in confidence, or for maintaining the authority and impartiality of the judiciary.

Unlike the freedom of thought, the right to freedom of expression does not entail an unconditional right. Instead, all rights are subject to the exceptions outlined in Article 10(2) ECHR.[177] The right to freedom of expression entails both a positive and negative aspect. As Harris et al. write:

> Albeit sparse in the case law, Article 10 guarantees to some extent the negative aspect of freedom of expression, namely the right not to be compelled to express oneself. One notable example is the right to remain silent.[178]

The previous section argued that – in their current understandings – unlike Article 9 ECHR, Article 10 ECHR is able to cover both the current and future brain-reading applications. In line with this argument, the present section examines the legal implications of Article 10 ECHR in respect of coercive brain-reading. Section 5.4.2 considers the general meaning and scope of Article 10 ECHR and discusses the right to freedom of non-expression. Section 5.4.3 considers coercive brain-reading in light of this right. Section 5.4.4 draws conclusions.

[177] Van Rijn 2018, pp. 767, 784

[178] Harris et al. 2018, p. 595. See also Bychawska-Siniarska 2017, pp. 13 and 18; Jackson & Summers 2012, pp. 249, 268; Trechsel 2005, pp. 242–243.

5.4.2 *The Right to Freedom of Non-expression (Article 10 ECHR)*

Although closely related,[179] the freedom of thought and the freedom to hold opinions, receive, and impart information and ideas are two distinctive rights. Unlike Article 10 ECHR, Article 9 ECHR does not comprise a right to *manifest* or *express thoughts*. As Evans notes, 'there can be no question of manifesting or "actualizing" thought or conscience under Article 9. Expressions of thought or conscience are the exclusive preserve of Article 10'.[180]

The scope of Article 10 ECHR is wider than of Article 9 ECHR. The Grand Chamber approaches the freedom of *thought* somewhat restrictively.[181] It only encompasses thoughts that attain a certain threshold. Meanwhile, the Court refuses to confine the scope of 'information, ideas and opinions' in the meaning of Article 10 ECHR in a similar way.[182] Apart from some very few exceptions,[183] the content of an expression is irrelevant to the applicability of the right to freedom of expression: 'it is applicable not only to "information" or "ideas" that are favourably received or regarded as inoffensive or as a matter of indifference, but also to those that offend, shock or disturb'.[184]

Rainey, McCormick, and Ovey note that the right to freedom of expression is 'extremely broad'.[185] Among others, it encompasses value statements and simple facts,[186] television commercials,[187] and advertisements in newspapers.[188] As Lester writes, the freedom of expression extends to all forms of expression that impart or convey opinions, ideas, or information, irrespective of the content or mode of communication.[189] Similarly, Harris et al. argue that Article 10(1) ECHR must be interpreted broadly, 'so as to encompass not only the substance of information and ideas,

179 European Commission of Human Rights, *Preparatory Work on Article 10 of the European Convention on Human Rights*, Strasbourg, 17 August 1959, p. 21; Van Rijn 2018, p. 781; Rainey, McCormick & Ovey 2021, pp. 461, 488; Bublitz 2014, pp. 4–6; Fawcett 1987, p. 261.

180 Evans 1997, p. 285. Cf. Alegre 2017, p. 224; Bublitz 2014, p. 2; Murdoch 2012, p. 16.

181 Van Rijn 2018, p. 781.

182 Cf. ECtHR 28 March 1990, appl.no. 10890/84 (*Groppera Radio AG and Others/Switzerland*), § 55.

183 Van Rijn 2018, p. 772. Exceptional examples are hate speech, incitement to violence, promoting the Nazi ideology and denying the Holocaust: ECtHR (GC) 17 December 2004, appl.no. 33348/96 (*Cumpănă and Mazăre/Romania*), § 115; ECtHR 23 September 1998, appl.nos. 55/1997/839/1045 (*Lehideux and Isorni/France*), § 53; EComHR 26 June 1996, appl.no. 26551/95 (*D.I./Germany*).

184 ECtHR (GC) 7 February 2012, appl.no. 39954/08 (*Axel Springer AG/Germany*), § 78. Also ECtHR (GC) 20 May 1999 appl.no. 21980/93 (*Bladet Tromsø and Stensaas/Norway*), § 62; ECtHR 16 April 2019, appl.no. 10257/17 (*Rebechenko/Russia*), § 19; ECtHR 7 December 1976, appl.no. 5493/72 (*Handyside/UK*), § 49.

185 Rainey, McCormick & Ovey 2021, p. 488. See also Van Rijn 2018, p. 771.

186 ECtHR 16 November 2004, appl.no. 56767/00 (*Selistö/Finland*); ECtHR 23 October 2018, appl.no. 26892/12 (*Wanner/Germany*); Van Rijn 2018, p. 770.

187 ECtHR (GC) 30 June 2009, appl.no. 32772/02 (Verein gegen Tierfabriken Schweiz (VgT)/Switzerland (no. 2)).

188 ECtHR 11 December 2003, appl.no. 39069/97 (*Krone Verlag GmbH & Co. KG/Austria (no. 3)*).

189 Lester 1993, p. 469. Also Rainey, McCormick & Ovey 2021, pp. 488–489.

but a diverse variety of forms and means in which they are manifested, transmitted, and received'.[190]

This view is reflected in the Grand Chamber's case-law, holding that Article 10 ECHR 'protects not only the substance of the ideas and information expressed, but also the form in which they are conveyed'.[191] The mode of conveyance can vary from speech, poetry, and painting to radio, film and even disrupting foxhunting by diverting the dogs' attention through blowing a hunting horn.[192]

In sum, Article 10(1) ECHR guarantees a broad right to freedom of expression. It covers opinions, ideas, facts, value statements, and other information of almost *any content*, transmitted through practically *any means*. At the same time, this broad freedom also entails the freedom *not* to transmit through any means information, ideas, and opinions. As the EComHR considered in *Strohal/Austria*, the right to freedom of expression also implies a 'negative right'. A right not to be compelled to express oneself. A right to remain silent.[193] A bit more nuanced, the Grand Chamber:

> does not rule out that a negative right to freedom of expression is protected under Article 10 of the Convention, but finds that this issue should be properly addressed in the circumstances of a given case.[194]

To date, this negative freedom not to express ourselves has most prominently been developed in cases where journalists were legally obliged to reveal the identity of their sources, for example in the context of a civil or criminal trial.

In *Goodwin/UK*, the applicant received information as a journalist about financial problems of a company named *Tetra Ltd*. In order to check the facts and request for comments, the applicant reached out to the company. It appeared that the received information was derived from a draft of the company's confidential corporate plan, which was 'strictly confidential'. On the company's request, the High Court of Justice restrained the applicant from publishing any information derived from the corporate plan and ordered to identify the source of the information. Since

[190] Harris et al. 2018, p. 594. See also Van Rijn 2018, pp. 772–773.

[191] ECtHR (GC) 15 December 2005, appl.no 73797/01 (*Kyprianou/Cyprus*), § 174. Also ECtHR (GC) 6 May 2003, appl.no. 48898/99 (*Perna/Italy*), § 39; ECtHR (GC) 8 July 1999, appl.no. 23168/94 (*Karataş/Turkey*), § 49.

[192] ECtHR (GC) 15 December 2005, appl.no 73797/01 (*Kyprianou/Cyprus*) (speech); ECtHR (GC) 8 July 1999, appl.no. 23168/94 (*Karataş/Turkey*) (poetry); ECtHR 24 May 1988, appl.no. 10737/84 (*Müller and others/Switzerland*) (painting); ECtHR 28 March 1990, appl.no. 10890/84 (*Groppera Radio AG and Others/Switzerland*) (radio); ECtHR 20 September 1994, appl.no. 13470/87 (*Otto-Preminger-Institut/Austria*) (film); ECtHR 25 November 1999, appl.no. 25594/94 (*Hashman and Harrup/UK*) (blowing a hunting horn).

[193] EComHR 7 April 1994, appl.no. 20871/92 (*Strohal/Austria*). See also EComHR 1 March 1993, appl. no. 17488/90 (*Goodwin/UK*), § 48; EComHR 13 October 1992 appl.no. 16002/90 (*K./Austria*), § 45.

[194] ECtHR (GC) 3 April 2012, appl.no. 41723/06 (*Gillberg/Sweden*), § 86. Cf. ECtHR 23 October 2018, appl.no. 26892/12 (*Wanner/Germany*), § 39–42.

the applicant refused to disclose the identity of his source, the High Court fined him £5,000 for contempt of court.[195]

The Grand Chamber takes account of the importance of protecting journalistic sources for press freedom in a democratic society. It refers to the potentially chilling effects that orders of source disclosure have on the exercise of press freedom. Such measures cannot be compatible with Article 10 ECHR, unless they are justified by an overriding requirement in the public interest.[196]

Ultimately, the Grand Chamber considered the disclosure order disproportionate to the legitimate aim of protecting the rights of the company. Both the order to reveal the source and the fine imposed upon the applicant for refusal, violated the right to freedom of expression pursuant to Article 10 ECHR.[197]

The Grand Chamber in this case did not take an explicit position on whether Article 10(1) ECHR comprises a *negative* right to freedom of non-expression. Yet, the Commission clearly recognised such a right in its report:

> There are circumstances in which a 'negative right' is to be implied in Article 10 (Art. 10) not to be compelled to give information or to state an opinion. Compulsion to provide information as to a journalist's sources must in particular constitute a restriction in the capacity of a journalist freely to receive and impart information without interference by a public authority.[198]

In *Becker/Norway*, the applicant, also a journalist, was ordered to testify as a witness in a criminal trial about her contact with the defendant in that case. The suspect was accused of market manipulation and insider trading by providing false information to the applicant about the financial situation of a particular company. That information had been published by the applicant, resulting in a stock fall of 4.1 per cent. In this case, the applicant was not explicitly ordered to reveal the identity of her source. In fact, the suspect had already admitted being the source. Still, the Court considered that the possible effects of the order to testify were of such a nature that the general principles regarding source disclosure were applicable to this case.[199] In the Court's view, the applicant's obligation to testify infringed her right to freedom of expression. The infringement served the legitimate aim of preventing crime and disorder.[200] Whether the order to testify was necessary in a democratic society,

195 ECtHR (GC) 27 March 1996, appl.no. 17488/90 (*Goodwin/UK*), § 10–19.

196 Ibid, § 39. See also ECtHR (GC) 14 September 2010, appl.no. 38224/03 (*Sanoma Uitgevers B.V./The Netherlands*), § 50–51; ECtHR 15 December 2009, appl.no. 821/03 (*Financial Times Ltd and Others/UK*), § 63.

197 ECtHR (GC) 27 March 1996, appl.no. 17488/90 (*Goodwin/UK*), § 46. Cf. ECtHR 15 December 2009, appl.no. 821/03 (*Financial Times Ltd and Others/UK*). For more references see Harris et al. 2018, pp. 618–621; Van Rijn 2018, p. 796.

198 EComHR 1 March 1993, appl.no. 17488/90 (*Goodwin/UK*), § 48. See also Council of Europe 2007, p. 17, footnote 31.

199 ECtHR 5 October 2017, appl.no. 21272/12 (*Becker/UK*), § 72.

200 Ibid, § 60.

largely depended on the need of the witness testimony as evidence in this case.[201] Because the applicant's refusal to disclose her source did not in any way hinder the progress of the case, the Court was not convinced that the impugned order was justified by an 'overriding requirement in the public interest'. Article 10 ECHR had been violated.[202]

Compelling a witness in a criminal case to disclose the identity of a journalistic source does not always violate the right to freedom of expression. In *Nordisk Film & TV A/S/Denmark*, journalists went undercover and infiltrated in a paedophile association in order to produce a programme on paedophilia in Denmark. One of the journalists became befriended with members of the paedophile association. Those members made various incriminating statements, including advice on how to induce a child to chat over the internet. They made comments about how difficult it was to procure sexual acts from children and how easy it was to procure children in Eastern Europe and India. One of the journalist's 'friends' recommended a specific hotel, run by a Danish paedophile in India, where he had sex with Indian boys in the past. To produce evidence of serious child abuse, the Danish Supreme Court ordered the applicant company to hand over a limited part of the non-anonymised footage and notes to the police. The requested information would reveal the identity of the journalist's sources.[203]

The ECtHR considered that since most of the filmed and interviewed individuals had neither knowingly assisted the journalist nor consented to be filmed or recorded, they could not be regarded as sources of journalistic information in the traditional sense. Hence, the applicant company was not coerced to disclose its journalistic source. Rather, they were ordered to hand over a part of their own research-material.[204] Nonetheless, compelling the applicant company to hand over the unedited footage constituted an infringement of Article 10(1) ECHR. This infringement was prescribed by law and pursued the legitimate aims of preventing disorder or crime and protecting the rights of others. Regarding the necessity, the Court reiterated that the ECHR obliges States to provide effective protection to ensure that individuals within their jurisdiction are not subjected to ill-treatment, such as sexual child abuse. In this respect, and given the fact that the disclosure order was limited to footage of particular individuals, the order was not disproportionate. The Court qualified the complaint as manifestly ill-founded and declared it inadmissible.[205]

In *British Broadcasting Corporation/UK*, the BBC was summoned as a witness in the context of a criminal trial. The trial concerned two police officers accused of

[201] Ibid, § 78.
[202] Ibid, § 80–84. See also ECtHR 22 November 2007, appl.no. 64752/01 (*Voskuil/The Netherlands*).
[203] ECtHR 8 December 2005, appl.no. 40485/02 (*Nordisk Film & TV A/S/Denmark*).
[204] Ibid, p. 11. As Harris et al. 2018 explain, these two situations are different in that the former involves freedom of expression of both the journalist and his source, whereas the latter only concerns freedom of expression of the journalist himself (p. 620).
[205] ECtHR 8 December 2005, appl.no. 40485/02 (*Nordisk Film & TV A/S/Denmark*), pp. 11–13.

obstructing the investigation into the death of an individual during a major riot in London. On request of the defence, the BBC was ordered to disclose all film material that had been taken during the riot. The Commission 'assumed' an infringement of the BBC's right to freedom of expression.[206] However, it conceived the duty to give evidence as a normal civic duty in a democratic society.[207] In addition, it argued that domestic judges can only consider the evidence and assess its relevance and admissibility when they have powers to require the production of evidence in the first place, such as through summoning witnesses. The order to disclose the BBC's footage was considered necessary for maintaining the authority and impartiality of the judiciary. The application was found inadmissible.[208]

As these examples illustrate, the right not to convey information pursuant to Article 10(1) ECHR has mainly been addressed in (criminal) cases regarding *journalist* witnesses. Meanwhile, the Court has also considered the freedom of non-expression regarding obligations on 'regular' witnesses to testify in a criminal case. In *Wanner/Germany* (discussed in Section 5.3.3), the applicant was threatened with detention if he did not comply with the obligation to reveal the identity of the co-perpetrators of an aggravated assault (for which the applicant had already been irrevocably convicted). The Court assumed that the negative aspect of the right to freedom of expression was applicable. Yet, it declared the application inadmissible: all the applicant had to do was testifying about the names of his accomplices, without any risk of further prosecution. The Court reiterates that the duty to give evidence in criminal proceedings is ordinarily a normal civic duty in a democratic society. Such a duty cannot be regarded disproportionate to the aims of preventing crime and maintaining the authority of the judiciary.[209] Although the obligation to testify in court infringed the right not to express oneself, it did not constitute a violation. Similarly, in the cases of *K./Austria* and *Strohal/Austria*, complaints about obligations to produce information as a witness in legal proceedings were considered under Article 10 ECHR.[210]

In conclusion, the right to freedom of expression offers a wide range of legal protection. It comprises almost any type of information, idea, and opinion, irrespective of their content and how they are communicated. The right also entails a negative freedom: the freedom of non-expression. Coercing a witness to disclose a simple fact such as a person's name infringes this negative freedom. Depending on all

[206] EComHR 18 January 1996, appl.no. 25798/94 (*British Broadcasting Corporation/UK*).

[207] Cf. ECtHR 22 November 2007, appl.no. 64752/01 (*Voskuil/The Netherlands*), § 86.

[208] EComHR 18 January 1996, appl.no. 25798/94 (*British Broadcasting Corporation/UK*).

[209] ECtHR 23 October 2018, appl.no. 26892/12 (*Wanner/Germany*), § 40–44. Cf. ECtHR 22 November 2007, appl.no. 64752/01 (*Voskuil/The Netherlands*), § 86; EComHR 7 April 1994, appl.no. 20871/92 (*Strohal/Austria*); EComHR 13 October 1992 appl.no. 16002/90 (*K./Austria*).

[210] EComHR 13 October 1992 appl.no. 16002/90 (*K./Austria*), § 45; EComHR 7 April 1994, appl.no. 20871/92 (*Strohal/Austria*). Moreover, in Ireland, the right to silence and the privilege against self-incrimination are considered as a corollary of the constitutional right to freedom of expression: Daly 2021.

circumstances of the individual case, infringements could sometimes be justified under Article 10(2) ECHR. The next section considers the legal protection offered by Article 10 ECHR in respect of coercive brain-reading in criminal law.

5.4.3 *Coercive Forensic Brain-Reading under the Freedom of Non-expression*

The right to freedom of expression protects the transmission – and non-transmission – of information by an individual. Every individual is free not to impart, convey, and disclose information, ideas, and opinions. The right not to be compelled to *express* ourselves[211] suggests that for Article 10 ECHR to be applicable, a person should be compelled to *act* in a way that she *expresses herself*, that is, that she *imparts, conveys*, or *discloses* certain information, ideas, or opinions.[212] Therefore, this right is unlikely to apply to brain-reading applications that do not involve any kind of participation of the subject, such as an MRI-scan for diagnosing traumatic brain injury. At least, to date, no convincing indications exist to assume the applicability of the freedom of non-expression to means of data-acquisition that bypass any exertion of the subject. For example, Article 10 ECHR has not been considered in respect of taking photographs, fingerprints, and DNA samples in criminal law.[213] Therefore, the analysis below focusses on brain-reading applications that involve some kind of cooperation on the part of the subject. Meanwhile, if the right to freedom of non-expression appears applicable to 'passive' brain-reading applications after all, the considerations provided in this section will also be relevant to those types of brain-reading.

In view of the right to freedom of expression, we can draw a similar analogy as in the context of the closely related right to freedom of thought: an analogy with obligatory witness testimony.[214] Clearly, there are many legally relevant differences between obliging a *witness to speak* and coercing a *defendant or convicted offender to participate in brain-reading*. Still, in light of Article 10 ECHR, case-law about obligatory witness testimonies may provide helpful directions for the debate on coercive brain-reading. Obliging witnesses to give testimony and coercing defendants and

[211] As it is formulated in EComHR 7 April 1994, appl.no. 20871/92 (*Strohal/Austria*); EComHR 1 March 1993, appl.no. 17488/90 (*Goodwin/UK*), § 48; EComHR 13 October 1992 appl.no. 16002/90 (*K./Austria*), § 45. See also Harris et al. 2018, p. 595; Bychawska-Siniarska 2017, pp. 13 and 18.

[212] Cf. the freedom not to be compelled to *engage in conduct* from which it might be inferred that one does (not) have certain religious convictions under Article 9 ECHR: ECtHR 3 June 2010, appl.nos. 42837/06, 3237/07, 3269/07, 35793/07, and 6099/08 (*Dimitras and others/Greece*), § 78; ECtHR 21 February 2008, appl.no. 19516/06 (*Alexandridis/Greece*), § 38; ECtHR 15 June 2010, appl.no. 7710/02 (*Grzelak/Poland*), § 87.

[213] In specific cases on *press freedom*, searching a journalist's home and workplace and seizing materials by the State could infringe Article 10 ECHR: Harris et al. 2018, pp. 620–621. This should be understood in light of the great weight the Court attaches to freedom of press for the concept of democracy, fulfilling a vital role as public watchdog. See Van Rijn 2018, pp. 774, 796. See also ECtHR 1 April 2021, appl.no. 42634/18 (*Sedletska/Ukraine*).

[214] See Section 5.3.2.

convicted offenders to participate in brain-reading are both means that impart similar kind of information in the context of criminal procedures.[215]

The sparse case-law about the freedom of *non*-expression mainly concerns obligations on witnesses to give information in legal procedures. But the right to non-expression is a generic right that applies to anyone, including witnesses, defendants, and convicted offenders. Moreover, it pertains to the transmission of information *through any means*.[216] Therefore, the obligation to disclose information through participating in a *brain-reading test* will most likely be covered by the freedom of non-expression.[217]

Article 10 ECHR protects almost any information, opinion, and idea, regardless their precise content. Therefore, it is likely that the freedom of non-expression covers the results of forensic brain-reading, such as whether a suspect recognises a murder weapon, whether the defendant lies about his alibi, and whether the convicted offender still hears commanding voices. Moreover, this broad 'content-insensitive-approach' may also enable to protect against the non-consensual expression of *emotions*,[218] which can be disclosed through brain-reading applications. For instance, brain-reading could identify neural correlates of distress, sexual arousal, or aggressive responses to particular stimuli.

Altogether, coercing a defendant or convicted offender to cooperate in brain-reading that discloses whether one recognises, lies, or how one feels (about) something is likely to *infringe* the right not to be compelled to express oneself under Article 10(1) ECHR – similar to the coerced transmission of such mental states via other means, like through mandatory witness testimony.[219] The next question is whether such infringements could be justified via Article 10(2) ECHR. That is, whether they (1) are prescribed by law, (2) serve a legitimate interest, and (3) are necessary in a democratic society.

As to the legitimate interest, Article 10(2) ECHR accepts the following objectives: national security, territorial integrity or public safety, prevention of disorder or crime, protection of health or morals, protection of the reputation or rights of others, preventing the disclosure of information received in confidence, and maintaining the authority and impartiality of the judiciary. Although the exceptions of Article 10(2) ECHR are formulated broadly, they must be interpreted narrowly.[220]

[215] Ibid.

[216] Even covering the distraction of a dog by blowing a hunting horn to express one's opinion about foxhunting: ECtHR 25 November 1999, appl.no. 25594/94 (*Hashman and Harrup/UK*).

[217] Cf. Roskies 2015, pp. 686–687.

[218] Cf. ECtHR (GC) 8 July 1999, appl.no. 23168/94 (*Karataş/Turkey*).

[219] ECtHR 23 October 2018, appl.no. 26892/12 (*Wanner/Germany*); EComHR 7 April 1994, appl.no. 20871/92 (*Strohal/Austria*); EComHR 13 October 1992 appl.no. 16002/90 (*K./Austria*).

[220] ECtHR 19 December 1994, appl.no. 15153/89 (*Vereinigung demokratischer Soldaten Österreichs and Gubi/Austria*), § 37; Harris et al. 2018, pp. 592–593.

As long as coercive brain-reading is regulated by accessible and foreseeable legislation and employed in view of a legitimate interest, such as the prevention of crime, the first two requirements need not give rise to basic objections. Similar to Article 8(2) ECHR,[221] Article 10(2) ECHR may require member States to develop new laws, setting out criteria for yielding information through coercive brain-reading. However, in principle, these are no insurmountable obstacles.

The third requirement – whether coercive brain-reading in criminal law would be necessary in a democratic society – is likely to give rise to more fundamental debates.[222] This section aims to deduce some helpful insights from the limited amount of Strasbourg case-law on the freedom of non-expression, which insights can provide further directions in developing an approach on coercive brain-reading in light of Article 10 ECHR.

Of note, regarding *defendants in criminal proceedings*, it is – to say the least – questionable whether the Court would actually consider complaints about coercive brain-reading under the head of Article 10 ECHR. In its case-law on Article 6 ECHR – concerning the privilege against self-incrimination – the Court has developed a comprehensive approach tailored to coercing defendants to produce information in criminal trials.[223]

For example, in *Heany and McGuinness/Ireland*, the applicants had been sentenced to six-month imprisonment for refusing to give account of their movements during a terrorist attack. Apart from a violation of their right not to incriminate themselves under Article 6 ECHR, the applicants complained about their 'correlative right not to speak or furnish information guaranteed by Article 10'.[224] The Court considered that the essential issue concerned the compulsion to respond to the questions of police officers in the investigation of a serious criminal offence. The Court dealt with this matter under Article 6 ECHR. Therefore, the applicants' complaints under Article 10 ECHR did not give rise to any separate issue.[225]

Similarly, in *Quinn/Ireland*, the applicant had been sentenced to six-month imprisonment for refusing to give account of his movements during the time of a murder. Besides a violation of Article 6 ECHR, he complained about his right to not to speak or to furnish information guaranteed by Article 10 ECHR.[226] In his complained, the applicant referred to *K./Austria*, where a witness had refused to give testimony in view of the criminal proceedings pending against him, resulting in a fine and five-day detention. In that case, the Commission reported that Article 10(1) ECHR implicated a right not to be compelled to express oneself; a right to remain

[221] See Chapter 4, Section 4.3.

[222] Cf. Harris et al. 2018, p. 593.

[223] The implications of coercive brain-reading under the privilege against self-incrimination pursuant to Article 6 ECHR are discussed in Chapter 6.

[224] ECtHR 21 December 2000, appl.no. 34720/97 (*Heaney and McGuinness/Ireland*), § 62.

[225] Ibid, § 63.

[226] ECtHR 21 December 2000, appl.no. 36887/97 (*Quinn/Ireland*).

silent. Sentencing the witness for not giving testimony infringed this right.[227] Since the Commission considered the infringement not necessary in a democratic society, Article 10 ECHR had been violated.[228] However, like in *Heaney and McGuinness/ Ireland*, the Court in *Quinn/Ireland* held that the central issue of compelling the applicant to answering questions in the course of criminal proceedings against him was already dealt with under Article 6 ECHR. The complaints under Article 10 ECHR did not give rise to a separate issue.[229]

In view of these considerations, it seems unlikely that coercing *defendants* to express themselves through brain-reading will be considered by the Court under Article 10 ECHR. The Court may rather address such complaints under the privilege against self-incrimination. Meanwhile, we cannot exclude the potential relevance of Article 10 ECHR in this context.[230] Moreover, as will be argued later on, applying the privilege to emerging brain-reading technologies raises fundamental questions, whilst the freedom of non-expression is in fact well equipped to offer adequate legal protecting in this regard.[231] So, for the sake of our examination, let us here assume that the Court might possibly consider complaints about coercive brain-reading of both defendants and convicted offenders under the head of Article 10 ECHR. Which factors should the Court take into account when assessing proportionality and striking a fair balance?

A first relevant factor, presented by case-law on obligatory witness testimonies, concerns the risk of *self-incrimination*. In considering the necessity of infringing the right to non-expression in *Wanner/Germany*, the Court explicitly referred to the *absence* of any risk of self-incrimination:

> There was no indication that this could lead to the revelation of any further offences involving him [the applicant]. In these circumstances, the domestic courts' decision not to exempt him from the statutory obligation of any witness to give evidence in the context of criminal investigations and, eventually, at trial against third parties cannot be regarded as disproportionate to the aims of the prevention of crime and of maintaining the authority of the judiciary.[232]

Meanwhile, in *K./Austria*, such a risk *did* exist. At the time of obliging the applicant to testify as a witness, criminal proceedings were pending against him. As the Commission argued under the head of Article 10 ECHR:

[227] EComHR 13 October 1992 appl.no. 16002/90 (*K./Austria*), § 45–46.
[228] Ibid, § 49–53.
[229] ECtHR 21 December 2000, appl.no. 36887/97 (*Quinn/Ireland*), § 63. See also ECtHR 20 October 1997, appl.nos. 20225/92 (*Serves/France*), § 54–55.
[230] For example, in Ireland, the right to silence and the privilege against self-incrimination are considered as a corollary of the constitutional right to freedom of expression: Daly 2021.
[231] See Chapter 8, Sections 8.4.2 and 8.4.3.
[232] ECtHR 23 October 2018, appl.no. 26892/12 (*Wanner/Germany*), § 42–43.

> The Government argue that nevertheless in the present case the interests of the judiciary and the public in general to have the true facts in an important criminal case established as well as the interests of the accused possibly to prove their innocence prevailed over the applicant's interest in protection against self-incrimination. (…) In these particular circumstances, and without expressing an opinion on whether in all arguable cases the risk of self-incrimination precludes the duty to testify, the Commission does not find that the interference with the applicant's right to remain silent was 'necessary in a democratic society'.[233]

These examples illustrate that when the right to freedom of non-expression has been infringed, the self-incriminating nature of the expressed mental states can be a relevant factor when balancing the competing interests at stake. As Jackson infers from *K./Austria*: when a person is required to incriminate himself out of his own mouth, this involves a particular intrusion, entitled to a particular weighting under Article 10(2) ECHR.[234] Often, a risk of self-incrimination will exist when suspects are coerced to co-operate in brain-reading in the course of their criminal proceedings.

Meanwhile, it is unclear whether and, if so, how we could extrapolate a similar argument to brain-reading of *convicted offenders*. This could be relevant in legal procedures regarding prison regimes, probation, or parole. A central question would be how to define 'self-incrimination' in this context. Should information only qualify as such if it reveals an offender's involvement in another crime?[235] Or also when it indicates a high risk of reoffending, resulting in the rejection of probation requests, or in the extension of a hospitalisation order?

Often, high risks of recidivism result in longer periods of deprivation of liberty. These are potentially far-reaching consequences. Accordingly, one could argue that coercing convicted offenders into neuroprediction entails a certain risk to 'incriminate' oneself, somewhat similar to self-incrimination at trial. In both cases, the subject imparts personal information that can result in an infringement of his fundamental rights, either by imposing or by extending deprivation of liberty.[236]

Perhaps, in an individual case, this could be a relevant argument in contending that neuroprediction of a detainee should be considered disproportionate. Meanwhile, to counter this argument, one can emphasise that refusing cooperation in brain-based risk assessment could increase the risk of serious harm to others. Think of an offender with neural deficits who refuses neuroprediction and commits a crime during probation.[237] Such risks are worth being taken into account when

[233] EComHR 13 October 1992 appl.no. 16002/90 (*K./Austria*), § 49–52.
[234] Jackson 2009, p. 841. Cf. Redmayne 2007, pp. 221–222; Lamberigts 2016, pp. 424–425; Jackson & Summers 2012, p. 273.
[235] Using such coercively acquired information in a subsequent criminal trial might raise an issue under the privilege against self-incrimination pursuant to Article 6 ECHR. See Chapter 6, Section 6.3.2.
[236] Cf. Morse 2012, p. 170.
[237] Cf. the risk of miscarriages of justice when exempting witnesses to testify: ECtHR 23 October 2018, appl.no. 26892/12 (*Wanner/Germany*), § 43.

considering the necessity of neuroprediction in penal law. This is especially relevant regarding offenders convicted of severe crimes, when reoffending may result in ill-treatment or even death of others. Member States have positive obligations to safeguard the lives and physical and psychological integrity of their residents. For this purpose, States should enact efficient criminal-law provisions and include requirements related to the effectiveness of criminal investigation.[238]

As the case of *Nordisk Film & TV A/S/Denmark* illustrates, such positive obligations put weight in balancing the competing interests under Article 10(2) ECHR. The applicant company in this case complained that the obligation to disclose information about serious child abuse had violated Article 10 ECHR. In determining the necessity of the infringement, the Court referred to the State's positive obligation under Article 3 ECHR. States should 'take measures designed to ensure that individuals within their jurisdiction are not subjected to torture or inhuman or degrading treatment, including such ill-treatment administered by private individuals'.[239] Such measures should provide effective protection and include reasonable steps to prevent ill-treatment of which the authorities had or ought to have had knowledge. In the case of *Nordisk Film & TV*, the Court argued that coercing the company to hand over a limited amount of unedited footage was not disproportionate to the legitimate aims of preventing disorder or crime and protecting the rights of others.

Interestingly, the case of *Goodwin/UK* suggests another relevant factor for striking a fair balance under Article 10(2) ECHR: the *chilling effect* a restricting measure could have on exercising the freedom of non-expression.[240] The Court has acknowledged a 'chilling-effect-principle' as a relevant factor of special regard in balancing interests, especially in case-law on the freedom of expression.[241] Examples concern cases about obligations to disclose journalistic sources, as in *Goodwin*,[242] and cases regarding the imposition of prison sentences for defamation or insult.[243]

According to Fathaigh, the chilling-effect-principle 'seems to be based on the idea that certain interferences with freedom of expression must be considered not only in the light of the individual applicant, but also [in view of the] the broader effect this interference has on freedom of expression generally'.[244] Arai-Takahashi explains that even when restricting measures are to be considered as the least burdensome, their very necessity should be called into question if they have a deterrent impact on the freedom of expression.[245] As Baumbach holds, the term 'chilling

[238] ECtHR 22 June 2021, appl.no. 22597/16 (*R.B./Estonia*), § 78–84.
[239] ECtHR 8 December 2005, appl.no. 40485/02 (*Nordisk Film & TV A/S/Denmark*), p. 12.
[240] ECtHR (GC) 27 March 1996, appl.no. 17488/90 (*Goodwin/UK*), § 39.
[241] Fathaigh 2013; Baumbach 2018; Harris et al. 2018, p. 621. The Court has also referred to the chilling effect of restricting measures in light of other Convention rights, such as in cases on prohibiting abortion under Article 8 ECHR. E.g. ECtHR 20 March 2007, appl.no. 5410/03 (*Tysiąc/Poland*), § 116.
[242] ECtHR (GC) 27 March 1996, appl.no. 17488/90 (*Goodwin/UK*), § 39.
[243] ECtHR (GC) 17 December 2004, appl.no. 33348/96 (*Cumpănă and Mazăre/Romania*), § 116.
[244] Fathaigh 2013, p. 312.
[245] Arai-Takahashi 2002, p. 134.

effect' in Strasbourg case-law is a legal concept that 'indicates that something striking is at stake'.[246] It is a relevant factor reserved to special circumstances, not referred to randomly.[247]

Coercing people into brain-reading may well entail such special circumstances, requiring the inclusion of its chilling effects when balancing all competing interests at stake. Coercing individuals to express their mental content through neurotechnology could have a chilling effect on the public at large. It could deter *other* people from thinking what they want to think and from wishing not to express their mental content.[248] Together with the risk of self-incrimination and the public interest in prosecuting and preventing crime, the potential chilling effect of coercive brain-reading is likely a relevant factor when balancing the competing interests under Article 10(2) ECHR.

5.4.4 *Synthesis*

The most important finding is that the right to freedom of expression pursuant to Article 10(1) ECHR comprises a negative aspect: the right not to be compelled to express ourselves. Under this negative freedom, individuals are free not to convey, impart, and disclose information, ideas, and opinions through any means. Coercive brain-reading in criminal law is likely to infringe this freedom of non-expression under Article 10 ECHR.

Such infringements can be justified when they are in accordance with domestic law and necessary in the legitimate interest of, for example, the detection, prosecution, and prevention of crime. The limited number of case-law on freedom of non-expression suggests at least three relevant factors that put weight in balancing the competing interests at stake. These concern (1) the self-incriminating nature of brain-reading, (2) the existence of positive obligations to prosecute and prevent the crime concerned, and (3) the chilling effect of coercive brain-reading on the public at large. Whether these and, perhaps, other interests can outweigh the importance of crime control in individual cases is hard to predict. Specifying the yet under-elaborated freedom of non-expression to coercive brain-reading certainly entails challenges. For instance, how would the legal protection afforded by Article 10 ECHR relate to the privilege against self-incrimination and to the right to respect for private life? These and other challenges will be discussed in Chapter 8.

5.5 CONCLUSION

This chapter examined the legal implications of coercive brain-reading in light of the right to freedom of thought and the right to freedom of expression guaranteed

[246] Baumbach 2018, p. 111.
[247] Ibid.
[248] Roskies 2015, pp. 686–687; Kraft & Giordano 2017, p. 3; Lavazza 2018, p. 4.

by Articles 9 and 10 ECHR. The analysis shows that two basic approaches are conceivable. In the first approach, coercive brain-reading is considered under the right not to disclose thoughts as guaranteed by the absolute *forum internum* of Article 9(1) ECHR. However, to qualify as a 'thought', mental states should attain a certain level of cogency, seriousness, cohesion, and importance. This approach will not offer robust protection regarding present brain-reading applications. Normally, they do not yield 'thoughts' as protected by the *forum internum*.

The data that forensic brain-reading applications can currently yield, such as information about lies and memories relating to a crime or to other specific events, are more akin to the mental states and content acquired through obligatory witness testimonies. The technique may reveal whether one recognises the victim or whether one has been present at the crime scene. Complaints about obligations to reveal such information as a witness in court have been considered under the negative aspect of the right to freedom of expression pursuant to Article 10 ECHR. Not under the freedom of thought.

This leads to the second approach, where coercive brain-reading is covered by the freedom of non-expression. Coercing individuals to convey information through participating in brain-reading infringes the right not to express oneself. Such infringements can be justified when in accordance with the law and necessary for a legitimate interest, such as the detection, prosecution, and prevention of crime. When balancing the competing interests at stake, the Court should take cognizance of risks of self-incrimination, chilling effects, and severity of the crime concerned. Regarding defendants, it is an open question whether the Court would actually consider complaints about brain-reading under article 10 ECHR, or whether it would address this issue in light of the privilege against self-incrimination pursuant to Article 6 ECHR. The legal implications of the privilege against self-incrimination for forensic brain-reading will be discussed in the following chapter.

6

Coercive Brain-Reading and the Privilege against Self-incrimination

Article 6 ECHR

6.1 INTRODUCTION

A central right that should guarantee the fairness of criminal proceedings is the right to remain silent and, more broadly, the right not to incriminate oneself. These rights have deep historical roots, leading back to the abolition of violent methods of interrogation, such as the thumbscrew and the rack.[1] While the Convention does not explicitly recognise these rights as such,[2] the Grand Chamber considers that 'The right to remain silent under police questioning and the privilege against self-incrimination are generally recognised international standards which lie at the heart of the notion of a fair procedure under Article 6'.[3]

Brain-reading does not require subjects to speak. Rather, questions are 'asked' directly to the brain. Nonetheless, as this chapter will show, coercive brain-reading raises profound questions regarding the privilege against self-incrimination.[4] The outline of this chapter is as follows. Section 6.2 discusses the meaning, scope, and rationales of the privilege, followed by an examination of its legal implications for coercive brain-reading in section 6.3. Section 6.4 draws conclusions.

1 Levy 1968, pp. 33, 326–327; Waldron 2005, p. 1731; Alschuler 1997, pp. 190–192.

2 Both rights are recognised in Article 7 of Directive (EU) 2016/343, 'on the strengthening of certain aspects of the presumption of innocence and of the right to be present at the trial in criminal proceedings'. Consideration 27 of this directive states that 'In order to determine whether the right to remain silent or the right not to incriminate oneself has been violated, the interpretation by the European Court of Human Rights of the right to a fair trial under the ECHR should be taken into account'. See Pivaty et al. 2021a.

3 ECtHR (GC) 13 September 2016, appl.nos. 50541/08, 50571/08, 50573/08, and 40351/09 (*Ibrahim and others/UK*), § 266.

4 Cf. Meijer & Van Toor 2021; Ligthart et al. 2020; Pardo & Patterson 2015, p. 161 et seq.; Shen 2013; Farahany 2012a; Van Toor 2017.

6.2 THE PRIVILEGE AGAINST SELF-INCRIMINATION (ARTICLE 6 ECHR)

6.2.1 *Introduction*

Anyone charged with a criminal offence has the right 'to remain silent and not to contribute to incriminating himself'.[5] The privilege against self-incrimination has been recognised and developed by the Court in the casuistic case-law under Article 6 ECHR. Due to its casuistic nature, the most convincing interpretation of this case-law – and thus of the meaning and scope of the privilege – is open to debate.[6] Interpretative differences have given rise to diverging approaches across member States.[7]

Two central approaches are to be distinguished: (1) a means-based approach and (2) a material-based approach.[8] This distinction relates to the applicability of the privilege. In a means-based account, the privilege applies to certain *means of obtaining information*. It prohibits the authorities from requiring suspects to produce self-incriminating evidence.[9] In a material-based understanding, however, the privilege is thought to apply to a *particular type of information*, rather than to certain means of obtaining evidence.[10] As Redmayne put it, the privilege then protects answers to questions as opposed to physical material.[11] As I will argue below, a means-based approach appears predominant in Strasbourg case-law.

6.2.2 *Applicability of the Privilege*

In *Ibrahim and others/UK*, the Grand Chamber summarised some 'general principles' that are central to Strasbourg case-law on the privilege against self-incrimination. As the Grand Chamber stresses:

> The right not to incriminate oneself is primarily concerned with respecting the will of an accused person to remain silent and presupposes that the prosecution in a criminal case seek to prove their case without resort to evidence obtained through methods of coercion or oppression in defiance of the will of the accused.[12]

[5] ECtHR 25 February 1993, appl.no. 10828/84 (*Funke/France*), § 44.

[6] For example, Trechsel 2005, pp. 342–355; Peçi 2006; Redmayne 2007; Ashworth 2008; Jackson 2009; Jackson & Summers 2012, pp. 241–272; Lamberigts 2016.

[7] Lamberigts 2016, p. 429. See, for example, Pivaty et al. 2021b; Choo 2013; Meijer & Van Toor 2021, p. 110.

[8] Redmayne 2007.

[9] Ibid., p. 216.

[10] Pivaty, Ter Vrugt & De Vocht 2021, p. 4.

[11] Redmayne 2007, p. 215.

[12] ECtHR (GC) 13 September 2016, appl.nos. 50541/08, 50571/08, 50573/08, and 40351/09 (*Ibrahim and others/UK*), § 266. Also: ECtHR (GC) 10 March 2009, appl.no. 4378/02 (*Bykov/Russia*), § 92; ECtHR (GC) 11 July 2006, appl.no. 54810/00 (*Jalloh/Germany*), § 102; ECtHR (GC) 17 December 1996, appl. no. 19187/91 (*Saunders/UK*), § 68–69.

Accordingly, the privilege aims, primarily, to protect the *will* of the accused to remain silent.[13] It serves to protect the *freedom* of any suspect to *choose* whether to speak or not when questioned by the police.[14] As Judges Martens and Kuris put it, roughly speaking, the privilege against self-incrimination entails the right not to be obliged to *produce* evidence against oneself.[15] In other words, in criminal prosecutions, the authorities themselves should do the work of obtaining and providing the evidence against the accused. They should refrain from defying the accused's will by coercing him to give evidence.[16]

These considerations are a first indication that the privilege is primarily concerned with *means* of obtaining evidence, rather than with protecting particular types of information.[17] It protects against those means that do not respect the accused's freedom in choosing a defence strategy. As the Court puts it: it protects against '*methods* of coercion or oppression in defiance of the will of the accused'.[18]

The right to silence and the privilege against self-incrimination have not been introduced out of thin air. There are foundational rationales behind these legal principles.[19] The Grand Chamber provides the following justification:

> Their rationale lies, *inter alia*, in the protection of the accused against improper compulsion by the authorities, thereby contributing to the avoidance of miscarriages of justice and to the fulfilment of the aims of Article 6[20]

Let us consider the rationales in some more detail. The first rationale – *protecting against improper compulsion* – relates, historically, to human dignity and to the prohibition of torture and ill-treatment as means of criminal investigation.[21] Under Article 3 ECHR, the Court holds that with respect to people deprived of their liberty, resource to physical force that has not been made strictly necessary by a person's own conduct, diminishes human dignity, and infringes the prohibition of ill-treatment.[22] Providing suspects with a right not to incriminate themselves under Article 6 ECHR delegitimises the use of harmful methods to enforce self-incriminating evidence.[23]

13 Jackson & Summers 2012, p. 266; Jackson 2009, p. 842.

14 ECtHR 5 November 2002, appl.no. 48539/99 (*Allan/UK*), § 50.

15 Dissenting opinion Judges Martens and Kuris under ECtHR (GC) 17 December 1996, appl.no. 19187/91 (*Saunders/UK*), point 4.

16 Lamberigts 2016, pp. 425–426.

17 Cf. Myjer, comment to *HR* 26 November 2019, *NJ* 2020/103.

18 ECtHR (GC) 13 September 2016, appl.nos. 50541/08, 50571/08, 50573/08, and 40351/09 (*Ibrahim and others/UK*), § 266 (emphasis added).

19 For a discussion of coercive forensic brain-reading in light of the privilege's rationales, see Section 6.3.4.

20 ECtHR (GC) 13 September 2016, appl.nos. 50541/08, 50571/08, 50573/08, and 40351/09 (*Ibrahim and others/UK*), § 266. See also ECtHR (GC) 1 June 2010, appl.no. 22978/05 (*Gäfgen/Germany*), § 168; ECtHR (GC) 10 March 2009, appl.no. 4378/02 (*Bykov/Russia*), § 92.

21 Waldron 2005, p. 1731; Alschuler 1997, pp. 190–192; Ölçer 2008, p. 101; Myjer 1978.

22 ECtHR 3 May 2012, appl.no. 23880/05 (*Salikhov/Russia*), § 78.

23 Dissenting opinion Judges Martens and Kuris under ECtHR (GC) 17 December 1996, appl.no. 19187/91 (*Saunders/UK*), point 8.

This idea is closely linked to the second rationale – *avoiding miscarriages of justice*. The use of coercion or even ill-treatment to elicit confessions from suspects entails a serious risk of producing unreliable information. Using such information at trial could manifest in miscarriages of justice.[24] As the Court put it, 'experience has all too often shown that the victim of torture will say anything – true or not – as the shortest method of freeing himself from the torment of torture'.[25]

In the meaning of the ECHR, 'miscarriage of justice' has been defined as 'some serious failure in the judicial process involving grave prejudice to the convicted person'.[26] It refers to cases where a person has been convicted by a final decision for a crime that he did not commit. It refers to 'wrongful convictions'.[27] By prescribing to respect the will of suspects not to speak or otherwise produce evidence, the privilege aims to reduce the risk of wrongful convictions.

In addition to these two distinctive – though interconnected – rationales that are explicitly recognised by the Court, a third implicit pillar of justification has arguably been accepted in the literature: *the individual's autonomy*.[28] As the rationale of preventing improper compulsion, the autonomy rationale relates to the concept of human dignity too. Judges Martens and Kuris describe this rationale as follows:

> respect for human dignity and autonomy requires that every suspect should be completely free to decide which attitude he will adopt with respect to the criminal charges against him. On this view it would be improper, because incompatible with such respect, to compel an accused to cooperate in whatever way in bringing about his own conviction.[29]

Linking the autonomy rationale to human dignity aligns with the very essence of the ECHR – that is, respecting human dignity and human freedom.[30] Yet, beyond

24 Drizin & Leo 2004.

25 ECtHR 12 January 2012, appl.no. 8139/09 (*Othman (Abu Qatada)/UK*), § 264.

26 Explanatory Report to Article 3, Protocol No. 7 to the ECHR, paras. 22–23.

27 Harris et al. 2018, pp. 961–962; Flinterman 2018. Cf. ECtHR 8 February 2011, appl.no. 35863/10 (*Judge/UK*); ECtHR (GC) 13 September 2016, appl.nos. 50541/08, 50571/08, 50573/08, and 40351/09 (*Ibrahim and others/UK*), § 255, 267. But in contrast: ECtHR 23 October 2018, appl.no. 26892/12 (*Wanner/Germany*), § 43.

28 See, for example, Harris et al. 2018, p. 423; Choo 2013, p. 8; Jackson & Summers 2012, pp. 273–277; Jackson 2009, pp. 849–854; Ashworth 2008, pp. 767–768; Redmayne 2007, p. 225; Trechsel 2005, pp. 347–349; Peçi 2006, pp. 79–80.

29 Dissenting opinion Judges Martens and Kuris under ECtHR (GC) 17 December 1996, appl.no. 19187/91 (*Saunders/UK*), point 9. Cf. ECtHR 5 November 2002, appl.no. 48539/99 (*Allan/UK*), § 50: 'The right (…) serves in principle to protect the freedom of a suspected person to choose whether to speak or to remain silent when questioned by the police. Such freedom of choice is effectively undermined in a case in which, the suspect having elected to remain silent during questioning, the authorities use subterfuge to elicit, from the suspect, confessions or other statements of an incriminatory nature, which they were unable to obtain during such questioning and where the confessions or statements thereby obtained are adduced in evidence at trial'.

30 ECtHR (GC) 13 December 2012, appl.no. 39630/09 (*El-Masri/Former Yugoslav republic of Macedonia*), § 248.

a basic minimum core,[31] the concept of human dignity does not provide a clear, principled basis in interpreting and applying human rights.[32] Meanwhile, personal autonomy is an important principle for the interpretation of the Convention guarantees,[33] including the privilege against self-incrimination.

The autonomy rationale is reflected by the Grand Chamber's consideration that the privilege is primarily concerned with respecting the *will* of the accused, safeguarding his *choice* to set up a preferred defence strategy. The prosecution should prove their case without resort to evidence obtained through methods of coercion or oppression *in defiance of the suspect's will*.[34]

According to Martens and Kuris, the autonomy rationale often seems the main justification for the privilege.[35] At the same time, all three rationales are interrelated.[36] *Improper compulsion* adversely affects the accused's *autonomy* in not producing self-incriminating information, thereby increasing the risk of producing unreliable evidence and *miscarriages of justice*. The stronger the exerted pressure, the greater the risk of breaking the accused's will and of eliciting unreliable information. Meanwhile, when the authorities do not restrict a suspect's autonomy, but *bypass* his will not to provide information, no risk will exist of the suspect producing unreliable evidence.[37] Although often discussed separately, the three central pillars of justification are to some extent intertwined. Their relative significance may well vary across individual cases.

In *Ibrahim and others/UK*, the Grand Chamber stresses that the privilege does not protect suspects against the making of an incriminating statement *per se*. Rather, it protects 'against the *obtaining of evidence by coercion or oppression*. It is the *existence of compulsion* that gives rise to concerns as to whether the privilege against self-incrimination has been respected'.[38] In essence, the privilege aims to protect

[31] From a human rights perspective, McCrudden 2008, p. 679 has identified three elements of this minimum core: (1) every human being possesses an intrinsic worth, merely by being human; (2) this intrinsic worth should be recognised and respected by others, and some forms of treatment are inconsistent with, or required by, respect for this intrinsic worth; (3) recognising the intrinsic worth of the individual requires that the State should be seen to exist for the sake of the individual human being, not *vice versa*. Among others, this minimum core has been at stake in cases on women's freedom to have an abortion and in cases on ill-treatment. In the same vein, this minimum core is reflected in the first rationale of the privilege: preventing from harmful methods in the course of criminal investigations.

[32] McCrudden 2008.

[33] ECtHR (GC) 11 January 2006, appl.nos. 52562/99 and 52620/99 (*Sørensen and Rasmussen/Denmark*), § 54.

[34] Also: Lamberigts 2016, p. 428; Trechsel 2005, p. 148; Ashworth 2008, pp. 767–768; Dissenting opinion Judges Martens and Kuris under ECtHR (GC) 17 December 1996, appl.no. 19187/91 (*Saunders/UK*), point 9.

[35] Cf. Ashworth 2008, pp. 767–772.

[36] Koops 2000, pp. 45–46; Koops & Stevens 2003, p. 287.

[37] Think of examining closed-circuit television (CCTV) records of a crime scene, instead of coercing the suspect to testify about whether she has ever been there to prepare and commit a bank-robbery.

[38] ECtHR (GC) 13 September 2016, appl.nos. 50541/08, 50571/08, 50573/08, and 40351/09 (*Ibrahim and others/UK*), § 267 (emphasis added). See also ECtHR 5 November 2002, appl.no. 48539/99 (*Allan/UK*), § 50.

the way in which evidence in criminal proceedings is collected by the authorities: it protects against the employment of direct and indirect[39] coercion that disrespects or breaches the suspect's will not to produce the requested information.[40] As phrased by Jackson and Summers, the privilege can best be equated with the immunity from *wilfully participating* in one's own conviction.[41] According to Redmayne, the privilege is *means*-based. It protects against the obligation to cooperate with the authorities by providing them with self-incriminating evidence.[42]

However, sometimes, it is allowed to use coercion in order to obtain information in a criminal investigation. In *Saunders/UK*, the Grand Chamber has formulated an exception to the privilege's applicability:

> The right not to incriminate oneself is primarily concerned, however, with respecting the will of an accused person to remain silent. (…) it does not extend to the use in criminal proceedings of material which may be obtained from the accused through the use of compulsory powers but which has an existence independent of the will of the suspect such as, *inter alia*, documents acquired pursuant to a warrant, breath, blood and urine samples and bodily tissue for the purpose of DNA testing.[43]

In general, the privilege does not apply to the acquisition of information that 'exists independently of the will of the suspect'. Although the precise implications of this consideration may not immediately be clear, the essence is rather logical in light of a means-based approach of the privilege.

Within a means-based approach, the privilege primarily protects from obtaining evidence in a way that disrespects or breaches the suspect's will not to produce information. However, to obtain information that 'exists independently of the will of the suspect', such as blood and fingerprints, the suspect is not required to produce anything at all. Rather, the authorities can recover the information *without any cooperation* of the accused, for example by pulling out a hair for DNA analysis.[44] Accordingly, to obtain such evidence, the *will* of the suspect *not to cooperate* should not be breached. The suspect is not required to do or produce anything at all.

39 See ECtHR (GC) 29 June 2007, appl.nos. 15809/02 and 25624/02 (*O'Halloran and Francis/UK*), § 57 ('direct compulsion'); ECtHR (GC) 8 February 1996, appl.no. 18731/91 (*John Murray/UK*), § 49–50 and ECtHR 6 June 2000, appl.no. 36408/97 (*Averill/UK*), § 48 ('indirect compulsion'). Cf. ECtHR 5 November 2002, appl.no. 48539/99 (*Allan/UK*), § 50: 'While the right to silence and the privilege against self-incrimination are primarily designed to protect against improper compulsion by the authorities and the obtaining of evidence through methods of coercion or oppression in defiance of the will of the accused, the scope of the right is not confined to cases (…) where the will of the accused has been directly overborne in some way'. See also Pitcher 2018a, p. 36, footnote 109; Jackson & Summers 2012, pp. 253 and 255–256.

40 Cf. Redmayne 2007, pp. 215 and 225; Jackson 2009, pp. 842 and 844; Ashworth 2008, pp. 759–760; Trechsel 2005, p. 354; Lamberigts 2016, pp. 425–426.

41 Jackson & Summers 2012, p. 269.

42 Redmayne 2007, p. 225.

43 ECtHR (GC) 17 December 1996, appl.no. 19187/91 (*Saunders/UK*), § 69.

44 Ashworth 2008, p. 759; Redmayne 2007, p. 215.

Instead, the authorities *bypass* the suspect's will not to provide the information: they gather the information all by themselves. To such means of obtaining evidence, the privilege will not typically apply.

Meanwhile, sometimes, the acquisition of evidence *does require* some kind of cooperation of the suspect, either actively or rather passively.[45] In those cases, the authorities cannot obtain the evidence through bypassing the suspect's reluctance to cooperate. Then, the authorities can only obtain the information they seek if and only if the suspect chooses to cooperate. When a suspect refuses his essential assistance and decides not to produce the requested evidence, only one measure of last resort remains to the authorities: coercing the suspect and breaking his will not to provide the evidence. Such means of obtaining evidence are proscribed by the privilege.[46]

The precise scope of the *Saunders*-formula is open to debate. In order to assess when the privilege applies, we must determine what the Court exactly means with 'information that has an existence independent of the will of the suspect'. The unclarity in this regard originates from the way in which the cases of *Saunders/UK*, *J.B./Switzerland*, and *Funke/France* relate to each other.[47] In *Saunders*, the Court suggests that the coercive acquisition of documents pursuant to a warrant exceeds the scope of the privilege, because such documents exist independently of the will of the suspect. However, the obligations in *J.B.* and *Funke* to submit all kind of pre-existing documents and to provide bank statements, followed by the imposition of financial sanctions for non-compliance, violated the privilege.[48] So, whereas the Court in *Saunders* seems to exclude documents from the privilege's scope, the sanctions imposed on *Funke* and *J.B* for not handing over documents did constitute a violation. How should we understand this case-law?

The cases of *Funke* and *J.B.* had in common that the authorities were not certain about either the existence or the precise scope of the documents they had requisitioned.[49] They only *assumed* the existence of certain documents with certain content. Still, the applicants were the only persons who actually knew about the existence and content of the documents. Only *they* were able to provide those

45 To be clear: with 'rather passive' cooperation I have not in mind methods such as taking fingerprints or collecting DNA samples. In such cases, cooperation of the suspect is not *required* at all; the suspect's assistance is no *condicio sine qua non* to obtain the information. Rather, I think of lying in an functional magnetic resonance imaging (fMRI) scan very calmly, without making any movements that will distort the scan results. Such 'passive cooperation' of the subject is necessary to obtain functional brain-reading data.

46 ECtHR (GC) 13 September 2016, appl.nos. 50541/08, 50571/08, 50573/08, and 40351/09 (*Ibrahim and others/UK*), § 266.

47 Redmayne 2007, pp. 214–215; Lamberigts 2016, p. 430.

48 ECtHR 3 May 2001, appl.no. 31827/96 (*J.B./Switzerland*), § 68–71; ECtHR 25 February 1993, appl.no. 10828/84 (*Funke/France*), § 44. Cf. ECtHR 5 April 2012, appl.no. 11663/04 (*Chambaz/Switzerland*), § 53–58.

49 ECtHR 25 February 1993, appl.no. 10828/84 (*Funke/France*), § 44; ECtHR 3 May 2001, appl.no. 31827/96 (*J.B./Switzerland*), § 69.

documents. Their cooperation was essential. As the Court held in *J.B.*, such documents do not qualify as 'having an existence independent of the will of the suspect'. Therefore, they are not excluded from legal protection under the privilege:

> The Court notes that in its judgment of 7 July 1995 the Federal Court referred to various provisions in criminal law obliging a person to act in a particular way so as to enable the authorities to obtain his conviction, for instance the obligation to install a tachograph in lorries, or to submit to a blood or a urine test. In the Court's opinion, however, the present case does not involve material of this nature which, like that considered in *Saunders*, has an existence independent of the person concerned and is not, therefore, obtained by means of coercion and in defiance of the will of that person.[50]

At first glance, the *Saunders*-formula might suggest a material-based approach of the privilege. It suggests that *particular types of information* are excluded from the privilege's scope – that is, information that exists in a physical way independently of the will of the suspect (DNA, fingerprints, etc.). However, the cases of *J.B.* and *Funke* rather indicate a means-based approach: the criterion is whether the information can be *acquired* independently of the suspect's will.[51] The documents in *J.B.* and *Funke*, both concerning former investments, did *exist* in a physical way, whether the applicants liked it or not. Yet in order to *obtain* them, *cooperation* of the applicants was required.[52] When a suspect in such cases refuses cooperation, only one last resort exists to obtain the information: breaking the will of the suspect not to cooperate, coercing him to provide the evidence after all. As the Court phrased it in *Funke*:

> Being unable or unwilling to procure them by some other means, they [the government] attempted to compel the applicant himself to provide the evidence of offences he had allegedly committed.[53]

Such use of compulsion is not in accordance with the privilege, which prescribes to respect the suspect's will not to cooperate in producing evidence. The prosecution should prove their cases without resort to evidence obtained through methods of coercion or oppression in defiance of the will of the accused.[54]

Sometimes, people resist coercion, persisting in their choice not to provide the requested information. In those cases, the will of the suspect not to give evidence

[50] ECtHR 3 May 2001, appl.no. 31827/96 (*J.B./Switzerland*), § 68.

[51] Lamberigts 2016, p. 431; Ashworth 2008, pp. 759–760; Redmayne 2007, p. 215; Trechsel 2005, p. 354.

[52] See also Redmayne 2007, p. 215: 'It is true that the language in *Saunders* is confusing – pre-existing documents handed over by the suspect do have "an existence independent of the will"; it is their production that depends on the will. But let us interpret charitably, and assume that what the privilege should protect us from is some sort of requirement to cooperate'.

[53] ECtHR 25 February 1993, appl.no. 10828/84 (*Funke/France*), § 44.

[54] For example, ECtHR (GC) 13 September 2016, appl.nos. 50541/08, 50571/08, 50573/08, and 40351/09 (*Ibrahim and others/UK*), § 266; ECtHR (GC) 10 March 2009, appl.no. 4378/02 (*Bykov/Russia*), § 92; ECtHR (GC) 11 July 2006, appl.no. 54810/00 (*Jalloh/Germany*), § 102; ECtHR (GC) 17 December 1996, appl.no. 19187/91 (*Saunders/UK*), § 68–69.

shall not be breached. However, if a person's choice not to produce information is sanctioned, her autonomous decision in this regard will be disrespected as well. In this way, the imposed sanctions in *J.B.* and *Funke* violated the right against self-incriminating pursuant to Article 6 ECHR.[55]

In conclusion, on the face of it, the cases of *J.B.* and *Funke* may conflict with the exception formulated in *Saunders*. But these three cases can be reconciled within a means-based approach of the privilege. That is, when we understand the *Saunders*-formula as applying to evidence that can be *obtained* independently of the will of the accused.[56] As the Grand Chamber puts it, 'self-incrimination', in the broader meaning given to that term in *Funke* and *J.B.*, involves 'cases in which *coercion to hand over* incriminatory evidence was in issue'.[57]

Accordingly, when the collection of evidence does *not require* cooperation of the suspect, but the evidence can be recovered independently of the suspect's will ('will-independent information'), the coercive acquisition of the evidence will not normally raise an issue under privilege. Meanwhile, when obtaining evidence *does require the suspect's cooperation*, that is, when her will to produce information is essential to obtain the evidence ('will-dependent information'), the privilege does apply.

At this point, one could raise the question: would this means-based understanding also cover the coercive acquisition of real evidence such as blood samples and fingerprints when obtained via a legal *obligation to cooperate*? The Court in *Saunders* suggests a negative answer. It argues that the privilege does not extend to the use in criminal proceedings of will-independent information that *could* (but not necessarily have to) be obtained from the accused through the use of compulsory powers, such as forcibly taking blood and fingerprints.[58] In this regard, Redmayne notes that:

> one thing that distinguishes bodily samples from testimony is that the police can obtain them by force. Getting them does not have to involve co-opting the suspect. Thus under the Police and Criminal Evidence Act 1984, the police have the power to obtain fingerprints and non-intimate bodily samples by force. On the theory being developed here, this does not infringe the privilege against self-incrimination.[59]

55 ECtHR 3 May 2001, appl.no. 31827/96 (*J.B./Switzerland*), § 71; ECtHR 25 February 1993, appl.no. 10828/84 (*Funke/France*), § 44. Cf. ECtHR 5 April 2012, appl.no. 11663/04 (*Chambaz/Switzerland*), § 53–58. See also ECtHR (GC) 29 June 2007, appl.no. 25624/02 (*Francis/UK*); ECtHR 21 December 2000, appl.no. 34720/97 (*Heaney and McGuinness/Ireland*); ECtHR 21 December 2000, appl.no. 36887/97 (*Quinn/Ireland*).

56 Redmayne 2007, p. 215.

57 ECtHR (GC) 29 June 2007, appl.nos. 15809/02 and 25624/02 (*O'Halloran and Francis/UK*), § 54 (emphasis added).

58 Cf. Redmayne 2007, p. 215.

59 Redmayne 2007, p. 215.

As Trechsel puts it, '[t]he privilege only covers assistance from the suspect which could not be substituted by employing direct force'.[60]

To be clear, the pre-existing documents in *Funke* and *J.B.* are different from blood, hair, and fingerprints. Unlike the latter, the documents in *Funke* and *J.B.* could *not* be obtained through the use of compulsory powers, such as a search warrant. The authorities *did not know* exactly what they were looking for. Similarly, in *Van Weerelt/The Netherlands*,[61] the applicant had been obliged to provide tax information through either an oral or written statement. He was also required to provide all documented information regarding his relation to a particular financial entity. Without cooperation of the applicant, the tax authorities would have been unable to obtain the requested information. According to the Court, the applicant had been compelled 'to give information that could not be obtained from any other source than the applicant himself'.[62] Such information is covered by the privilege.[63]

In conclusion, according to a means-based approach, the privilege only covers the coercive acquisition of information when such requires cooperation; when the information *cannot be obtained from any other source than the cooperating suspect*. Examples from Strasbourg case-law concern the acquisition of oral and written statements[64] and documents of which the existence and/or precise scope are unclear to the authorities.[65]

Meanwhile, when information could also be obtained through the use of compulsory powers (such as direct force) – not requiring the suspect's cooperation – the privilege will normally not apply. As examples, the Court mentions bodily tissue for DNA testing, blood, hair, breath, urine, voice samples, documents acquired pursuant to a warrant, and tachograph data.[66]

Regarding blood, hair, voice samples, tachograph data, and documents obtained through a search warrant, it may be clear that such information can be acquired without the suspect's cooperation. The authorities can obtain such information all

60 Trechsel 2005, p. 354.

61 ECtHR 16 June 2015, appl.no. 784/14 (*Van Weerelt/The Netherlands*).

62 Ibid., § 61. See also ECtHR 10 June 2021, appl.no. 2833/13 (*Bajić/North Macedonia*), § 72.

63 ECtHR 16 June 2015, appl.no. 784/14 (*Van Weerelt/The Netherlands*), § 61–64.

64 ECtHR (GC) 17 December 1996, appl.no. 19187/91 (*Saunders/UK*), § 69–76; ECtHR 14 October 2010, appl.no. 1466/07 (*Brusco/France*), § 52–55; ECtHR 4 October 2005, appl.no. 6563/03 (*Shannon/UK*), § 36–41; ECtHR 27 April 2004, appl.no. 21413/02 (*Kansal/UK*), § 29; ECtHR 21 December 2000, appl.no. 36887/97 (*Quinn/Ireland*), § 54–56.

65 ECtHR 16 June 2015, appl.no. 784/14 (*Van Weerelt/The Netherlands*), § 5–24, 55, 6–61; ECtHR 5 April 2012, appl.no. 11663/04 (*Chambaz/Switzerland*), § 53–58; ECtHR 3 May 2001, appl.no. 31827/96 (*J.B./Switzerland*), § 68–71; ECtHR 25 February 1993, appl.no. 10828/84 (*Funke/France*), § 44.

66 For example, ECtHR (GC) 17 December 1996, appl.no. 19187/91 (*Saunders/UK*), § 69; ECtHR 15 May 2018, appl.no. 41079/16 (*Caruana/Malta*), § 36; ECtHR 25 September 2001, appl.no. 44787/98 (*P.G. and J.H./UK*), § 80; ECtHR 15 June 1999, appl.no. 43486/98 (*Tirado Ortiz and Lozano Martin/Spain*); European Commission of Human Rights (EComHR) 9 April 1997, appl.no. 30551/96 (*Cartledge/UK*).

by themselves, for example, by pulling out a hair, tapping the suspect's phone, or through a search and seizure. However, concerning breath and urine, one might argue that their acquisition *does require* some kind of cooperation: the suspect has to produce a particular amount of breath and urine in accordance with the prescribed procedure.[67] This raises the question: why does the privilege not apply to the coercive acquisition of breath and urine while they do require the suspect's participation? I presume this is because the essential information to be obtained, such as blood alcohol content and drug metabolites, can also be recovered without the suspect's cooperation, for instance, by taking blood, saliva, or pulling out a hair.[68] The mere fact that the essential information in an individual case has been recovered with coerced cooperation should not as a rule imply that obtaining the evidence *depends* on the will of the accused.

The same holds true for documents, drugs, weapons, and other physical objects. For example, imagine the police receiving tip-offs that someone collects old, deactivated though illegal guns at home. The next day, the police visit the suspect and require him to hand over the guns as evidence on pain of a EUR 3,000 fine. If the suspect complies, the evidence will be obtained through coerced cooperation. However, this does not allow for the conclusion that the guns therefore qualify as evidence obtained 'dependent of the will of the suspect', which *could not have been obtained from any other source than the cooperating suspect himself.* The police could also have searched the suspect's home and seized the guns without any cooperation whatsoever. The mere fact that they opted for a less intrusive method, involving the suspect's cooperation, should not detract from this.[69]

Following a similar line of reasoning, it is arguable that the information obtained from breath and urine can also be obtained without the suspect's cooperation – independently of his will – through more intrusive methods such as taking blood and pulling out a hair. Such information normally exceeds the scope of the privilege.

However, exceptions do exist. In *Jalloh/Germany*, the coercive acquisition of will-independent information (a swallowed pellet of cocaine) did raise an issue regarding the privilege.[70] The Grand Chamber considered:

> In the Court's view, the evidence in issue in the present case, namely, drugs hidden in the applicant's body which were obtained by the forcible administration of emetics, could be considered *to fall into the category of material having an existence*

67 Dissenting opinion Judges Martens and Kuris under ECtHR (GC) 17 December 1996, appl.no. 19187/91 (*Saunders/UK*), point 12; Jackson & Summers 2012, p. 254.

68 Cf. Redmayne 2007, p. 215.

69 Meanwhile, when the police only assume that someone possesses illegal goods, perhaps guns, drugs, or stolen watches and that these products are stored somewhere in (or even outside) Europe, the police will often be unable to obtain the evidence by themselves. If the evidence cannot be obtained from any other source than the cooperating suspect, coercing the suspect to hand over the illegal products as evidence shall infringe the privilege in a means-based approach.

70 Cf. ECtHR (GC) 11 July 2006, appl.no. 54810/00 (*Jalloh/Germany*), § 113–116.

> *independent of the will of the suspect, the use of which is generally not prohibited in criminal proceedings.*[71]

Nonetheless, according to the Grand Chamber, there were several reasons that distinguished this case from the examples of will-independent material listed in *Saunders* (blood, hair, bodily tissue, etc.).

First, similar to the acquisition of documents in *Funke* and *J.B.*, the use of coercion in *Jalloh* aimed at obtaining 'real evidence' in defiance of the applicant's will. The Court contrasts this kind of real evidence with the bodily material listed in *Saunders*. Unlike documents and a pellet of cocaine, bodily material is generally obtained by coercion for the purpose of forensic examination, with a view of detecting, for example, the presence of alcohol or drugs.[72]

Second, the Court stressed that the degree of force used in *Jalloh* differed significantly from the degree of compulsion that is normally required to obtain the will-independent information as mentioned in the *Saunders*-formula. For example, to obtain blood, hair, or bodily tissue, a defendant is only obliged to endure passively a minor interference with his physical integrity. And if some kind of cooperation is required (e.g. to produce urine or breath), the Court infers from *Saunders* that this concerns material produced by the normal functioning of the body. By contrast, compelling the applicant in *Jalloh* to regurgitate the swallowed pellet of cocaine involved the forcible introduction of a tube into his stomach. Emetics were administered to provoke a pathological reaction, involving serious health risks.[73]

Third, closely related to the second point, the evidence in *Jalloh* was obtained in breach of Article 3 ECHR.[74] In light of these considerations, the Grand Chamber finds the privilege against self-incrimination applicable, regardless the will-independent nature of obtaining the pellet of cocaine.[75]

The persuasiveness of the Court's reasoning in *Jalloh* is open to debate.[76] First, it is questionable whether the pellet of drugs did indeed not require any further forensic examination to be usable as evidence against the applicant. Assessing whether the acquired white powder did actually constitute cocaine will require some further research, such as performing a narcotest. Moreover, it is not clear why it should be relevant to the applicability of the privilege whether the obtained information requires further forensic examination or can be used directly as 'real evidence' against the defendant. Should the '*Jalloh*-like' acquisition of blood for DNA testing, using brute force and violating Article 3 ECHR, be excluded from the privilege

71 Ibid., § 113 (emphasis added).

72 Ibid.

73 Ibid., § 114.

74 Ibid., § 115.

75 Ibid., § 116. See also ECtHR (GC) 29 June 2007, appl.nos. 15809/02 and 25624/02 (*O'Halloran and Francis/UK*), § 54.

76 Stevens 2007.

merely because additional forensic research is required to use the information as evidence? The Court's own case-law suggests a negative answer. The privilege applies to anyone charged with a criminal offence and is not limited to directly incriminating evidence.[77]

Although not essential to this case, the Court introduced a novel sub-category of evidence: evidence produced by the normal functioning of the body. However, the Court refrains from explaining the normative relevance of this descriptive qualification. Moreover, the scope of this qualification is obscure. Apparently, providing breath and urine in accordance with particular test protocols qualifies as evidence 'produced by the normal functioning of the body'. But then, what about *watching*, *listening*, *nodding*, *writing*, and *speaking*?[78] The Court does not provide any clarification whatsoever. To date, this normal-functioning-of-the-body-qualification has not been reiterated in Strasbourg case-law.

Most likely, we should understand the case of *Jalloh* in light of the *excessive force* employed to obtain the drugs, thereby restricting the suspect's autonomy.[79] As discussed, the rationale of the privilege lies in (1) the protection of the accused against improper compulsion, (2) avoiding miscarriages of justice, and (3) respecting the suspect's autonomy in choosing a preferred defence strategy. Regarding the second rationale, the case of *Jalloh* did not raise particular concerns. The obtained drugs constituted objective, reliable real evidence. Meanwhile, the first rationale – protecting the accused against improper compulsion – had been gravely disrespected, thereby restricting the suspect's autonomy over his own physical reactions that produced the evidence.

In conclusion, the case of *Jalloh* shows that some (narrow) exceptions exist to the general rule that the privilege does not apply to the coercive acquisition of information that can be obtained without cooperation of the suspect. Sometimes, the use of excessive force to recover such information can trigger legal protection under the privilege against self-incrimination. As the Grand Chamber holds in *Ibrahim and others/UK*, different situations can give rise to concerns as to improper compulsion in breach of Article 6 ECHR. One of those situations is where the authorises obtain information by using 'physical or psychological pressure, often in the form of treatment which breaches Article 3 of the Convention'.[80]

Finally, it is important to note that the privilege does not protect from imposing sanctions upon the suspect for providing *false information*, regardless of whether the

77 ECtHR (GC) 13 September 2016, appl.nos. 50541/08, 50571/08, 50573/08, and 40351/09 (*Ibrahim and others/UK*), § 268; ECtHR (GC) 17 December 1996, appl.no. 19187/91 (*Saunders/UK*), § 71; ECtHR 25 February 1993, appl.no. 10828/84 (*Funke/France*), § 44.

78 Watching and listening can produce evidence, for example, in the course of a CIT or in neuroprediction. Cf. ECtHR 14 March 2000, appl.no. 39195/98 (*Jager/The Netherlands*).

79 Jackson & Summers 2012, p. 255.

80 ECtHR (GC) 13 September 2016, appl.nos. 50541/08, 50571/08, 50573/08, and 40351/09 (*Ibrahim and others/UK*), § 267; ECtHR 10 June 2021, appl.no. 2833/13 (*Bajić/North Macedonia*), § 65.

false statements were given under a duty to cooperate. In *Allen/UK*, the tax authorities required the applicant to provide a certified statement concerning his assets and liabilities over a particular period. When the applicant failed to comply, he was officially warned that subsequent failure to provide the information rendered him liable to a minor financial penalty. In response, the applicant delivered a schedule of his assets as was required. This information appeared incorrect and the applicant was convicted of 'cheating the public revenue of income tax and corporation tax' – that is, making a false declaration of his assets. Regarding the applicability of the privilege, the Court considered:

> In other words, he lied, or perjured himself through giving inaccurate information about his assets. This was not an example of forced self-incrimination about an offence which he had previously committed; it was the offence itself. It may be that the applicant lied in order to prevent the Inland Revenue uncovering conduct which might possibly be criminal and lead to a prosecution. However, the privilege against self-incrimination cannot be interpreted as giving a general immunity to actions motivated by the desire to evade investigation by the revenue authorities.[81]

The case of *Allen/UK* clearly illustrates that the privilege does not apply to the imposition of sanctions for providing false information. Neither does it prohibit the drawing of adverse inferences from statements of the accused that appear untrue.[82]

6.2.3 *Violating the Privilege against Self-incrimination: Three Relevant Factors*

The privilege against self-incrimination is not absolute.[83] It does not proscribe all coercive measures that encourage people to produce information in the course of their criminal proceedings.[84] In determining whether the coercive acquisition of evidence has *violated* the privilege, the Court has regard to three central factors: (1) the nature and degree of the coercion that has been employed to obtain the evidence, (2) the existence of any relevant safeguards in the procedure, and (3) the use to which the information has been put.[85]

[81] ECtHR 10 September 2002, appl.no. 76574/01 (*Allen/UK*), p. 5. See also ECtHR 8 April 2003, appl. no. 13881/02 (*King/UK*), p. 10.

[82] ECtHR 4 July 2000, appl.no. 43149/98 (*Kok/The Netherlands*), p. 22. Cf. ECtHR 26 April 1991, appl. no. 12398/86 (*Asch/Austria*), § 29–32.

[83] ECtHR (GC) 13 September 2016, appl.nos. 50541/08, 50571/08, 50573/08, and 40351/09 (*Ibrahim and others/UK*), § 269; ECtHR 21 December 2000, appl.no. 34720/97 (*Heaney and McGuinness/Ireland*), § 47.

[84] ECtHR 10 September 2002, appl.no. 76574/01 (*Allen/UK*), p. 5; ECtHR 4 October 2005, appl.no. 6563/03 (*Shannon/UK*), § 36. See, for example, ECtHR 10 January 2008, appl.no. 58452/00 and 61920/00 (*Lückhof and Spanner/Austria*); ECtHR (GC) 29 June 2007, appl.nos. 15809/02 and 25624/02 (*O'Halloran and Francis/UK*).

[85] ECtHR (GC) 13 September 2016, appl.nos. 50541/08, 50571/08, 50573/08, and 40351/09 (*Ibrahim and others/UK*), § 269; ECtHR (GC) 10 March 2009, appl.no. 4378/02 (*Bykov/Russia*), § 92; ECtHR (GC) 29 June 2007, appl.nos. 15809/02 and 25624/02 (*O'Halloran and Francis/UK*), § 55; ECtHR (GC) 11 July 2006, appl.no. 54810/00 (*Jalloh/Germany*), § 117.

In *Jalloh/Germany*, the Court referred to a fourth factor: (4) the weight of the public interest in the investigation and punishment of the offence in issue. However, in subsequent cases, the Court has not reiterated this factor of public interest anymore. Moreover, in *O'Halloran and Francis/UK*, the Grand Chamber discusses its own *Jalloh* judgement, only recalling the first three factors mentioned above:

> In the light of the principles contained in its *Jalloh* judgment, and in order to determine whether the essence of the applicants' right to remain silent and privilege against self-incrimination was infringed, the Court will focus on the nature and degree of compulsion used to obtain the evidence, the existence of any relevant safeguards in the procedure, and the use to which any material so obtained was put.[86]

Although it has been argued that the Court in *O'Halloran and Francis/UK* has played the 'public interest card' implicitly,[87] it appears no central factor in assessing whether the privilege has been violated.[88] This aligns with the Court's central view that:

> The general requirements of fairness contained in Article 6 apply to all criminal proceedings, irrespective of the type of offence at issue. Public-interest concerns cannot justify measures which extinguish the very essence of an applicant's defence rights, including the privilege against self-incrimination guaranteed by Article 6 of the Convention.[89]

The three central factors that are relevant to the determination of a violation are discussed below.

I. Nature and degree of coercion

The Grand Chamber holds that 'not all direct compulsion will destroy the very essence of the privilege against self-incrimination and thus lead to a violation of Article 6'.[90] Meanwhile, the Court is reluctant to define which means of coercion do and which do not violate the privilege.[91]

At least it is clear that the permissible level and means of coercion depend on the kind of evidence that is recovered. When the acquisition of information does

86 ECtHR (GC) 29 June 2007, appl.nos. 15809/02 and 25624/02 (*O'Halloran and Francis/UK*), § 55.

87 Dissenting opinion judge Meyjer under ECtHR (GC) 29 June 2007, appl.nos. 15809/02 and 25624/02 (*O'Halloran and Francis/UK*), point 6. See also Ashworth 2008, p. 763–764. Cf. ECtHR 10 January 2008, appl.no. 58452/00 and 61920/00 (*Lückhof and Spanner/Austria*), § 51–59.

88 This also follows from later cases such as ECtHR (GC) 13 September 2016, appl.nos. 50541/08, 50571/08, 50573/08, and 40351/09 (*Ibrahim and others/UK*), § 269; ECtHR (GC) 10 March 2009, appl.no. 4378/02 (*Bykov/Russia*), § 92; ECtHR 25 June 2013, appl.no. 25333/03 (*Niculescu/Romania*), § 111; ECtHR 1 April 2010, appl.no. 42371/02 (*Pavlenko/Russia*), § 100.

89 ECtHR (GC) 10 March 2009, appl.no. 4378/02 (*Bykov/Russia*), § 93. Also ECtHR (GC) 11 July 2006, appl.no. 54810/00 (*Jalloh/Germany*), § 97. Cf. Ashworth 2007, pp. 720–721.

90 ECtHR (GC) 13 September 2016, appl.nos. 50541/08, 50571/08, 50573/08, and 40351/09 (*Ibrahim and others/UK*), § 269.

91 ECtHR (GC) 8 February 1996, appl.no. 18731/91 (*John Murray/UK*), § 46.

not require the suspect's cooperation, the authorities are allowed to employ more serious means and levels of coercion than when they seek to obtain information that can only be produced by the accused.[92] Let us consider both types of evidence gathering below.

Will-dependent information. Arresting a suspect and eliciting a confession by regular police interrogation during custody will not typically raise an issue under Article 6 ECHR (provided that all fair trial requirements are complied with). Meanwhile, enforcing a confession through physical coercion in breach of Article 3 ECHR will violate the privilege.[93] It is also clear that threatening with and imposing six-month imprisonment with a view of coercing suspects to give testimony (about their movements during particular periods of time) attains a level of coercion that destroys the very essence of the privilege and the right to remain silent.[94] However, in between these clear examples of legitimate versus illicit means of coercion, the area is grey.

For example, threatening with or imposing financial sanctions in the amount of EUR 1,638; EUR 3,599; EUR 4,738; and EUR 33,638, to coerce the applicants to provide information about their financials, has violated the privilege.[95] Meanwhile, in *O'Halloran and Francis/UK*, the applicants were informed that, as registered keepers of their vehicles, they were required to provide the full name and address of the driver at the time that a traffic offence had been registered. Failure to provide the information constituted a criminal offence, threatened with a fine up to EUR 1,446 and disqualification from driving or endorsement of three penalty points on their driving licence. One of the applicants, Mr Francis, refused to give evidence. As a consequence, he was ordered to pay a fine of EUR 1,218 and received three penalty points to his driver licence.[96] According to the Court, the penalties that were threatened with (EUR 1,446) and actually imposed (EUR 1,218) qualified as 'moderate and non-custodial', not destroying the very essence of the right to remain silent and the privilege against self-incrimination.[97] Similarly, threatening with fines up to EUR 2,180 in order to obtain information about the driver's identity did not violate Article 6 ECHR in *Lückhof and Spanner/Austria*.[98]

[92] Meijer & Van Toor 2021, p. 108.

[93] For example, ECtHR 21 April 2011, appl.no. 42310/04 (*Nechiporuk and Yonkalo/Ukraine*), § 260.

[94] ECtHR 21 December 2000, appl.no. 34720/97 (*Heaney and McGuinness/Ireland*), § 55; ECtHR 21 December 2000, appl.no. 36887/97 (*Quinn/Ireland*), § 56. Cf. ECtHR 4 October 2005, appl.no. 6563/03 (*Shannon/UK*).

[95] Respectively ECtHR 25 February 1993, appl.no. 10828/84 (*Funke/France*), § 9–15 and 44; ECtHR 5 April 2012, appl.no. 11663/04 (*Chambaz/Switzerland*), § 9–13, 50–58 and 75; ECtHR 3 May 2001, appl. no. 31827/96 (*J.B./Switzerland*), § 15–21, 65–71; ECtHR 21 April 2009, appl.no. 19235/03 (*Marttinen/Finland*), § 10 and 73.

[96] See also ECtHR 10 January 2008, appl.no. 58452/00 and 61920/00 (*Lückhof and Spanner/Austria*), § 54.

[97] ECtHR (GC) 29 June 2007, appl.nos. 15809/02 and 25624/02 (*O'Halloran and Francis/UK*), § 56–62.

[98] ECtHR 10 January 2008, appl.nos. 58452/00 and 61920/00 (*Lückhof and Spanner/Austria*), § 53–59.

So, whereas the imposition of a EUR 1,638 fine in *Funke* for not providing documents did violate the privilege, threats of imposing fines in the amount of EUR 1,446 and EUR 2,180 to enforce testimony are to be considered 'moderate' and thus acceptable. How should we understand these differences?

First, what seems important is whether the nature and degree of the coercion can reasonably destroy the essence of the privilege. That is, whether the employed coercion *can reasonably break the will of the suspect* not to cooperate in producing evidence. It appears from Strasbourg case-law that custodial sanctions (to obtain will-dependent information) do indeed constitute coercion of such nature and degree. As to financial sanctions, the Court draws a distinction between moderate and non-moderate sanctions. Of these, only the latter seem able to extinguish the essence of the privilege. The implicit argument, it seems, is that moderate financial sanctions do not impose *such a level of pressure* as to break a person's will not to provide evidence. Threats of moderate financial sanctions can reasonably be resisted. They should not necessarily diminish autonomy or elicit false confessions out of fearing the sanctions threatened with. As the Court considered in *Allen/UK*:

> not every measure taken with a view to encouraging individuals to give the authorities information which may be of potential use in later criminal proceedings must be regarded as improper compulsion.[99] The applicant faced the risk of imposition of a penalty of a maximum of GBP 300 if he persisted in refusing to make a declaration of assets, which may be contrasted with the position in the Saunders case, where a two year prison sentence was the maximum penalty.[100]

Apart from the ability of breaking the suspect's will, a second consideration appears relevant. This concerns the *scope and content of the information* that the suspect has to produce. In *O'Halloran and Francis/UK*, the Court argued that a relevant aspect of the employed coercion concerned the 'limited nature of the inquiry'.[101] In this case, the inquiry consisted in threatening with fines up to EUR

99 'Improper compulsion' not in the meaning of the first rationale of the privilege, but in the meaning of whether the nature and degree of the employed pressure are acceptable or 'improper' because able to destroy the essence of the privilege; whether it is able to disrespect the suspect's will in not providing evidence.

100 ECtHR 10 September 2002, appl.no. 76574/01 (*Allen/UK*), p. 5. Cf. Joint dissenting opinion of Judges Hajiyev & Jebens under ECtHR 24 March 2005, appl.no. 63207/00 (*Rieg/Austria*), point 3: 'the degree of compulsion [fine of ± EUR 110 or two days imprisonment] imposed on the applicant was, in our opinion, at a level that actually destroyed the very essence of the right to remain silent and the privilege against self-incrimination. In this respect we would like to note that the applicant had no other choice than either to break her silence and provide possibly incriminating information or to have a fine or term of imprisonment imposed on her for failure to provide such information. There was therefore no way in which the applicant could have avoided to give full information, and still not be penalized'. Cf. ECtHR (GC) 8 February 1996, appl.no. 18731/91 (*John Murray/UK*), § 48.

101 ECtHR 21 December 2000, appl.no. 34720/97 (*Heaney and McGuinness/Ireland*), § 58.

1,446 to obtain the name and address of the car driver. In *Lückhof and Spanner/Austria*, concerning a similar legal obligation under road traffic law, the Court reiterated that:

> the requirement to state a simple fact, namely who the driver of the car was, was not in itself incriminating. Indeed, this distinguishes cases concerning the registered car keeper's obligation to disclose the identity of the driver from other cases, in which the authorities were entitled to seek comprehensive information or to subject the applicants to extensive questioning.[102]

Apparently, imposing financial sanctions, in this case a fine of EUR 2,180, will not violate the privilege when the information the authorities seek to obtain constitutes just a simple fact. Such simple facts should not be considered incriminatory.

However, similar to the 'name and address of the person who was the driver', one could argue that the obligation upon a suspect to provide the 'name of the person who killed the victim' also merely requires to state 'a simple fact'. Yet, no one would deny that such a simple fact – *I killed the victim* – is highly incriminating.[103]

Moreover, the privilege cannot be confined to statements that are directly incriminating. Rather, 'exculpatory remarks or mere information on questions of fact, may be deployed in criminal proceedings in support of the prosecution case, for example to contradict or cast doubt upon other statements of the accused or evidence given by him during the trial, or to otherwise undermine his credibility'.[104]

As it appears, it is hard to align the Court's 'simple-fact-reasoning' in cases concerning road traffic legislation with its more general considerations on the aim and essence of the privilege. Presumably, we should understand this reasoning in light of the specific context of road traffic law.[105] This presumption seems to be confirmed by Court:

> Those who choose to keep and drive motor cars can be taken to have accepted certain responsibilities and obligations as part of the regulatory regime relating to motor vehicles, and in the legal framework of the United Kingdom these responsibilities include the obligation, in the event of suspected commission of road-traffic offences, to inform the authorities of the identity of the driver on that occasion.[106]

102 ECtHR 10 January 2008, appl.nos. 58452/00 and 61920/00 (*Lückhof and Spanner/Austria*), § 55. See also ECtHR 24 March 2005, appl.no. 63207/00 (*Rieg/Austria*), § 31–32.

103 Cf. Ashworth 2008, pp. 771–772.

104 ECtHR (GC) 13 September 2016, appl.nos. 50541/08, 50571/08, 50573/08, and 40351/09 (*Ibrahim and others/UK*), § 268. See also ECtHR (GC) 17 December 1996, appl.no. 19187/91 (*Saunders/UK*), § 71; ECtHR 18 February 2010, appl.no. 39660/02 (*Aleksandr Zaichenko/Russia*), § 54.

105 ECtHR 10 January 2008, appl.nos. 58452/00 and 61920/00 (*Lückhof and Spanner/Austria*), § 53; ECtHR 18 March 2010, appl.no. 13201/05 (*Krumpholz/Austria*), § 36. Cf. Jackson & Summers 2012, p. 274.

106 ECtHR (GC) 29 June 2007, appl.nos. 15809/02 and 25624/02 (*O'Halloran and Francis/UK*), § 57.

In sum, to incite suspects to provide information that requires their cooperation, like a confession, some means of coercion are clearly impermissible. These concern physical coercion and threatening with or imposing custodial sanctions. At the other end of the spectrum, it is clear that regular interrogations in the context of an arrest are acceptable. In between, the area is apparently grey. To determine the permissibility of the nature and degree of coercion in this grey zone, Strasbourg case-law suggests the following criterion: are the negative consequences threatened with or imposed moderate sanctions, or can they reasonably break the subject's will not to provide evidence?

Will-independent information. Normally, the privilege will not apply to information that can be obtained without the suspect's cooperation. For instance, threatening with a twelve-month prison sentence to coerce the applicants to provide breath for a breathalyser test did not even raise an issue under the privilege.[107] Yet not all means of coercion are permitted in such cases. Using excessive force, especially in the form of ill-treatment contrary to Article 3 ECHR, may raise an issue and violate the privilege after all.[108]

II. Procedural safeguards

The Grand Chamber finds it inherent to the privilege and the right to remain silent that any person charged with a criminal offence should have the right to be informed of these rights.[109] Without such information, the guaranteed protection would not be practical and effective.[110] Furthermore, procedural safeguards should exist when the suspect simply does not have neither could have the information the authorities seek to obtain.[111] Examples of such safeguards concern the law preventing from imposing sanctions or providing legal remedies to challenge any sanction imposed for not providing the requested information.[112]

107 ECtHR 15 June 1999, appl.no. 43486/98 (*Tirado Ortiz and Lozano Martin/Spain*).

108 ECtHR (GC) 13 September 2016, appl.nos. 50541/08, 50571/08, 50573/08, and 40351/09 (*Ibrahim and others/UK*), § 267; ECtHR (GC) 11 July 2006, appl.no. 54810/00 (*Jalloh/Germany*), § 118–123. Cf. ECtHR (GC) 1 June 2010, appl.no. 22978/05 (*Gäfgen/Germany*), § 167.

109 Cf. Article 3 of Directive 2012/13/EU, on the right to information in criminal proceedings.

110 ECtHR (GC) 9 November 2018, appl.no. 71409/10 (*Beuze/Belgium*), § 128–130; ECtHR (GC) 13 September 2016, appl.nos. 50541/08, 50571/08, 50573/08, and 40351/09 (*Ibrahim and others/UK*), § 272; ECtHR (GC) 27 November 2008, appl.no. 36391/02 (*Salduz/Turkey*), § 54.

111 Think of the obligation of registered car keepers to provide the name and address of the driver at the time a traffic offence had been registered. If one can show that the car had been stolen at the time of the offence, sanctions should not be imposed. Other examples could concern requests of particular documents, over which the individual has no control, for example, because he is not authorised.

112 ECtHR (GC) 29 June 2007, appl.nos. 15809/02 and 25624/02 (*O'Halloran and Francis/UK*), § 59; ECtHR 21 December 2000, appl.no. 34720/97 (*Heaney and McGuinness/Ireland*), § 51; ECtHR 18 March 2010, appl.no. 13201/05 (*Krumpholz/Austria*), § 36–40.

When the coercive acquisition of information interferes with the applicant's physical integrity, such as taking a blood sample, the Court also takes into account whether the procedure has been employed *lege artis*. In such cases, medical supervision appears a relevant factor.[113] Similarly, regarding the prohibition of ill-treatments under Article 3 ECHR, the Court holds that any forcible medical procedure to obtain evidence should be accompanied by medical supervision, both before and during the procedure.[114]

III. Use of the information

Finally, the way the authorities use the enforced information in the course of a criminal trial is essential.[115] When the information will not be used in the determination of a criminal charge, no issue will arise regarding the privilege.[116] For instance, enforcing a pretrial confession through measures in breach of Article 3 ECHR did not violate the privilege in *Gäfgen/Germany*, because the confession was excluded from evidence.[117] The Court considered that no causal chain existed leading from the prohibited methods of investigation to the applicant's conviction and sentence.[118] When the enforced evidence is not excluded, but is allowed to be used at trial, a violation of Article 6 ECHR is likely to arise.[119] Meanwhile, excluding or simply not using the evidence obtained by means of coercion will not always prevent a violation of Article 6 ECHR. Ultimately, this will depend on whether the criminal proceedings as a whole were fair.[120]

The Court not only takes account of the question of *whether* enforced information has been used in the determination of a criminal charge. Sometimes, it also considers *how* such information contributed to the suspect's conviction and/or

113 ECtHR (GC) 11 July 2006, appl.no. 54810/00 (*Jalloh/Germany*), § 120.

114 See Chapter 3, Section 3.3.3, Factors 4 and 5.

115 ECtHR (GC) 13 September 2016, appl.nos. 50541/08, 50571/08, 50573/08, and 40351/09 (*Ibrahim and others/UK*), § 269; ECtHR (GC) 17 December 1996, appl.no. 19187/91 (*Saunders/UK*), § 71.

116 For example, ECtHR 16 June 2015, appl.no. 784/14 (*Van Weerelt/The Netherlands*), § 60–64; ECtHR 8 April 2004, appl.no. 38544/97 (*Weh/Austria*), § 54; ECtHR 8 April 2003, appl.no. 13881/02 (*King/UK*), pp. 9–10.

117 ECtHR (GC) 1 June 2010, appl.no. 22978/05 (*Gäfgen/Germany*), § 186. The derivative physical evidence was not considered decisive to the ultimate conviction.

118 Ibid., § 179–187.

119 For example, ECtHR 3 May 2001, appl.no. 31827/96 (*J.B./Switzerland*); ECtHR 21 December 2000, appl.no. 34720/97 (*Heaney and McGuinness/Ireland*). Cf. ECtHR (GC) 11 July 2006, appl.no. 54810/00 (*Jalloh/Germany*), § 122: 'allowing the use at the applicant's trial of evidence obtained by the forcible administration of emetics infringed his right not to incriminate himself and *therefore* rendered his trial as a whole unfair. Accordingly, there has been a violation of Article 6 § 1 of the Convention' (emphasis added). See also Pitcher 2018a, pp. 39–40, 52, 58–59, 99; Kuiper 2014, p. 453. Cf. Ölçer 2008, p. 90.

120 ECtHR (GC) 9 November 2018, appl.no. 71409/10 (*Beuze/Belgium*); ECtHR (GC) 13 September 2016, appl.nos. 50541/08, 50571/08, 50573/08, and 40351/09 (*Ibrahim and others/UK*).

sentencing. For example, in *Saunders/UK*, the Court paid attention to the 'extensive use' of the enforced statements. Those statements formed 'a significant part' of the prosecution's case.[121] Meanwhile, in *O'Halloran and Francis/UK*, concerning the specific question of identifying a driver in respect of traffic road offences, the Court argued that 'the identity of the driver is only one element in the offence of speeding, and there is no question of a conviction arising in the underlying proceedings in respect solely of the information obtained'.[122]

Whereas it is clear that the use of enforced evidence at trial will likely raise an issue under the privilege, it is less clear whether the privilege allows the use of enforced evidence to merely induce further criminal investigation, which could eventually lead to a criminal conviction. Case-law on this particular issue is scarce. With caution, the Court seems to suggest that such use of enforced information will not raise an issue under the privilege as long as the evidence is not actually admitted to trial. For example, in the case of *Gäfgen/Germany*, the police had threatened the applicant with the infliction of considerable pain if he did not disclose the whereabouts of an abducted child. In response, the applicant gave testimony that led the authorities to the child's body and some additional real evidence. The domestic court excluded the applicant's statements. The real evidence was, however, admitted to trial. Eventually, the applicant confessed the murder, which confession was central to his conviction. Although the evidence used in this case resulted either directly or indirectly from the enforced pretrial statements, those statements had not been used at trial. The privilege against self-incrimination had not been violated.[123] This suggests that the privilege does not as such prohibit the admission to trial of evidence *derived* from statements obtained through coercion. It suggests that coerced confessions may be used in the criminal investigation, but not at trial.

This suggestion is strengthened by the case of *Saunders/UK*. Saunders had been involved in a business battle to take over another company. In that regard, he had induced people into purchasing shares of his own company in order to maintain or inflate its quoted share price. In response to allegations and rumours, the Department of Trade and Industry appointed specific inspectors to investigate the affair. In this administrative procedure, Saunders was obliged to answer the questions of the inspectors in the course of nine lengthy interviews. Eventually, the transcripts and documents obtained during those interviews were passed on to the police and Saunders was charged with and convicted for various criminal offences. In considering Saunders' complaint about the privilege against self-incrimination, the Court held that the 'sole concern in the present case is with the use made of the

[121] ECtHR (GC) 17 December 1996, appl.no. 19187/91 (*Saunders/UK*), § 71.
[122] ECtHR (GC) 29 June 2007, appl.nos. 15809/02 and 25624/02 (*O'Halloran and Francis/UK*), § 60.
[123] ECtHR (GC) 1 June 2010, appl.no. 22978/05 (*Gäfgen/Germany*), § 186.

relevant statements *at the applicant's criminal trial*'.[124] This suggests that the use of enforced statements to initiate a criminal investigation is not the primary concern of the right against self-incrimination.[125]

6.2.4 *Conclusion*

The right to a fair trial pursuant to Article 6 ECHR encompasses the privilege against self-incrimination. This right protects the will of suspects not to produce self-incriminating information. It aims to (1) protect against improper compulsion, (2) avoid miscarriages of justice, and (3) respect the suspect's autonomy.

In present case-law of the Court, a means-based approach of the privilege appears predominant. In the Strasbourg account, the privilege is applicable when the *coercive acquisition of self-incriminating information requires cooperation of the suspect.* Most common examples are the obligation to produce an oral or written statement, or to submit written documents or other evidence that no one else can deliver.

Meanwhile, in general, the privilege will not apply when the information can also be obtained without cooperation of the suspect, such as a blood sample and tachograph data. As an exception to this rule, sometimes, the privilege could protect against the collection of will-independent information by using excessive force (e.g. in the form of ill-treatment in breach of Article 3 ECHR).

When the privilege applies to a particular means of obtaining evidence, the Court will determine whether the privilege has been violated. That is, whether the authorities have extinguished the very essence of the privilege. In examining this question, the Court has regard to (1) the nature and degree of the employed coercion, (2) the existence of any relevant safeguards in the procedure, and (3) the use of the enforced information.

6.3 COERCIVE FORENSIC BRAIN-READING UNDER THE PRIVILEGE AGAINST SELF-INCRIMINATION

6.3.1 *Introduction*

Could coercive brain-reading be permitted under the privilege against self-incrimination? And if so, under which conditions? These questions are central to the analysis below. Section 6.3.2 examines the applicability of the privilege to each brain-reading technique central to this book. Section 6.3.3 considers whether coercive use of brain-reading would violate the privilege. Section 6.3.4 discusses coercive brain-reading in respect of the privilege's rationales.

[124] ECtHR (GC) 17 December 1996, appl.no. 19187/91 (*Saunders/UK*), § 67 (emphasis added).

[125] A relevant distinction with *Gäfgen/Germany*: Gäfgen was coerced to testify in the determination of a criminal charge; Saunders was obliged to answer questions in an administrative procedure.

6.3.2 *Applicability of the Privilege to Coercive Forensic Brain-Reading*

6.3.2.1 Introduction

The privilege against self-incrimination accrues to anyone charged with a criminal offence in the meaning of Article 6 ECHR.[126] It does not protect against the making of an incriminating statement *per se*, but against the acquisition of evidence via coercion or oppression.[127] In the Strasbourg approach, the privilege normally only applies to means of obtaining evidence that require cooperation of the subject. Altogether, whether the privilege protects against coercive brain-reading in an individual case depends on (1) whether brain-reading is employed in relation to a criminal charge, (2) whether it involves coercion or oppression, and (3) whether it requires cooperation of the subject. The following sections consecutively discuss these factors in respect of brain-reading.

6.3.2.2 Criminal Charge

A 'criminal charge' in the autonomous meaning of the ECHR 'exists from the moment that an individual is officially notified by the competent authority of an allegation that he has committed a criminal offence, or from the point at which his situation has been substantially affected by actions taken by the authorities as a result of a suspicion against him'.[128] Among others, a criminal charge arises if a person is repeatedly being questioned by the police about a particular crime; if the authorities employ coercion to provide information about one's involvement in a crime; and when an individual is arrested on the suspicion of having committed an offence.[129] Subjecting someone to a forensic examination in relation to a criminal offence can also be a relevant factor in assessing whether a criminal charge exists.[130]

The criminal limb of Article 6 ECHR, including the privilege against self-incrimination, does not apply to State actions that do not involve the determination of a criminal charge, such as placing people under 'special police supervision' with the aim of *preventing* crime.[131] Similarly, measures and procedures employed in the

126 ECtHR 25 February 1993, appl.no. 10828/84 (*Funke/France*), § 44.

127 ECtHR (GC) 13 September 2016, appl.nos. 50541/08, 50571/08, 50573/08, and 40351/09 (*Ibrahim and others/UK*), § 267; ECtHR 5 November 2002, appl.no. 48539/99 (*Allan/UK*), § 50.

128 ECtHR (GC) 12 May 2017, appl.no. 21980/04 (*Simeonovi/Bulgaria*), § 110. Also ECtHR (GC) 13 September 2016, appl.nos. 50541/08, 50571/08, 50573/08, and 40351/09 (*Ibrahim and others/UK*), § 249; ECtHR 27 February 1980, appl.no. 6903/75 (*Deweer/Belgium*), § 44.

129 ECtHR 5 October 2017, appl.no. 22059/08 (*Kalēja/Latvia*), § 38–40; ECtHR (GC) 29 June 2007, appl. nos. 15809/02 and 25624/02 (*O'Halloran and Francis/UK*), § 35; ECtHR 21 December 2000, appl.no. 34720/97 (*Heaney and McGuinness/Ireland*), § 42. See also Barkuyzen et al. 2018, pp. 524–526; Harris et al. 2018, pp. 379–381 with further references.

130 ECtHR 8 April 2014, appl.no. 36259/04 (*Blaj/Romania*), § 74.

131 ECtHR (GC) 23 February 2017, appl.no. 43395/09 (*De Tommaso/Italy*), § 143.

context of the *execution* of criminal sanctions, such as penal proceedings regarding prison regimes, conditional release, or amnesty requests, do not involve the determination of a criminal charge.[132] As soon as one has been convicted irrevocably – and the sanction has been fixed definitively[133] – one is no longer *charged* with a criminal offence. The charge has then been determined.[134] However, although no criminal charge may exist when enforcing information, such as in prison, the use of coercively obtained information in subsequent criminal proceedings might raise an issue under the privilege after all.[135]

In sum, coercive brain-reading will only elicit protection from the privilege when the data are used in the determination of a criminal charge. This will be the case when the authorities use brain-reading in examining the subject's guilt (including the search for evidence through police investigation), in assessing criminal responsibility (including the examination of psychiatric and neural disorders), and when imposing criminal sanctions. Coercive brain-reading in the *execution* of criminal sanctions, like in penal procedures, will in most cases exceed the scope of the privilege.

6.3.2.3 Coercion or Oppression

The privilege protects against the acquisition of evidence by 'coercion' or 'oppression'. It is the existence of 'compulsion' that raises an issue under the privilege.[136] Although coercion, oppression, and compulsion are often considered distinctive concepts, the Court seems to use them somewhat interchangeably. As it appears, the Court's main message is that for the privilege to be applicable, at least some level of coercion or pressure is required.[137]

Regarding *coercive* brain-reading, this requirement shall in most cases not give rise to much debate. Both *physical coercion* and making *legal threats* to obtain information clearly constitute a level of coercion that raises an issue under the privilege.[138]

Meanwhile, brain-reading could also be proposed as an *offer*. For example, the authorities could offer a CIT in return for conditional release from pretrial detention. A defendant could accept such an offer by *consenting* to the brain-reading test. In such

[132] ECtHR (GC) 17 September 2009, appl.no. 74912/01 (*Enea/Italy*), § 97; ECtHR 30 October 2003, appl.no. 41576/98 (*Ganci/Italy*), § 20–22; ECtHR (GC) 3 April 2012, appl.no. 37575/04 (*Boulois/Luxembourg*), § 85; EComHR 7 May 1990, appl.no. 16266/90 (*H.A./Austria*); Harris et al. 2018, p. 380.

[133] ECtHR 15 July 1982, appl.no. 8130/78 (*Eckle/Germany*), § 77.

[134] Harris et al. 2018, p. 380.

[135] See, for example, ECtHR (GC) 17 December 1996, appl.no. 19187/91 (*Saunders/UK*). Cf. ECtHR 10 July 2012, appl.no. 29353/06 (*Vidgen/The Netherlands*).

[136] ECtHR (GC) 13 September 2016, appl.nos. 50541/08, 50571/08, 50573/08, and 40351/09 (*Ibrahim and others/UK*), § 267; ECtHR 5 November 2002, appl.no. 48539/99 (*Allan/UK*), § 50.

[137] Jackson & Summers 2012, pp. 252–253.

[138] For example, ECtHR (GC) 11 July 2006, appl.no. 54810/00 (*Jalloh/Germany*), § 113–116; ECtHR (GC) 29 June 2007, appl.nos. 15809/02 and 25624/02 (*O'Halloran and Francis/UK*), § 53.

cases, one could argue that by consensually cooperating in brain-reading, the subject waives his right not to incriminate oneself. Would such an argument be compelling?

The Court holds that neither the letter nor the spirit of Article 6 ECHR prevents individuals from waiving of their own free will, either explicitly or tacitly,[139] the entitlement to the guarantees of a fair trial.[140] Regarding the validity of such a waiver, the Court considers that:

> a waiver must be established in an unequivocal manner and be attended by minimum safeguards commensurate with its importance. A waiver need not be explicit, but it must be voluntary and constitute a knowing and intelligent relinquishment of a right. Before an accused can be said to have implicitly, through his conduct, waived an important right under Article 6, it must be shown that he could reasonably have foreseen what the consequences of his conduct would be. Moreover, the waiver must not run counter to any important public interest.[141]

In addition, it follows from the knowing-and-intelligent-waiver-standard that a suspect should be aware of his right not to incriminate oneself, before he can effectively waive that right. Any person charged with a criminal offence has the right to be notified of the privilege against self-incrimination.[142]

Regarding the case of waiving the privilege by consenting to forensic brain-reading in response to an offer, the most pressing question concerns the *voluntariness* of such a 'waiver'.[143] Can we consider the subject's choice to cooperate in brain-reading voluntary, or should we rather think of him being coerced into (consenting to) the brain-reading test?

We saw that in philosophy,[144] there are basically two positions: (1) offers are never coercive and (2) offers can be coercive sometimes, and if they are they will negate voluntariness and invalidate consent. Relevant considerations to position 2 are power asymmetry, vulnerability, interference by the consent-seeker in the baseline position of the consent-giver, and/or when in fact no other options exist but to consent.

In the context of Article 6 ECHR, the Court seems to sympathise the second approach rather than the first. At least, it accepts that vulnerability and power asymmetry are relevant factors in assessing the validity of a voluntary waiver. In *Panovits/Cyprus*, the Court stressed that:

139 ECtHR 26 January 2017, appl.no. 52009/07 (*Lena Atanasova/Bulgaria*), § 52.

140 ECtHR (GC) 18 December 2018, appl.no. 36658/05 (*Murtazaliyeva/Russia*), § 117; ECtHR (GC) 20 October 2015, appl.no. 25703/11 (*Dvorski/Croatia*), § 100; ECtHR (GC) 1 March 2006, appl.no. 56581/00 (*Sejdovic/Italy*), § 86.

141 ECtHR (GC) 18 December 2018, appl.no. 36658/05 (*Murtazaliyeva/Russia*), § 117. See also ECtHR (GC) 20 October 2015, appl.no. 25703/11 (*Dvorski/Croatia*), § 100.

142 ECtHR (GC) 13 September 2016, appl.nos. 50541/08, 50571/08, 50573/08, and 40351/09 (*Ibrahim and others/UK*), § 272. Cf. ECtHR 18 February 2010, appl.no. 39660/02 (*Aleksandr Zaichenko/Russia*), § 55. See also Trechsel 2005, p. 352; Jackson 2009, p. 860.

143 Cf. Chapter 3, Section 3.3.4, factor 3; Chapter 4, Section 4.3.4.3. See also Knack, Chandler & Fedoroff 2020; Bachmaier 2018; Pugh 2018.

144 Chapter 2, Section 2.7.

> given the *vulnerability* of an accused minor and the *imbalance of power to which he is subjected by the very nature of criminal proceedings*, a waiver by him or on his behalf of an important right under Article 6 can only be accepted where it is expressed in an unequivocal manner after the authorities have taken all reasonable steps to ensure that he or she is fully aware of his rights of defence and can appreciate, as far as possible, the consequence of his conduct.[145]

The issue of indirect pressure due to power asymmetry in criminal justice was also essential in the case of *Allan/UK*. This case concerned the use of a cellmate informant in order to elicit incriminating information from the accused applicant, who had earlier invoked the right to remain silent during police interrogations. The Court stressed that the right to remain silent and the privilege against self-incrimination serve in principle to protect the freedom of the accused to choose whether to speak or to remain silent when questioned by the police. This freedom, the Court continues, is not confined to cases where the will of the accused has been *directly* overborne in some way. Instead, the protected freedom of choice can also be effectively undermined when the authorities use subterfuge to elicit self-incriminating statements.[146] The Court considered that the applicant has been:

> subjected to psychological pressures which impinged on the 'voluntariness' of the disclosures allegedly made by the applicant to H. [the informant]: he was a suspect in a murder case, in detention and under direct pressure from the police in interrogations about the murder, and would have been susceptible to persuasion to take H., with whom he shared a cell for some weeks, into his confidence. In those circumstances, the information gained by the use of H. in this way may be regarded as having been obtained in defiance of the will of the applicant and its use at trial impinged on the applicant's right to silence and privilege against self-incrimination.[147]

The authorities in this case did not use any physical coercion or legal threats. Still, the psychological pressure that partly arose from detention and the criminal proceedings as such did affect the voluntariness of the accused's statements.[148]

[145] ECtHR 11 December 2008, appl.no. 4268/04 (*Panovits/Cyprus*), § 68 (emphasis added). See also Aall 2011, p. 253. Cf. ECtHR 18 February 2010, appl.no. 39660/02 (*Aleksandr Zaichenko/Russia*), § 55; ECtHR 10 June 2021, appl.no. 2833/13 (*Bajić/North Macedonia*), § 72.

[146] ECtHR 5 November 2002, appl.no. 48539/99 (*Allan/UK*), § 50.

[147] Ibid., § 52. Cf. ECtHR (GC) 10 March 2009, appl.no. 4378/02 (*Bykov/Russia*), § 102: 'Unlike the applicant in the Allan case, the applicant was not detained on remand but was at liberty on his own premises attended by security and other personnel. (…) In other words, the applicant was free to see V. and to talk to him, or to refuse to do so. (…) Thus, the Court is not convinced that the obtaining of evidence was tainted with the element of coercion or oppression which in the Allan case the Court found to amount to a breach of the applicant's right to remain silent'. Cf. ECtHR 14 October 2010, appl.no. 1466/07 (*Brusco/France*), § 52–55. See also Aall 2011, p. 253.

[148] Cf. Jackson & Summers 2012, pp. 55–56; Choo 2013, p. 80; Dennis 1995, p. 350.

This idea, that the privilege not only protects from *direct* but also from *indirect* pressure, finds its origin in the case of *John Murray/UK*. In this earlier case, the Grand Chamber had to consider the permissibility of drawing adverse inferences from a suspect's silence. It argued that a legal system that allows the drawing of adverse inferences, when taken in conjunction with the weight of the case against the accused, 'involves a certain level of indirect compulsion'.[149] Such indirect pressure can raise an issue under the privilege against self-incrimination.[150]

In the same vein, informing an accused that adverse inferences may be drawn from his refusal to cooperate in brain-reading will entail a certain level of indirect pressure. As will the notification that such refusal could obstruct the possibilities of conditional release. Suppose, for instance, that the authorities *offer* an accused in pretrial detention to participate in brain-based diagnostics. They explain that if the accused cooperates during the test, he would increase his chances of conditional release. Meanwhile, refusal is likely to reduce those chances to zero. It is clear that such an offer entails a certain level of pressure, especially when taken into account the imbalance of power in criminal proceedings and the vulnerable position of people in pretrial detention. Strasbourg case-law seems to allow for arguing that offers like these could exert some level of indirect pressure and could therefore negate the voluntariness of the accused's choice to cooperate in brain-reading.[151]

Whether the Court would consider a specific 'brain-reading offer' coercive remains hard to predict. At least, case-law shows that any claim regarding the absence of coercion calls for a critical analysis of the subject's voluntariness. In this respect, the imbalance of power and the subject's vulnerability are relevant factors.[152]

6.3.2.4 Cooperation of the Subject

Finally, the applicability of the privilege will depend on whether the acquisition of brain-reading data *requires cooperation* of the subject. In order to assess whether the subject's cooperation is needed to obtain the relevant information, we should first determine which information should exactly be central to our analysis. There are three possibilities, respectively focussing on (1) the brain features that are identified by the neuroimaging assessment (brain activity and anatomy), (2) the ultimate results of the test (such as the recognition of a gun or a predisposition to aggressive behaviour), or (3) both.[153]

[149] ECtHR (GC) 8 February 1996, appl.no. 18731/91 (*John Murray/UK*), § 49–50. Also ECtHR 6 June 2000, appl.no. 36408/97 (*Averill/UK*), § 48.

[150] See also Pitcher 2018a, p. 36, footnote 109; Jackson & Summers 2012, p. 253.

[151] Similarly, when determining the validity of consent under Articles 3 and 8 ECHR, the Court takes into account the vulnerability of people deprived of their liberty. See Chapter 3, Section 3.3.4, factor 3 and Chapter 4, Section 4.3.4.2.

[152] Cf. Jackson & Summers 2012, pp. 267, 276.

[153] These positions can lead to different normative conclusions. Cf. Shen 2013.

The Strasbourg case-law suggests the second approach (yet some authors follow option 3, as will be discussed below). When assessing whether evidence can be obtained independently of the will of the suspect, the Court focusses on the ultimate information the authorities seek to obtain, rather than on the source of the information. Although obtaining breath and urine in the context of a non-consensual alcohol and drug test requires cooperation of the individual, the Court qualifies such means of obtaining evidence as 'independent of the will of the suspect'. As previously discussed,[154] this can be explained as follows. In the context of alcohol and drug testing, breath and urine are only one of the sources of the ultimate information the authorities seek to obtain. They contain blood alcohol content and drug metabolites. Unlike breath and urine, blood alcohol content and drug metabolites can also be obtained without cooperation of the suspect – independently of one's will – by taking blood, saliva, or pulling out a hair. Although obtaining breath and urine as one of the sources of the essential information requires cooperation, the central information the authorities seek to recover can also be yielded without any cooperation whatsoever. Therefore, the collection of such evidence exceeds the scope of the privilege.

In the course of forensic brain-reading, the relevant information the authorities seek to obtain concerns the person's mental states and content, emotional traits, and neural or mental disorders. The mere identification of the person's brain features – brain activity and brain anatomy – will often be meaningless.[155] Rather, those brain features function as a source from which the essential information can be derived. They provide the rough data that enable the authorities to draw inferences about particular mental content or about emotional or mental traits. If one would like to draw an analogy, brain features would be akin to breath and urine; the identified mental content to blood alcohol content and the presence of drug metabolites.

Considering the CIT, Van Toor follows a different approach. In determining whether the privilege applies, Van Toor includes *both* biological brain features, which he calls the 'biological trace', and the ultimate test results regarding mental content, the 'cognitive trace'.[156] Van Toor qualifies the cognitive trace (recognition of an object) as 'testimonial evidence' and the biological trace (the P300 signal) as 'physical evidence'.[157] For reasons set out below, the analysis in this section will not follow a similar approach.

Van Toor's argument appears to be inspired by US literature on the permissibility of coercive brain-reading in light of the self-incrimination clause pursuant to the Fifth Amendment.[158] In that debate, focussing on the US legal system, some scholars

[154] Section 6.2.2.
[155] Exceptions do exist, such as the identification of a brain tumour.
[156] Meijer & Van Toor 2021, p. 111; Van Toor 2017, pp. 433–437.
[157] Meijer & Van Toor 2021, p. 115; Van Toor 2017, p. 116.
[158] Stating that 'No person shall be held to answer for a capital, or otherwise infamous crime (…) nor shall be compelled in any criminal case to be a witness against himself'.

consider the information yielded through brain-reading to be hybrid. On the one hand, these techniques yield information about physical processes in (blood vessels of) the brain – qualifying as *physical evidence*. On the other hand, they also enable the authorities to acquire information about mental content, such as recognition, knowledge, and emotions – qualifying as *testimonial evidence*.[159]

The reason that some authors qualify brain-reading data as hybrid, originates from US case-law and doctrine on the self-incrimination clause. This right only applies to 'testimonial communications', not to 'physical evidence'.[160] When information should exactly qualify as 'testimonial' is open to debate. According to one of the advocated approaches, information is testimonial *if it relates to mental content*. That is, if the information reveals the content of a person's cognition. In this view, information is testimonial when it discloses knowledge, thoughts, memories, motivations, or emotions.[161]

Within that particular approach of the US self-incrimination clause, it is conceived possible to argue that information is on the one hand physical, because it relates to, for example, haemodynamics in the brain, while on the other hand it is testimonial, since it reveals mental content like the recognition of a particular pistol. Following this line of reasoning, brain-reading data yielded through lie detecting and CITs can be considered physical by nature, but testimonial for their content.[162] As long as brain-reading does not reveal any mental content whatsoever, but, for example, only detects the activity of a brain area for the purpose of diagnosing a disorder, both nature and content of the yielded data qualify as physical. Such data fall outside the scope of the self-incrimination clause pursuant to the Fifth Amendment – regardless of whether cooperation of the subject is required to obtain the information.[163]

However, unlike US case-law, the ECtHR does not use a physical-or-testimonial-criterion to determine the applicability of the privilege against self-incrimination. Whether coercively obtained information is either physical, testimonial, or hybrid is not decisive in Strasbourg case-law. Instead, as of *Saunders/UK*, the applicability of the privilege mainly depends on whether obtaining evidence *requires cooperation* of the suspect. Besides, one of the rationales of the privilege against self-incrimination lies in avoiding miscarriages of justice.[164] The specific approach of the US self-incrimination clause considered above explicitly rejects this rationale.[165]

[159] Van Toor 2017, pp. 435–436 refers to Farahany 2012a and Fox 2009. See also Pardo & Patterson 2015, p. 161; Kilbride & Iuliano 2015, pp. 177–178 and 186; Pustilnik 2012, p. 10; Morse 2012, p. 167; Holloway 2008, p. 166; Pardo 2006, pp. 331–332. See also Meijer & Van Toor 2021, pp. 112–113.

[160] *Fisher* v. *United States*, 425 U.S. 391 (1976); *Schmerber* v. *California*, 384 U.S. 757 (1966). For an exhaustive discussion, see Allen & Mace 2004.

[161] Allen & Mace 2004, pp. 266–277; Pardo & Patterson 2015, pp. 164–167.

[162] Pardo & Patterson 2015, pp. 161–162.

[163] Ibid., p. 169; Morse 2012, pp. 170.

[164] See Section 6.2.2.

[165] Allen & Mace 2004, pp. 264–266; Pardo & Patterson 2015, pp. 172–173.

In sum, unlike the case-law and doctrine on the Fifth Amendment, the Strasbourg approach of the privilege under Article 6 ECHR does not refer to 'testimonial' or 'physical' evidence. Therefore, there are no convincing reasons to consider brain-reading evidence 'physical' on the one hand while 'testimonial' on the other hand. Accordingly, there is no reason to examine whether the privilege will apply to *both* physical brain features and to the ultimate test results about mental content (approach 3). Instead, as explained above, we should determine whether the acquisition of the ultimate information about mental content, behavioural and mental traits *requires cooperation* of the subject (approach 2). If not, the privilege shall normally not apply to the brain-reading test.

Finally, it is important to reiterate that the privilege does not pertain to the imposition of sanctions for providing *false* information, nor to the drawing of adverse inferences from untrue statements. Above we discussed the case of *Allen/UK*,[166] where the applicant provided the tax authorities with false information and was therefore convicted for 'cheating the public revenue of income tax and corporation tax'. The Court held that the privilege against self-incrimination does not entail a general immunity to actions motivated by the desire to evade investigation.[167]

The applicant in *Allen/UK* cheated by providing false information about his taxes. In the course of brain-reading, one can cheat by deploying countermeasures. However, to a certain extent, such countermeasures can be identified.[168] As Rosenfeld et al. note, information about the subject's attempted manipulation could provide additional evidence of a subject's involvement in a crime.[169] If it appears that a suspect has tried to manipulate the test results, the authorities could draw adverse inferences from this. Moreover, when detectable, the use of countermeasures can be threatened with adverse legal consequences.

Drawing adverse inferences from countermeasures and threatening countermeasure use with sanctions will most likely exceed the scope of the privilege. After all, the privilege cannot be interpreted as giving a general immunity to actions motivated by the intention to lie, cheat, or evade criminal investigation.

In conclusion, the privilege protects against the coercive acquisition of information in the determination of a criminal charge. It does not typically apply when the information sought can also be obtained independently of the will of the suspect. Thus, we must determine (1) whether completing a brain-reading test requires cooperation of the subject, and (2) whether the mental content, behavioural or mental traits that the test seeks to identify could also be obtained through other means that do not require the subject's cooperation. Below, we will consider the four brain-reading applications central in this book.

[166] See Section 6.2.2.
[167] ECtHR 10 September 2002, appl.no. 76574/01 (*Allen/UK*), p. 5.
[168] Rosenfeld et al. 2013, p. 121; Ambach & Gamer 2018, p. 27.
[169] Rosenfeld et al. 2013, p. 121.

BRAIN-BASED LIE DETECTION. Brain-based lie detection requires active participation of the subject. He must *observe* each presented question and answer it in a yes-or-no fashion.[170] In order to accomplish the test successfully, the subject should furthermore refrain from manipulating the test by using countermeasures.[171] Therefore, determining whether a person lies through brain-based lie detection requires cooperation from the subject.

Could the authorities also obtain information about arguable deceptive mental content without the subject's cooperation? This may well depend on the exact lie the authorities aim to identify. Imagine a defendant who argues not having been near the crime scene during the day of the offence. Instead, he was visiting his parents on the other side of the country. Suppose that CCTV records show the suspect walking around close to the crime scene on the day of the offence. Those records allow the authorities to infer that the defendant is lying. This will not require any cooperation of the suspect whatsoever. Similarly, footprints, fingerprints, DNA, bank accounts, and witness testimonies sometimes provide very valuable information indicative for a person's deceptiveness. Meanwhile, they do not actually reveal the individual's deceptive mental properties.

Lie detection will normally only add value to the determination of a criminal charge when no other means exist that enable the authorities to verify the truthfulness of the accused's statements. The use of brain-based lie detection shall usually be limited to such cases. When no other means exist to identify the subject's truthful or deceptive mental content in response to particular questions, the privilege will be applicable to coercive brain-based lie detection.

P300-BASED CONCEALED INFORMATION TEST. A P300-based CIT detects a brain wave that occurs *automatically* in 300 to 800 milliseconds after observing a meaningful stimulus. Therefore, some have argued that the subject cannot control the information the test seeks to yield, similar to the acquisition of fingerprints and blood samples.[172] Accordingly, the acquisition of P300 responses has been considered not to require the subject's cooperation.[173]

This argument, however, ignores three essential features of the P300-based CIT. First, a CIT requires the subject to visually *observe* each presented stimulus. This requires some form of cooperation. Still, one could argue that a CIT can also be applied with auditorily presented stimuli,[174] and, at least in theory, even when the

170 See Chapter 2, Section 2.2.2. Cf. Shen 2013, p. 704; Nugent 2012b, p. 293; Greely & Wagner 2011, p. 791; Holley 2009, p. 20; Holloway 2008, p. 167.

171 Cf. Holley 2009, p. 20.

172 Meixner Jr. 2018, p. 424; Hurd 2012, pp. 237–238; Greely & Wagner 2011, pp. 791–792; Holley 2009, p. 20.

173 Stoller & Wolpe 2007, pp. 368–369; Thompson 2007, p. 347; Van Toor 2017, p. 433.

174 Van Toor 2017, p. 433.

subject is asleep.[175] However, apart from the fact that *visual* CITs appear most accurate,[176] it is hard to imagine how an auditory test can be effective in the context of criminal law.

Suppose that the police subject a defendant, accused of murder, to a CIT. They aim to examine whether the defendant recognises the murder weapon: a 'Glock G44 .22LR 4.02 inch'. It is relatively easy to visually present a picture of this pistol within a set of images of comparable pistols. Meanwhile, it is hard to envisage how such relevant and irrelevant items could be presented auditorily – requiring a detailed description of each pistol. Apart from the question of whether an offender is actually aware of the precise brand and type of the pistol he has used, it is not clear whether such a detailed and fine-grained auditory presentation of stimuli would enable the accurate identification of recognition. Clearly, this would be even more complex when the murder weapon consists of a regular bread knife or claw hammer, many of which look like each other very much.[177] In sum, when applied with visual stimuli, a CIT will require cooperation on the part of the subject.[178]

Second, the subject should not merely observe the presented stimuli. She must observe them *attentively*.[179] One must stay focussed to the test. This requires active participation.[180] Moreover, certain test paradigms aim to realise attentive participation through requiring the subject to *press* a button after observing particular stimuli.[181] These features of the test provide further evidence for the fact that cooperation is required.

Third, the subject can *manipulate* the test by deploying countermeasures. To be clear, one cannot *supress* P300 when recognising relevant items (i.e. 'probes', such as the murder weapon). The P300 will occur automatically. Because the subject cannot prevent the occurrence of P300 in response to relevant items, Van Toor holds that the CIT works in fact independently of the subject's will.[182]

However, while a subject cannot suppress the P300, she can deliberately create additional brain activity (P300) in response to the irrelevant stimuli that she does not recognise.[183] An effective strategy is to recall emotional memories when observing the irrelevant items. When using techniques like these successfully, the test will

[175] Meijer & Van Toor 2021.

[176] Rosenfeld et al. 2015a; Van der Cruyssen et al. 2021. See also Rosenfeld et al. 2015b; Ambach et al. 2010, p. 266.

[177] This might be different in case of an extraordinary murder weapon, such as a pink pistol or purple bread knife.

[178] See also Chapter 2, Section 2.3.2.

[179] Picton 1992, p. 456.

[180] Cf. Shen 2013, p. 704; Nugent 2012b, p. 293; Greely & Wagner 2011, p. 791; Holley 2009, p. 20; Holloway 2008, p. 167.

[181] Meixner & Rosenfeld 2014, p. 1997; Rosenfeld et al. 2013, p. 120; Farwell, Richardson & Richardson 2013, p. 268.

[182] Van Toor 2017, p. 433.

[183] See Chapter 2, Section 2.3.2.

show similar P300 amplitudes to all stimuli. Consequently, it is no longer possible to identify the stimulus that evoked the 'real' P300 signal. The measurement is therefore effectively distorted. As Meixner and Rosenfeld put it:

> Thus, when a guilty subject performs a countermeasure to an irrelevant item, he creates a large P300 in response to that item. Because the primary statistical comparison of the CIT is between probe and irrelevant items, as irrelevant P300 amplitude increases, accuracy decreases.[184]

Prior to assessing the implications of such countermeasures in light of the privilege, we must identify with great precision which information a CIT aims to yield: (1) the P300 reaction in response to the relevant stimuli (the actual murder weapon, etc.), or (2) the interrelationship between the P300 reactions to relevant and irrelevant items?

As the quotation of Meixner and Rosenfeld clearly shows, the CIT is not merely concerned with individual P300 amplitudes in relation to the relevant stimuli. Rather, this test is about statistically *comparing* the P300 responses to relevant items with the responses to irrelevant items. The difference between the subject's P300 reactions to the actual murder weapon and to other irrelevant pistols is crucial here.[185] Not cooperating by using countermeasures in respect of irrelevant stimuli will disturb the essential measurements. As Kraphol highlights, the final piece to a successful CIT is whether the examinee *cooperates* with the testing process; whether the guilty subject could engage in countermeasures that will affect the results.[186]

In conclusion, a P300-based CIT requires cooperation. To date, we cannot determine whether a person recognises specific stimuli through other means that do not involve cooperation of the subject. Therefore, the privilege is applicable to P300-based CITs.

Advances in the neural representation of real-time thoughts might affect this conclusion. In the future, it may become possible to detect real-time thoughts while no external input is required (such as presenting the murder weapon). And perhaps, such 'next-step' brain-reading could allow for identifying memories or knowledge *without any task performed by the subject*. However, similar to present brain-reading applications, it might well be that the neural identification of real-time thoughts will only be effective when the subject refrains from countermeasures.

BRAIN-BASED DIAGNOSTICS AND NEUROPREDICTION. Brain-based diagnostics and neuroprediction can be used with either functional or structural neuroimaging. *Structural* neuroimaging (visualising brain anatomy) does, in general, not require cooperation of the subject. One should just lie in the scanner, without making any movements that frustrate the scan results. In fact, this can be achieved without

[184] Meixner & Rosenfeld 2010, p. 57.

[185] Meixner & Rosenfeld 2014, p. 6; Verschuere & Meijer 2014, p. 164. See also Chapter 2, Section 2.3.2.

[186] Kraphol 2011, p. 160 (emphasis added). Cf. Verschuere & Meijer 2014, p. 166.

any form of cooperation, for example, by means of chemical restraint. If physical coercion is actually employed, the means and level of force could possibly elicit protection under the privilege after all, especially when such gives rise to an issue under Article 3 ECHR.[187]

Regarding diagnostics and neuroprediction with *functional* neuroimaging, the level of required cooperation will much depend on the aim of the examination.[188] For example, PET and SPECT can be used to detect *structural* brain anomalies, such as a brain tumour and particular forms of dementia. Apart from lying in the scanner calmly, which can also be realised through administering sedatives, such use of PET and SPECT does not require the subject's cooperation, similar to structural neuroimaging. In the course of PET and SPECT, the injection of contrast agent is required, but this can also be realised without the subject's cooperation. Accordingly, the privilege will normally not cover these types of brain-reading.

Depending on the design of the test, functional neuroimaging can also be performed to examine brain activity while the subject performs a *task*. Clearly, such task-based neuroimaging requires active cooperation of the subject.[189] Some brain-reading tests examine brain activity in a state of rest, for instance with the aim of increasing the accuracy of risk assessment.[190] Although such resting-state imaging does not require active cooperation (there is no task to be performed), it does require passive cooperation: the subject has to lie in the scanner calmly, keeping his brain in a state of rest, and refraining from any mental or physical actions that will frustrate the imaging results. This is also a task. Although passive, such resting-state brain-reading *does require* cooperation of the subject.[191]

The mental characteristics that functional neuroimaging aim to identify in the course of diagnostics or prediction, such as aggressive traits or emotional deficits, cannot normally be disclosed by other means, which do not require the subject's participation. These types of neuroimaging will in general be covered by the privilege.

Interestingly, following a *material*-based approach of the privilege could possibly lead to different conclusions concerning functional neuroimaging in order to identify brain activity, either resting-state or task-based. In a material-based understanding, the privilege applies to *particular types of information*, rather than to certain means of obtaining evidence. Within such an approach, the exception formulated in *Saunders/UK*[192] comes down to the following rule: the privilege does not cover

[187] Cf. ECtHR (GC) 11 July 2006, appl.no. 54810/00 (*Jalloh/Germany*); ECtHR (GC) 13 September 2016, appl.nos. 50541/08, 50571/08, 50573/08 and 40351/09 (*Ibrahim and others/UK*), § 267. See also Chapter 3, Section 3.3.4.

[188] Chapter 2, Section 2.4.2.

[189] Ibid. Cf. Shen 2013, p. 704.

[190] For example, Delfin et al. 2019.

[191] Chapter 2, Section 2.4.2.

[192] Discussed in Section 6.2.2.

information that exists independently of the will of the suspect, such as DNA and fingerprints.[193] Does the existence of a brain disorder or an emotional trait depend on what a defendant wishes?

Clearly, it does not. In the course of diagnostics and neuroprediction, the subject cannot undo the existence of the information about the mental characteristics the test aims to identify. These brain-reading applications aim to yield information about the inactivity of the person's prefrontal cortex,[194] increased amygdala response,[195] or the activity of the anterior cingulate cortex that is elicited by a simple task.[196] Such information allows for drawing inferences about the individual's mental properties, like emotional deficits, aggressive traits, or sexual proclivities.

Mental features like these *exist* – whether the subject likes it or not. People just have certain behavioural traits or emotional characteristics. The existence of such mental properties does not depend on the will of the individual, similar to DNA. Therefore, in a material-based understanding, the privilege is not likely to apply to functional neuroimaging in the context of diagnostics and neuroprediction, regardless the fact that the test requires cooperation of the subject.

Still, in a material-based approach, one could possibly argue that the authorities might not always be certain about what they are looking for, going on a 'fishing expedition' in the subject's brain. Perhaps, sometimes, this could elicit protection under the privilege after all. For example, in case-law of the Dutch Supreme Court, which has been considered predominantly material-based,[197] fishing expeditions may sometimes elicit protection from the privilege, regardless of whether the evidence exists independently the subject's will.[198] Such protection could be triggered, for instance, when the authorities oblige a person to provide a bunch of unspecified, potentially self-incriminating, but pre-existing documents.[199] In such cases, so the argument goes, providing the documents can be equated with a *confession* to which the privilege applies: 'yes, indeed, I do have documents containing incriminating information'.[200]

Rusconi and Mitchener-Nissen have warned against 'fishing trips' by the police through the use of brain-reading technologies.[201] Similarly, Pardo does not exclude the risk of 'mental fishing expeditions'.[202] As Nugent argues:

193 Van Toor 2016; Ligthart 2019c.
194 For example, Glenn & Raine 2014, p. 56.
195 For example, Blair 2010.
196 For example, Aharoni et al. 2013.
197 Pivaty, Ter Vrugt & De Vocht 2021, p. 4; Ligthart 2019c; Van Toor 2016.
198 In the Strasbourg approach, the privilege will apply to such fishing expeditions if they require cooperation of the suspect: ECtHR 25 February 1993, appl.no. 10828/84 (*Funke/France*), § 44; ECtHR 3 May 2001, appl.no. 31827/96 (*J.B./Switzerland*), § 69.
199 *HR* 24 April 2015, *NJ* 2015/265, m.nt. Zwemmer, para. 4.3.3; *HR* 24 April 2015, ECLI:NL:HR:2015:1129, para. 3.7.3.
200 Stevens 2005, p. 136; Van Toor 2017, p. 423; Corstens/Borgers & Kooijmans 2021, p. 372–373.
201 Rusconi & Mitchener-Nissen 2013, p. 8.
202 Pardo 2006, p. 327. Cf. Morse 2004, p. 188.

> a defense counsel that objects to the use of neuroimaging techniques on its client also might argue that the prosecution is constitutionally precluded from going on an 'expedition' into the defendant's brain to search for any neurological anomalies that are statistically connected to the *mens rea* or *actus reus* (the 'criminal act') at issue, particularly if the prosecution would not be able to, as the Fourth Amendment requires, 'particularly describ[e] the place to be searched' within the brain.[203]

However, arguing that brain-based diagnostics and neuroprediction may well qualify as a mental fishing expedition is not convincing. Admittedly, in most cases, the authorities will not be familiar with the precise structure and activity of a person's brain. Still, they will be quite sure about the existence, approximate shape, and general functioning of the brain of the subject. Moreover, science teaches us that different parts of the brain are involved in different mental states and emotions. The only thing that may be unclear prior to diagnostic or predictive brain-reading concerns the exact brain responses and the precise information about mental properties that can be inferred from the brain-derived data. In the same vein, although the police will not be familiar with a suspect's fingerprint, DNA profile, or blood type, they do know that such material exists and where to find it. Similar to determining an individual's DNA profile, the identification of specific mental capacities with brain-based diagnostics and neuroprediction can hardly qualify as a 'fishing expedition'. Hence, using these tests with coercion shall normally exceed the scope of the privilege in a material-based approach (as opposed to the means-based approach, discussed above).

6.3.2.5 Synthesis

The privilege against self-incrimination protects against the use of direct and indirect coercion to obtain information from an individual charged with a criminal offence. Coercive brain-reading in the *execution* of criminal sanctions – without a criminal charge – will normally exceed the scope of the privilege.[204]

Coercive brain-reading in the determination of the subject's guilt, in the assessment of criminal responsibility, and/or in the imposition of criminal sanctions can raise questions under the privilege. Whether such brain-reading will indeed raise an issue depends on the exact means of recovering brain-derived information; it depends on whether obtaining the information requires cooperation of the subject. Therefore, we must carefully consider the specific features of the test.

The privilege is applicable to coercive brain-based lie detection, CITs, and to brain-based diagnostics and neuroprediction through the detection of brain activity. The privilege will not typically apply to diagnostics and neuroprediction through visualising structural brain features, except when excessive means of coercion will be used.

[203] Nugent 2012b, p. 294.

[204] Though Articles 3, 8, and 10 ECHR do offer legal protection in this regard: see Chapters 3, 4, and 5.

6.3.3 *Violating the Privilege?*

In determining whether the privilege has been violated, the Court has regard to (1) the nature and degree of the coercion, (2) the existence of any relevant safeguards in the procedure, and (3) how the information has been used.[205] This section discusses these factors with regard to coercive brain-reading. The analysis in this section focusses on those brain-reading applications to which the privilege applies – that is, determining a criminal charge with the use of lie detection, CITs, and brain-based diagnostics and neuroprediction through the identification of brain activity.

I. Nature and Degree of Coercion

Regarding brain-based lie detection, CITs, and brain-based diagnostics and neuroprediction through the detection of brain activity, the use of *physical coercion* will be ineffective. The reason is that these tests require participation of the subject. Meanwhile, making legal *threats* or *offering* brain-reading could involve an effective incentive for the subject to participate in these brain-reading tests.[206] Whether such direct or indirect volitional coercion will be able to destroy the very essence of the privilege will depend on the degree of the coercion used. Could it reasonably break the subject's will not to cooperate in the brain-reading test?

Threatening with imprisonment to enforce the production of self-incriminating evidence is likely to violate the privilege.[207] This should be a relevant consideration too regarding offers to which any refusal *de facto* results into (extended) custody. Threatening with and actually imposing non-custodial and moderate financial sanctions, such as a fine up to EUR 1,446,[208] will not necessarily extinguish the essence of the privilege.[209] Neither will various forms of *indirect* pressure, such as warning the accused that adverse inferences may be drawn from any refusal to cooperate in a brain-reading test.[210]

As yet, the Court has not developed a well-defined generic approach on which degrees of coercion are acceptable and which are not.[211] Therefore, current case-law does not provide much guidance in determining whether particular threats or offers

[205] See Section 6.2.3.

[206] See also Chapter 2, Section 2.7.

[207] See, for example, ECtHR 21 December 2000, appl.no. 34720/97 (*Heaney and McGuinness/Ireland*), § 55; ECtHR 21 December 2000, appl.no. 36887/97 (*Quinn/Ireland*), § 56.

[208] Threatening with such moderate sanctions is not likely to be effective if the ultimate sanctions to be imposed for the criminal offence are non-moderate, such as imprisonment or commitment to a forensic healthcare institution.

[209] ECtHR (GC) 29 June 2007, appl.nos. 15809/02 and 25624/02 (*O'Halloran and Francis/UK*), § 56–62.

[210] Cf. ECtHR (GC) 8 February 1996, appl.no. 18731/91 (*John Murray/UK*); ECtHR 6 June 2000, appl. no. 36408/97 (*Averill/UK*).

[211] ECtHR (GC) 8 February 1996, appl.no. 18731/91 (*John Murray/UK*), § 46; Corstens/Borgers & Kooijmans 2021, p. 373.

are permissible to enforce brain-reading.[212] As long as the Court refrains from providing further clarification on this issue, we should assess in each case whether (1) the employed pressure has reasonably breached the will of the subject not to cooperate in the brain-reading assessment,[213] or (2) could have done so, but the subject resisted the exerted pressured and has therefore been sanctioned (either directly or indirectly).[214] When applying this criterion, we should not only focus on the means of coercion or oppression but also take into account the imbalance of power and the level of vulnerability to which suspects are subjected by the very nature of criminal proceedings and, in some cases, through custody.[215]

II. Procedural Safeguards

Any suspect who is about to participate in forensic brain-reading must be informed about his right not to incriminate oneself, especially where access to a lawyer is delayed. In addition, since brain-reading interferes with the subject's physical integrity,[216] the Court can take into account whether the procedure has been employed *lege artis* and whether a medical specialist has been involved.[217] Earlier, we saw that medical supervision is also relevant in light of Article 3 ECHR.[218]

Strasbourg case-law further suggests that procedural safeguards should exist when the suspect simply has not and could not have the information the authorities seek to obtain. In such cases, the law could exclude the imposition of sanctions for not providing the requested information.[219] Regarding brain-reading, this will not be essential. Sanctions are most likely be imposed for refusing cooperation, rather than for claiming not to have the information the authorises seek to obtain. Whether the subject 'has' the information or not will be determined by the test itself.

III. Use of the Information

Finally, whether coercive brain-reading will violate the privilege will depend on how the data will be used in the criminal proceedings against the subject. Violations can be avoided when the results are excluded as evidence from trial.[220]

[212] Cf. Jackson & Summers 2012, p. 253.

[213] Cf. ECtHR (GC) 17 December 1996, appl.no. 19187/91 (*Saunders/UK*); ECtHR 5 November 2002, appl.no. 48539/99 (*Allan/UK*); ECtHR 27 April 2004, appl.no. 21413/02 (*Kansal/UK*).

[214] Cf. ECtHR 21 April 2009, appl.no. 19235/03 (*Marttinen/Finland*); ECtHR 3 May 2001, appl.no. 31827/96 (*J.B./Switzerland*); ECtHR 21 December 2000, appl.no. 34720/97 (*Heaney and McGuinness/Ireland*).

[215] See Section 6.3.2.3.

[216] See also Chapter 4, Section 4.3.4.2.

[217] See also Cf. ECtHR (GC) 11 July 2006, appl.no. 54810/00 (*Jalloh/Germany*), § 120.

[218] Chapter 3, Section 3.3.4, factor 4 and 5.

[219] ECtHR (GC) 29 June 2007, appl.nos. 15809/02 and 25624/02 (*O'Halloran and Francis/UK*), § 59; ECtHR 21 December 2000, appl.no. 34720/97 (*Heaney and McGuinness/Ireland*), § 51.

[220] Cf. ECtHR (GC) 1 June 2010, appl.no. 22978/05 (*Gäfgen/Germany*), § 186; ECtHR 16 June 2015, appl. no. 784/14 (*Van Weerelt/The Netherlands*), § 60–64.

When brain-reading data do contribute to the subject's conviction and/or sentencing, a violation of the privilege is likely to occur.[221] Especially when the data are put to extensive use or form a significant part of the ultimate prosecution.[222]

In some cases, brain-reading data may only relate to mere questions of fact or peripheral details – such as whether the subject has ever stolen something before, or whether he recognises the car of one of the employees of the robbed jewellery. Although such information may not immediately seem incriminating, its use at trial could result in a violation of the privilege. The privilege cannot be confined to information that is directly incriminating. This is because *prima facie* non-incriminating information – such as exculpatory remarks and mere information about questions of fact – might also be used to support the prosecution case. Such information can contradict or cast doubt upon other statements of the accused or otherwise undermine his credibility.[223]

In conclusion, a violation of the privilege is likely to arise when the coercively obtained brain-reading data are used in the determination of a criminal charge against the subject. Both physical coercion and threatening with imprisonment will be unacceptable. Threatening with non-custodial and moderate sanctions, or making certain offers, shall not always necessarily destroy the essence of the privilege, but could sometimes be permissible when accompanied with sufficient procedural safeguards. The ultimate judgement on whether Article 6 ECHR has been respected will depend on whether the criminal proceedings as a whole were fair.[224]

6.3.4 *The Privilege's Rationales*

There is a reason behind the right against self-incrimination. As discussed, there are in fact three reasons, which are to some extent intertwined and relate to the values of human dignity and human freedom as the central notions underlying the Convention.[225] The three rationales of the privilege concern (1) the protection of the accused against improper compulsion, (2) avoiding miscarriages of justice, and (3) respecting the suspect's autonomy. This section looks at coercive brain-reading in light of the rationales of the privilege. As will be argued, two of the three rationales do not appear relevant regarding the brain-reading technologies we discussed. We focus on those types of coercive brain-reading to which the privilege will, in general,

[221] See, for example, ECtHR 21 December 2000, appl.no. 34720/97 (*Heaney and McGuinness/Ireland*); ECtHR 21 December 2000, appl.no. 36887/97 (*Quinn/Ireland*); ECtHR 3 May 2001, appl.no. 31827/96 (*J.B./Switzerland*).

[222] See, for example, ECtHR (GC) 17 December 1996, appl.no. 19187/91 (*Saunders/UK*), § 71. Cf. ECtHR (GC) 29 June 2007, appl.nos. 15809/02 and 25624/02 (*O'Halloran and Francis/UK*), § 60.

[223] ECtHR (GC) 17 December 1996, appl.no. 19187/91 (*Saunders/UK*), § 71.

[224] ECtHR (GC) 9 November 2018, appl.no. 71409/10 (*Beuze/Belgium*); ECtHR (GC) 13 September 2016, appl.nos. 50541/08, 50571/08, 50573/08, and 40351/09 (*Ibrahim and others/UK*). See also Chapter 7.

[225] See Section 6.2.2.

be applicable: brain-based lie detection, CITs, and brain-based diagnostics and neuroprediction through the detection brain activity.

Rationale 1. Preventing improper compulsion

Physical coercion will be ineffective as far as brain-reading requires cooperation of the subject.[226] For these techniques, States should probably resort to the use of volitional coercion: either legal threats or offers. Making such threats and offers to enforce participation will not typically involve serious physical or mental harm. In fact, deploying such forms of direct and indirect pressure is very common and often considered lawful in the context of criminal proceedings. Similar levels of coercion are used regarding defendants in day-to-day criminal practices, for instance, to yield a blood sample for DNA testing,[227] to provide breath,[228] and, to some extent, even as an incentive to testify about a person's involvement in a criminal offence (such as police custody).[229] Moreover, functional neuroimaging is considered safe. fMRI and EEG are commonly used in research on brain-reading. Both are not physically invasive. Usually, they do not pose any risks to the subject's health.[230] PET and SPECT involve injection of radioactive contrast agent, constituting a minor interference with the subject's body.[231]

Employing these technologies with volitional coercion is unlikely to amount to 'improper compulsion' in the sense of the first rationale. As discussed,[232] this rationale relates to human dignity and the prohibition of torture and ill-treatment. Employing physical force to people deprived of their liberty, while such force was not strictly necessary in view of the person's own conduct, diminishes human dignity, and violates the prohibition of ill-treatment pursuant to Article 3 ECHR.[233] The right against self-incrimination delegitimises the use of harmful methods to enforce self-incriminating evidence. However, enforcing brain-reading through legal threats or offers will in most cases be harmless. At least it will not entail any level of force that even comes close to degrading or inhuman treatment, being capable of diminishing human dignity. Volitionally coerced brain-reading clearly differs from threatening with and/or imposing physical pain – such as using the thumbscrew and the rack, in whose abolition the idea of the privilege is thought to find its historical roots.[234] It clearly differs from enforcing regurgitation in order to obtain evidence,

[226] See also Chapter 2, Section 2.7.2.
[227] For example, ECtHR 4 June 2013, appl.nos. 7841/08 and 57900/12 (*Peruzzo/Germany and Martens/Germany*).
[228] For example, ECtHR 15 June 1999, appl.no. 43486/98 (*Tirado Ortiz and Lozano Martin/Spain*).
[229] Cf. Corstens/Borgers & Kooijmans 2021, p. 317.
[230] Chapter 2, Section 2.2.2.
[231] See also Chapter 4, Section 4.3.4.3.
[232] See Section 6.2.2.
[233] For example, ECtHR 3 May 2012, appl.no. 23880/05 (*Salikhov/Russia*), § 78.
[234] Levy 1968, pp. 33, 326–327; Waldron 2005, p. 1731; Alschuler 1997, pp. 190–192.

which raised an issue regarding the first rationale in *Jalloh*.[235] As such, in respect of brain-reading, the first rationale seems not immediately relevant.

Can we conceive the obligation to either participate in brain-reading or otherwise suffer adverse consequences to be harmful in another way? Perhaps, psychologically? Arguing from human dignity, some authors have tried to justify the privilege by claiming that it is somehow inhuman or 'cruel' to confront defendants with the following trilemma: provide the authorities with self-incriminating evidence, be sanctioned for refusing cooperation, or lie and commit perjury.[236] However, this rationale of 'cruel choices' is not convincing.[237] As Judges Martens and Kuris argue in *Saunders/UK*:

> Such 'rationales' cannot justify the immunities under discussion since they obviously presuppose that the suspect is guilty, for an innocent suspect would not be subjected to such choices nor bring about his own ruin by answering questions truthfully! Innocent suspects are, therefore, not treated cruelly or unethically, whilst guilty suspects should not complain that society does not allow them to escape conviction by refusing to answer questions or otherwise hiding evidence.[238]

In the same vein, Bentham has argued that the rationale of cruel choices only serves guilty suspects.[239] Yet, guilty suspects should not complain when they must answer questions or give evidence. According to Bentham, the claim of facing guilty suspects with cruel choices is an 'old woman's reason'.[240] Perhaps, confronting defendants with such choices is harsh, at most.[241] Yet, hardly anyone would object to such harshness when something as important as prosecuting and preventing crime is at stake.[242] In criminal law, we often do 'harsh' things to facilitate criminal prosecution.[243] We deprive suspects of their liberty and send them to pretrial detention. We accept body cavity searches. And we allow law enforcement officials to shave a suspect's hair when such pursues the interest of the criminal investigation.[244]

[235] ECtHR (GC) 11 July 2006, appl.no. 54810/00 (*Jalloh/Germany*).

[236] Redmayne 2007, p. 221; O'Brien 1978, pp. 43–45; Van Toor 2017, p. 382. Examples of authors who endorse this cruel choices rationale are Greenawalt 1981, p. 39; Koops 2000, pp. 44–45.

[237] Redmayne 2007, pp. 221–224; Jackson & Summers 2012, pp. 268–270.

[238] Judges Martens and Kuris under ECtHR (GC) 17 December 1996, appl.no. 19187/91 (*Saunders/UK*), point 4, fn. 4.

[239] Bentham 1978, p. 238.

[240] Ibid., p. 230.

[241] Ibid: 'Hard it is upon a man, it must be confessed, to be obliged to do anything that he does not like. That he should not much like to do what is meant by his criminating himself, is natural enough; for what it leads to, is, his being punished. What is not less hard upon him, is, that he should be punished. (…) Whatever hardship there is in a man's being punished, that, and no more, is there in his thus being made to criminate himself'.

[242] Ibid., pp. 230–231. See also Redmayne 2007, p. 221.

[243] Redmayne 2007, p. 221. Think also of civil cases, where people may be obliged to disclose information that will lead to the deprivation of parental authority.

[244] Article 61a Dutch Code of Criminal Procedure.

In response, proponents of the cruel choice rationale may argue that the level of harshness of these examples is much lower compared with coercing a suspect to give evidence against himself, facilitating his own conviction and self-imposing criminal sanctions. In this view, the 'cruelty' lies not so much in the trilemma a guilty suspect faces, but rather in imposing a standard of conduct that runs counter to the basic human instinct of self-preservation.[245] In other words: it is cruel or even inhuman to coerce people into dragging themselves into prison by giving testimony at trial, or to punish them for not doing so.

However, this argument is even less compelling. It is not merely limited to *guilty* suspects, but it only pertains to *guilty* suspects who have committed a *serious offence*. Only they can talk themselves into prison or towards other severe criminal sanctions by being coerced to tell the truth. Consider a defendant who has stolen one bottle of beer, therefore risking a EUR 150 fine. It is very hard to imagine how being obliged to tell the truth – or otherwise be punished – runs counter to the defendant's basic human instinct of self-preservation. It is hard to conceive how such an obligation is cruel and diminishes human dignity.[246]

In conclusion, neuroimaging technologies are generally safe. The use of volitional coercion in this regard will not even come close to inhuman or degrading treatment. It will not cause any psychical or psychological harm as to diminish human dignity. Therefore, the first rationale of the privilege does not appear relevant regarding coercive brain-reading.[247] At least, not regarding the brain-reading applications that will normally be covered by the privilege: lie detection, CITs, and diagnosing brain anomalies and neuroprediction by detecting brain activity.[248]

Rationale 2. Avoiding miscarriages of justice

It might be clear that coercing defendants to testify through an oral or written statement could increase the risk of *unreliable testimonies* and thus of miscarriages of justice, that is, wrongful convictions. This is, to say the least, less clear regarding coercive brain-reading. If a person is threatened, for instance with non-moderate financial sanctions or with (extended) custody, that person may lie just to please the interrogator and to avoid adverse consequences.[249] This could well result in

[245] Dolinko 1986, p. 1095; Redmayne 2007, pp. 224–226; Corstes/Kooijmans & Borgers 2021, p. 316.

[246] Examples from Strasbourg case-law where human dignity had been at stake concerned non-consensual sterilisation under Article 3 ECHR and racial violence under Article 8 ECHR: ECtHR 8 November 2011, appl.no. 18968/07 (*V.C./Slovakia*), § 106–120; ECtHR 6 July 2005, appl.nos. 43577/98, and 43579/98 (*Nachova and Others/Bulgaria*), § 145.

[247] This could be different when threats or coercive offers could impose long periods of deprivation of a person's liberty.

[248] Cf. Van Toor 2017, p. 432 et seq.

[249] Cf. ECtHR 12 January 2012, appl.no. 8139/09 (*Othman (Abu Qatada)/UK*), § 264: 'Indeed, experience has all too often shown that the victim of torture will say anything – true or not – as the shortest method of freeing himself from the torment of torture'.

wrongful convictions. However, the risk of giving false information does not seem to be increased by the use of brain-reading. Rather, these technologies will *reduce* the risk of unreliable testimonies.

Valid and accurate brain-reading provides an *objective* assessment of the person's subjective mental states. In principle, this technology could be a very helpful tool to *circumvent* the individual's possibility to lie and deceive, thus decreasing the risk of false statements.[250] Brain-reading tests such as lie detection and, to some extent, CITs explicitly aim to *verify the reliability* of people's statements. And brain-based diagnostics and neuroprediction aim to *improve the accuracy* of forensic assessments.[251] As a consequence, unlike coercing defendants to testify, obliging them to participate in brain-reading may rather *improve reliability* and therefore help avoid miscarriages of justice.[252] Therefore, the second rationale does not appear relevant in respect of brain-reading.[253]

Admittedly, the use of countermeasures by the subject could manipulate the test results. However, such countermeasures, if successful, will *benefit* the subject (help him to hide the truth), rather than facilitate his wrongful conviction. They aim to *conceal* the actual recognition of the murder weapon or to *obstruct* the identification of a neural anomaly in order to *avoid* criminal sanctions. In some cases, countermeasures may prevent a guilty subject from being convicted. Would such a 'wrongful *acquittal*' affect the second rationale? Probably not. In the meaning of the ECHR, 'miscarriage of justice' refers to cases where someone has been convicted by a final decision for a crime that he did not commit. It refers to 'wrongful *convictions*'.[254] Avoiding wrongful *acquittals* – ensuring guilty suspects of being convicted – seems not to align with the nature of the privilege: protecting the accused against the State by providing defence rights. Indeed, convicting and sentencing guilty defendants responds to the public interest of punishing and preventing crime. However, such considerations about public interest are not central to the privilege against self-incrimination.[255]

In addition, countermeasure use is, to some extent, detectable. Although countermeasures could manipulate the reliability of the test, the authorities will at least be able to identify the manipulation and act upon it accordingly, for example

[250] Meynen 2020; Ligthart, Kooijmans & Meynen 2021a, p. 124.

[251] See, for example, Delfin et al. 2019; Zijlmans 2021.

[252] Cf. Ferrua 2020, p. 404. Presumably, this advantage of brain-reading will only increase when the technology further develops and accuracy rates improve. Of course, the accuracy of these technologies will not be 100 per cent, but on average, they should have a positive value concerning truth finding, otherwise they should not be allowed in the criminal justice process.

[253] Cf. Van Toor 2017, p. 375.

[254] Harris et al. 2018, pp. 961–962; Flinterman 2018; Explanatory Report to Article 3, Protocol No. 7 to the ECHR, paras. 22–23. Cf. ECtHR 8 February 2011, appl.no. 35863/10 (*Judge/UK*); ECtHR (GC) 13 September 2016, appl.nos. 50541/08, 50571/08, 50573/08, and 40351/09 (*Ibrahim and others/UK*), § 255, 267. In contrast: ECtHR 23 October 2018, appl.no. 26892/12 (*Wanner/Germany*), § 43.

[255] ECtHR (GC) 10 March 2009, appl.no. 4378/02 (*Bykov/Russia*), § 93.

by excluding the test results from trial (as opposed to, for example, lying during police interrogation). Altogether, the second rationale will not apply to coercive brain-reading.

Rationale 3. Autonomy

The third rationale does apply to brain-reading technology. Clearly, *coercing* someone to participate in a brain-reading assessment restricts the subject's autonomy in choosing a preferred defence strategy. Similarly, the imposition of sanctions for refusing cooperation too will disrespect the subject's autonomous choice in how to defend himself.[256]

In conclusion, the first and second rationales do not appear relevant to coercive brain-reading in criminal law. In fact, brain-reading even aims to increase the reliability of evidence. In that way, it will contribute to *avoiding* miscarriages of justice, contributing to one of the rationales the Court attaches to the privilege. If we are to proscribe coercive brain-reading under the privilege, we can only rely on the third rationale: respecting the subject's autonomy.

Would the autonomy rationale alone be sufficient to support the right against self-incrimination in view of brain-reading? Or, would this right be seriously weakened as far as coercive brain-reading is concerned? These questions relate to the broader issue about the sustainability of the privilege's foundations in view of emerging technology.[257] I will delve into these questions in Chapter 8, when discussing the challenges coercive brain-reading poses for European human rights law.

6.4 CONCLUSION

This chapter examined the legal implications of coercive brain-reading in light of the privilege against self-incrimination pursuant to Article 6 ECHR. At a foundational level, this right aims to prevent the use of improper compulsion by law enforcements authorities, avoiding miscarriages of justice, and to respect the suspect's autonomy.

The privilege only applies in relation to a criminal charge. It usually not covers the employment of brain-reading in the *execution of criminal sanctions*. In the Strasbourg approach, the privilege applies to certain means of obtaining information. It only protects means that require cooperation of the subject, while no other means are available to bypass the person's participation. Therefore, in most cases, the privilege will not protect against coercive brain-based diagnostics and

[256] Perhaps, technological developments might change this view. If it will be possible in the future to read out real-time thoughts without considerable participation of the subject, one's will not to *provide* incriminating mental content could potentially be bypassed, similar to, for example, structural brain-reading.

[257] Ligthart & Meynen 2021.

neuroprediction through the detection of *structural* brain features. Such brain-reading can be accomplished without any cooperation of the subject.

The privilege will apply to coercive brain-based lie detection, CITs, and brain-based diagnostics and neuroprediction through the identification of brain activity. These tests require cooperation. Whether these types of coercive brain-reading will *violate* the privilege shall depend on the nature and degree of the employed pressure, the existence of any relevant safeguards in the procedure, and on the use of the information.

We also looked at the foundations of the right against self-incrimination in light of brain-reading technology. As it turned out, the first and second rationales of the privilege do not appear relevant to coercive brain-reading in criminal law. Therefore, proscribing coercive brain-reading under the privilege can only be grounded on the third rationale: respecting the subject's autonomy.

7

Procedural Implications of Brain-Reading in Breach of the ECHR: Excluding Unlawfully Obtained Evidence?

Article 6 ECHR

7.1 INTRODUCTION

When brain-reading in the determination of a criminal charge violates one of the rights and freedoms discussed in the previous chapters, Article 6 ECHR could impose procedural obligations to the State.[1] The present chapter aims to determine these procedural implications. It examines whether 'unlawful' brain-reading raises fundamental questions regarding the right to a fair trial, focussing on the exclusion of unlawfully obtained evidence.

This chapter proceeds as follows. Section 7.2 discusses the Court's approach to excluding evidence obtained in breach of the Convention in light of Article 6 ECHR. Section 7.3 examines whether brain-reading evidence obtained in breach of the Convention should be excluded from evidence to preserve trial fairness. Section 7.4 draws conclusions.

7.2 UNLAWFULLY OBTAINED EVIDENCE AND THE RIGHT TO A FAIR TRIAL (ARTICLE 6 ECHR)

7.2.1 *Introduction*

Routinely, the Grand Chamber of the European Court of Human Rights (ECtHR) remarks that the Court's only duty under Article 19 ECHR is to ensure the

[1] When brain-reading is used for other purposes than the determination of a 'criminal charge', such as neuroprediction in penal procedures, Article 6 ECHR will not normally apply. In those cases, procedural implications of Convention violations will largely follow from the general requirement of States to guarantee an effective remedy (in terms of Article 13 ECHR) before a national authority in respect of arguable claims of such violations. See Chapter 8, Section 8.4.3. On Article 13 ECHR see Pitcher 2018a, p. 65 et seq; Barkhuysen & Van Emmerik 2018; Harris et al. 2018, Ch. 16; Rainey, McCormick & Ovey 2021, Ch. 7.

observance of the engagements undertaken by the member States. In particular, the Court considers itself

> not competent to deal with an application alleging that errors of law or fact have been committed by domestic courts, except where it considers that such errors might have involved a possible violation of any of the rights and freedoms set out in the Convention. While Article 6 guarantees the right to a fair hearing, it does not lay down any rules on the admissibility of evidence as such, which is primarily a matter for regulation under national law.[2]

As the Court continues, it is not its role to determine, as a matter of principle, whether particular types of evidence – such as unlawfully obtained evidence – are admissible in criminal proceedings. The question to be answered by the Court is whether the proceedings as a whole, including the obtaining of evidence, were fair. This involves an examination of the unlawfulness in question and, where a violation of another Convention right is concerned, of the nature of that violation.[3]

Whether the use of evidence obtained in breach of the ECHR renders the trial unfair in an individual case may well depend on the nature of the violated right at issue.[4] The present Strasbourg approach on excluding unlawfully obtained evidence is limited to evidence obtained in breach of Articles 6, 8, and 3 ECHR. Therefore, the analysis in this section focusses on the three central though diverging lines in Strasbourg case-law concerning the use of evidence obtained in breach of (1) the suspect's defence rights under Article 6 ECHR, (2) the rights and freedoms guaranteed by Article 8 ECHR, and (3) the prohibition of ill-treatment pursuant to Article 3 ECHR. Meanwhile, introducing coercive brain-reading in criminal law could possibly give rise to complaints about evidence gathering in breach of Article 9 or 10 ECHR.[5] Therefore, Section 7.3 explores whether the Court's current position to violations of Articles 6, 8, and 3 ECHR provides helpful directions for developing similar approaches in respect of Articles 9 and 10 ECHR.

7.2.2 *Evidence Obtained in Breach of Article 6 ECHR: The Privilege against Self-incrimination*

Article 6(1) ECHR guarantees to anyone charged with a criminal offence the right to a 'fair hearing'. Unlike the other guarantees enshrined in this provision, the right

2 ECtHR (GC) 17 October 2019, appl.nos. 1874/13 and 8567/13 (*López Ribalda and Others/Spain*), § 149; ECtHR (GC) 1 June 2010, appl.no. 22978/05 (*Gäfgen/Germany*), § 162; ECtHR (GC) 10 March 2009, appl.no. 4378/02 (*Bykov/Russia*), § 88.

3 ECtHR (GC) 17 October 2019, appl.nos. 1874/13 and 8567/13 (*López Ribalda and Others/Spain*), § 150; ECtHR (GC) 1 June 2010, appl.no. 22978/05 (*Gäfgen/Germany*), § 163; ECtHR (GC) 10 March 2009, appl.no. 4378/02 (*Bykov/Russia*), § 89.

4 See, for example, ECtHR (GC) 11 July 2006, appl.no. 54810/00 (*Jalloh/Germany*), § 99, stating that different considerations apply to evidence recovered by measures in breach of Article 3 ECHR, compared with Article 8 ECHR. See also Harris et al. 2018, p. 420; Pitcher 2018a, p. 59.

5 See Chapter 5, Sections 5.3.3 and 5.4.3.

to a fair hearing has an 'open-ended, residual quality'.[6] It allows for adding specific rights not explicitly enshrined in Article 6 ECHR but essential to a fair trial, such as the privilege against self-incrimination. In determining whether the right to a fair trial has been respected, the Court follows a holistic approach. It evaluates the *overall fairness* of the criminal proceedings.

But what exactly constitutes a 'fair trial'? This cannot be captured by one single rule. It depends on the circumstances of the particular case.[7] Consequently, compliance with the requirements of a fair trial must be examined in each individual case, having regard to the development of the proceedings as a whole – not on the basis of an isolated consideration of one particular aspect or one particular incident.[8]

In assessing the overall fairness of the criminal process, the Court takes into account, if appropriate, the minimum rights listed in Article 6(3) ECHR. These rights exemplify the requirements of a fair trial in respect of typical procedural situations in criminal cases.[9] Those minimum rights, meanwhile, are not ends in themselves: their intrinsic aim is to contribute to ensuring the fairness of the criminal proceedings as a whole.[10]

In accordance with these general considerations, the Court has developed various approaches regarding the use at trial of evidence obtained in defiance of different rights under Article 6 ECHR. Think of Strasbourg case-law on the use of confessions obtained during police interrogation without prior access to a lawyer[11] and of the admission of evidence secured by entrapment.[12] On several occasions, the Court has also dealt with the admission of evidence obtained in breach of the privilege against self-incrimination. As this book addresses the legal implications of the privilege for the use of brain-reading, this section is confined to the admissibility of evidence obtained in breach of the privilege.

The privilege against self-incrimination is not an absolute right. Not just any coercive measure taken with a view of encouraging the accused to produce

6 Harris et al. 2018, pp. 410–411.

7 ECtHR (GC) 9 November 2018, appl.no. 71409/10 (*Beuze/Belgium*), § 120; ECtHR (GC) 13 September 2016, appl.nos. 50541/08, 50571/08, 50573/08, and 40351/09 (*Ibrahim and others/UK*), § 250. See also Barkhuysen et al. 2018, pp. 561–562; Rainey, McCormick & Ovey 2021, p. 295.

8 ECtHR (GC) 9 November 2018, appl.no. 71409/10 (*Beuze/Belgium*), § 120–121; ECtHR (GC) 13 September 2016, appl.nos. 50541/08, 50571/08, 50573/08, and 40351/09 (*Ibrahim and others/UK*), § 250–151.

9 ECtHR (GC) 9 November 2018, appl.no. 71409/10 (*Beuze/Belgium*), § 122; ECtHR (GC) 13 September 2016, appl.nos. 50541/08, 50571/08, 50573/08, and 40351/09 (*Ibrahim and others/UK*), § 251.

10 Ibid.

11 See, for example, ECtHR (GC) 27 November 2008, appl.no. 36391/02 (*Salduz/Turkey*); ECtHR (GC) 13 September 2016, appl.nos. 50541/08, 50571/08, 50573/08, and 40351/09 (*Ibrahim and others/UK*); ECtHR (GC) 9 November 2018, appl.no. 71409/10 (*Beuze/Belgium*); Pitcher 2018a, pp. 30–34; Harris et al. 2018, pp. 473–482.

12 See, for example, ECtHR 9 June 1998, appl.no. 44/1997/828/1034 (*Teixeira de Castro/Portugal*); ECtHR (GC) 5 February 2008, appl.no. 74420/01 (*Ramanauskas/Lithuania*); ECtHR 2 October 2012, appl.nos. 23200/10, 24009/07, and 556/10 (*Veselov and Others/Russia*); Pitcher 2018a, pp. 44–48; Harris et al. 2018, pp. 428–430.

self-incriminating evidence will always violate the privilege.[13] However, if the use of certain evidence violates the privilege against self-incrimination, it will therefore render the criminal proceedings as a whole unfair.[14] As the Grand Chamber concludes in *Jalloh/Germany*, 'allowing the use at the applicant's trial of evidence obtained by the forcible administration of emetics infringed his right not to incriminate himself and *therefore* rendered his trial as a whole unfair. Accordingly, there has been a violation of Article 6 § 1 of the Convention'.[15] This conclusion – that the admission of evidence obtained in breach of the privilege will therefore render the trial as a whole unfair – is hardly surprising. The Court deduces the privilege directly from the right to a fair trial: together with the right to remain silent, the privilege 'lies at the heart' of the notion of a fair procedure pursuant to Article 6(1) ECHR.[16]

7.2.3 *Evidence Obtained in Breach of Article* 8 *ECHR*

A breach of Article 8 ECHR will not automatically render the trial unfair under Article 6 ECHR. The birth of this approach is to be found in the case of *Khan/UK*.[17] There, Article 8 ECHR had been violated because the use of a covered listening device was not sufficiently regulated by domestic law. Regarding Article 6 ECHR, the applicant complained that the use as sole evidence in his case of the information obtained in breach of Article 8 ECHR was incompatible with the requirements of a 'fair hearing'. Here, the Court built upon the case of *Schenk/Switzerland*, where the use of a recorded telephone conversation obtained in breach of *domestic law* had not violated Article 6 ECHR.[18] In reaching that conclusion, the Court considered that the applicant had ample opportunity to challenging the authenticity and the use of the recording. It 'attached weight' to the fact that the recording was not the only evidence on which the conviction was based.[19]

As in *Schenk*, the Court stresses in *Khan* that its only duty under Article 19 ECHR is to ensure the observance of the engagements undertaken by the member States.

[13] Chapter 6, Section 6.2.3. See, for example, ECtHR (GC) 13 September 2016, appl.nos. 50541/08, 50571/08, 50573/08, and 40351/09 (*Ibrahim and others/UK*), § 269; ECtHR (GC) 29 June 2007, appl. nos. 15809/02 and 25624/02 (*O'Halloran and Francis/UK*).

[14] Pitcher 2018a, pp. 39–40, 52, 58–59, 99; Kuiper 2014, p. 453. Cf. Ölçer 2008, p. 90.

[15] ECtHR (GC) 11 July 2006, appl.no. 54810/00 (*Jalloh/Germany*), § 122 (emphasis added). See also: ECtHR 4 October 2005, appl.no. 6563/03 (*Shannon/UK*), § 41; ECtHR 5 November 2002, appl.no. 48539/99 (*Allan/UK*), § 52–53; ECtHR (GC) 17 December 1996, appl.no. 19187/91 (*Saunders/UK*), § 76, 80–81.

[16] ECtHR (GC) 13 September 2016, appl.nos. 50541/08, 50571/08, 50573/08, and 40351/09 (*Ibrahim and others/UK*), § 266; ECtHR (GC) 1 June 2010, appl.no. 22978/05 (*Gäfgen/Germany*), § 168.

[17] ECtHR 12 May 2000, appl.no. 5394/97 (*Khan/UK*).

[18] ECtHR 12 July 1988, appl.no. 10862/84 (*Schenk/Switzerland*). Cf. ECtHR 22 September 2015, appl.no. 16184/06 (*Niţulescu/Romania*) and, by contrast, ECtHR 25 February 2010, appl.no. 20100/06 (*Lisica/Croatia*).

[19] ECtHR 12 July 1988, appl.no. 10862/84 (*Schenk/Switzerland*), § 39–49.

Although Article 6 ECHR guarantees the right to a fair hearing, it does not lay down any rules on the admissibility of evidence as such. This is primarily a matter for regulation under national law. It is not the role of the Court to determine, as a matter of principle, whether particular types of evidence – such as evidence obtained in breach of the law – are admissible or not. The question that must be answered, the Court reiterates, is whether the proceedings as a whole, including the way in which the evidence was obtained, were fair. This involves an examination of the unlawfulness in question and, where a violation of another Convention right is concerned, the nature of the violation found.[20]

As to the unlawfulness, the Court notes that, unlike in the case of *Schenk*, obtaining the recordings was not in breach with *domestic* law (since no domestic legal basis existed). The unlawfulness in *Khan* exclusively related to the fact that the interference with private life was not 'in accordance with the law' as Article 8(2) ECHR requires.[21] Next, the Court noted that the contested evidence was in fact the sole evidence in this case. It argued that the relevance of this observation depends on the circumstances of the individual case: 'In the present circumstances, where the tape recording was acknowledged to be very strong evidence, and where there was no risk of it being unreliable, the need for supporting evidence is correspondingly weaker'.[22]

Ultimately, the Court answered the central question of whether the proceedings as a whole were fair in the affirmative: in all instances, the domestic courts assessed the effects of admitting the unlawfully obtained evidence on the overall fairness of the trial. The fact that the applicant's arguments appeared unsuccessful makes no difference. In addition, the Court considers that if the domestic courts would have found the admission of the evidence to render the trial unfair, they would have had a discretion to exclude that evidence based on domestic law. Altogether, the use of evidence obtained in breach of Article 8 ECHR did not violate the right to a fair trial pursuant to Article 6 ECHR.[23]

Following a similar line of reasoning in *P.G. and J.H./UK*, the Court argued that the admission of voice recordings obtained in breach of Article 8 ECHR did not violate the right to a fair trial pursuant to Article 6 ECHR.[24] Again, the Court considered that the 'unlawfulness' related exclusively to the fact that the infringement of Article 8(1) ECHR was not 'in accordance with the law'.[25] Yet, unlike the case of *Khan*, the contested evidence was not the only evidence against the applicants. What both cases did have in common, concerned the fact that the applicants had ample *opportunity to challenge* both the authenticity and the use of the recordings.

[20] ECtHR 12 May 2000, appl.no. 5394/97 (*Khan/UK*), § 34.

[21] Ibid., § 36.

[22] Ibid., § 37. See also ECtHR 3 March 2016, appl.no. 7215/10 (*Prade/Germany*), § 40; ECtHR 31 October 2017, appl.no. 22767/08 (*Dragoş Ioan Rusu/Romania*), § 54.

[23] ECtHR 12 May 2000, appl.no. 5394/97 (*Khan/UK*), § 38–40.

[24] ECtHR 25 September 2001, appl.no. 44787/98 (*P.G. and J.H./UK*), § 76–81.

[25] Ibid., § 78. Cf. ECtHR (GC) 10 March 2009, appl.no. 4378/02 (*Bykov/Russia*), § 91.

Although the applicants were unsuccessful in their arguments, the domestic courts would have had the discretion to exclude the evidence if such were necessary to preserve the fairness of the trial.[26]

After reiterating these considerations in *Allan/UK*,[27] the Grand Chamber explicitly recognised them as 'general principles' in *Jalloh/Germany*. In examining the fairness of the proceedings as a whole, which involves an examination of the unlawfulness in question and the nature of the violation of the Convention right in question, regard must be had to whether a person's defence rights have been respected.

> It must be examined in particular whether the applicant was given the opportunity of challenging the authenticity of the evidence and of opposing its use. In addition, the quality of the evidence must be taken into consideration, including whether the circumstances in which it was obtained cast doubts on its reliability or accuracy. While no problem of fairness necessarily arises where the evidence obtained was unsupported by other material, it may be noted that where the evidence is very strong and there is no risk of its being unreliable, the need for supporting evidence is correspondingly weaker.[28]

To determine the overall fairness of the criminal proceedings, the weight of the public interest in investigating and punishing the criminal offence can be taken into consideration as well. The public interest can be weighed against the individual's interest that the evidence against him will be gathered lawfully.[29] Meanwhile, the Court stresses that considerations of public interest cannot justify measures that extinguish the very essence of the applicant's defence rights, including the privilege against self-incrimination.[30]

In later cases, the Grand Chamber has not reiterated its considerations on public interest as a general principle.[31] Yet, it did play an explicit role in the case of *Prade/Germany*.[32] A search warrant had been issued with respect to the applicant's home on suspicion of an intellectual property crime. Although the police found none of the items they were searching for, they did coincidentally find 463.73 grams of hashish,

[26] ECtHR 25 September 2001, appl.no. 44787/98 (*P.G. and J.H./UK*), § 79. Cf. by contrast ECtHR 16 February 2021, appl.no. 69762/12 (*Budak/Turkey*), § 81–89; ECtHR 25 February 2010, appl.no. 20100/06 (*Lisica/Croatia*), § 49–62.

[27] ECtHR 5 November 2002, appl.no. 48539/99 (*Allan/UK*), § 42–43.

[28] ECtHR (GC) 11 July 2006, appl.no. 54810/00 (*Jalloh/Germany*), § 96. See also ECtHR (GC) 17 October 2019, appl.nos. 1874/13 and 8567/13 (*López Ribalda and Others/Spain*), § 150–151; ECtHR (GC) 10 March 2009, appl.no. 4378/02 (*Bykov/Russia*), § 90.

[29] ECtHR (GC) 11 July 2006, appl.no. 54810/00 (*Jalloh/Germany*), § 97.

[30] Ibid.

[31] ECtHR (GC) 17 October 2019, appl.nos. 1874/13 and 8567/13 (*López Ribalda and Others/Spain*), § 150–151; ECtHR (GC) 1 June 2010, appl.no. 22978/05 (*Gäfgen/Germany*), § 162–165; ECtHR (GC) 10 March 2009, appl.no. 4378/02 (*Bykov/Russia*), § 89–91. Moreover, in *Bykov* (§ 93) the Grand Chamber noted that 'The general requirements of fairness contained in Article 6 apply to all criminal proceedings, irrespective of the type of offence at issue'.

[32] ECtHR 3 March 2016, appl.no. 7215/10 (*Prade/Germany*).

containing 39.09 grams of pure tetrahydrocannabidinol (THC). Eventually, the applicant was convicted for possessing a substantial quantity of drugs. The encountered hashish were in effect the only evidence.

Regarding Article 6 ECHR, the applicant complained that searching his flat had violated Article 8 ECHR and that the admission of the hashish as sole evidence therefore conflicted with the right to a fair trial. The Court noted that the house search 'was not in accordance with the domestic law'.[33] However, the Court held that the applicant had the effective opportunity to challenge the use of the evidence and that his arguments were given due consideration by the courts in all three instances.[34] Nothing casted doubts on the reliability and accuracy of the contested sole evidence. Since the evidence was strong with no risk of it being unreliable, the need for supporting evidence was correspondingly weaker.[35] Regarding the public interest in investigating and punishing drug crimes, the Court considered that:

> the national courts addressed in detail the applicant's arguments regarding the use of the evidence and thoroughly reasoned why they were of the opinion that the evidence, although obtained by an unlawful house search, could be used as evidence in the criminal proceedings at issue. They weighed the public interest in prosecuting the crime of drugs possession against the applicant's interest in respect for his home. (…) In these circumstances, and further given that the considerable amount of hashish which had been detected (in contrast to the case of *Jalloh* in which only a small amount of cocaine was found) was taken into consideration by the domestic courts, their conclusion that the public interest outweighed the applicant's basic rights was carefully and thoroughly reasoned and did not disclose any appearance of arbitrariness or disproportionality.[36]

The Court did not find a violation of Article 6(1) ECHR. As the considerations on public interest indicate, the Court appears to accept the 'seriousness of a crime' as a valid argument in favour of admitting evidence obtained in breach of Article 8 ECHR.[37]

The Court's reference to *Jalloh* in this case seems bit odd though. In *Prade*, the hashish had been obtained by a violation of Article 8 ECHR. Meanwhile, in *Jalloh*, the evidence had been recovered in breach of the absolute prohibition of Article 3 ECHR. Moreover, the forcible administration of emetics in *Jalloh* violated the privilege against self-incrimination. *Therefore*, using the so obtained pellet of cocaine as evidence had rendered the trial unfair.[38] In light of these differences, it is unclear

33 Ibid., § 37. The Court did not explicitly determine a violation of Article 8 ECHR because the applicant's complaint in this regard was lodged beyond the six-month time limit (§ 44–45).

34 Ibid., § 38.

35 Ibid., § 39–40.

36 Ibid., § 41.

37 See also Thommen & Samadi 2016.

38 ECtHR (GC) 11 July 2006, appl.no. 54810/00 (*Jalloh/Germany*), § 122.

how the cases of *Prade* and *Jalloh* can be compared when determining the fairness of the proceedings and weighing the public interest of prosecuting drug offences.[39]

Still, the public interest in prosecuting and preventing crime appears a relevant factor in determining the fairness of the proceedings when evidence has been obtained in breach of Article 8 ECHR. Similar to *Prade/Germany*, the Court concluded in *Heglas/Czech Republic* that the use as evidence of a telephone conversation obtained in breach of Article 8 ECHR did not violate the applicant's right to a fair trial. Significant to this conclusion was the fact that the contested evidence related to a serious offence causing harm to a third party (theft), for which ultimately a nine-year prison sentence was imposed.[40]

The Court's approach on the admissibility of evidence obtained in breach of Article 8 ECHR, including its considerations on public interest, has been criticised. The criticism will be discussed in Section 7.2.5.

7.2.4 *Evidence Obtained in Breach of Article 3 ECHR*

The use at trial of evidence obtained in breach of one of the core and absolute rights guaranteed by the ECHR will always raise serious issues as to the fairness of the proceedings.[41] Even when the admission of such evidence was not decisive in securing a conviction. It follows from Article 6 ECHR that domestic courts should only admit evidence after having verified, in view of all elements specific to the case, that the evidence has not been secured by means of ill-treatment in breach of Article 3 ECHR.[42] This requirement is inherent in the domestic courts' responsibility to ensure fair trials and to verify whether the overall fairness is not affected by the acquisition of evidence on which they rely.[43] But when exactly will the admission of evidence obtained in breach of Article 3 ECHR render the proceedings as a whole unfair?

First of all, the admission of *confessions* obtained in breach of Article 3 ECHR – regardless the classification as either torture, inhuman, or degrading treatment – will automatically render the trial as a whole unfair in breach of Article 6 ECHR.[44] This

39 Moreover, when comparing the drug offences in *Prade* and *Jalloh*, the Court only refers to the differences in the *amounts* of drugs in both cases. Yet, it seems to neglect the distinction between 'hard drugs', such as cocaine, and 'soft drugs', like hashish.

40 ECtHR 1 March 2007, appl.no. 5935/02 (*Heglas/Czech Republic*), § 91.

41 ECtHR (GC) 1 June 2010, appl.no. 22978/05 (*Gäfgen/Germany*), § 165; ECtHR (GC) 11 July 2006, appl.no. 54810/00 (*Jalloh/Germany*), § 99; ECtHR 30 July 2009, appl.no. 2807/04 (*Gladyshev/Russia*), § 75; ECtHR 11 February 2014, appl.no. 9278/06 (*Cēsnieks/Latvia*), § 65 (with further references).

42 ECtHR 25 September 2012, appl.no. 649/08 (*El Haski/Belgium*), § 89, 99.

43 Ibid. See also Partly dissenting opinion of Judge Bošnjak under ECtHR 26 January 2021, appl.nos. 73313/17 and 20143/19 (*Zličić/Serbia*), point. 52–53.

44 ECtHR (GC) 13 September 2016, appl.nos. 50541/08, 50571/08, 50573/08, and 40351/09 (*Ibrahim and others/UK*), § 254; ECtHR (GC) 1 June 2010, appl.no. 22978/05 (*Gäfgen/Germany*), § 166, 173; ECtHR

rule applies irrespective of the probative value and decisiveness of a confession in securing the defendant's conviction.[45] Here, the Court has adopted a stricter exclusionary rule compared with Article 15 of the United Nations Convention against Torture and Other Cruel, Inhuman or Degrading Treatment or Punishment (UNCAT). Article 15 UNCAT only prescribes that *statements* obtained by *torture* should never be relied upon as evidence.[46] The Strasbourg rule also pertains to inhuman and degrading treatment.

Second, the use in criminal proceedings of *real evidence* (tangible evidence) obtained as a direct result of *torture* will always undermine the fairness of the proceedings, irrespective of their probative value.[47] As the Grand Chamber holds:

> Any other conclusion would only serve to legitimise, indirectly, the sort of morally reprehensible conduct which the authors of Article 3 of the Convention sought to proscribe or, in other words, to 'afford brutality the cloak of law'.[48]

However, the use at trial of *real evidence* obtained as a result of *inhuman* or *degrading treatment* in breach of Article 3 ECHR will only render the trial unfair if it has been shown that the violation of Article 3 ECHR had a bearing on the outcome of the proceedings against the defendant.[49] That means: if it had impact on the conviction or sentence.[50]

The Court first adopted this approach in *Gäfgen/Germany*. In that case, the police had threatened the applicant with 'intolerable pain' in order to obtain information about the whereabouts of an abducted child. In response to those threats, which amounted to inhuman treatment, the applicant guided the police to a location where they found the child's body, together with other real evidence, including tyre tracks of the applicant's car and the victim's backpack and clothes. According to the Grand Chamber, this *real evidence* was secured as a direct result of *inhuman treatment*.[51]

25 September 2012, appl.no. 649/08 (*El Haski/Belgium*), § 85. But, in contrast ECtHR 17 January 2012, appl.no. 20212/05 (*Alchagin/Russia*), § 67–74, which in later case-law has been considered 'the only exception' to the line in Strasbourg case-law on the use of confessions obtained in defiance of Article 3 ECHR: ECtHR 23 June 2013, appl.nos. 33192/07 and 33194/07 (*Kaçiu and Kotorri/Albania*), § 125. Cf. ECtHR 11 February 2014, appl.no. 9278/06 (*Cēsnieks/Latvia*), § 68. See also Pitcher 2018a, pp. 26–28; Rainey, McCormick & Ovey 2021, pp. 321–323.

45 See also Pitcher 2018a, p. 23 et seq. with further references.

46 Cf. ECtHR (GC) 11 July 2006, appl.no. 54810/00 (*Jalloh/Germany*), § 105.

47 ECtHR (GC) 1 June 2010, appl.no. 22978/05 (*Gäfgen/Germany*), § 173; ECtHR 25 September 2012, appl.no. 649/08 (*El Haski/Belgium*), § 85.

48 ECtHR (GC) 1 June 2010, appl.no. 22978/05 (*Gäfgen/Germany*), § 167. Also ECtHR (GC) 11 July 2006, appl.no. 54810/00 (*Jalloh/Germany*), § 105; ECtHR 28 June 2007, appl.no. 36549/03 (*Harutyunyan/Armenia*), § 63; ECtHR 17 January 2012, appl.no. 8139/09 (*Othman (Abu Qatada)/UK*), § 264–267.

49 Cf. ECtHR (GC) 11 July 2006, appl.no. 54810/00 (*Jalloh/Germany*), § 107–108.

50 ECtHR 26 January 2021, appl.nos. 73313/17 and 20143/19 (*Zličić/Serbia*), § 119; ECtHR 5 February 2020, appl.no. 31454/10 (*Ćwik/Poland*), § 75–76; ECtHR 25 September 2012, appl.no. 649/08 (*El Haski/Belgium*), § 85.

51 ECtHR (GC) 1 June 2010, appl.no. 22978/05 (*Gäfgen/Germany*), § 171.

The applicant had requested the domestic court to exclude the real evidence obtained by ill-treatment. Yet, his request had been denied; all items were admitted. The next day at trial, the applicant confessed that he had killed the eleven-year-old victim.[52] The real evidence was adduced. At the end of trial, the applicant again admitted that he had intended to kill the victim. In his view, giving confession was 'the only way to accept his deep guilt', being the 'greatest possible apology for the murder of the child'.[53] The domestic court convicted the applicant of murder and kidnapping with extortion causing the death of the victim. Life imprisonment was imposed.

In determining the fairness of the criminal proceedings, the Grand Chamber stressed that unlike Article 3 ECHR, Article 6 ECHR does not guarantee an absolute right. As a consequence, when criminal evidence is obtained in breach of Article 3 ECHR, it is to be determined by the Court which procedural measures are necessary and sufficient for securing effective protection of the rights and freedoms pursuant to Article 6 ECHR.[54] The Grand Chamber acknowledges that when evidence obtained in violation of Article 3 ECHR is allowed at trial, this might be an incentive for law-enforcement officials to employ unlawful methods of investigation, regardless of whether they are absolutely prohibited by Article 3 ECHR. Therefore, the effective protection against the use of investigative methods that violate Article 3 ECHR may also require, as a rule, the exclusion of real evidence that has been obtained as a result[55] of *any* violation of Article 3 ECHR – be that either torture, inhuman, or degrading treatment. Otherwise, the proceedings as a whole will be unfair.[56] However, the Grand Chamber holds that both the fairness of the criminal proceedings and the effective protection of Article 3 ECHR within the context of those proceedings will only be at stake when the breach of Article 3 ECHR had a bearing on the outcome of the proceedings against the defendant. In other words: when it had impact on the conviction or sentence.[57]

In *Gäfgen/Germany*, the Grand Chamber concluded that the real evidence obtained through inhuman treatment was not *necessary nor used* to prove the applicant's guilt and to determine the sentence. Rather:

> the Regional Court expressly based its findings of fact concerning the execution of the crime committed by the applicant – and thus the findings decisive for the applicant's conviction for murder and kidnapping with extortion – exclusively on the new, full confession made by the applicant at the trial (…). Moreover, that

[52] Ibid., § 31.
[53] Ibid., § 32.
[54] Ibid., § 178.
[55] Direct or indirect: 'even though that evidence is more remote from the breach of Article 3 than evidence extracted immediately as a consequence of a violation of that Article'. (ECtHR (GC) 1 June 2010, appl.no. 22978/05 (*Gäfgen/Germany*), § 178).
[56] ECtHR (GC) 1 June 2010, appl.no. 22978/05 (*Gäfgen/Germany*), § 178.
[57] Ibid.

> court also considered the new confession the essential, if not the only, basis for its findings of fact concerning the planning of the crime, which likewise played a role in the applicant's conviction and sentence (….). The additional [real] evidence admitted at the trial was not used by the Regional Court against the applicant to prove his guilt, but only to test the veracity of his confession. The Regional Court further referred to corroborative evidence which had been secured independently of the first confession (…) which was 'untainted' by the breach of Article 3.[58]

According to the Grand Chamber, there had been 'a break in the causal chain leading from the prohibited methods of investigation to the applicant's conviction and sentence in respect to the impugned real evidence'.[59] Consequently, the right to a fair trial had not been violated. As it appears, to affect the overall fairness of the criminal proceedings, real evidence obtained by inhuman or degrading treatment must have *direct* impact on either the conviction or sentence.

Both scholars and dissenting Judges have considered it impossible to argue that the real evidence in *Gäfgen* had no bearing whatsoever on the outcome of the case.[60] Criminal proceedings are to be considered as an organic process. We cannot deny that the admission of the real evidence had affected the applicant's confession and influenced the perception of the domestic judges. Nonetheless, the Court has repeatedly reiterated the general considerations provided in *Gäfgen*. Recently, it has summarised its approach of admitting evidence obtained in breach of Article 3 ECHR as follows:

> the use in criminal proceedings of statements obtained as a result of a violation of Article 3 – irrespective of the classification of the treatment as torture, inhuman or degrading treatment – renders the proceedings as a whole automatically unfair, in breach of Article 6 (…). This also holds true for the use of real evidence obtained as a direct result of acts of torture (…); the admission of such evidence obtained as a result of an act qualified as inhuman treatment in breach of Article 3, but falling short of torture, will only breach Article 6, however, if it has been shown that the breach of Article 3 had a bearing on the outcome of the proceedings against the defendant, that is, had an impact on his or her conviction or sentence.[61]

58 Ibid., § 179. See also § 183–184. Cf. ECtHR 26 January 2021, appl.nos. 73313/17 and 20143/19 (*Zličić/Serbia*), § 121; ECtHR 17 January 2012, appl.no. 20212/05 (*Alchagin/Russia*), § 67–74; ECtHR 18 October 2011, appl.no. 26088/06 (*Stanimirović/Serbia*), § 52; ECtHR 28 June 2007, appl.no. 36549/03 (*Harutyunyan/Armenia*), § 65.

59 ECtHR (GC) 1 June 2010, appl.no. 22978/05 (*Gäfgen/Germany*), § 180.

60 For example, Joint partly dissenting opinion of Judges Rozakis, Tulkens, Jebens, Ziemele, Bianku, and Power, ECtHR (GC) 1 June 2010, appl.no. 22978/05 (*Gäfgen/Germany*), points 5–7; Partly dissenting opinion of Judge Bošnjak under ECtHR 26 January 2021, appl.nos. 73313/17 and 20143/19 (*Zličić/Serbia*), point 64. See also point 33 et seq; Harris et al. 2018, p. 421; Muller 2009, para. 9.

61 ECtHR 26 January 2021, appl.nos. 73313/17 and 20143/19 (*Zličić/Serbia*), § 119. See also ECtHR 5 February 2020, appl.no. 31454/10 (*Ćwik/Poland*), § 75–76; ECtHR 25 September 2012, appl.no. 649/08 (*El Haski/Belgium*), § 85.

These principles apply not only where the victim of ill-treatment concerns the defendant but also when third parties such as witnesses are treated in breach of Article 3 ECHR. They also apply when the ill-treatment has been inflicted not by State officials but by private individuals.[62]

The Court's approach on the admission of evidence obtained in breach of Article 3 ECHR has received fundamental critique, which is discussed in the following section.

7.2.5 *Reflecting on the Court's Approach*

7.2.5.1 Rationales for Excluding Evidence Obtained in Breach of Fundamental Rights

In order to enable a well-grounded reflection on the Strasbourg approach to the exclusion of evidence secured in violation of the ECHR, the present section first identifies the rationales that the Court accepts for excluding such evidence. In the literature, scholars distinguish different justifications. Most central are:

(1) deterrence (aiming to prevent future violations of fundamental rights in similar situations),
(2) the integrity principle (safeguarding the integrity of the criminal justice system in accordance with the rule of law and guaranteeing judicial integrity and legitimacy of the verdict),
(3) the protective principle (protecting right holders from being disadvantaged by a breach of their rights), and
(4) the reliability of evidence (excluding unlawfully obtained evidence if it is unreliable).[63]

Let us take a closer look whether and, if so, how these or other considerations are reflected in the Court's case-law on excluding evidence obtained in breach of Articles 3, 6, and 8 ECHR.

DETERRENCE. It is clear that the Court accepts 'deterrence' of law enforcement as a valid rationale to exclude unlawfully obtained evidence.[64] As the Grand Chamber considers in *Gäfgen/Germany*, admitting evidence obtained by conduct in breach

[62] ECtHR 5 February 2020, appl.no. 31454/10 (*Ćwik/Poland*), § 77 and 89.

[63] See, for example, Ashworth 1977; Mirfield 1997; Ashworth 2003; Roberts & Zuckerman 2010, pp. 179–191; Jackson & Summers 2012, pp. 153–158; Roberts 2012; Chau 2016; Pitcher 2018b; Turner & Weigend 2019; Corstens/Borgers & Kooijmans 2021, pp. 869–871; Pitcher & Samadi 2018; Kuiper 2014, pp. 44–45.

[64] Thommen & Samadi 2016, p. 82.

of Article 3 ECHR could be an incentive for law-enforcement officials to use similar methods of investigation in future cases.[65] The repression of and the effective protection against the use of investigation methods that violate Article 3 ECHR may therefore require, as a rule, the exclusion of evidence so obtained.[66] In respect of excluding evidence obtained in breach of Article 8 ECHR, deterrence appears no central consideration to the ECtHR.[67]

INTEGRITY PRINCIPLE. In the Court's view, the exclusion of evidence obtained by torture is also required to protect the integrity of the criminal proceedings and to respect the rule of law.[68] As the Court puts it in *Othman (Abu Qatada)/UK*:

> no legal system based upon the rule of law can countenance the admission of evidence – however reliable – which has been obtained by such a barbaric practice as torture. The trial process is a cornerstone of the rule of law. Torture evidence damages irreparably that process; it substitutes force for the rule of law and taints the reputation of any court that admits it. Torture evidence is excluded to protect the *integrity* of the trial process and, ultimately, the rule of law itself.[69]

In the same vein, the Grand Chamber stressed in *Jalloh* and *Gäfgen* that the admission of evidence secured as a result of torture would only serve to legitimise, indirectly, the sort of morally reprehensible conduct that Article 3 ECHR aims to proscribe.[70] As the Court argues in *Gäfgen*, there is 'a vital public interest in preserving the integrity of the judicial process and thus the values of civilised societies founded upon the rule of law'.[71] Apart from excluding torture evidence, it has been argued that the Court's position towards the admission of evidence obtained by entrapment, violating Article 6(1) ECHR,[72] is also predominantly motivated by considerations of moral integrity.[73] Regarding the use at trial of evidence obtained

65 See also Partly dissenting opinion of Judge Bošnjak under ECtHR 26 January 2021, appl.nos. 73313/17 and 20143/19 (*Zličić/Serbia*), point 41.

66 ECtHR (GC) 1 June 2010, appl.no. 22978/05 (*Gäfgen/Germany*), § 178.

67 For example, ECtHR 3 March 2016, appl.no. 7215/10 (*Prade/Germany*); ECtHR 5 November 2002, appl.no. 48539/99 (*Allan/UK*); ECtHR 25 September 2001, appl.no. 44787/98 (*P.G. and J.H./UK*); ECtHR 12 May 2000, appl.no. 5394/97 (*Khan/UK*).

68 See also Thommen & Samadi 2016, p. 83; Jackson & Summers 2012, p. 162; Pitcher & Samadi 2018, pp. 742–743; Concurring opinion of Judge Yudkivska in ECtHR 22 October 2020, appl.no. 6739/11 (*Bokhonko/Georgia*), points 15–18.

69 ECtHR 17 January 2012, appl.no. 8139/09 (*Othman (Abu Qatada)/UK*), § 264 (emphasis added).

70 ECtHR (GC) 1 June 2010, appl.no. 22978/05 (*Gäfgen/Germany*), § 167; ECtHR (GC) 11 July 2006, appl. no. 54810/00 (*Jalloh/Germany*), § 105. Also ECtHR 28 June 2007, appl.no. 36549/03 (*Harutyunyan/Armenia*), § 63.

71 ECtHR (GC) 1 June 2010, appl.no. 22978/05 (*Gäfgen/Germany*), § 175. See also Turner & Weigend 2019, pp. 258–259.

72 ECtHR (GC) 5 February 2008, appl.no. 74420/01 (*Ramanauskas/Lithuania*); ECtHR 9 June 1998, appl.no. 44/1997/828/1034 (*Teixeira de Castro/Portugal*).

73 Choo 2008, p. 148; Pitcher & Samadi 2018, p. 742.

in breach of Article 8 ECHR, the Court pays no explicit attention to the integrity of the criminal proceedings.[74]

PROTECTIVE PRINCIPLE. Unlike deterrence and integrity, the protective principle – aiming to vindicate fundamental rights – appears *no* relevant consideration for the Court to exclude unlawfully obtained evidence under the right to a fair trial. Rather, the Court seems to follow the opposite approach, which Ashworth has called the *separation thesis*.[75] Under this thesis, one conceives the requirements of a fair trial pursuant to Article 6 ECHR and violations of other Convention rights as two entirely separate matters.[76]

The Court's affinity with the separation thesis is clearly illustrated by its position on the use of evidence obtained in defiance of Article 8 ECHR. Violations of Article 8 ECHR and the fairness of criminal proceedings are considered two separate issues.[77] Protecting individuals against violations of Article 8 ECHR appears no relevant factor when determining the overall trial fairness. Moreover, in the context of Article 6 ECHR, the suspects' interest in having their fundamental rights protected can be outweighed by the public interest in the investigation and punishment of particular crimes.[78] As a result, disadvantaging suspects by admitting evidence secured in violation of their rights pursuant to Article 8 ECHR will only very seldom render the criminal proceedings unfair.[79]

The Court's preference for the separation thesis over the exclusion of evidence to vindicate fundamental rights is also reflected in its position on the admission of *real evidence* secured by *inhuman and degrading treatment* contrary to Article 3 ECHR. The use at trial of such evidence will not necessarily affect the overall fairness of the criminal proceedings, unless the evidence had direct impact on the conviction or sentence.[80] As it appears, sometimes, defendants may be disadvantaged by a violation of their absolute right not to be ill-treated, when the evidence so obtained is allowed to be used against them at trial, as in the case of Gäfgen.[81] Indeed, victims of ill-treatment can be granted compensation. However, if the evidence obtained in breach

74 For example, ECtHR 3 March 2016, appl.no. 7215/10 (*Prade/Germany*); ECtHR 5 November 2002, appl.no. 48539/99 (*Allan/UK*); ECtHR 25 September 2001, appl.no. 44787/98 (*P.G. and J.H./UK*); ECtHR 12 May 2000, appl.no. 5394/97 (*Khan/UK*).

75 Ashworth 2003, pp. 113–115.

76 Ashworth 2012, p. 157; Ashworth 2003, pp. 113–115; Ölçer 2008, p. 105; Kuiper 2014, p. 473.

77 See Section 7.2.3.

78 Cf. Thommen & Samadi 2016, pp. 84–85.

79 For example, ECtHR 16 February 2021, appl.no. 69762/12 (*Budak/Turkey*). See also Thommen & Samadi 2016, p. 80; Ölçer 2013, p. 379; Kuiper 2014, p. 470. Cf. *Rb.* Midden-Nederland 17 February 2021, ECLI:NL:RBMNE:2021:602.

80 ECtHR (GC) 1 June 2010, appl.no. 22978/05 (*Gäfgen/Germany*), § 175–188; ECtHR 26 January 2021, appl.nos. 73313/17 and 20143/19 (*Zličić/Serbia*), § 119; ECtHR 5 February 2020, appl.no. 31454/10 (*Ćwik/Poland*), § 75–76; ECtHR 25 September 2012, appl.no. 649/08 (*El Haski/Belgium*), § 85.

81 See also ECtHR 26 January 2021, appl.nos. 73313/17 and 20143/19 (*Zličić/Serbia*), § 121.

of Article 3 ECHR has (indirectly) contributed to a criminal conviction and/or to the imposition of sanctions, the mere award of damages cannot undo such disadvantage.[82]

Altogether, the Court appears not to accept the protective principle as a rationale for excluding evidence obtained in breach of the Convention. Rather, it tends to adhere the separation thesis. As Ashworth summarises the Strasbourg approach: 'breaches of Article 8 or the "inhuman or degrading treatment" limb of Article 3 [with respect to real evidence] are regarded as separate matters, calling for discrete remedies divorced from trial fairness'.[83]

RELIABILITY. Finally, together with deterrence, the integrity principle, and the separation thesis, the Court takes account of the reliability of evidence obtained in breach of fundamental rights. When determining the fairness of the trial, the Court conceives it relevant whether evidence obtained in defiance of Article 8 ECHR constitutes 'strong evidence' and whether there is any risk of it being unreliable.[84] Regarding the admission of confessions obtained in violation of Article 3 ECHR, the Court considers their unreliability a 'compelling reason' for exclusion.[85] Statements made in disregard of Article 3 ECHR are inherently unreliable;[86] 'experience has all too often shown that the victim of torture will say anything – true or not – as the shortest method of freeing himself from the torment of torture'.[87] Regarding the exclusion of evidence obtained in breach of the privilege against self-incrimination, reliability plays an implicit role as well, as one of the privilege's rationales lies in avoiding miscarriages of justice.[88]

7.2.5.2 Criticising the Strasbourg Approach

The Strasbourg approach on excluding evidence obtained in breach of the ECHR (henceforth: 'unlawfully obtained evidence') has been criticised. As Judges Pinto de Albuquerque and Bošnjak note in their separate opinion to *Dragoş Ioan Rusu/*

[82] See Section 7.2.5.2, under the heading *The separation thesis.*

[83] Ashworth 2012, p. 158.

[84] ECtHR 12 May 2000, appl.no. 5394/97 (*Khan/UK*), § 37; ECtHR 3 March 2016, appl.no. 7215/10 (*Prade/Germany*), § 40; ECtHR 31 October 2017, appl.no. 22767/08 (*Dragoş Ioan Rusu/Romania*), § 49, 54. See also ECtHR (GC) 11 July 2006, appl.no. 54810/00 (*Jalloh/Germany*), § 96; ECtHR (GC) 17 October 2019, appl.nos. 1874/13 and 8567/13 (*López Ribalda and Others/Spain*), § 150–151; ECtHR (GC) 10 March 2009, appl.no. 4378/02 (*Bykov/Russia*), § 90; ECtHR (GC) 1 June 2010, appl.no. 22978/05 (*Gäfgen/Germany*), § 164–165.

[85] ECtHR 17 January 2012, appl.no. 8139/09 (*Othman (Abu Qatada)/UK*), § 264.

[86] ECtHR 6 October 2015, appl.no. 4722/09 (*Turbylev/Russia*), § 90; ECtHR 21 September 2006, appl. no. 46661/99 (*Söylemez/Turkey*), § 122.

[87] ECtHR 17 January 2012, appl.no. 8139/09 (*Othman (Abu Qatada)/UK*), § 264, 267. See also with regard to real evidence: ECtHR 22 October 2020, appl.no. 6739/11 (*Bokhonko/Georgia*), § 96–99.

[88] ECtHR (GC) 1 June 2010, appl.no. 22978/05 (*Gäfgen/Germany*), § 168; ECtHR (GC) 10 March 2009, appl.no. 4378/02 (*Bykov/Russia*), § 92.

Romania: 'the Court's case-law on the use of illegally obtained evidence in criminal proceedings lacks persuasiveness, coherence and clarity and needs to be revisited'.[89] To structure the debate, I discuss the central critiques within the context of the rationales for (not) excluding unlawfully obtained evidence as are reflected in case-law of the Court: (1) deterrence, (2) the integrity principle, (3) the separation thesis, and (4) the reliability of evidence.

DETERRENCE. From the outset of the Court's approach, critics have pointed to its incompatibility with the idea of deterrence. As Judge Loucaides stressed in *Khan/UK*: 'If violating Article 8 can be accepted as 'fair' then I cannot see how the police can be effectively deterred from repeating their impermissible conduct'.[90] In other words, when the evidence obtained by unlawful car searches, illegal secret surveillance, or in breach with the suspect's bodily integrity can still be used at trial, then there will be no strong incentive for the police to refrain from such practices. In her partly dissenting opinion to *P.G. and J.H./UK*, Judge Tulkens agrees,[91] as does Judge Spielmann, joined by Rozakis, Tulkens, Casadevall, and Mijović in the partly dissenting opinion to *Bykov/Russia*.[92] They all draw attention to the fact that the Court itself underlines

> the need to ensure that the police exercise their powers to control and prevent crime in a manner which fully respects the due process and *other guarantees* which legitimately place restraints on the scope of their action to investigate crime and bring offenders to justice, including the guarantees contained in Articles 5 and 8 of the Convention.[93]

Similar concerns have been raised regarding the Court's approach to *real evidence* obtained by *inhuman or degrading treatment*, the admission of which does not necessarily render the trial as a whole unfair.[94] The partly dissenting Judges Rozakis, Tulkens, Jebens, Ziemele, Bianku, and Power stress in *Gäfgen/Germany* that the

89 Joint partly concurring opinion of Judges Pinto de Albuquerque and Bošnjak under ECtHR 31 October 2017, appl.no. 22767/08 (*Dragoş Ioan Rusu/Romania*), point 1. Cf. Goss 2016, p. 59; Jackson & Summers 2012, p. 195.

90 Partly concurring, partly dissenting opinion of Judge Loucaides, under ECtHR 12 May 2000, appl. no. 5394/97 (*Khan/UK*), p. 16.

91 Partly dissenting opinion of Judge Tulkens, under ECtHR 25 September 2001, appl.no. 44787/98 (*P.G. and J.H./UK*), point 5.

92 Partly dissenting opinion of Judge Spielmann, joined by Judges Rozakis, Tulkens, Casadevall, and Mijović, under ECtHR (GC) 10 March 2009, appl.no. 4378/02 (*Bykov/Russia*), points 12–13. Cf. Concurring opinion of Judge Cabral Barreto, under ECtHR (GC) 10 March 2009, appl.no. 4378/02 (*Bykov/Russia*), points 3.1–3.4.

93 ECtHR 5 September 2019, appl.no. 20147/15 (*Olewnik-Cieplińska and Olewnik/Poland*), § 119 (emphasis added). Also ECtHR 24 July 2012, appl.no. 41526/10 (*Đorđević/Croatia*), § 139; ECtHR 28 October 1998, appl.no. 87/1997/871/1083 (*Osman/UK*), § 116.

94 See, for example, ECtHR (GC) 1 June 2010, appl.no. 22978/05 (*Gäfgen/Germany*), § 175–188.

prohibition of Article 3 ECHR is absolute. All violations are serious. The most effective way to guarantee this absolute prohibition, they contend, is a strict application of the exclusionary rule under Article 6 ECHR. Such an approach would leave State agents who are tempted to employ inhuman treatment in no doubt about the futility of engaging in such prohibited conduct. This will deprive the authorities of any potential incentive for treating suspects contrary to Article 3 ECHR.[95] Allowing evidence obtained in violation of Article 3 ECHR weakens the protection of the absolute prohibition. It signals a certain ambivalence about the scope of that protection.[96]

Meanwhile, deterrence is not the only rationale the Court takes into account. It recognises that different competing interests are at stake when excluding unlawfully obtained evidence. Especially when reliable, excluding evidence can hamper the effective prosecution of crime.[97]At the same time, a vital public interest exists in preserving the integrity of the proceedings and respecting the rule of law.[98] The Court also takes account of the distinctive nature of substantive right violations on the one hand and the requirements of a fair trial pursuant to Article 6 ECHR on the other hand. Let us take a closer look at the Strasbourg approach on excluding unlawfully obtained evidence in view of the other rationales endorsed by the Court.

THE INTEGRITY PRINCIPLE. Even more fundamental than the incompatibility with deterrence is the argument that the Court's approach disregards the integrity of criminal proceedings and the judicial process, undermining the rule of law. Since the case of *Khan*,[99] dissenting Judges in *P.G. and J.H.*, *Jalloh*, *Bykov*, *Gäfgen*, and *Dragoş Ioan Rusu* have repeatedly stressed that they cannot accept a trial to be 'fair' in the meaning of Article 6 ECHR if a person's guilt for any offence is established through evidence obtained in violation of the human rights guaranteed by the ECHR. They argue that the term 'fairness' in the context of the ECHR implies observance with the rule of law. Thus, fairness presupposes respect for human rights guaranteed by the Convention, which it is the Court's very task to scrutinise.[100] Ashworth agrees, arguing

95 Joint partly dissenting opinion of Judges Rozakis, Tulkens, Jebens, Ziemele, Bianku, and Power, under ECtHR (GC) 1 June 2010, appl.no. 22978/05 (*Gäfgen/Germany*), point 10. See also Partly dissenting opinion of Judge Bošnjak under ECtHR 26 January 2021, appl.nos. 73313/17 and 20143/19 (*Zličić/Serbia*), points 41, 64–68; Concurring opinion of Judge Cabral Barreto, under ECtHR (GC) 10 March 2009, appl.no. 4378/02 (*Bykov/Russia*), point 3.1. See also Harris et al. 2018, p. 421.

96 Joint partly dissenting opinion of Judges Rozakis, Tulkens, Jebens, Ziemele, Bianku, and Power, under ECtHR (GC) 1 June 2010, appl.no. 22978/05 (*Gäfgen/Germany*), point 8. Cf. Kuiper 2014, p. 451.

97 ECtHR (GC) 1 June 2010, appl.no. 22978/05 (*Gäfgen/Germany*), § 175.

98 Ibid.

99 Cf. *Schenk*, with regard to the admission of evidence obtained in breach of *domestic* law: Joint dissenting opinion of Judges Pettiti, Spielmann, De Meyer, and Carrillo Salcedo, under ECtHR 12 July 1988, appl.no. 10862/84 (*Schenk/Switzerland*).

100 Partly concurring, partly dissenting opinion of Judge Loucaides, under ECtHR 12 May 2000, appl.no. 5394/97 (*Khan/UK*), p. 15; Partly dissenting opinion of Judge Tulkens, under ECtHR 25 September

that the admission of evidence obtained in breach of Article 8 ECHR compromises the integrity of the judicial process.[101]

Such a position would align with the Court's considerations on excluding torture evidence. In the Court's view, not excluding such evidence would only serve to legitimise indirectly the sort of morally reprehensible conduct that the authors of the ECHR sought to proscribe,[102] tainting the reputation of the Court that admits such evidence.[103] Similarly, using evidence obtained in violation of any other Convention right, be that either Article 8, 9, or 10 ECHR, will also indirectly legitimise the objectionable conduct that the Convention aims to outlaw.[104] Judge Loucaides underlines that member States have an obligation under Article 1 ECHR to secure the rights and freedoms defined in Section I of the Convention. This obliges domestic courts not to admit or rely on evidence that has been obtained in breach of the Convention – especially if that evidence is the only evidence against the accused.[105]

Regarding evidence obtained in breach of Article 3 ECHR, Judges Rozakis, Tulkens, Jebens, Ziemele, Bianku, and Power emphasise that societies founded upon the rule of law should not tolerate, or sanction directly, indirectly, or otherwise, any form of ill-treatment prohibited by Article 3 ECHR. Neither the wordings of Article 3 ECHR nor of any other provision of the ECHR distinguishes between the consequences that should be attached to torture, inhuman, and degrading treatment. The Convention provides no legal basis to make such a distinction: 'Neither "a break in the causal chain" nor any other intellectual construct can overcome the inherent wrong that occurs when evidence obtained in violation of Article 3 is admitted into criminal proceedings'.[106]

2001, appl.no. 44787/98 (*P.G. and J.H./UK*), point 1; Concurring opinion of Judge Bartza, under ECtHR (GC) 11 July 2006, appl.no. 54810/00 (*Jalloh/Germany*), p. 37; Partly dissenting opinion of Judge Spielmann, joined by Judges Rozakis, Tulkens, Casadevall, and Mijović, under ECtHR (GC) 10 March 2009, appl.no. 4378/02 (*Bykov/Russia*), points 6–7; Joint partly dissenting opinion of Judges Rozakis, Tulkens, Jebens, Ziemele, Bianku, and Power, under ECtHR (GC) 1 June 2010, appl.no. 22978/05 (*Gäfgen/Germany*), points 2, 9, and 12; Joint partly concurring opinion of Judges Pinto de Albuquerque and Bošnjak under ECtHR 31 October 2017, appl.no. 22767/08 (*Dragoş Ioan Rusu/Romania*), points 3–4 and 6.

101 Ashworth 2012, p. 157. Cf. Choo 2008, p. 127; Lawson 2004, pp. 201–203.

102 ECtHR (GC) 1 June 2010, appl.no. 22978/05 (*Gäfgen/Germany*), § 167; ECtHR (GC) 11 July 2006, appl.no. 54810/00 (*Jalloh/Germany*), § 105; ECtHR 28 June 2007, appl.no. 36549/03 (*Harutyunyan/Armenia*), § 63.

103 ECtHR 17 January 2012, appl.no. 8139/09 (*Othman (Abu Qatada)/UK*), § 264.

104 Cf. Turner & Weigend 2019, p. 264, who argue that for the integrity principle, the type of right violated should not be decisive, since all rights and freedoms that are part of a legal system require equal respect.

105 Partly concurring, partly dissenting opinion of Judge Loucaides, under ECtHR 12 May 2000, appl. no. 5394/97 (*Khan/UK*), p. 15. Also Lawson 2004, p. 204.

106 Joint partly dissenting opinion of Judges Rozakis, Tulkens, Jebens, Ziemele, Bianku, and Power, under ECtHR (GC) 1 June 2010, appl.no. 22978/05 (*Gäfgen/Germany*), point 9. See also point 12.

Indeed, Article 15 UNCAT distinguishes between evidence obtained by torture and by other types of cruel, inhuman, or degrading treatment: it prescribes to exclude *torture* evidence. However, Article 15 UNCAT only refers to statements. It is open to debate whether it also applies to real evidence.[107] Meanwhile, in developing and applying its approach on excluding real evidence obtained in breach of Article 3 ECHR, the Court does not rely on Article 15 UNCAT.[108] Rather, the Court refers to considerations of moral integrity: using real evidence obtained by torture shall only legitimise the morally objectionable behaviour that the authors of the Convention intended to prohibit.[109] It is unclear why this argument should only pertain to real evidence obtained by torture as opposed to inhuman or degrading treatment. All three types of conduct are proscribed in absolute terms by the same Article 3 ECHR.

THE SEPARATION THESIS. In addition to the arguments from integrity – and closely related to the considerations on deterrence – Judge Loucaides cannot accept the Court's preference for the separation thesis over the protective principle:

> Moreover, if it is accepted that the admission of evidence obtained in breach of the Convention against an accused person is not necessarily a breach of the required fairness under Article 6, then the effective protection of the rights under the Convention will be frustrated. (…) The exclusion of evidence obtained contrary to the protected right to privacy should be considered as an essential corollary of the right, if such right is to be of any value. It should be recalled here that the Court has on many occasions stressed 'that the Convention is intended to guarantee not rights that are theoretical or illusory but rights that are practical and effective'.[110]

A similar argument has been made by Judge Tulkens and reiterated by Judge Spielmann, joined by Judges Rozakis, Tulkens, Casadevall, and Mijović,[111] worth of citing here at length:

> With regard to the nature and scope of the Court's scrutiny, the Court rightly reiterates that 'its duty, according to Article 19 of the Convention, is to ensure the observance of the engagements undertaken by the Contracting States to the

[107] Monina 2019, Section 3.1.2; Pattenden 2006.

[108] ECtHR (GC) 1 June 2010, appl.no. 22978/05 (*Gäfgen/Germany*), § 167, 173–178; ECtHR 26 January 2021, appl.nos. 73313/17 and 20143/19 (*Zličić/Serbia*), § 119–121. Cf. ECtHR (GC) 11 July 2006, appl.no. 54810/00 (*Jalloh/Germany*), § 107, where the Court notes that Article 15 UNCAT 'provides that statements which are established to have been made as a result of torture shall not be used in evidence in proceedings against the victim of torture'.

[109] ECtHR (GC) 1 June 2010, appl.no. 22978/05 (*Gäfgen/Germany*), § 167; ECtHR (GC) 11 July 2006, appl.no. 54810/00 (*Jalloh/Germany*), § 105.

[110] Partly concurring, partly dissenting opinion of Judge Loucaides, under ECtHR 12 May 2000, appl. no. 5394/97 (*Khan/UK*), p. 16.

[111] Partly dissenting opinion of Judge Spielmann, joined by Judges Rozakis, Tulkens, Casadevall, and Mijović, under ECtHR (GC) 10 March 2009, appl.no. 4378/02 (*Bykov/Russia*), points 8–9.

> Convention' (...). Accordingly, and I firmly share this observation, 'it is not its function to deal with errors of fact or of law allegedly committed by a national court unless and in so far as they may have infringed rights and freedoms protected by the Convention'. Similarly, although it is not 'the role of the Court to determine, *as a matter of principle*, whether particular types of evidence – for example, unlawfully obtained evidence – may be admissible', the position is different, however, where, as in this case, the evidence has been obtained in breach of a right guaranteed by the Convention because it is the Court's very duty, where the taking of evidence is concerned, to ensure that the commitments entered into under the Convention are honoured by the Contracting States.[112]

As Tulkens continues,[113] by considering a criminal trial fair under Article 6 ECHR regardless of whether the admitted evidence has been obtained in violation of Article 8 ECHR, the Court renders Article 8 ECHR completely ineffective.[114] However, she stresses, the rights enshrined in the ECHR cannot remain purely theoretical or virtual, since, in the Court's own words, 'the Convention must be interpreted and applied in such a way as to guarantee rights that are practical and effective'.[115] But what will remain of fundamental rights, when law-enforcement officials may violate those rights in order to prosecute the right holders?[116]

Judge Spielmann and the joining Judges point to the Court's approach of reading the Convention as a coherent whole, which must be interpreted as to promote internal consistency and harmony between the various provisions.[117] Any interpretation of the rights and freedoms guaranteed by the ECHR must be consistent with the general spirit of the Convention, 'an instrument designed to maintain and promote the ideals and values of a democratic society'.[118]

Admittedly, we can also maintain and promote rights and values by other, less far-reaching means than excluding unlawfully obtained evidence, for example, through

[112] Partly dissenting opinion of Judge Tulkens, under ECtHR 25 September 2001, appl.no. 44787/98 (*P.G. and J.H./UK*), point 2.

[113] Ibid., point 4.

[114] Cf. Ashworth 2012, p. 157 who thinks that this claim ('completely ineffective') goes too far.

[115] See, for example, ECtHR (GC) 27 November 2008, appl.no. 36391/02 (*Salduz/Turkey*), § 51; ECtHR (GC) 6 April 2000, appl.no. 35382/97 (*Comingersoll S.A./Portugal*), § 35. See for a similar argument Lawson 2004, pp. 203–204.

[116] De Hert & Koops 2001, p. 974. Cf. Ashworth 1977, p. 735: 'the primary question remains whether we are willing to recognize rights in suspect and accused persons and to protect them; recognition without any protection would be a pretence'.

[117] Partly dissenting opinion of Judge Spielmann, joined by Judges Rozakis, Tulkens, Casadevall, and Mijović, under ECtHR (GC) 10 March 2009, appl.no. 4378/02 (*Bykov/Russia*), point 6. See, for example, ECtHR (GC) 8 July 2019, appl.no. 54012/10 (*Mihalache/Romania*), § 91.

[118] See, for example, ECtHR (GC) 17 July 2014, appl.nos. 32541/08 and 43441/08 (*Svinarenko and Slyadnev/Russia*), § 118. Cf. ECtHR 27 June 1968, appl.no. 2122/64 (*Wemhoff/Germany*), § 8: 'Given that it is a law-making treaty, it is also necessary to seek the interpretation that is most appropriate in order to realise the aim and achieve the object of the treaty, not that which would restrict to the greatest possible degree the obligations undertaken by the Parties'. See also Harris et al. 2018, pp. 6–7.

reducing sentence or granting financial compensation.[119] However, such forms of compensation alone cannot protect right holders from being disadvantaged by a breach of their fundamental rights. Regardless of reducing sentences or granting financial compensation, the unlawfully obtained evidence – if not excluded – can be used to prosecute the right holder whose Convention rights have been violated. Arguing from the protective principle, as the above-mentioned Judges do, this would be – at least *prima facie* – unacceptable. If legal systems recognise and endorse fundamental rights, then suspects whose rights have been violated should not thereby be disadvantaged through using evidence so obtained against them at trial.[120] By ratifying the ECHR, member States have defined boundaries for lawful State conduct, including the acquisition of evidence in criminal cases. Beyond those self-imposed boundaries, States should abstain from intrusion and respect individual values such as human dignity and personal autonomy. As a consequence, excluding evidence obtained in breach of the Convention puts the prosecution in the exact position the member States have envisaged: deprived of evidence secured by violating fundamental rights guaranteed by the Convention.[121]

In their partly concurring opinion to *Dragoş Ioan Rusu/Romania*, Judges Pinto de Albuquerque and Bošnjak agree with the above-mentioned arguments of both Loucaides and Tulkens. Focussing on the Court's balancing of public interest under Article 6 ECHR, they draw attention to the fact that criminal evidence is often secured by infringing rights and freedoms guaranteed by the ECHR, such as the right to respect for private life and physical integrity. Such means of investigation will not amount to a violation as long as they are compatible with the requirements of the Convention right in question, such as the requirements of Article 8(2) ECHR. The purpose of these requirements, they continue, is to ensure a fair balance between the rights of the individual and the interests of society. However, when, in a specific case, the rights of the individual prevail over the interests of society and Article 8 ECHR has therefore been violated, it is hard to conceive how such a violation can nonetheless be validated under Article 6 ECHR in the same public interest of prosecuting and convicting the accused individual.[122]

Indeed, victims, their families, and the public at large have an interest in the prosecution and punishment of criminal offenders. We must convict and prevent crime. At the same time, there is an equally vital, compelling and competing public interest in the preservation of the values of civilised societies founded upon the rule of law.[123] It follows from the rule of law that infringing Article 8 ECHR requires

[119] Cf. ECtHR 10 March 2015, appl.nos. 14097/12, 45135/12, 73712/12, 34001/13, 44055/13, and 64586/13 (*Varga and Others/Hungary*), § 109.

[120] Ashworth 1977, p. 725.

[121] Roberts & Zuckerman 2010, p. 182.

[122] Joint partly concurring opinion of Judges Pinto de Albuquerque and Bošnjak under ECtHR 31 October 2017, appl.no. 22767/08 (*Dragoş Ioan Rusu/Romania*), point 5. See also point 10.

[123] ECtHR (GC) 1 June 2010, appl.no. 22978/05 (*Gäfgen/Germany*), § 175.

an accessible and foreseeable legal basis. Such infringements must be 'in accordance with the law'. Article 8(2) ECHR also prescribes that infringements should serve a legitimate public interest and must be necessary in a democratic society. These requirements echo and respond to the relevant public and private interests at stake. When balancing those interests forces us to determine a violation of Article 8 ECHR, what can then still legitimatise another, deviating balance of those interests under Article 6 ECHR?[124] To catch it in one phrase, as Judge Spielmann and the joining Judges did under *Bykov*: 'what is prohibited under one provision (Article 8) cannot be accepted under another (Article 6)'.[125]

Ashworth seems to be on the same page: if fundamental rights are to be taken seriously, there should at least be a presumption that violating the ECHR leads to the inadmissibility of the evidence resulting from it.[126] Such a '*prima facie* rule', he argues, appropriately prioritises fundamental rights, while it leaves open the possibility not to exclude evidence in cases where sufficient, strong countervailing factors exist. Similar *prima facie* approaches have been suggested by Ormerod and by Judge Cabral Barreto in the concurring opinion to *Bykov*.[127]

Apart from these principle objections to the separation thesis, it has been argued that the Court is inconsistent in its adherence to this separating approach. On the one hand, the Court routinely remarks that it is not its role to determine as a matter of principle whether unlawfully obtained evidence would be admissible. It considers breaches of Article 8 and violations of the 'inhuman and degrading' limb of Article 3 ECHR in respect of real evidence as separate matters from trial fairness. However, at the same time, the Court holds that any use of evidence obtained by torture does automatically – as a matter of principle – render the trial unfair.[128] Similarly, the use of evidence obtained in defiance of the privilege against self-incrimination *ipso facto* violates the right to a fair trial.[129] Regarding evidence obtained by entrapment, the Grand Chamber holds that 'for the trial to be fair within the meaning of Article 6 § 1 of the Convention, all evidence obtained as a result of police incitement *must be excluded*'.[130]

124 Cf. Joint partly concurring opinion of Judges Pinto de Albuquerque and Bošnjak under ECtHR 31 October 2017, appl.no. 22767/08 (*Dragoş Ioan Rusu/Romania*), point 5.

125 Partly dissenting opinion of Judge Spielmann, joined by Judges Rozakis, Tulkens, Casadevall, and Mijović, under ECtHR (GC) 10 March 2009, appl.no. 4378/02 (*Bykov/Russia*), point 10.

126 Ashworth 2003, pp. 120–121. See also Ashworth 1977. Cf. Choo 2008, pp. 126–127.

127 Ormerod 2003; Concurring opinion of Judge Cabral Barreto, under ECtHR (GC) 10 March 2009, appl.no. 4378/02 (*Bykov/Russia*), point 3.4.

128 Ashworth 2012, pp. 157–158, 159–160; Goss 2016, pp. 60–61.

129 Pitcher 2018a, pp. 39–40, 52, 58–59, 99; Ölçer 2008, p. 90; Kuiper 2014, p. 453. Cf. the use of incriminating statements made during police interrogation in breach of the right to counsel: ECtHR (GC) 27 November 2008, appl.no. 36391/02 (*Salduz/Turkey*), § 55.

130 ECtHR (GC) 5 February 2008, appl.no. 74420/01 (*Ramanauskas/Lithuania*), § 60 (emphasis added). See also ECtHR 26 October 2006, appl.no. 59696/00 (*Khudobin/Russia*), § 133.

Another inconsistency concerns the balancing of public interest under the head of Article 6 ECHR. On the one hand, the Court is keen in stressing that public interests cannot justify the use of evidence obtained (1) in violation of the privilege against self-incrimination,[131] (2) in breach of the prohibition of ill-treatment,[132] or (3) as a result of police incitement.[133] Meanwhile, it does accept that the seriousness of the offence and the public interest in prosecuting it can 'outweigh the applicant's basic rights' in light of Article 6 ECHR when the evidence is obtained in breach of Article 8 ECHR.[134]

These inconsistencies raise questions regarding the arguable hierarchy of the fundamental rights and freedoms guaranteed by the Convention. Why is the balancing of public and private interest under Article 6 ECHR permitted when evidence is obtained contrary to Article 8 ECHR, but not when the evidence is secured (1) in violation of the privilege, (2) in breach of Article 3 ECHR, or (3) as a result of entrapment? And why does the use of real evidence obtained by torture automatically violate Article 6 ECHR, while similar evidence, obtained through similar conduct but only (a little) less severe, therefore qualifying as either inhuman, degrading, or breaching Article 8 ECHR, may under certain circumstances be admitted into criminal proceedings?[135]

As Judges Tulkens notes: where and how should we draw the line? And according to which hierarchy among Convention rights?[136] Indeed, the Court considers the right to life as the supreme value in the hierarchy of human rights.[137] Meanwhile, most other rights, such as the prohibition of ill-treatment,[138] the right to respect for private life,[139] the right to a fair trial,[140] the freedom of thought, conscience, and

[131] ECtHR (GC) 10 March 2009, appl.no. 4378/02 (*Bykov/Russia*), § 93; ECtHR 21 December 2000, appl. no. 34720/97 (*Heaney and McGuinness/Ireland*), § 58.

[132] ECtHR (GC) 1 June 2010, appl.no. 22978/05 (*Gäfgen/Germany*), § 176; ECtHR (GC) 11 July 2006, appl.no. 54810/00 (*Jalloh/Germany*), § 106.

[133] ECtHR (GC) 5 February 2008, appl.no. 74420/01 (*Ramanauskas/Lithuania*), § 54; ECtHR 9 June 1998, appl.no. 44/1997/828/1034 (*Teixeira de Castro/Portugal*), § 36.

[134] ECtHR 3 March 2016, appl.no. 7215/10 (*Prade/Germany*), § 41.

[135] Cf. Ashworth 2012, pp. 154–155; Ölçer 2013, p. 380.

[136] Partly dissenting opinion of Judge Tulkens, under ECtHR 25 September 2001, appl.no. 44787/98 (*P.G. and J.H./UK*), point 5.

[137] ECtHR (GC) 20 October 2015, appl.no. 35343/05 (*Vasiliauskas/Lithuania*), § 158.

[138] ECtHR (GC) 1 June 2010, appl.no. 22978/05 (*Gäfgen/Germany*), § 87: 'The Court reiterates that Article 3 of the Convention enshrines one of the most fundamental values of democratic societies'.

[139] ECtHR (GC) 11 July 2002, appl.no. 28957/95 (*Christine Goodwin/UK*), § 90: 'Nonetheless, the very essence of the Convention is respect for human dignity and human freedom. Under Article 8 of the Convention in particular, where the notion of personal autonomy is an important principle underlying the interpretation of its guarantees, protection is given to the personal sphere of each individual, including the right to establish details of their identity as individual human beings'.

[140] ECtHR (GC) 12 February 2004, appl.no. 47287/99 (*Perez/France*), § 64: 'the Court notes that the right to a fair trial holds so prominent a place in a democratic society that there can be no justification for interpreting Article 6 § 1 restrictively'.

religion,[141] and the freedom of expression,[142] are all considered essential within the Convention and critical to democratic societies.[143]

Moreover, according to which criterion should we assess the hierarchy of different aspects of the same absolute provision, such as the prohibition of torture, inhuman, and degrading treatment pursuant to Article 3 ECHR?[144] Judge Cabral Barreto argues that the difference between torture and inhuman and degrading treatment is often difficult to determine. The nuances are sometimes tiny.[145] As a rule, each type of treatment prohibited by Article 3 ECHR involves blunders by the authorities against people in positions of inferiority.[146] Hence, Cabral Barreto argues that the Grand Chamber should state firmly that the use of any evidence obtained in violation of Article 3 ECHR will always infringe Article 6 ECHR, even if the evidence was not decisive.[147] Judge Bratza has drawn the same conclusion, stressing that the borderline between the various forms of ill-treatment is neither immutable nor capable of precise definition, as has been recognised by the Court itself.[148]

Perhaps, the inconsistency in the Court's approach on evidence obtained in breach of Article 8 ECHR compared with Article 3 ECHR and specific defence rights relates to 'the unlawfulness in question' and 'the nature of the violation found'.[149] Both factors are relevant when determining the overall fairness in cases on unlawfully obtained evidence.[150] At least, it is notable that in cases such as *Khan*, *P.G. and J.H*, and *Bykov*, the violation of Article 8 ECHR 'related exclusively' to the fact that the infringement was not 'in accordance with the law'.[151] In assessing whether the criminal proceedings as a whole were fair, the Court in *P.G. and J.H* stressed that:

141 ECtHR (GC) 26 October 2000, appl.no. 30985/96 (*Hasan and Chaush/Bulgaria*), § 60: 'The Court recalls that freedom of thought, conscience and religion is one of the foundations of a democratic society within the meaning of the Convention'.

142 ECtHR (GC) 29 March 2016, appl.no. 56925/08 (*Bédat/Switzerland*), § 48: 'Freedom of expression constitutes one of the essential foundations of a democratic society and one of the basic conditions for its progress and for each individual's self-fulfilment'.

143 See also Goss 2016, p. 62; Lawson 2004, p. 190.

144 Cf. Ashworth 2012, p. 161; Jackson & Summers 2012, pp. 168–169.

145 See also Harris et al. 2018, p. 421.

146 Concurring opinion of Judge Cabral Barreto, under ECtHR (GC) 10 March 2009, appl.no. 4378/02 (*Bykov/Russia*), point 3.1.

147 Ibid.

148 Concurring opinion Judge Bratza, under ECtHR (GC) 11 July 2006, appl.no. 54810/00 (*Jalloh/Germany*), p. 38. See also Joint partly dissenting opinion of Judges Rozakis, Tulkens, Jebens, Ziemele, Bianku, and Power, under ECtHR (GC) 1 June 2010, appl.no. 22978/05 (*Gäfgen/Germany*), point 9.

149 Lawson 2004, pp. 197–198.

150 ECtHR (GC) 17 October 2019, appl.nos. 1874/13 and 8567/13 (*López Ribalda and Others/Spain*), § 150; ECtHR (GC) 1 June 2010, appl.no. 22978/05 (*Gäfgen/Germany*), § 163; ECtHR (GC) 10 March 2009, appl.no. 4378/02 (*Bykov/Russia*), § 89.

151 ECtHR 12 May 2000, appl.no. 5394/97 (*Khan/UK*), § 36; ECtHR 25 September 2001, appl.no. 44787/98 (*P.G. and J.H./UK*), § 78; ECtHR (GC) 10 March 2009, appl.no. 4378/02 (*Bykov/Russia*), § 82. See also ECtHR 22 September 2003, appl.no. 50210/99 (*Doerga/the Netherlands*).

> It is not established that any substantive precondition for the police exercising their surveillance powers was not in fact complied with. *The 'unlawfulness' in the present case therefore relates exclusively to the fact that there was no statutory authority for the interference with the applicants' right* to respect for private life and that, accordingly, such interference was not 'in accordance with the law', as that phrase has been interpreted in Article 8 § 2 of the Convention.[152]

Similarly, when outlining the general principles in *Hambardzumyan/Armenia*, and referring to *Khan, P.G. and J.G*, and *Bykov*, the Court held that:

> As regards, in particular, the examination of the nature of the Convention violation found, the Court observes that in several cases it has found the use of covert listening devices to be in breach of Article 8 *since such interference was not 'in accordance with the law'*. Nonetheless, the admission in evidence of information obtained thereby did not in the circumstances of a particular case conflict with the requirements of fairness guaranteed by Article 6 § 1.[153]

Does the Court suggest here that the *seriousness* of a Convention violation can be a relevant factor when determining the overall fairness of a trial?[154] And if we would accept this claim, should we then regard infringements with private life without or in defiance of a proper legal basis less serious compared with infringements that are 'in accordance with the law', but not 'necessary in a democratic society' for any 'legitimate interest'?[155]

This is not clear from Strasbourg case-law. Indeed, in most cases on excluding evidence obtained in breach of Article 8 ECHR, the violation related to the law-test.[156] However, in some cases, the Court considered the contested covert surveillance

[152] ECtHR 25 September 2001, appl.no. 44787/98 (*P.G. and J.H./UK*), § 78 (emphasis added). See also ECtHR 12 May 2000, appl.no. 5394/97 (*Khan/UK*), § 36.

[153] ECtHR 5 December 2019, appl.no. 43478/11 (*Hambardzumyan/Armenia*), § 77 (emphasis added). See also ECtHR 15 January 2015, appl.no. 68955/11 (*Dragojević/Croatia*), § 130.

[154] Cf. Lawson 2004, p. 198.

[155] See, for example, Lawson 2004, p. 198; Ormerod 2003, pp. 73–74, both challenging this hierarchy of private life violations. Cf. Ashworth 2003, pp. 119–120. By contrast, see, for example, Concurring opinion of Judge Cabral Barreto, under ECtHR (GC) 10 March 2009, appl.no. 4378/02 (*Bykov/Russia*), point 3.4.

[156] ECtHR 5 December 2019, appl.no. 43478/11 (*Hambardzumyan/Armenia*); ECtHR 1 March 2018, appl.no. 50049/12 (*Parazajder/Croatia*); ECtHR 7 November 2017, appl.no. 59589/10 (*Konstantin Moskalev/Russia*); ECtHR 7 November 2017, appl.no. 21200/05 (*Akhlyustin/Russia*); ECtHR 31 October 2017, appl.no. 22767/08 (*Dragoş Ioan Rusu/Romania*); ECtHR 31 January 2017, appl.no. 40233/07 (*Kalnėnienė/Belgium*); ECtHR 18 October 2016, appl.no. 61838/10 (*Vukota-Bojić/Switzerland*); ECtHR 2 December 2014, appl.no. 3082/06 (*Taraneks/Latvia*); ECtHR 25 June 2013, appl.no. 25333/03 (*Niculescu/Romania*); ECtHR 23 June 2013, appl.no. 18540/04 (*Valentino Acatrinei/Romania*); ECtHR 8 March 2011, appl.no. 12739/05 (*Goranova-Karaeneva/Bulgaria*); ECtHR 26 April 2007, appl.no. 71525/01 (*Dumitru Popescu/Roumanie (no 2)*); ECtHR 1 March 2007, appl.no. 5935/02 (*Heglas/Czech Republic*).

measures also not 'necessary within a democratic society'.[157] Examples are *Dragojević/Croatia* and *Bašić/Crotatia*.[158] In these cases, the violation of Article 8 ECHR did not exclusively relate to the law-test. Nonetheless, referring to *Khan*, *P.G. and J.H*, and *Bykov*, the Court applied its standard formula, considering the reliability of the evidence together with the applicants' opportunity to contest the evidence and accepting the balancing of public interest. In both cases, the Court considered the use of evidence obtained in breach of Article 8 ECHR not to render the trial as a whole unfair.[159] Although in *Dragojević* and *Bašić* the violation of Article 8 ECHR consisted in the incompatibility with *both* the law-test and the requirement of necessity, the Court approached these cases under Article 6 ECHR just like any other case on the admission of evidence obtained in defiance of Article 8 ECHR.

Perhaps, the seriousness of a Convention violation in the acquisition of evidence may be a relevant factor in determining the overall fairness of the trial. But this is not clearly illustrated by Strasbourg case-law. Nor is it clear that the seriousness of a violation of Article 8 ECHR should be determined according to the precise requirements of Article 8(2) ECHR that are not complied with. There are no reasons to assume that interfering with people's private life without a legal basis is less severe than when the interference has a legal basis, but is not necessary in a democratic society in the meaning of Article 8(2) ECHR.[160]

Ölçer suggests another explanation for the Court's inconsistent adherence to the separation thesis. In the first place, she argues that the non-derogable Article 3 ECHR hierarchically outranks Articles 8 and 6 ECHR in the general structure of the Convention. In that sense, Ölçer thinks it is not remarkable that evidence obtained in violation of Article 3 ECHR has profound implications.[161] However, apart from the issue of the arguable hierarchy of Convention rights, this argument cannot explain the diverging approach of real evidence obtained by torture as opposed to inhuman and degrading treatment – both consisting non-derogable prohibitions, enshrined in the same provision.

Second, Ölçer argues that unlike pretrial rights such as the right to 'non-incitement' and the right to counsel, privacy violations in pretrial procedures stand 'somewhat isolated' from the sphere of a fair trial. Therefore, they do not necessarily require a remedy within the criminal procedure.[162] The validity of this claim directly

157 Both requirements – the law test and the necessity – are sometimes closely related: ECtHR (GC) 4 December 2008, appl.nos. 30562/04 and 30566/04 (*S. & Marper/UK*), § 99; ECtHR 13 February 2020, appl.no. 45245/15 (*Gaughran/UK*), § 73.

158 ECtHR 15 January 2015, appl.no. 68955/11 (*Dragojević/Croatia*), § 101–102; ECtHR 25 October 2016, appl.no. 22251/13 (*Bašić/Crotatia*), § 34–36.

159 ECtHR 25 October 2016, appl.no. 22251/13 (*Bašić/Crotatia*), § 49; ECtHR 15 January 2015, appl.no. 68955/11 (*Dragojević/Croatia*), § 134.

160 Cf. Kuiper 2014, p. 471.

161 Ölçer 2008, pp. 100–101.

162 Ibid.; Ölçer 2013, p. 380.

touches upon the very essence of the critique on the Strasbourg approach – that is, that the term 'fairness' within the context of the ECHR presupposes respect for the rule of law and for all human rights set out in the Convention.[163]

Closely related to her second claim, Ölçer notes that whereas privacy violations are somewhat isolated from Article 6 ECHR, there is a logical and close relationship between Article 3 ECHR and criminal procedures. Legal proceedings, she argues, are a civilised replacement of the resolution of conflicts by uncivilised physical prevalence. Foremost, they aim to abandon violence in solving disputes.[164] According to Ölçer, the very nature of Article 3 ECHR almost automatically touches procedural fairness. To a large extent, Articles 3 and 6 ECHR overlap, most evidently within the context of the privilege against self-incrimination and the right to remain silent.[165] This overlap is also reflected in one of the foundations of the privilege – preventing improper compulsion – which closely relates to the prohibition of ill-treatment and to the broader concept of human dignity.[166]

Although not referred to by the Court, perhaps, an arguable overlap and closer relationship between Articles 3 and 6 ECHR could explain the inconsistency in separating different substantive rights violations from the notion of a fair trial. At the same time, this argument cannot explain the distinctive approach of *real evidence* obtained by inhuman and degrading treatment as opposed to torture.[167] Both types of ill-treatment are absolutely prohibited by Article 3 ECHR.

RELIABILITY. In examining the fairness of the proceedings when evidence is obtained in breach of Article 8 ECHR, the Court takes into account the quality of the evidence. It considers whether the circumstances of acquisition cast doubts as to the reliability or accuracy of evidence. For example, in *Khan* and *Dragoş Ioan Rusu*,

[163] Partly concurring, partly dissenting opinion of Judge Loucaides, under ECtHR 12 May 2000, appl.no. 5394/97 (*Khan/UK*), p. 15; Partly dissenting opinion of Judge Tulkens, under ECtHR 25 September 2001, appl.no. 44787/98 (*P.G. and J.H./UK*), point 1; Concurring opinion of Judge Bartza, under ECtHR (GC) 11 July 2006, appl.no. 54810/00 (*Jalloh/Germany*), p. 37; Partly dissenting opinion of Judge Spielmann, joined by Judges Rozakis, Tulkens, Casadevall, and Mijović, under ECtHR (GC) 10 March 2009, appl.no. 4378/02 (*Bykov/Russia*), points 6–7; Joint partly dissenting opinion of Judges Rozakis, Tulkens, Jebens, Ziemele, Bianku, and Power, under ECtHR (GC) 1 June 2010, appl.no. 22978/05 (*Gäfgen/Germany*), points 2, 9 and 12; Joint partly concurring opinion of Judges Pinto de Albuquerque and Bošnjak under ECtHR 31 October 2017, appl. no. 22767/08 (*Dragoş Ioan Rusu/Romania*), points 3–4 and 6. Also Lawson 2004, pp. 201–203; Ashworth 2012, p. 157.

[164] Ölçer 2008, p. 101.

[165] Cf. Partly dissenting opinion of Judge Bošnjak under ECtHR 26 January 2021, appl.nos. 73313/17 and 20143/19 (*Zličić/Serbia*), point 18.

[166] Levy 1968, pp. 33, 326–327. See Chapter 6, Section 6.2.2.

[167] Partly dissenting opinion of Judge Bošnjak under ECtHR 26 January 2021, appl.nos. 73313/17 and 20143/19 (*Zličić/Serbia*), points 18–23, 63–69.

the Court 'attached weight' to the fact that the unlawfully obtained evidence was strong and that there was no risk of unreliability.[168]

As Judge Loucaides explains in *Khan*, the basic argument not to exclude unlawfully obtained though reliable evidence is the pursuit of the truth. It relates to the public interest in effective criminal law enforcement and in preventing guilty suspects to escape punishment. However, as Loucaides argues: 'Breaking the law, in order to enforce it, is a contradiction in terms and an absurd proposition'.[169] As noted by Judges Rozakis et al., the exclusion of reliable evidence obtained in breach of Article 3 ECHR may indeed compromise the effective prosecution of a crime or result in a lower sentence. However, the ultimate responsibility of any such 'advantage' to the defendant lies firmly with the State authorities who permit ill-treatment, taking the risk of compromising criminal proceedings.[170]

Moreover, Judges Pinto de Albuquerque and Bošnjak have stressed that seeking the truth is not the only objective of criminal proceedings. As demonstrated by the long-standing case-law of the Court, protecting individuals against the unlimited, disproportionate, and arbitrary use of State powers in criminal law is of equal historical importance.[171] States should respect the rule of law. Thus, they must respect human rights. As a consequence, investigative powers entail legal conditions and procedures, governing the infringements of people's rights and balancing those rights against the interests of society. Often, methods of criminal investigation should correspond to the requirements pursuant to Article 8(2) ECHR. If the domestic courts disregard such legal conditions by admitting evidence obtained in breach of them, the balance will be lost, impairing the fairness of criminal proceedings. Therefore, Pinto de Albuquerque and Bošnjak contend that the probative value of a particular piece of evidence should not be a sufficient argument to override the need to protect human rights and fundamental freedoms.[172]

7.2.6 Synthesis

The Court seems to accept at least four central rationales for either excluding or admitting unlawfully obtained evidence under Article 6 ECHR. These are: (1) deterrence, (2) the integrity principle, (3) the separation thesis, and (4) the reliability of evidence.

[168] ECtHR 12 May 2000, appl.no. 5394/97 (*Khan/UK*), § 37; ECtHR 31 October 2017, appl.no. 22767/08 (*Dragoş Ioan Rusu/Romania*), § 54.

[169] Judge Loucaides, under ECtHR 12 May 2000, appl.no. 5394/97 (*Khan/UK*), p. 16.

[170] Joint partly dissenting opinion of Judges Rozakis, Tulkens, Jebens, Ziemele, Bianku, and Power, under ECtHR (GC) 1 June 2010, appl.no. 22978/05 (*Gäfgen/Germany*), point 11. Also: Partly dissenting opinion of Judge Bošnjak under ECtHR 26 January 2021, appl.nos. 73313/17 and 20143/19 (*Zličić/Serbia*), point 68.

[171] Judges Pinto de Albuquerque and Bošnjak under ECtHR 31 October 2017, appl.no. 22767/08 (*Dragoş Ioan Rusu/Romania*), point 10.

[172] Ibid.

Meanwhile, the Court appears reluctant to develop from these abstract rationales a more concrete, central approach on excluding evidence obtained in breach of the rights and freedoms guaranteed by the ECHR. Instead, the Court keeps stressing that it is not its role to determine as a matter of principle whether such unlawfully obtained evidence should be admissible or not under Article 6 ECHR. The question to be answered in each case is whether the proceedings as a whole, including the acquisition of evidence, were fair. In this regard, the Court has developed various diverging approaches under Article 6 ECHR on the use at trial of evidence obtained in breach of Article 3, 8 and particular defence rights such as the privilege against self-incrimination.

These approaches, both on their own and taken together, align not very well with the central rationales for excluding evidence as are endorsed by the Court. Perhaps most telling is the Court reiterating its guiding principle of not being competent to determine, as a rule, whether unlawfully obtained evidence may be admissible under Article 6 ECHR. At the same time, it has formulated exact such absolute exclusionary rules, for example, regarding evidence obtained by torture and entrapment.

Furthermore, while endorsing the importance of deterrence and the integrity principle, the Court limits, in my view without convincing reasons, the implications of these rationales to evidence obtained in breach of Article 3 ECHR. It even makes an artificial distinction between the exclusion of real evidence obtained by torture and real evidence obtained through inhuman or degrading treatment – which are both prohibited in absolute terms under Article 3 ECHR. Further inconstancies have been identified in the Court's adherence to the separation thesis.

Clearly, crime must be combated. States have positive obligations to enact effective provisions of criminal law and to apply them in practice through effective investigation and prosecution,[173] which obligations could be jeopardised by the exclusion of evidence in criminal proceedings.[174] Meanwhile, States are bound to the rule of law and to the self-imposed restrictions of human rights. They should prevent and prosecute crime while respecting the fundamental rights and freedoms guaranteed by the ECHR. When reliable evidence has been obtained in breach of the Convention, domestic courts are sometimes confronted with a difficult dilemma: *admit* the evidence and prosecute crime based on a human rights violation, or *exclude* the evidence, respecting the rule of law, deterring law-enforcement and vindicate human rights, while hampering the effective prosecution of crime.

Current Strasbourg case-law does not provide clear guidance to the domestic courts. Recalling the observation of Judges Pinto de Albuquerque and Bošnjak, the Court's approach lacks persuasiveness, coherence, and clarity. These judges

[173] See, for example, ECtHR 4 December 2003, appl.no. 39272/98 (*M.C./Bulgaria*), § 153; ECtHR 22 June 2021, appl.no. 22597/16 (*R.B./Estonia*), § 78–84.

[174] ECtHR 22 June 2021, appl.no. 22597/16 (*R.B./Estonia*), § 101–104.

argue that the Court should therefore revise its current position.[175] In the same vein, Goss considers the present position of the Court incoherent and poorly explained; the Court fails to appreciate the complexity of the framework outlined in its own case-law.[176]

A clearer approach would be valuable to domestic courts in searching for a fair balance between effectively combatting crime and respecting human rights. Think of the *prima facie* rule suggested by Ashworth. According to such a rule, there should at least be a presumption that violating the Convention leads to the inadmissibility of the evidence resulting from it.[177] Meanwhile, when sufficient, strong countervailing factors exist, the use at trial of such evidence could sometimes be allowed in an individual case.

Reconsidering the Strasbourg position on excluding unlawfully obtained evidence under Article 6 ECHR would exceed the scope of this book. The present chapter analyses the procedural implications of brain-reading in breach of the Convention. Although the Strasbourg approach is not free from principle objections, the member States must comply with the minimum standards the Court determines under Article 6 ECHR. But of course, in guaranteeing the rights and freedoms enshrined in the Convention, the member States are free to provide stronger legal protection.[178] They may adopt stricter rules relating to the exclusion of evidence obtained in defiance of fundamental rights. As Myjer noted in response to *Khan/UK*, if it were not for the self-respecting member States to exceed the minimum requirements determined by the Strasbourg institutions, *Khan* could have been the end of many domestic doctrines on excluding evidence obtained in breach of human rights.[179]

7.3 FORENSIC BRAIN-READING IN BREACH OF THE ECHR: EXCLUDING EVIDENCE UNDER ARTICLE 6 ECHR?

7.3.1 *Introduction*

In 2001, De Hert and Koops considered the legal implications of the Strasbourg approach on excluding unlawfully obtained evidence as was adopted by the Court in *Khan/UK*. Fantasising about a brilliant new tool that captures brain waves and reads thoughts, breaching Article 8 ECHR but yielding reliable evidence, the

175 Joint partly concurring opinion of Judges Pinto de Albuquerque and Bošnjak under ECtHR 31 October 2017, appl.no. 22767/08 (*Dragoş Ioan Rusu/Romania*), point 1.

176 Goss 2016, p. 59. See also Jackson & Summers 2012, p. 195

177 Ashworth 2003, pp. 120–121. See also Ashworth 1977. Cf. Choo 2008, pp. 126–127; Ormerod 2003; Concurring opinion of Judge Cabral Barreto, under ECtHR (GC) 10 March 2009, appl.no. 4378/02 (*Bykov/Russia*), point 3.4.

178 See Article 53 ECHR.

179 Myjer 2000, p. 1255.

authors speculated that such privacy violations shall not render the trial unfair under the Strasbourg position as adopted in *Khan*.[180] This section examines whether the Court's approach on excluding evidence obtained in breach of the Convention will indeed allow the admission of evidence obtained by unlawful brain-reading.

As discussed in the previous chapters, coercive brain-reading has the potential of not only raising issues under Articles 8, 3, and 6 ECHR but also under Article 10 and, possibly, Article 9 ECHR. Violations of the Convention by 'traditional' methods of criminal investigation are normally limited to privacy, ill-treatment, and defence rights. As a consequence, the Strasbourg account on excluding unlawfully obtained evidence has yet not been specified to the use at trial of evidence obtained in defiance of the freedom of expression and the freedom of thought. This section explores whether the Court's current position to breaches of Articles 8, 3, and 6 ECHR provides helpful insights for developing similar sub-approaches in respect of Articles 9 and 10 ECHR.

The next sections discuss the issue of excluding brain-reading evidence obtained in breach of, respectively, (1) the privilege against self-incrimination, (2) the prohibition of ill-treatment, (3) the right to freedom of thought, (4) the right to respect for private life, and (5) the freedom of non-expression.

7.3.2 *Violating the Privilege against Self-incrimination (Article 6 ECHR)*

The use at trial of evidence obtained in breach of the privilege against self-incrimination will always render the trial as a whole unfair. Coercive brain-reading in criminal law will not raise fundamental questions in this regard. To preserve the fairness of the criminal proceedings, brain-reading data secured in defiance of the privilege should be excluded from evidence.

However, regarding the rationales of excluding evidence obtained in breach of the privilege, one could argue that these are less compelling in respect of forensic brain-reading. These rationales can be traced back to the privilege's foundations – that is, (1) protecting from improper compulsion, (2) pursuing the use of reliable evidence, and (3) respecting the suspect's autonomy.[181] However, earlier we saw that coercive brain-reading is generally safe and will not typically involve improper compulsion. Moreover, it can provide a valuable contribution to increase the reliability of criminal evidence.[182] Accordingly, *excluding* brain-reading data obtained in defiance of the privilege cannot be justified by protecting against improper compulsion, nor by the pursuit of using only reliable evidence at trial. Still, the exclusion of evidence could be grounded in preserving the integrity of the criminal proceedings and respecting the rule of law. Similarly, it has been argued that the exclusion of

[180] De Hert & Koops 2001, p. 974.
[181] Section 7.2.2.
[182] Chapter 6, Section 6.3.4.

evidence obtained by entrapment is predominantly motivated by considerations of moral integrity.[183]

Will the integrity principle alone be compelling enough to exclude brain-reading evidence obtained in breach of the privilege, when that breach is exclusively grounded in infringing the suspect's autonomy?[184] This is an open question, touching upon the general issue of valuing autonomy in the context of Article 6 ECHR. I will delve deeper into this question in Chapter 8, when discussing the challenges coercive brain-reading poses for European human rights law.

7.3.3 *Violating the Prohibition of Ill-Treatment (Article 3 ECHR)*

Enforcing brain-reading with physical coercion entails a serious risk of causing physical discomfort, pain, distress, and/or mental suffering, capable of attaining the threshold of Article 3 ECHR.[185] Such brain-reading could amount to inhuman and/or degrading treatment. When extreme levels of physical coercion are used, causing 'serious and cruel suffering', forensic brain-reading could even attain to torture.

The admission of evidence obtained in breach of Article 3 ECHR will always raise serious issues regarding the fairness of the proceedings, even if the evidence is not decisive in securing a conviction.[186] It is clear from Strasbourg case-law that using brain-reading evidence obtained by torture will render the criminal proceedings as a whole unfair: 'no legal system based upon the rule of law can countenance the admission of evidence – however reliable – which has been obtained by such a barbaric practice as torture'.[187]

Whether the use of evidence secured by *inhuman and/or degrading treatment* will render the trial unfair depends, however, on the nature of the evidence so obtained. Regarding *confessions*, using such evidence will always violate the right to a fair trial under Article 6 ECHR. As to *real evidence*, the criminal proceedings will only be unfair when the violation of Article 3 ECHR had direct impact on the conviction or sentence.[188] How should we qualify brain-reading evidence in this respect?

Typically, neuroimaging techniques, such as (f)MRI, CT, EEG, and PET, do not produce a confession. They neither yield any real, tangible evidence (such as a knife, fingerprints, and blood samples). In fact, they produce brain-derived data that

[183] Choo 2008, p. 148; Pitcher & Samadi 2018, p. 742.

[184] As discussed in Chapter 6, Section 6.3.4.

[185] Chapter 3.

[186] ECtHR (GC) 1 June 2010, appl.no. 22978/05 (*Gäfgen/Germany*), § 165.

[187] ECtHR 17 January 2012, appl.no. 8139/09 (*Othman (Abu Qatada)/UK*), § 264. Cf. ECtHR (GC) 1 June 2010, appl.no. 22978/05 (*Gäfgen/Germany*), § 166–167, 173; ECtHR (GC) 11 July 2006, appl. no. 54810/00 (*Jalloh/Germany*), § 105; ECtHR 25 September 2012, appl.no. 649/08 (*El Haski/ Belgium*), § 85.

[188] ECtHR 26 January 2021, appl.nos. 73313/17 and 20143/19 (*Zličić/Serbia*), § 119; ECtHR (GC) 1 June 2010, appl.no. 22978/05 (*Gäfgen/Germany*), § 166, 167, 178.

enable the examiner to draw certain inferences about brain and mental states.[189] How should we approach such brain-reading data, obtained by means of inhuman and/or degrading treatment, in the context of excluding evidence under Article 6 ECHR?

Equating them with confessions is not persuasive. The Court's predominant rationale for excluding, under Article 6 ECHR, confessions obtained in breach of Article 3 ECHR, lies in their inherent unreliable nature.[190] Victims of ill-treatments may often say anything, truthful or not, as the shortest way of freeing themselves from the pain and suffering inflicted on them.[191] However, unlike subjective confessions, the reliability of objective data yielded through brain-reading will hardly be affected by the employment of ill-treatment.[192] In view of the results, it will normally be immaterial whether a CT-scan to diagnose a brain tumour or an MRI-scan to asses brain anomalies associated with violent behaviour is performed either volitionally or via the use of inhuman and degrading treatment (e.g. through general anaesthesia). In both cases, if present, the brain tumour will be diagnosed and the brain anomaly identified.

Admittedly, this may be different regarding functional neuroimaging, which is sensitive to countermeasures and can be distorted by physical force. Meanwhile, since the Court has even qualified a written document signed under force as real evidence in this context,[193] equating the results of functional neuroimaging with confessions is unlikely to be compelling.

Approaching brain-reading data along the lines of real evidence may therefore be more convincing. Regarding the exclusion of real evidence obtained through inhuman and degrading treatment, the Grand Chamber relies predominantly on considerations of deterrence. It argues that the repression of and the effective protection from such prohibited treatment may require, as a rule, the exclusion of real evidence obtained as a result of any violation of Article 3 ECHR, including inhuman and degrading treatment.[194] Excluding brain-reading data along the lines of real evidence, that is, for the purpose of deterring law-enforcement officials from inflicting ill-treatment, is persuasive.

However, if we equate brain-reading data with real evidence, the use of these data, obtained by *degrading or inhuman treatment*, will not as a rule render the proceedings as a whole unfair. The admission of real evidence so obtained only

[189] Cf. the descriptive qualification of 'demonstrative evidence'.

[190] ECtHR 9 February 2016, appl.no. 40852/05 (*Shlychkov/Russia*), § 82–88; ECtHR 6 October 2015, appl. no. 4722/09 (*Turbylev/Russia*), § 90–98; ECtHR 21 September 2006, appl.no. 46661/99 (*Söylemez/Turkey*), § 122. Cf.

[191] Cf. ECtHR 17 January 2012, appl.no. 8139/09 (*Othman (Abu Qatada)/UK*), § 264.

[192] Cf. Mirfield 1997, p. 7. Provided that the brain technology is valid and accurate.

[193] ECtHR 26 January 2021, appl.nos. 73313/17 and 20143/19 (*Zličić/Serbia*), § 121.

[194] ECtHR (GC) 1 June 2010, appl.no. 22978/05 (*Gäfgen/Germany*), § 178.

breaches Article 6 ECHR when it had direct impact on the conviction or sentence. Consider the following example.

> *Guilty Gabriel.* Gabriel stands trial for robbing a bank. She pleads not guilty. In order to examine whether Gabriel recognises essential details of the crime, she is obliged to a concealed information test. To ensure Gabriel's full cooperation, the police abuse her physically prior to the test and guarantee that if she refuses cooperation or engages in countermeasures, they will subject her to intolerable pain. As it turns out, Gabriel recognises the crime scene, the victim that opened the safe, the sports bag with money found nearby, and the getaway car recorded by CCTV. Suppose that the test results have been obtained by inhuman treatment in breach of Article 3 ECHR. Therefore, Gabriel argues to exclude the brain-reading data from evidence. The court declines this motion. At trial, Gabriel is confronted with the results of the concealed information test. In response, she confesses. Based on this confession and some additional evidence, Gabriel is convicted and sentenced to four years imprisonment.

If we equate brain-reading data with real evidence, the current Strasbourg approach forces us to conclude that Gabriel's right to a fair trial has not been undermined by admitting and using the outcomes of the concealed information test at trial. Although the test results had been obtained by inhuman treatment, they were not decisive in proving guilt or determining sanctions.[195] They were 'only' used to verify Gabriel's statements.[196] Echoing the case of *Gäfgen*, the Court would probably argue that there had been a break in the causal chain leading from the proscribed means of investigation to Gabriel's conviction and sentence. Admitting the brain-reading data to trial will therefore not render the proceedings as a whole unfair contrary to Article 6 ECHR. Meanwhile, if Gabriel had invoked her right to remain silent and the brain-reading results had actually been used as evidence in her conviction, the right to a fair trial would have been violated. Then, the unlawfully obtained evidence had a direct impact on the conviction or sentence.

In conclusion, if brain-reading data have been obtained in breach of Article 3 ECHR, it may be most persuasive to treat such evidence along the lines of real evidence when determining the overall fairness of the criminal proceedings. Yet although such an approach is most convincing in light of Strasbourg case-law, it will be susceptible to the fundamental critique that any kind of evidence obtained in defiance of any kind of ill-treatment contrary to Article 3 ECHR should always be excluded to preserve the integrity of the proceedings and to respect the rule of law.[197]

[195] Cf. ECtHR 26 January 2021, appl.nos. 73313/17 and 20143/19 (*Zličić/Serbia*), § 121; ECtHR (GC) 1 June 2010, appl.no. 22978/05 (*Gäfgen/Germany*), § 179.

[196] Cf. ECtHR (GC) 1 June 2010, appl.no. 22978/05 (*Gäfgen/Germany*), § 179.

[197] See Section 7.2.5.2.

7.3.4 *Violating the Right to Freedom of Thought (Article 9 ECHR)*

Present forensic brain-reading applications will not typically reveal mental content that qualifies as a 'thought' in the meaning of Article 9(1) ECHR. Perhaps, technological developments might enable the non-consensual acquisition of such information in the future. When they do, the absolute protection of the *forum internum* kicks in, prohibiting any form of coercion to reveal a person's thoughts, conscience, or religious adherence.

Traditional means of criminal investigation are not normally considered to violate Article 9 ECHR. As a consequence, the Court has yet abstained from taking position in this matter under Article 6 ECHR. In developing an approach on excluding evidence obtained in violation of Article 9 ECHR, the Court's considerations on excluding evidence in breach of Article 3 ECHR could provide helpful insights and directions.

Under Article 6 ECHR, the Court's central concern is whether the proceedings as a whole, including the way in which the evidence was obtained, were fair. Where a violation of another Convention right is concerned, the Court takes into account the nature of the violation found. In respect of Article 3 ECHR, the Court stresses: 'The use of such evidence, secured as a result of a violation of one of the core and absolute rights guaranteed by the Convention, always raises serious issues as to the fairness of the proceedings, even if the admission of such evidence was not decisive in securing a conviction'.[198]

Similar to Article 3 ECHR, the right to freedom of thought as enshrined in the *forum internum* is an absolute right. It qualifies as one of the foundations of a democratic society within the meaning of the Convention.[199] The Convention is to be interpreted as promoting internal consistency and harmony between the various provisions.[200] Therefore, it is arguable that the use of evidence obtained by a violation of other core and absolute rights – such as the right to freedom of thought – will always raise serious issues regarding the fairness of the proceedings, similar to evidence obtained in breach of Article 3 ECHR.

Excluding brain-reading evidence obtained in breach of the right to freedom of thought can be grounded in similar reasons as the Court provides for excluding evidence obtained in violation of Article 3 ECHR. Similar to the admission of evidence obtained in breach of Article 3 ECHR,[201] the use at trial of evidence secured in violation of the right to freedom of thought could be an incentive for law-enforcement officials to use similar methods of investigation in future cases – regardless of whether they are absolutely prohibited by Article 9 ECHR. The repression of and

198 ECtHR (GC) 1 June 2010, appl.no. 22978/05 (*Gäfgen/Germany*), § 165.
199 ECtHR (GC) 26 October 2000, appl.no. 30985/96 (*Hasan and Chaush/Bulgaria*), § 60.
200 ECtHR (GC) 8 July 2019, appl.no. 54012/10 (*Mihalache/Romania*), § 91.
201 ECtHR (GC) 1 June 2010, appl.no. 22978/05 (*Gäfgen/Germany*), § 178. See also Thommen & Samadi 2016, p. 82.

the effective protection from means of police investigation that violate the *forum internum* may also require, as a rule, the exclusion of evidence obtained in breach of Article 9 ECHR. This would align with the idea expressed in the *travaux préparatoires*, that the right to freedom of thought protects 'from those abominable methods of police enquiry or judicial process which rob the suspect or accused person of control of his intellectual faculties and of his conscience'.[202]

Similar to Article 3 ECHR,[203] it is compelling to exclude evidence secured in violation of the freedom of thought in order to preserve the integrity of the judicial process and thus to protect the values of civilised societies founded upon the rule of law. The freedom of thought is to be considered one of the core foundations of present democratic societies.[204] As France argued during the codification of the Universal Declaration of Human Rights, freedom of thought is a 'sacred and inviolable right'. It is the basis and origin of all other rights and liberties.[205] In discussing its historical, legal-philosophical glances, Bublitz argues that without exaggeration the right to freedom of thought is one of the central elements of the Enlightenment, foundational to liberal democracies.[206] As Harris et al. contend, such a right, largely exercised inside an individual's heart and mind, falls beyond the jurisdiction of the State.[207]

It is hardly conceivable how the use at trial of evidence obtained in violation of the freedom of thought would serve anything else but to 'legitimise, indirectly, the kind of morally reprehensible conduct that the authors of Article 9 ECHR sought to proscribe'.[208] Among others, this right seeks to prohibit those methods in both *police enquiry* and *judicial process* that rob the defendant of controlling her mental capacities.[209] Excluding evidence obtained in defiance of the absolute right to freedom of thought could therefore be required to protect the integrity of the criminal process and, ultimately, the rule of law itself.[210] As Judges Rozakis, Tulkens, Jebens, Ziemele, Bianku, and Power have argued in *Gäfgen/Germany*,

202 European Commission of Human Rights (EComHR), *Preparatory Work on Article 9 of the European Convention on Human Rights*, Strasbourg, 16 August 1959, pp. 3–4. See also Vermeulen & Roosmalen 2018, p. 738–739.

203 ECtHR 17 January 2012, appl.no. 8139/09 (*Othman (Abu Qatada)/UK*), § 264; ECtHR (GC) 1 June 2010, appl.no. 22978/05 (*Gäfgen/Germany*), § 175.

204 ECtHR (GC) 26 October 2000, appl.no. 30985/96 (*Hasan and Chaush/Bulgaria*), § 60; Rainey, McCormick & Ovey 2021, p. 461; McCarthy-Jones 2019, p. 2.

205 Schabas 2013, pp. 1766–1767.

206 Bublitz 2014, pp. 4–5.

207 Harris et al. 2018, p. 573.

208 Cf. ECtHR (GC) 1 June 2010, appl.no. 22978/05 (*Gäfgen/Germany*), § 167; ECtHR (GC) 11 July 2006, appl.no. 54810/00 (*Jalloh/Germany*), § 105; ECtHR 28 June 2007, appl.no. 36549/03 (*Harutyunyan/Armenia*), § 63.

209 EComHR, *Preparatory Work on Article 9 of the European Convention on Human Rights*, Strasbourg, 16 August 1959, pp. 3–4.

210 Cf. ECtHR 17 January 2012, appl.no. 8139/09 (*Othman (Abu Qatada)/UK*), § 264; ECtHR (GC) 1 June 2010, appl.no. 22978/05 (*Gäfgen/Germany*), § 167, 175; ECtHR (GC) 11 July 2006, appl.no. 54810/00 (*Jalloh/Germany*), § 105.

> There is, in addition, a critical public interest in ensuring and maintaining the integrity of the judicial process and the admission into a trial of evidence obtained in violation of an absolute human right would undermine and jeopardise the integrity of that process.[211]

Approaching evidence obtained in breach of Article 9(1) ECHR analogous to evidence secured by ill-treatment could raise another question. Should the Court value violations of the different aspects of the *forum internum* – that is, freedom of *thought*, *conscience*, and *religion* – differently under Article 6 ECHR, as it does in respect of real evidence obtained through torture, inhuman, and degrading treatment?

Apart from the general critique on considering separate aspects of one single absolute right distinctively under the right to a fair trial,[212] the text of Article 9(1) ECHR cannot give any reasons for such artificial distinction. As demonstrated by the initial drafting process of the right to freedom of thought conscience, and religion pursuant to Article 18 UDHR, no internal hierarchy exists among these protected notions. The reason that 'thought' is mentioned first is because freedom of thought has historically preceded freedom of belief. Therefore, China suggested mentioning freedom of thought prior to the freedom of religion and conscience.[213]

Alternative approaches on excluding evidence obtained in violation of Article 9 ECHR are conceivable as well. Perhaps, the Court could align with its approach on excluding evidence obtained in violation of the privilege against self-incrimination. When a suspect is coerced to testify in breach of the privilege, his spoken or written words should be excluded to ensure a fair trial. Intuitively, it seems reasonable that when a suspect is coerced to participate in brain-reading in breach of Article 9 ECHR, the unspoken words – his 'thoughts' – should likewise be excluded to assure fair proceedings.

One could object to this view by referring to the separation thesis that the Court tends to adhere. According to this thesis, the requirements of a fair trial under Article 6 ECHR and violations of other Convention rights are two separate matters.[214] As a consequence, there would be no compelling reason to exclude evidence obtained in breach of Article 9 ECHR in a similar way as evidence yielded in breach of the privilege, guaranteed by Article 6 ECHR. The privilege lies at the heart of a fair trial; the *forum internum* of Article 9 ECHR does not.

Meanwhile, as the *travaux préparatoires* suggest, fair trials and the freedom of thought are not *entirely* unrelated. Among other things, the freedom of thought protects against means of police investigation and judicial process that restrict our free disposal over mental capacities.[215] Can we consider a trial fair in the

[211] Joint partly dissenting opinion of Judges Rozakis, Tulkens, Jebens, Ziemele, Bianku, and Power, under ECtHR (GC) 1 June 2010, appl.no. 22978/05 (*Gäfgen/Germany*), point 12.

[212] Section 7.2.5.2.

[213] Schabas 2013, p. 1768.

[214] Ashworth 2012, p. 157; Ashworth 2003, pp. 113–115; Ölçer 2008, p. 105; Kuiper 2014, p. 473.

[215] See also Levy 1968, p. 4; UN Special Rapporteur on Freedom of Religion or Belief 2021, para. 26.

meaning of Article 6 ECHR when the evidence has been obtained by such illicit means of police enquiry? Or should any limitation of the suspect's autonomy in disclosing 'thoughts' result in excluding the evidence so obtained? The answer to this question partly depends on how much weight we should attach to the concept of autonomy under the head of Article 6 ECHR. This issue will be discussed in Chapter 8.

7.3.5 *Violating the Right to Respect for Private Life (Article 8 ECHR)*

Coercive brain-reading can be in accordance with the right to respect for private live as long as the law provides sufficient safeguards against arbitrary use and abuse.[216] Yet, cases where forensic brain-reading would violate Article 8 ECHR are easy to conceive. Think of employing brain-reading without or in defiance of a national legal basis; yielding sensitive medical brain data to solve trivial offences; or retaining, indefinitely, neuropredictive data from acquitted suspects.

In most such cases, where forensic brain-reading violates Article 8 ECHR, the use at trial of evidence so obtained shall not render the proceedings as a whole unfair under Article 6 ECHR – provided that the defendant had ample opportunity to challenging both the authenticity and use of the brain-reading data.[217] The Court will take into account the quality of the evidence, including whether the circumstances of acquisition cast doubts on its reliability or accuracy.[218]

When a brain-reading test is considered both valid and accurate, the 'mere' fact that it has been employed in defiance of Article 8 ECHR, for example, without a sufficient legal basis, shall not cast any doubts as to the reliability or accuracy of the yielded information. This may, however, be different when the breach of Article 8 ECHR consists in the use of physical force, violating the subject's right to respect for bodily integrity. For example, during a resting-state fMRI, the use of chemical or physical restraint might affect the subject's brain activity and thereby the ultimate results.[219] Moreover, muscular movements of the subject, such as physically resisting means of restraint, generate 'noise'. Especially in the course of functional neuroimaging such as EEG and fMRI, such noise could invalidate the

[216] Chapter 4.

[217] Cf., *inter alia*, ECtHR (GC) 10 March 2009, appl.no. 4378/02 (*Bykov/Russia*), § 94–98; ECtHR 5 December 2019, appl.no. 43478/11 (*Hambardzumyan/Armenia*), § 79–81; ECtHR 31 January 2017, appl.no. 40233/07 (*Kalnėnienė/Belgium*), § 48–54; ECtHR 15 January 2015, appl.no. 68955/11 (*Dragojević/Croatia*), § 131–135; ECtHR 26 September 2002, appl.no. 63831/00 (*Chalkley/UK*), pp. 15–16; ECtHR 26 September 2002, appl.no. 63737/00 (*Perry/UK*), pp. 10–11; ECtHR 25 September 2001, appl.no. 44787/98 (*P.G. and J.H./UK*), § 79; ECtHR 12 May 2000, appl.no. 5394/97 (*Khan/UK*), § 38–40.

[218] ECtHR (GC) 17 October 2019, appl.nos. 1874/13 and 8567/13 (*López Ribalda and Others/Spain*), § 150–151; ECtHR (GC) 10 March 2009, appl.no. 4378/02 (*Bykov/Russia*), § 90; ECtHR 31 October 2017, appl.no. 22767/08 (*Dragoş Ioan Rusu/Romania*), § 49, 54.

[219] See, for example, Mhuircheartaigh et al. 2010; Paasonen et al. 2018; Roskies 2013a, p. 47; Korponay & Koenigs 2016, p. 16.

data set.[220] In those cases, a breach of Article 8 ECHR can give rise to exclude the data so obtained.

7.3.6 *Violating the Right to Freedom of Non-expression (Article 10 ECHR)*

Similar to the right to freedom of thought, complaints about traditional means of criminal investigation are not typically addressed under the right to freedom of expression. As a consequence, the Court has not specified an individual approach on the use at trial of evidence secured in violation of Article 10 ECHR. Meanwhile, the freedom of non-expression may well develop into one of the central human rights regulating coercive brain-reading in criminal law.[221]

Although Article 10(2) ECHR allows for some exceptions, violating the freedom of non-expression by coercive brain-reading is easy to imagine. Think of brain-reading without a legal basis in domestic law. In such cases, where brain-reading violates the right not to express oneself pursuant to Article 10 ECHR, the question will arise whether the admission of the evidence renders the trial as a whole unfair under Article 6 ECHR.

As a qualified right, Article 10(2) ECHR allows for various exceptions that are in accordance with the law and necessary in a democratic society in view of the legitimate interest pursued, similar to Article 8 ECHR.[222] Considering complaints about the use at trial of evidence obtained in breach of the Convention, the Court takes account of the nature of the violated right at issue. As mentioned earlier,[223] the Convention must be interpreted systematically, pursuing both internal consistency and harmony among the Convention provisions. Since Articles 10 and 8 ECHR are both qualified rights, it seems reasonable to develop an approach on excluding evidence obtained in breach of Article 10 ECHR in conformity with the Court's position on evidence secured in defiance of Article 8 ECHR. That means (1) putting emphasis on the opportunity of challenging the authenticity of the evidence and of opposing its use, (2) taking into account the quality of the evidence, and (3) leaving room for the balancing of public interests.

At the same time, from a more substantive point of view, the use of evidence obtained in breach of the right *not to express oneself* could also be approached along the lines of admitting evidence secured in breach of the right *not to incriminate oneself*. Basically, both rights guarantee the same substantive freedom: the freedom not to speak or furnish certain information.[224]

220 Mecacci & Haselager 2019, p. 455; Kanwisher 2009, p. 12.

221 See Chapter 8, Section 8.4.3.

222 Cf. Lavrysen 2018, p. 308; Ashworth 2012, p. 147; Barkhuysen & Van Emmerik 2018, p. 1057.

223 Cf. Section 7.3.4.

224 See, for example, ECtHR 21 December 2000, appl.no. 34720/97 (*Heaney and McGuinness/Ireland*), § 62, speaking of the 'correlative right not to speak or furnish information guaranteed by Article 10',

Meanwhile, whereas both rights provide defendants in criminal proceedings with similar freedoms, one could object to this view by emphasising their distinctive origins. Whereas the privilege derives directly from the right to a fair trial,[225] the freedom of non-expression follows from the broader interest of enabling public debates, vital for a well-functioning democracy and for each individual's self-fulfilment.[226] Concerning the privilege against self-incrimination, it may be obvious that the admission of evidence obtained in violation of this legal principle – lying at the heart of the notion of a fair trial – will automatically render the criminal proceedings as whole unfair. Such a strict approach is less evident in respect of rights and freedoms that primarily protect fundamental values somewhat isolated from the notion of a fair trial, like the right to private life and the freedom of expression.[227] Whether the admission of evidence obtained in defiance of such 'somewhat isolated' human rights will affect the notion of a fair trial depends on the circumstances of the individual case. In light of the separation thesis, which appears predominant in present Strasbourg case-law, it is unlikely that the Court would approach the use of evidence obtained in violation of Article 10 ECHR along the lines of evidence secured in breach of the privilege against self-incrimination.

The exact procedural implications of using brain-reading evidence obtained in breach of Article 10 ECHR shall also depend on the Court's substantive approach of brain-reading in this regard. When specifying the yet underdeveloped freedom of non-expression to coercive brain-reading, the Court could possibly adopt considerations relating to the notion of a fair trial, for example, by referring to its case-law on the 'correlative right' not to incriminate oneself.[228] Violations of the freedom of non-expression might then be considered 'less isolated' from Article 6 ECHR compared with violations of the right to respect for private life. In that case, it could be reasonable to exclude evidence obtained in breach of the freedom of non-expression pursuant to Article 10 ECHR. Alternatively, the Court could also develop a substantive approach on the freedom to non-expression by relying, predominantly, on the origins of Article 10 ECHR, referring to mental privacy and to the importance of fostering democracy and the individual's self-fulfilment.[229] Breaches of Article 10 ECHR should then rather be conceived as remote from the fairness of an individual

which did not give rise to a separate issue, since the essential issue of coercing the defendants to testify had been considered under the privilege against self-incrimination pursuant to Article 6 ECHR. See also ECtHR 21 December 2000, appl.no. 36887/97 (*Quinn/Ireland*), § 63.

225 ECtHR (GC) 13 September 2016, appl.nos. 50541/08, 50571/08, 50573/08, and 40351/09 (*Ibrahim and others/UK*), § 266; ECtHR (GC) 1 June 2010, appl.no. 22978/05 (*Gäfgen/Germany*), § 168.

226 ECtHR (GC) 29 March 2016, appl.no. 56925/08 (*Bédat/Switzerland*), § 48; Van Rijn 2018, p. 765; Harris et al. 2018, pp. 592–593; Rainey, McCormick & Ovey 2021, pp. 488–489; Bublitz 2014, pp. 4–6.

227 Cf. Ölçer 2008, pp. 100–101; Ölçer 2013, p. 380.

228 Cf. ECtHR 21 December 2000, appl.no. 34720/97 (*Heaney and McGuinness/Ireland*), § 62; ECtHR 21 December 2000, appl.no. 36887/97 (*Quinn/Ireland*), § 63.

229 Cf. Jackson & Summers 2012, p. 249.

criminal trial. In that case, the arguments to exclude evidence obtained through a violation of Article 10 ECHR shall be less compelling.

7.4 CONCLUSION

When forensic brain-reading violates the Convention in the determination of a criminal charge, Article 6 ECHR sometimes requires judges to take action in order to preserve the fairness of the criminal proceedings. As De Hert and Koops predicted twenty years ago,[230] the admission of brain-reading evidence obtained in breach of Article 8 ECHR shall only very seldom render the criminal proceedings unfair under Article 6 ECHR. Yet, this observation should not imply that the authorities have *carte blanche* in using brain-reading evidence obtained in defiance of the Convention. Apart from the right to respect for private life, coercive brain-reading could elicit legal protection from the privilege against self-incrimination, the freedom of non-expression, the prohibition of ill-treatment and, potentially, the freedom of thought.

The use at trial of evidence obtained in defiance of the privilege against-self-incrimination will always render the trial as a whole unfair. To prevent a violation of Article 6 ECHR, such evidence should be excluded. And when brain-reading violates an absolute right, the admission of the evidence so obtained will therefore raise serious issues regarding the fairness of the proceedings, even when the evidence is not decisive in securing a conviction. In case of torture and, arguably, in case of violating the right to freedom of thought, the unlawfully obtained brain-reading data must be excluded from evidence on pain of rendering the trial as a whole unfair. The use of brain-reading evidence obtained through inhuman and/or degrading treatment will at least violate the right to a fair trial if it has direct impact on the ultimate conviction or sentence.

Meanwhile, the admission into evidence of brain-reading data obtained in breach of Article 8 ECHR shall not normally render the proceedings as a whole unfair. At least, not when the evidence is reliable and accurate and the defendant had ample opportunity to challenging both the authenticity and use of the data so obtained. Concerning violations of Article 10 ECHR, present case-law provides reasons to assume that the Court would be inclined to approach such evidence along the lines of evidence secured in breach of Article 8 ECHR. The precise procedural implications will also depend on the Court's substantive approach of forensic brain-reading under the yet underdeveloped freedom of non-expression. These conclusions follow from the Court's current position on admitting unlawfully obtained evidence in light of the right to a fair trial. This approach, however, is not free from fundamental criticism. It lacks persuasiveness, coherence, and clarity.

[230] De Hert & Koops 2001, p. 974.

8

Discussion and Perspectives

Emerging Challenges for European Human Rights Law

8.1 INTRODUCTION

The examination in the previous chapters focussed on the legal implications of coercive brain-reading in light of Articles 3, 6, 8, 9, and 10 ECHR. It provides an analysis of the legal possibilities and limitations of (1) using different means of pressure in order to (2) collect brain-data through neuroimaging in the context of criminal justice. The present chapter considers how the research findings so far could, together, disclose the first contours of a legal framework for coercive brain-reading in criminal law. Identifying such contours raises novel legal, ethical, political, societal, and technological questions. Considering all of these emerging issues would exceed the scope of this book. This chapter confines the discussion to *legal* questions regarding human rights protection against forensic brain-reading under the European Convention on Human Rights.

8.2 COERCION, MANIPULATION, AND PERSUASION

Different means of pressure are conceivable when enforcing brain-reading in criminal law. These range from physical force, such as mechanical and chemical restraint, over threatening with adverse legal consequences to making subtle offers.[1] It follows from the examination in the previous chapters that physical force will, in most cases, be impermissible in this context. Articles 3, 6, and, to some extent, Article 8 ECHR, will often prohibit the use of complete mechanical and chemical restraint. Moreover, such physical coercion will often be ineffective to enforce most brain-reading tests, since the majority requires at least some cooperation of the subject.

Article 3 ECHR only prohibits those means of coercion that attain a minimum level of severity. The privilege against self-incrimination also protects from other

[1] Chapter 2, Section 2.7.

forms of non-moderate compulsion, not necessarily attaining the threshold of Article 3 ECHR.[2] Thus, in cases where the privilege does not apply, like in the execution of criminal sanctions, the range of permissible means of physical coercion will be wider compared with cases that do elicit protection from the privilege.[3]

Since physical coercion will often be either ineffective or impermissible, States could resort to more subtle means of volitional coercion. This type of coercion ranges from making direct legal threats to offering brain-reading in a way that may favour the subject's personal interests. Think of offering neuroprediction in return for parole.

We saw that in philosophy it is generally accepted that threats coerce.[4] They undermine voluntariness and invalidate consent. Whether offers can coerce too is open to debate. We have considered two central positions: (1) offers never coerce and (2) offers could be coercive sometimes, like in cases of vulnerability, power asymmetry, and interference by the consent-seeker in the baseline position of the consent-giver.

To date, no such systematic thinking about coercion and consent has appeared under the ECHR.[5] For instance, concerning the privilege against self-incrimination, the Court refrains from developing a well-defined abstract approach on which types and degrees of pressure are acceptable and which are not.[6] Meanwhile, the previous chapters show that existing case-law cautiously suggest an implicit approach to different kinds of pressure in relation to informed consent to State interferences. At least it is clear that making legal threats to enforce cooperation with governmental investigations invalidates the voluntariness of consent and thus raises an issue under the human rights that apply in the particular context. We have discussed legal threats to participate in X-ray for tuberculosis screening,[7] to provide a urine sample for mandatory drug testing in prison,[8] to enable the acquisition of saliva for DNA testing,[9] to provide tax administration,[10] to give a detailed

[2] Article 8(1) ECHR will also cover the use of physical coercion that does not attain a minimum level of severity, but such use may potentially be justified under Article 8(2) ECHR.

[3] Think, for example, of the use of mechanical fixation in prison and psychiatric hospitals, which can sometimes be permissible. See, for example, Rule 68 of the European Prison Rules; CPT/Inf(2017)6.

[4] Chapter 2, Section 2.7.

[5] Buelens, Herijgers, & Illegems 2016. Cf. Richardson 2008, who concludes that European human rights law currently fails to capture much of the coercion experienced by patients in practice.

[6] Chapter 6, Section 6.3.3. See, for example, European Court of Human Rights (ECtHR) (GC) 8 February 1996, appl.no. 18731/91 (*John Murray/UK*), § 46.

[7] European Commission of Human Rights (EComHR) 10 December 1984, appl.no. 10435/83 (*Acmanne and others/Belgium*).

[8] EComHR 6 April 1994, appl.no. 21132/93 (*Peters/The Netherlands*); EComHR 9 September 1998, appl.no. 34199/96 (*Galloway/UK*); ECtHR 11 October 2005, appl.no. 60682/00 (*Young/UK*).

[9] ECtHR 14 April 2020, appl.no. 75229/10 (*Dragan Petrović/Serbia*), § 79.

[10] ECtHR 3 May 2001, appl.no. 31827/96 (*J.B./Switzerland*); ECtHR 25 February 1993, appl.no. 10828/84 (*Funke/France*).

account of one's movements during particular periods of time,[11] and to give evidence as a witness in court.[12]

In addition to these clear cases of legal threats, the Court appears to accept that the use of more subtle methods of indirect pressure could negate voluntariness as well, invalidating consent and raising an issue under the human rights in question. Examples we considered concern persistent requests for consent to gynaecological examination in prison,[13] informing a defendant about the law that allows for drawing adverse inferences from his silence,[14] and using subterfuge to elicit self-incriminating statements.[15]

Clearly, the sparse and casuistic case-law does not enable us to deduce a central approach on the coerciveness of offering certain means of investigation like brain-reading to people in a criminal legal context. Still, it shows that the very nature of criminal justice, either during police investigation,[16] at trial,[17] or in prison,[18] involves an imbalance of power and a certain level of vulnerability to which suspects and convicted offenders are subjected, calling for critical scrutiny of the voluntariness of consenting decisions.[19] Perhaps, this kind of vulnerability and power asymmetry may be insufficient to qualify 'brain-reading offers' as actually *coercive*. Nonetheless, in Strasbourg case-law, these factors appear able to invalidate the voluntariness of consent. Could it be possible that the Court accepts a broader continuum of (non-coercive) influences that could impinge on voluntariness and invalidate consent?

Such a continuum has been proposed by Faden, Beauchamp, and King.[20] They argue that sometimes, controlling influences fall short of coercion but still are able to restrict autonomy and invalidate consent. In such 'in between' cases, they argue, the exerted pressure qualifies as 'manipulation'.[21] Faden, Beauchamp, and King define manipulation in this sense as follows:

11 ECtHR 21 December 2000, appl.no. 34720/97 (*Heaney and McGuinnes/Ireland*); ECtHR 21 December 2000, appl.no. 36887/97 (*Quinn/Ireland*).

12 ECtHR 23 October 2018, appl.no. 26892/12 (*Wanner/Germany*).

13 ECtHR 13 May 2008, appl.no. 52515/99 (*Juhnke/Turkey*); ECtHR 22 July 2003, appl.no. 24209/94 (*Y.F./Turkey*); ECtHR 1 February 2011, appl.no. 36369/06 (*Yazgül Yılmaz/Turkey*).

14 ECtHR (GC) 8 February 1996, appl.no. 18731/91 (*John Murray/UK*); ECtHR 6 June 2000, appl.no. 36408/97 (*Averill/UK*).

15 ECtHR 5 November 2002, appl.no. 48539/99 (*Allan/UK*).

16 E.g. ECtHR 11 December 2008, appl.no. 4268/04 (*Panovits/Cyprus*), § 68; ECtHR 2 July 2019, appl. no. 65290/14 (*R.S./Hungary*), § 65.

17 E.g. ECtHR (GC) 8 February 1996, appl.no. 18731/91 (*John Murray/UK*), § 49–50; ECtHR 6 June 2000, appl.no. 36408/97 (*Averill/UK*), § 48.

18 E.g. ECtHR 13 May 2008, appl.no. 52515/99 (*Juhnke/Turkey*), § 76; ECtHR 1 February 2011, appl.no. 36369/06 (*Yazgül Yılmaz/Turkey*), § 45.

19 Cf. Buelens, Herijgers, & Illegems 2016, pp. 484–485; Bachmaier 2018; De Vries 2018, p. 694; Jackson & Summers 2012, p. 267.

20 Faden, Beauchamp, & King 1986, p. 259.

21 See also Noggle 2020, sect. 2.3.

> *Manipulation* is a catch-all category that includes any intentional and successful influence of a person by noncoercively altering the actual choices available to the person or by nonpersuasively altering the person's perceptions of those choices. The essence of manipulation is getting people to do what the manipulator intends by one of these two general means.[22]

In medical ethics, it is widely accepted that apart from coercion, some forms of manipulation interfere with autonomous decision-making and undermine informed consent.[23]

Manipulative influences come in different types. One of them concerns the *manipulation of options*. This involves direct modification of the options available to an individual, with the aim of modifying his behaviour or beliefs.[24] To this end, manipulators can decrease or increase the number of options or reward the behaviour they prefer. Often, these methods are employed together: 'The manipulator simultaneously creates a new option such as the 'opportunity' to participate in research or to receive a new medical treatment, and gerrymanders the reward structure so that the option presented is clearly preferable'.[25] Translating this strategy to brain-reading in criminal law: the prison director, aiming to subject the prisoner to neuroprediction, creates the opportunity of leaving on parole by participating in a brain assessment. Meanwhile, he informs the prisoner that reluctance to cooperate is likely to reduce the chances to parole significantly.

Feinberg has offered an account on manipulation as well. He argues that there are many ways of getting people to act as you wish. Some of these means can be situated on a spectrum of 'force', which includes, among others, physical compulsion, threats, offers, manipulation, persuasion, and incitement.[26] Similar to Faden, Beauchamp, and King, Feinberg holds that the line between forcing someone to act and merely getting someone to act lies somewhere in between manipulation and persuasion.[27]

With respect to brain-reading in criminal law: when exactly will the authorities either coerce, manipulate, or persuade subjects into a brain-reading assessment? As yet, the Court abstains from giving a more generic, sustainable approach on these distinctive forms of influences and their relation to informed consent. It only suggests that apart from making legal threats, more subtle means of indirect pressure could invalidate consent too, especially when exerted in cases of vulnerability and power asymmetry. It would be desirable to receive more guidance on this issue. The analysis in this book shows that brain-reading in criminal justice interferes with

22 Faden, Beauchamp, & King 1986, p. 261.
23 Noggle 2020, sect. 1.2 and 3.3.
24 Faden, Beauchamp, & King 1986, p. 355.
25 Ibid.
26 Feinberg 1989, p. 189.
27 Ibid.

personal interests protected by a variety of human rights. Valid informed consent can negate this wide-ranging legal protection. Therefore, it should be clear when consent to brain-reading can be considered free or not.

Developing a human rights-based account on coercion, manipulation, and rational persuasion will not only serve the regulation of brain-reading in criminal law. It will also be essential to normative analyses of other medical (technological) interventions in criminal justice, such as offering treatment or chemical castration in return for lowering sentences.[28] The issue of free and informed consent to treatment and neurotechnology in criminal justice has been under debate in moral philosophy for years.[29] It is time for the law to catch up.[30]

8.3 PROTECTING BRAINS AND MINDS

8.3.1 *Current Protection*

Current legal protection against the coercive acquisition of brain-reading data is anchored in a variety of human rights. In theory, the right to freedom of thought (Article 9 ECHR) could offer the strongest protection. This right has an absolute ring (*forum internum*), where any coercion to disclose thoughts, moral convictions, and religious adherence is prohibited unconditionally. When coercive brain-reading reveals one of these protected notions, it will violate Article 9 ECHR. However, the forensic application of brain-based diagnostics, neuroprediction, lie detection, and CITs will not typically yield information that allows for drawing inferences about the subject's religion, conscience, or thoughts in the meaning of Article 9 ECHR.[31] Therefore, the coercive employment of these brain-reading tests will most likely exceed the scope of the *forum internum*.

Possibly, in the future, technological advances might elicit absolute protection under Article 9 ECHR after all. If novel technologies will enable the identification of *real-time thoughts*, the possibility may arise that a subject, during such a test, unintentionally thinks about his political preference, moral convictions, or prays to his God, asking for favourable test results. The non-consensual acquisition of such collateral data will infringe the *forum internum* and thus violate Article 9(1) ECHR. However, as long as such brain-reading applications are only 'neuroscience fiction',

28 Cf. Forsberg 2021.

29 Cf. McMillan 2014; Wertheimer & Miller 2014; Shaw 2014; Douglas et al. 2013; Ryberg 2012; Focquaert, Van Assche, & Sterckx 2020; Knack, Chandler & Fedoroff 2020; Ryberg 2020, chap. 2; Pugh 2018; Bomann-Larsen 2013.

30 Close collaboration with ethics and philosophy would be desirable here: Ligthart, Kooijmans, & Meynen 2021a, p. 130. Cf. Ligthart et al. 2019.

31 Denoting only those views that attain a certain level of cogency, seriousness, cohesion, and importance: ECtHR (GC) 1 July 2014, appl.no. 43835/11 (S.A.S./*France*), § 55. See also ECtHR (GC) 26 April 2016, appl.no. 62649/10 (*İzzettin Doğan and others* v. *Turkey*), § 68.

Article 9 ECHR will, in its current understanding, not offer considerable protection against coercive brain-reading in criminal law.

In most cases, brain-reading will be covered by the generic right to respect for private life (Article 8 ECHR) and by the right not to express information, ideas, and opinions (Article 10 ECHR). These rights will not as such prohibit particular types of coercive brain-reading. Still, they impose certain legal boundaries, preventing from arbitrariness, abuse, and disproportionality, some of which overlap with the requirements under Article 3 ECHR, such as guaranteeing medical supervision. When specifying Articles 8 and 10 ECHR to forensic brain-reading, existing case-law on current methods of criminal investigation, such as DNA testing and obligatory witness testimonies, provides helpful insights and directions.

In some cases, the privilege against self-incrimination pursuant to Article 6 ECHR could provide additional, strong legal protection. The privilege will cover brain-reading tests that require cooperation of the subject[32] when employed with coercion in the determination of a criminal charge. The privilege will not normally apply when no criminal charge exists, like in the execution of criminal sanctions. Nor will it be applicable to brain-reading applications that do not require the subject's cooperation, such as diagnostics and neuroprediction through the detection of structural brain features.[33]

Whether coercive brain-reading in an individual case will violate the privilege shall depend on the nature and degree of the deployed coercion, the existence of relevant procedural safeguards, and on the use of the brain-derived data. As mentioned above,[34] the Court refrains from providing a general approach on the types and degrees of acceptable 'coercion' in this context.[35]

In conclusion, the human rights central to this book do not as such prohibit coercive brain-reading in criminal law.[36] Meanwhile, these rights and freedoms do establish normative limits, particularly Articles 8, 10, and, regarding defendants in criminal proceedings, Article 6 ECHR. Shall the scope of legal protection afforded by these existing rights and freedoms suffice to adequately protect from brain-reading in criminal law? This is an open question. Discussing this question involves legal, ethical, political, societal, and technological considerations. As to the legal debate, the following sections discuss two emerging challenges for European human rights law when protecting brains and minds within the existing framework of fundamental rights and freedoms.

32 While the information the authorities seek to obtain cannot be acquired by other means that do not involve the subject's cooperation. Examples of such brain-reading applications are brain-based lie detection, CITs, and brain-based diagnostics and neuroprediction through the identification of brain activity.

33 In those cases, coercive brain-reading will still be covered by Articles 8 and 10 ECHR.

34 Section 8.2.

35 ECtHR (GC) 8 February 1996, appl.no. 18731/91 (*John Murray/UK*), § 46.

36 Cf. Ienca & Andorno 2017; Ligthart et al. 2020.

8.3.2 *Reconsidering the Foundations of the Privilege against Self-incrimination*

When brain-reading requires cooperation of the subject, the privilege against self-incrimination will apply. The privilege then proscribes the use of non-moderate coercion to obtain self-incriminating data.[37] However, volitionally coerced brain-reading appears not to affect the first and second rationales of the privilege. It will not typically entail any level of force as to cause physical and/or mental harm, nor will it otherwise diminish human dignity.[38] Moreover, by providing an additional, objective source of information, brain-reading is likely to improve the reliability of criminal evidence, benefitting the second rationale of avoiding miscarriages of justice.[39] Therefore, I raised the question in Chapter 6 of whether only the third rationale – autonomy – would be strong enough to support the right against self-incrimination in cases of coercive brain-reading. Can we prohibit coercive brain-reading under the privilege, solely by relying on the subject's autonomy? Or will this right be seriously weakened as far as coercive brain-reading is concerned? In fact, these questions touch upon a more foundational issue: how much weight should we assign to the concept of autonomy when justifying the privilege against self-incrimination?[40]

Different positions are conceivable. For example, we could attach considerable weight to the autonomy rationale, arguing that there is just something inherently wrong with the State invading the 'sanctum of the mind' for the purpose of incriminating an individual.[41] Regarding coercive CITs, Van Toor argues that in order to respect the accused's autonomous decision about disclosing personal information (i.e. mental content), we should approach CITs in the same way as testimonies under the right not to incriminate oneself.[42] Moreover, regarding the theoretical example of performing a CIT to unconscious subjects – not requiring any participation whatsoever – Van Toor argues to consider such brain-reading along the lines of coerced confessions. Only then, the value of the privilege and the autonomous choice of suspects remain intact.[43]

This view, which attaches significant weight to autonomy and to the suspect's decision not to disclose personal information, echoes an alternative rationale of the privilege: the rationale of protecting mental privacy,[44] allowing suspects to decide which information they want to disclose about themselves.[45] As Galligan put it:

37 Chapter 6, Sections 6.3.2–6.3.3.
38 Chapter 6, Section 6.3.4.
39 Ibid.
40 Ligthart & Meynen 2021. Cf. Oshana 2003.
41 Jackson & Summers 2012, p. 270.
42 Van Toor 2017, p. 437.
43 Meijer & Van Toor 2021, p. 115.
44 Dolinko 1986, pp. 1109–1108; Lamberigts 2016, p. 427.
45 Gerstein 1970; Van Toor 2021. See also Redmayne 2007, p. 215; Pivaty, Ter Vrugt & De Vocht 2021.

> suppose that the police could find out all they need to know by plugging the suspect into a machine; the process is painless but it reveals everything about the suspect—his history, actions, thoughts, and desires. That would strike at the very centre of the zone of privacy. But there is no difference in principle between using the machine and requiring the suspect to disclose the same information through speech. The means differ but the objection is the same: the police have no claim on direct access to that information and it follows that they have no claim on the suspect to lower the shield of privacy. (…) both the right to silence and the privilege against self-incrimination *finally depend on the case from privacy*.[46]

A privacy-based approach of the privilege puts considerable emphasis on the freedom not to disclose personal information that is yet unknown to others, including the State.[47] In that way, it seems to move focus from the freedom not to *incriminate oneself in criminal proceedings*, to the broader freedom of *controlling personal information and of not expressing oneself*.[48]

However, as Lamberigts notes, privacy-based rationales are not compelling: they fail to explain why the privilege only applies in relation to a criminal charge. If privacy were the main justification, then why would the privilege only pertain to disclosing information that can be used in criminal proceedings, but not to the disclosure of otherwise damaging personal information?[49] For example, in tax procedures and divorce cases,[50] people may be obliged to disclose facts they would rather keep to themselves, as may be the case during obligatory witness testimonies in criminal trials. These examples do not fall within the ambit of the privilege.

One could argue that the difference lies in the interests at stake. Unlike in civil cases and administrative tax procedures, revealing personal information in the course of criminal law may well result in a criminal conviction and in the imposition of penal sanctions. Such potential adverse consequences of disclosing information are to be considered as much more severe compared with civil or administrative proceedings, justifying stricter protection of the freedom not to disclose personal information.[51]

But this argument it not convincing. Consider, for instance, civil cases where an obligation to provide information could result in loosing parental authority. Presumably, many people will value their loss of parental authority as much worse

[46] Galligan 1988, p. 89 (emphasis added).

[47] Cf. Galligan 1988, p. 89: 'the police are strangers to the suspect, which means that there are none of the duties of disclosure which result from special relationships. The only competing interest, therefore, is crime control'.

[48] These freedoms are also protected by Articles 8 and 10 ECHR. Cf. Ashworth 2008, p. 759.

[49] Lamberigts 2016, p. 427. See also Dolinko 1986, p. 1107 et seq; Dennis 1995, pp. 357–358.

[50] See, for example, Articles 21 and 22 of the Dutch Code of Civil Procedure.

[51] Redmayne 2007, p. 226.

compared with a criminal conviction for a minor offence and the imposition of, say, a EUR 300 fine.[52] Meanwhile, every suspect in any criminal case is entitled with the right not to incriminate herself. Parents in civil proceedings are not. This distinction cannot be justified by an appeal to privacy.

In the same vein, Jackson and Summers argue:

> It is hard to see why we should give specific priority to respecting the voluntariness of an accused's decision to hand over or reveal incriminating information over and above respecting an individual's general personal autonomy and freedom of action.[53]

Although not absolute, suspects are already protected against coercion to disclose personal information or to express certain opinions and ideas.[54] These interests are covered by the right to respect for private life and by the freedom of non-expression (Articles 8 and 10 ECHR). So, what is it that justifies additional, stronger protection under the privilege against self-incrimination?[55]

Whether the accused's *autonomy* is a convincing answer to this question is open to debate.[56] The legal significance of autonomy is not limited to the privilege and to defendants in criminal proceedings. Just like the notions of human dignity and human freedom,[57] personal autonomy is a central concept to the Convention as such. As the Grand Chamber holds, 'the notion of personal autonomy is an important principle underlying the interpretation of the Convention guarantees'.[58] When interpreting the right to respect for private life pursuant to Article 8 ECHR, personal autonomy has an important role.[59] Clearly, the *freedom* not to express oneself under Article 10 ECHR relates closely to autonomy as well.[60] As a consequence,

52 Cf. Dolinko 1986, pp. 1114–1115; Lamberigts 2016, p. 427, fn. 90.

53 Jackson & Summers 2012, p. 273.

54 Depending on the severity of coercion, even absolute protection may arise under Article 3 ECHR.

55 Jackson & Summers 2012, pp. 268, 270.

56 Cf. Jackson & Summers 2012, p. 269: 'Another problem with a rationale based on respecting the will of the accused is that it is difficult to find a clear and coherent dividing line between what state conduct may be said to respect the will and what does not. (…) We have seen that the best interpretation of the distinction made by the ECtHR is to be found by equating the privilege with immunity from wilfully participating in one's own incrimination. (…) There is still a problem, however, in finding a rationale which would justify handing over documents coming within the privilege, but not submitting to a blood test outside the privilege. In each case, there is compulsion in terms of restricting personal autonomy: in the one case by requiring the accused to act against his will; and in the other by requiring that he submit to interference with his body'.

57 ECtHR (GC) 13 December 2012, appl.no. 39630/09 (*El-Masri/Former Yugoslav republic of Macedonia*), § 248.

58 ECtHR (GC) 11 January 2006, appl.nos. 52562/99 and 52620/99 (*Sørensen and Rasmussen/Denmark*), § 54.

59 ECtHR (GC) 5 September 2017, appl.no. 61496/08 (*Bărbulescu/Romania*), § 70; ECtHR 5 July 2011, appl.no. 41588/05 (*Avram and Others/Moldova*), § 36.

60 Cf. EComHR 1 March 1993, appl.no. 17488/90 (*Goodwin/UK*), § 48: 'There are circumstances in which a 'negative right' is to be implied in Article 10 (Art. 10) not to be compelled to give information

it is hardly defensible that it is the suspect's *autonomy* alone that justifies *stronger protection under the privilege in criminal proceedings* compared with other situations where individuals are obliged to disclose personal information, covered by Articles 8 and 10 ECHR.

Perhaps, in understanding, justifying, and applying the privilege, we should not put too much emphasis on autonomy. Judges Martens and Kuris have defended such a position in *Saunders/UK*. As these Judges write, the third rationale of the privilege essentially 'boil[s] down to the proposition that respect for human dignity and autonomy requires that every suspect should be completely free to decide which attitude he will adopt with respect to the criminal charges against him'.[61] However, according to Martens and Kuris, the weight of this rationale should not be exaggerated.[62] As they argue:

> 'Human dignity and autonomy' have an absolute ring, but in our modern societies it must remain possible to protect the community against forms of crime, the effective combating of which makes it imperious to compel (specific categories of) suspects to cooperate in bringing about their own conviction. I believe that especially the broader privilege against self-incrimination may be restricted by law in order to protect legitimate interests of the community. In my opinion it is, in principle, open to the national law to compel (specific categories of) suspects by threat of punishment to contribute passively or actively to the creation of evidence, even decisive evidence, against themselves.[63]

This view appears more or less reflected in Strasbourg case-law on obliging registered car keepers to disclose the identity of the driver at the time a traffic offence was registered.[64] The applicability of the privilege to those cases strongly relies on the third rationale: the car keeper's autonomy not to provide the name of the driver. The level of volitional coercion in cases like these – that is, threatening with fines in the amount of EUR 2,000 – clearly not amounts to 'improper compulsion' in the meaning of the first rationale. The second rationale of avoiding miscarriages of justice neither provides much support. The authorities do not use coercion with

or to state an opinion. Compulsion to provide information (…) must in particular constitute a restriction in the capacity (…) to receive and impart information without interference by a public authority'.

61 Dissenting opinion Judges Martens and Kuris under ECtHR (GC) 17 December 1996, appl.no. 19187/91 (*Saunders/UK*), point 19.

62 Ibid., point 10. Cf. Groenhuijsen & Knigge 2004, p. 51.

63 Dissenting opinion Judges Martens and Kuris under ECtHR (GC) 17 December 1996, appl.no. 19187/91 (*Saunders/UK*), point 10.

64 See also Jackson & Summers 2012, pp. 273–275. Although the privilege applies in such cases, normally, it will not be violated: ECtHR (GC) 29 June 2007, appl.nos. 15809/02 and 25624/02 (*O'Halloran and Francis/UK*); ECtHR 10 January 2008, appl.nos. 58452/00 and 61920/00 (*Lückhof and Spanner/Austria*); ECtHR 24 March 2005, appl.no. 63207/00 (*Rieg/Austria*); ECtHR 8 April 2004, appl.no. 38544/97 (*Weh/Austria*).

the aim of obtaining a confession. The instruction is not: confess that *you* were the driver, or you will be punished. When a car keeper is innocent, for example because a friend borrowed his car and committed a traffic offence, the use of coercion should not lead to a wrongful conviction. Rather, in such cases, the car keeper will be coerced to disclose the identity of his friend.[65] When one *is* guilty, the obligation to inform the authorities accordingly will neither result in a *wrongful* conviction.

What remains in these cases is the third rationale. However, the autonomy rationale alone appears not strong enough to elicit effective protection from the privilege.[66] As previously cited, the Grand Chamber holds that:

> Those who choose to keep and drive motor cars can be taken to have accepted certain responsibilities and obligations as part of the regulatory regime relating to motor vehicles, and in the legal framework of the United Kingdom these responsibilities include the obligation, in the event of suspected commission of road-traffic offences, to inform the authorities of the identity of the driver on that occasion.[67]

Put differently, in these cases, the suspects' autonomy not to provide the requested information can be *outweighed* by the interest of prosecuting traffic offences.[68] In the words of Martens and Kuris, sometimes, national law should be able to compel suspects to contribute to the creation of evidence against themselves.[69]

Autonomy is an important value. It is a central consideration in interpreting the Convention guarantees[70] and in shaping criminal law.[71] Meanwhile, as the example of traffic offences shows, sometimes, autonomy may be *restricted*. In the context of criminal law, restricting autonomy often appears legitimate,[72] for example, to provide breath for a breathalyser test,[73] to participate in a line-up,[74] to share blood for DNA analysis,[75] and to unlock a suspect's smartphone with his fingerprint.[76]

65 Cf. ECtHR 10 January 2008, appl.nos. 58452/00 and 61920/00 (*Lückhof and Spanner/Austria*), § 55. See also ECtHR 24 March 2005, appl.no. 63207/00 (*Rieg/Austria*), § 31–32.

66 Cf., in contrast, ECtHR 3 May 2001, appl.no. 31827/96 (*J.B./Switzerland*), where the applicant was requested to submit all documents concerning the companies in which he had invested money.

67 ECtHR (GC) 29 June 2007, appl.nos. 15809/02 and 25624/02 (*O'Halloran and Francis/UK*), § 57.

68 Dissenting opinion judge Meyjer under ECtHR (GC) 29 June 2007, appl.nos. 15809/02 and 25624/02 (*O'Halloran and Francis/UK*), points 6 and 7. See also Jackson & Summers 2012, pp. 269, 274.

69 Cf. Jackson & Summers 2012, pp. 273–277; Redmayne 2007, p. 232.

70 ECtHR (GC) 11 January 2006, appl.nos. 52562/99 and 52620/99 (*Sørensen and Rasmussen/Denmark*), § 54.

71 Feinberg 1989; Foqué & 't Hart 1990.

72 Galligan 1988, pp. 87–88; Oshana 2003, pp. 112–114; Jackson & Summers 2012, p. 269; Ligthart, Kooijmans & Meynen 2021a, p. 129.

73 ECtHR 15 June 1999, appl.no. 43486/98 (*Tirado Ortiz and Lozano Martin/Spain*).

74 ECtHR 20 April 2010, appl.nos. 12315/04 and 17605/04 (*Laska and Lika/Albania*).

75 ECtHR 5 January 2006, appl.no. 2352/02 (*Schmidt/Germany*). See Chapter 4, Section 4.3.3.

76 *HR* 9 February 2021, *NJ* 2021/120, m.nt. Reijntjes; Stevens 2019.

Typically, these means of criminal investigation do not entail severe physical or psychological harm. They do not diminish human dignity.[77] Neither do they increase a risk of miscarriages of justice. They provide objective evidence, similar to brain-reading. Meanwhile, it is clear that all these means, when employed without valid consent, restrict the subject's autonomy, for example by requiring him to submit to interferences with his body.[78] Yet, these methods of non-consensual evidence gathering will not normally attract the guarantees of the privilege against self-incrimination.[79]

This suggests that the rationale of respecting autonomy is *in itself* not strong enough to justify this legal principle. Otherwise, the privilege would have protected each autonomous decision equally, including the decision not to confess a murder, not to testify about the name of a car driver, not to provide breath or urine, not to unlock one's smartphone, as well as the autonomous decision not to share one's DNA with the police.

When we look closely, it seems that restricting autonomy is only essential to the privilege when it (1) entails a risk of the authorities resorting to 'improper compulsion' and/or (2) when it increases the risk of producing unreliable evidence, which could manifest in 'miscarriages of justice'. It seems that protecting autonomy only serves as a legitimation of the privilege when respecting autonomy is necessary to prevent excessive force or to avoid wrongful convictions. If that is true, the autonomy rationale has no independent value. It only serves or strengthens the two rationales that the Court has endorsed explicitly: protecting the accused against improper compulsion by the authorities and thereby contributing to the avoidance of miscarriages of justice.[80]

Such understanding of autonomy – as a subordinate justification of the privilege – seems reflected in the substantive means-based approach the Court adheres. In this approach, the privilege protects against means of obtaining information that require the suspect's cooperation. It does not typically apply when the evidence can also be obtained independently of the suspect's will – that is, through *bypassing* his reluctance to cooperate.[81] Generally, the possibility of bypassing a suspect's cooperation takes away valid concerns regarding improper compulsion and miscarriages of justice. If a suspect decides not to produce evidence, for example, by refusing to provide breath for a breathalyser test, the authorities can

77 But when they do, the privilege against self-incrimination can offer protection anyway: ECtHR (GC) 13 September 2016, appl.nos. 50541/08, 50571/08, 50573/08, and 40351/09 (*Ibrahim and others/UK*), § 267; ECtHR (GC) 11 July 2006, appl.no. 54810/00 (*Jalloh/Germany*).

78 Jackson & Summers 2012, p. 269.

79 ECtHR (GC) 17 December 1996, appl.no. 19187/91 (*Saunders/UK*), § 69.

80 ECtHR (GC) 13 September 2016, appl.nos. 50541/08, 50571/08, 50573/08, and 40351/09 (*Ibrahim and others/UK*), § 266 (emphasis added); ECtHR (GC) 1 June 2010, appl.no. 22978/05 (*Gäfgen/Germany*), § 168.

81 See Chapter 6, Section 6.2.

simply circumvent that decision and take the evidence themselves, through taking a reliable blood sample with the use of proportionate force.[82] Obliging someone to produce breath as well as taking a blood sample without valid consent interfere with the person's autonomy. However, as the first two rationales do not apply, the mere issue of restricting autonomy appears unable to attract protection from the privilege against self-incrimination.[83]

To illustrate this subordinate role of autonomy in the Court's means-based approach, consider the example of the police who received tip offs about a guy collecting deactivated illegal guns at home.[84] The police require the suspect to hand over the guns on pain of a EUR 3,000 fine. Clearly, this requirement interferes with the suspect's autonomy; it disrespects his decision not to hand over self-incriminating evidence. Nevertheless, this obligation will not raise an issue under the privilege against self-incrimination. The evidence could also be obtained 'independently of the suspect's will', that is, without his cooperation, by searching his home and seizing the guns.[85] Because of this possibility of bypassing the suspect's assistance, hardly any risk exists of the police using harmful methods to coerce the suspect into handing over the guns. In cases like these, there is no real risk of the authorities resorting to 'improper compulsion'. If the suspect refuses cooperation, the police simply take the evidence themselves. In addition, as may be clear, the interference with autonomy in this case will not increase the risk of obtaining unreliable evidence. It will result in the police obtaining the guns. Accordingly, in this example, restricting the suspect's autonomy by obliging him to give evidence does not threaten the first or second rationale of the privilege against self-incrimination, nor does it otherwise elicit the applicability of the privilege to this case.

Meanwhile, suppose the police only assumed that the suspect possesses something illegal, perhaps guns, drugs, or stolen watches. Presumably, the illegal products are stored somewhere in (or even outside) Europe. Suppose that the police are unable to produce the evidence themselves. Therefore, they require the suspect to hand over the illegal products on pain of a EUR 3,000 fine. This requirement interferes with the suspect's autonomy in the same way as the first example; it disrespects his decision not to hand over self-incriminating evidence. But now the

82 In general, taking a blood sample, when employed *lege artis* by a medical doctor, is of very short duration, causes only minor bodily injury and cannot be said to cause intense physical or mental suffering: ECtHR 5 January 2006, appl.no. 2352/02 (*Schmidt/Germany*), pp. 4–5. Cf. ECtHR 20 January 2009, appl.no. 20689/08 (*W./The Netherlands*), p. 8; ECtHR 7 December 2006, appl.no. 29514/05 (*Van der Velden/The Netherlands*), p. 9; ECtHR 15 May 2018, appl.no. 41079/16 (*Caruana/Malta*), § 41.

83 E.g. ECtHR 15 June 1999, appl.no. 43486/98 (*Tirado Ortiz and Lozano Martin/Spain*).

84 See Chapter 6, Section 6.2.

85 Which will disrespect the suspect's autonomous decision of not providing the police with access to his private home and therefore interferes with Article 8(1) ECHR.

requirement to hand over evidence does raise an issue under the privilege.[86] Similar to the first example, the interference with autonomy will not typically increase the risk of obtaining unreliable evidence. But one crucial distinction exists between both cases. In the present case, the police cannot bypass the suspect's assistence. In order to obtain the evidence, they have no other option but to coerce the suspect into self-incrimination. If the suspect persists in refusing to produce the evidence, the authorities may well resource to more severe means of coercion, restricting the suspect's autonomy even further by breaking his will and obtain the evidence they seek. Because the police in this case cannot bypass the suspect's reluctance to provide evidence, the risk of 'improper compulsion' may be looming. The privilege against self-incrimination aims to protect the accused against improper compulsion; it delegitimises the use of harmful methods to enforce self-incriminating evidence.[87] Thereby, the application of the privilege to this case can be justified.

These examples illustrate that the interest of respecting autonomy is in itself not weighty enough to justify legal protection from the privilege. In my view, the autonomy rationale cannot explain why the privilege does not apply in the first example as opposed to the second. This difference in legal protection can, however, be justified by the rationale of preventing improper compulsion. Apparently, when restricting autonomy entails a risk of the authorities resorting to 'improper compulsion' in the meaning of the first rationale, the privilege starts to work.

Sometimes, restricting autonomy to obtain evidence will also increase the risk of producing false information and thus of miscarriages of justice, therefore justifying the privilege against self-incrimination. Interfering with a defendant's autonomy by coercing him to testify clearly attracts protection from the privilege.[88] Such use of coercion typically entails a risk of suspects giving false testimony.[89] And when the defendant is the only person who can produce the information the police seek to obtain, they may well resource to physical force or other means of improper compulsion to secure a confession.[90] Whereas restricting autonomy alone appears unable to justify the privilege, as in the case of obliging car keepers to testify about traffic offences, the privilege will apply when the interference with autonomy can typically manifest a wrongful conviction and/or in the use of improper compulsion.

In conclusion, brain-reading technology forces us to think about the centuries-old right against self-incrimination from a different angle. It puts autonomy at the centre. But it also raises the question of whether autonomy alone is sufficient as a

86 Cf. ECtHR 3 May 2001, appl.no. 31827/96 (*J.B./Switzerland*); ECtHR 25 February 1993, appl.no. 10828/84 (*Funke/France*).

87 Dissenting opinion Judges Martens and Kuris under ECtHR (GC) 17 December 1996, appl.no. 19187/91 (*Saunders/UK*), point 8.

88 ECtHR 21 December 2000, appl.no. 34720/97 (*Heaney and McGuinness/Ireland*).

89 Chapter 6, Sections 6.2.2 and 6.3.4.

90 Cf. ECtHR (GC) 1 June 2010, appl.no. 22978/05 (*Gäfgen/Germany*).

foundation of such a crucial right in criminal justice. I suggest it is not. Rather, restricting autonomy appears mainly relevant in direct relation to the rationales of preventing improper compulsion and avoiding miscarriages of justice. When these two rationales of the privilege do not apply – as in most cases of brain-reading – we should be critical about whether considerations of autonomy alone can justify strong protection under the right not to incriminate oneself.

When the use of harmless and reliable technologies in criminal proceedings increases, the natural significance of the privilege against self-incrimination might possibly decrease. Meanwhile, such emerging technologies could interfere with people's autonomy in novel ways. This calls for further research on the sustainability of the privilege's foundations and on the role of autonomy in this regard.[91] It is important to realise that 'autonomy' is not a clearly defined concept. Many different approaches exist.[92] When valuing the accused's autonomy in the context of the privilege against self-incrimination, we should seek for a clear definition of this concept in criminal proceedings.[93] In addition, we may want to think about whether the meaning of autonomy could or should vary across different Convention rights, such as under Articles 6, 8, and 10 ECHR.

8.3.3 *Specifying the Right to Freedom of Non-expression*

This book considered five types of brain-reading that can be used in the course of criminal law. Meanwhile, many more neurotechniques and fields of application are currently under debate, such as brain-reading devices in medicine, the military, education, and gaming.[94] These advances in neurotechnology are changing traditional boundaries of our brains and mental lives.

As mentioned earlier,[95] the majority of human rights traditionally pertain to physical actions and visible objects in the outside world. Far less they protect our internal lives, such as emotions, intentions, memories, and other mental states. A plausible explanation is that for many years our mental lives have been considered inaccessible to the outside world.[96] However, present-day developments in neurotechnology urge us to rethink the existing framework of human rights in view of protecting the mental aspects of life.[97] In order to guarantee adequate human rights protection in respect of technologies that may 'enter' human brains and unravel our minds, scholars have advocated various approaches. In general, two central positions can be distinguished.

91 Ligthart & Meynen 2021.
92 Feinberg 1989, Ch. 18; Pugh 2020, Ch. 1.
93 Ligthart 2021.
94 Goering et al. 2021; Rickli & Ienca 2021; Williamson 2019; Ienca, Haselager & Emanuel 2018.
95 Chapter 1, Section 1.1.
96 Bublitz & Merkel 2014, p. 61; Alegre 2017, p. 224.
97 Ienca 2021; Committee on Bioethics of the Council of Europe 2019, p. 9; Goering et al. 2021; Ienca & Andorno 2017; Yuste et al. 2017; UN Special Rapporteur on Freedom of Religion or Belief 2021;

1. Novel human rights are necessary

Scholars defending this position argue that existing human rights and freedoms are insufficient to offer adequate legal protection from emerging brain-reading technologies. At the time these rights were introduced, no one could have foreseen the possibilities neurotechnology currently offers to monitor our brains and to 'read' people's minds. As a consequence, in the development of traditional human rights, the intricacies of game changing neurotechnologies have not been taken into account. In order to fill this gap in legal protection, we should introduce novel human rights,[98] which are often referred to as 'neurorights'. Of particular importance to brain-reading is the proposed human right to mental privacy.[99]

2. Novel human rights are not necessary; interpretation is key

According to the second position, existing human rights and freedoms are in fact sufficient to offer adequate legal protection from neurotechnological brain-reading. Therefore, novel rights considerations are unnecessary. The precise level of legal protection just depends on how we interpret and specify traditional human rights, such as the right to respect for private life, the right to freedom of thought and, in criminal cases, the privilege against self-incrimination.[100]

This position aligns closely with the Court's conception that the European Convention on Human Rights is a 'living instrument'.[101] The rights and freedoms guaranteed by the Convention must be interpreted in light of current developments in society, including advances in technology and bioethics:

> What gives the Convention its strength and makes it extremely modern is the way the Court interprets it: dynamically, in the light of present-day conditions. By its case-law the Court has extended the rights set out in the Convention, such that its provisions apply today to situations that were totally unforeseeable and unimaginable at the time it was first adopted, including issues related to new technologies, bioethics or the environment.[102]

The analysis in this book supports the second position. It shows that, together, existing human rights have the ability of offering considerable protection against current and future types of brain-reading in criminal law. Indeed, the ECHR does not

Report of the International Bioethics Committee of UNESCO, Ethical Issues of Neurotechnology, SHS/BIO/IBC28/2021/3Rev. (15 December 2021).

98 Ienca & Andorno 2017; the NeuroRights Foundation, Colombia University (https://neurorightsfoundation.org/). Cf. Sommaggio & Mazzocca 2020; Sommaggio et al. 2017.

99 Ienca & Andorno 2017, pp. 11–17; Ligthart et al. 2020.

100 Michalowski 2020; Alegre 2017; Ligthart et al. 2020; Bublitz 2022.

101 ECtHR (GC) 19 February 2013, appl.no. 19010/07 (*X and others/Austria*), § 139.

102 Council of Europe 2020b, p. 7

guarantee specific 'neurorights' like a right to 'mental privacy'. Meanwhile, the right to respect for private life pursuant to Article 8 ECHR covers the protection of personal data, including data about brains, mental health, emotions, memories, lies, and other mental states.[103] Moreover, some types of brain-reading will be covered by the freedom of non-expression, guaranteed by Article 10 ECHR.[104] And in the determination of a criminal charge, the privilege against self-incrimination can offer even stricter protection under Article 6 ECHR, when brain-reading requires cooperation of the subject.[105] In addition, if brain-reading reveals 'thoughts' in the meaning of Article 9 ECHR, the *forum internum* proscribes the use of coercion in absolute terms.[106]

The precise level and scope of this human rights protection depend on how we *interpret* and *specify* these human rights in view of brain-reading in criminal law. For example, the right to respect for private life offers stronger protection when personal data are 'sensitive'. Some applications of brain-reading, like diagnostics, yield highly sensitive information about a person. Others, such as lie and memory detection, shall normally reveal information about more trivial mental states.[107] Accordingly, specifying Article 8 ECHR to forensic brain-reading will lead to different levels of legal protection across different types of techniques.

Regarding the right to freedom of thought, I have argued that a somewhat narrow understanding of this right is most convincing in light of legal history, current case-law, and the literature. This interpretation narrows the scope of legal protection offered by Article 9 ECHR: in general, it will not cover existing types of forensic brain-reading.[108] And while the privilege against self-incrimination has the potential of proving strict protection, its foundations seem less compelling when specified to brain-reading technology.[109]

By discussing the right to privacy, the freedom of thought, and the privilege against self-incrimination in view of brain-reading technology, the analysis in this book builds upon the current literature about fundamental that should protect our mental lives. Meanwhile, this study also introduces a novel perspective to the present debate: protecting brains and minds by specifying the right to freedom of non-expression pursuant to Article 10 ECHR.[110] Let us take a closer look at this possibility.

Article 10 ECHR comprises a negative aspect. It covers a right not to be compelled to express thoughts, impart opinions, convey ideas, or to give information.[111]

103 Chapter 4, Section 4.3.4.
104 Chapter 5, Section 5.4.3.
105 Chapter 6, Section 6.3.
106 Chapter 5, Section 5.3.3.
107 Chapter 4, Section 4.3.4.2.
108 Chapter 5, Section 5.3.3.
109 Chapter 7, Section 6.3.4 and Chapter 8, Section 8.4.2.
110 See also Ligthart 2020b.
111 Chapter 5, Section 5.4.

Whereas the scope of the freedom of thought pursuant to Article 9 ECHR is somewhat restricted, the freedom of expression is considered extremely broad.[112] Among others, it covers facts, value statements, and advertising. Moreover, Article 10 ECHR not only protects the substance of information, but also a diverse variety of forms and means by which information is manifested, transmitted, or received. These range from speech to poetry and painting over radio and film to disrupting foxhunting by blowing a hunting horn.[113]

In view of this broad scope, the existing right to freedom of non-expression is perfectly able to offer legal protecting in respect of forensic brain-reading, 'transmitting' brain-derived data that allows for drawing inferences about a variety of mental states and characteristics, such as memories and knowledge about simple facts, sexual proclivities, emotional states, neural disorders, and recidivism risks. In addition, Article 10(2) ECHR allows for balancing the right not to impart information against other interests, such as the prevention and prosecution of crime. Such a balancing of competing interests has been considered desirable in respect of disclosing individual mental states and content (think of obliging witnesses to testify at trial).[114] Altogether, Article 10 ECHR is well equipped to offer adequate legal protection in respect of forensic brain-reading. The scope of this protection will be broader compared with the closely related right to freedom of thought pursuant Article 9 ECHR.[115]

Considering coercive brain-reading under the freedom of non-expression will also provide valuable protection to our mental content next to the privilege against self-incrimination pursuant to Article 6 ECHR. Unlike Article 10 ECHR, the privilege only applies in the determination of a criminal charge: in general, it will not cover coercive brain-reading of, for example, convicted offenders, witnesses, and patients in involuntary civil commitment. Furthermore, through its casuistic case-law, the ECtHR has developed a long-standing and comprehensive, though complicated doctrine under the privilege, which may be thought unable to address the intricacies raised by emerging technologies such as brain-reading.[116] At least, in respect of brain-reading, the rationales of the privilege appear not immediately relevant,[117] except for respecting autonomy.[118] However, restricting autonomy in criminal law

[112] Rainey, McCormick & Ovey 2021, p. 488; Van Rijn 2018, pp. 771, 781.

[113] Chapter 5, Section 5.4.

[114] Cf. Bublitz 2014, p. 23; McCarthy-Jones 2019, pp. 7, 12–13. See also Jackson & Summers 2012, pp. 273–276.

[115] See Chapter 5, Sections 5.3.4 and 5.4.

[116] Cf. Farahany 2012a; Federspiel 2008; Stoller & Wolpe 2007; Shen 2013.

[117] Chapter 6, Section 6.3.4.

[118] The rationale of the freedom of expression is much broader, constituting 'one of the essential foundations of a democratic society and one of the basic conditions for its progress and for each individual's self-fulfilment'. According to Jackson & Summers 2012, p. 249, this rationale is arguably sounder to justify a right not to incriminate oneself compared with the rationales of the privilege

often calls for balancing the competing interests at stake.[119] Unlike the privilege,[120] Article 10(2) ECHR provides a clear framework within which the subject's autonomy can be balanced against the interests of criminal justice. This enables the development of a fine-grained framework of legal protection, distinguishing between different brain-reading technologies, applied in different contexts. For the purpose of balancing autonomy, it would be helpful to find a clear definition of autonomy in criminal proceedings.[121]

Importantly, under Article 10(2) ECHR, autonomy is not the only personal interest that should be taken into account. The potential self-incriminating nature of brain-reading data is likely a relevant factor too.[122] And sometimes, coercive brain-reading could involve a relevant risk of stigmatisation.[123] Another important factor concerns the potential chilling effect of reading individual brains on the public at large. Obliging people to express mental content through neurotechnology could deter other persons from thinking what they want to think and from wishing not to express those thoughts.[124] Presumably, other interests should be considered as well. The test of a fair balance in the meaning of Article 10 ECHR has been conceived as a flexible and open-ended weighing exercise. It allows the balancing of all relevant interests and arguments at stake.[125] The precise interests to be balanced shall depend on all relevant circumstances of each individual case.

Specifying the freedom of non-expression to coercive brain-reading perfectly aligns with the second position in the debate on neurorights discussed above, echoing the living-instrument-approach of the ECHR. Meanwhile, apart from Article 10 ECHR, scanning brains and reading minds without consent will often infringe the well-developed right to respect for private life under Article 8 ECHR.[126] Similar to Article 10(2), Article 8(2) ECHR entails a flexible and open-ended balancing of all relevant interests at stake. As case-law on DNA, GPS, and CCTV have shown,[127] the legal protection of private life offered by Article 8 ECHR is perfectly able to adapt to technological developments. So what would be the benefit of developing an

as are provided by the ECHR. In Ireland, for example, the right to silence and the privilege against self-incrimination are considered as a corollary of the constitutional right to freedom of expression: Daly 2021.

[119] See Section 8.4.2.

[120] ECtHR (GC) 10 March 2009, appl.no. 4378/02 (*Bykov/Russia*), § 93; ECtHR (GC) 17 December 1996, appl.no. 19187/91 (*Saunders/UK*), § 74.

[121] See also Section 8.4.2.

[122] See Chapter 5, Section 5.4.3.

[123] Chapter 4, Section 4.3.4.3.

[124] Chapter 5, Section 5.3.4.

[125] Sottiaux & Van der Shyff 2008, p. 131; Pirker 2013, p. 228; Christoffersen 2009, p. 76.

[126] Chapter 4, Section 4.3.4.2.

[127] ECtHR (GC) 4 December 2008, appl.nos. 30562/04 and 30566/04 (*S. & Marper/UK*); ECtHR 2 September 2010, appl.no. 35623/05 (*Uzun/Germany*); ECtHR 28 January 2003, appl.no. 44647/98 (*Peck/UK*).

additional approach on coercive brain-reading under the under-elaborated freedom of non-expression?

Sometimes, Articles 8 and 10 ECHR are closely connected.[128] For example, in cases concerning the right of prisoners to respect for their correspondence, Article 8 ECHR could absorb a prisoner's complaint about the freedom of expression guaranteed by Article 10 ECHR.[129] In such cases, the Commission has considered Article 8 ECHR as a *lex specialis*. No separate issues arise under Article 10 ECHR.[130] However, referring to these cases, Van Rijn underlines the distinctive aims of both provisions:

> in Article 8, the main point is the protection of the private character of the means of communication referred to, while in Article 10 its character as a means of expressing an opinion and of providing and receiving information is at issue.[131]

Perhaps, this distinction could sometimes result in different levels of legal protection afforded by Articles 8 and 10 ECHR to brain-reading in criminal law.

The balancing of interests under the right to respect for private life inextricably links to considerations of personal data and privacy sensitivity. Meanwhile, the right to non-expression is not primarily concerned with the sensitivity of brain-derived data. Rather, in more general terms, it protects the personal interest of not giving opinions, disclosing ideas, or furnishing all kind of information just because you don't want to express your mental content. Just because you don't wish to give other people access to the intimate spheres of your mental life.[132]

Yielding and using sensitive brain-reading data, for example concerning mental health, is likely to enjoy considerable protection under the right to respect for private life. The sensitivity of such brain-derived data puts weight to the balancing of interests, in favour of the coerced subject. At the same time, when brain-reading yields less sensitive information, for example, about the recognition of trivial objects, this will be a relevant factor too, potentially tipping the balance in favour of crime control.

Still, people may have good reasons not to disclose all kind of trivial opinions, frivolous ideas, or simple facts. For example, consider the following question: Did you like the Christmas dinner? The answer to this question is normally not conceived as highly sensitive in terms of privacy. But the inclination to actually disclose your critical thoughts may well depend on who is asking for your opinion: your mother-in-law, who prepared dinner, or the waitress of an expensive restaurant.

Presumably, Article 8 ECHR shall not offer much protection against the use of coercion to disclose simple facts or frivolous opinions in the course of criminal

[128] Van Rijn 2018, p. 780. Cf. O'Callaghan & Shiner 2021, p. 141.

[129] E.g. ECtHR 20 June 1988, appl.no. 11368/85 (*Schönenberger/Durmaz*), § 31; ECtHR 25 March 1983, appl.nos. 5947/72; 6205/73; 7052/75; 7061/75; 7107/75; 7113/75; 7136/75 (*Silver and others/UK*), § 107.

[130] EComHR 4 May 1989, appl.no. 9511/81 (*McCallum/UK*), § 63.

[131] Van Rijn 2018, p. 78. Cf. Van der Sloot 2015, p. 95.

[132] Cf. Goering et al. 2021; Van Toor 2017, p. 298.

procedures. Unlike Article 8, Article 10 ECHR is not intrinsically linked to privacy and sensitivity of personal data. It aims to protect 'expression' as a means of imparting information. Perhaps, this could justify a diverging 'fair balance' under Article 10 compared with Article 8 ECHR, putting less weight to the triviality of the information that is expressed. This nuance could be of particular importance regarding lie detection and CITs. After all, compared with DNA, medical data, and recidivism risks, the recognition of, say, a hammer or a sports bag is not highly sensitive as such.[133]

Admittedly, case-law and scholarship on the freedom of *non*-expression are still scarce. This lack of well-defined doctrine entails uncertainties regarding the scope of this right. But this could also be an advantage. The precise scope of the freedom of non-expression and the permissible limitations are yet to be defined. The intricacies of brain-reading technology can be taken into account as of the outset of specifying this right. This involves an important challenge for European human rights law.

Part of that challenge relates to the procedural implications of brain-reading in breach of the Convention. The use at trial of evidence obtained in violation of Article 10 ECHR will not necessarily render the criminal proceedings as a whole unfair. In view of the separation thesis, which the Court tends to adhere, the requirements of a fair trial on the one hand, and violations of Article 10 ECHR on the other hand, are to be considered as two separate matters.[134] However, the exact relation between the notion of a fair trial and the freedom of non-expression is as yet unclear. To what extent are both rights actually separated from each other? The answer to this question partly depends on how we specify the right not to convey information pursuant to Article 10 ECHR.[135]

One possibility is to develop and clarify the scope and boundaries of this right in a way that closely relates to Article 8 ECHR. In that case, the separation thesis will apply without prejudice. Another possibility is to specify the freedom of non-expression in a way that resembles the 'correlative'[136] freedom against self-incrimination.[137] In that case, the theoretical distinction between the right to a fair trial and a violation of Article 10 ECHR will arguably decrease.[138]

The exact substantive approach to be followed will affect the procedural implications of brain-reading in breach of Article 10 ECHR. The latter approach shall provide more opportunities to exclude such brain-reading evidence via Article 6

[133] Chapter 4, Section 4.3.4.2.
[134] Sections 7.2 and 7.3.6.
[135] Chapter 7, Section 7.3.6.
[136] ECtHR 21 December 2000, appl.no. 34720/97 (*Heaney and McGuinness/Ireland*), § 62; ECtHR 21 December 2000, appl.no. 36887/97 (*Quinn/Ireland*), § 63.
[137] Jackson 2009, p. 841; Jackson & Summers 2012, pp. 249, 268, 270, 273.
[138] Chapter 7, Section 7.3.6.

ECHR compared with the former. Again, deciding which path to take poses legal challenges. Part of those will touch upon the broader debate on excluding evidence obtained in breach of the Convention. As the preceding chapters show, the holistic protection against forensic brain-reading shall be anchored in the different rights and freedoms discussed in this book. Therefore, the debate on excluding unlawfully obtained brain-reading data should also include the use of such data yielded in breach of Articles 3, 8, 9 ECHR and in violation of the privilege against self-incrimination.

Finally, as briefly mentioned,[139] Article 13 ECHR prescribes additional, general procedural guarantees when brain-reading has violated one of the Convention rights.[140] It requires that, if anyone has an 'arguable claim' of being a victim of a violation of the ECHR, she should have an effective remedy before a national authority in order to deal with the substance of his claim and, if appropriate, to grant adequate relief.[141] The exact legal implications of this requirement will depend on the Convention right at stake.[142] Meanwhile, brain-reading is unlikely to raise novel, fundamental issues in this regard. For the purpose of Article 13 ECHR, it will not be critical whether a violation of, for example, Article 3 ECHR consists in the compulsory admission of emetics during police investigation or in brain-reading attaining a minimum level of severity. Concerning both violations, Article 13 ECHR prescribes similar kinds of effective remedies.[143] In determining the appropriateness of the relief to be afforded, all relevant circumstances of the case should be considered.[144] These will include the exact means of violating the Convention – that is, the precise brain-reading test and means of coercion. Yet, brain-reading shall not raise fundamental difficulties in this regard.

8.4 CONCLUSION

Introducing coercive brain-reading into criminal justice raises fundamental questions in view of different human rights and freedoms. This book examined those questions from a European perspective. It analysed the first contours of a legal framework for coercive brain-reading in criminal justice. Together, Articles 3, 6,

139 Chapter 7, Section 7.1.

140 On the relation between Articles 6 and 13 ECHR in criminal proceedings, see Pitcher 2018a, p. 65 et seq; Ormerod 2003, pp. 70–71. Cf. ECtHR 31 January 2017, appl.no. 40233/07 (*Kalnėnienė/Belgium*), § 60–63.

141 ECtHR (GC) 10 July 2020, appl.no. 310/15 (*Mugemangango/Belgium*), § 130; ECtHR 6 September 1978, appl.no. 5029/71 (*Klass and others/Germany*), § 64.

142 ECtHR (GC) 30 November 2004, appl.no. 48939/99 (*Öneryıldız/Turkey*), § 147; Harris et al. 2018, pp. 759–762; Barkhuysen & Van Emmerik 2018, pp. 1047–1052, both with further references.

143 The member States enjoy a margin of appreciation in this regard: ECtHR (GC) 26 October 2000, appl.no. 30210/96 (*Kudła/Poland*), § 154; ECtHR 8 March 2011, appl.no. 12739/05 (*Goranova-Karaeneva/Bulgaria*), § 57.

144 Cf. ECtHR 6 September 1978, appl.no. 5029/71 (*Klass and others/Germany*), § 69–72.

8, 9, and 10 ECHR cover all five types of coercive brain-reading discussed in this book. This finding supports the second position in the debate on establishing fundamental neurorights: existing human rights have the ability of offering adequate legal protection from neurotechnological brain-reading. The exact level of legal protection depends on how we – in particular the ECtHR – interpret and specify traditional human rights. Specifying the discussed human rights to the intricacies of brain-reading entails novel challenges for European human rights law. This chapter identified five such challenges:

(1) Developing a generic account on the validity of informed consent in relation to different means of influences, ranging from coercion over manipulation to rational persuasion.
(2) Seeking for a clear definition of the value of 'autonomy' in criminal proceedings.
(3) Reconsidering the foundations of the privilege against self-incrimination and revaluing the role of autonomy in this regard.
(4) Specifying the right to freedom of non-expression pursuant to Article 10 ECHR and determining its exact relation to other Convention rights, especially to Articles 8 and 9 ECHR and to the privilege against self-incrimination.
(5) Developing an approach under Article 6 ECHR on using evidence obtained in breach of Articles 9 and 10 ECHR. Specifying the current approach on evidence obtained in breach of the privilege and Articles 3 and 8 ECHR to brain-reading technologies.

In its Strategic Action Plan on Human Rights and Technologies in Biomedicine (2020–2025), the Committee on Bioethics of the Council of Europe stressed that there is a pressing need to embed human rights in novel technologies.[145] It highlighted the importance of tailoring the technology from the outset to protecting human rights. As the present chapter shows, this should not be a one-way-approach. Apart from developing technology towards protecting human rights, we should also reconsider and tailor those human rights in respect of emerging technologies that shape societies and change traditional means of criminal investigation.

[145] See Chapter 1, Section 1.1.

9

Concluding Observations

For centuries, we conceived our brains and minds as factually intangible to the outside world. When the European Convention on Human Rights was adopted in 1950, no one could have envisaged the possibilities brain-reading technologies offer today, enabling to examine our brains and read out mental states and emotions. As a growing body of evidence suggests, these technologies can contribute to answering central legal questions of criminal law in different meaningful ways. In fact, some types of brain-reading have already been used in criminal procedures all over the world. In the context of criminal justice, suspects and convicted offenders are often reluctant to cooperate with governmental investigations. This poses the pressing question: Is coercive brain-reading in criminal justice permissible in light of the European Convention on Human Rights and, if so, to what extent and under which legal conditions?

This study focussed on four technologies: (1) brain-based lie detection, (2) P300-based concealed information tests, (3) brain-based diagnostics of mental and neural disorders, and (4) neuroprediction. These types of brain-reading can inform legal decision-making in respect of the determination of guilt, legal responsibility, and in the imposition and execution of criminal sanctions. At the same time, coercive brain-reading in criminal law raises fundamental legal questions, particularly in light of:

(A) the prohibition of ill-treatment (Article 3 ECHR),
(B) the right to respect for private life (Article 8 ECHR),
(C) the right to freedom of thought (Article 9 ECHR),
(D) the right to freedom of expression (Article 10 ECHR), and
(E) the privilege against self-incrimination (Article 6 ECHR).

The central conclusion is that these rights and freedoms will not as such proscribe the use of coercive brain-reading in criminal law. Meanwhile, together, they offer a legal framework that delimits the permissible use of forensic brain-reading without valid consent. Technological advances such as in real-time thought-reading are likely to attract stricter protection under this framework of human rights.

A first delimitation relates to the use of coercion. Particular means of *physical* coercion to enforce brain-reading will, in most cases, be proscribed by the prohibition of ill-treatment and the privilege against self-incrimination. Examples are complete mechanical restraint and general anaesthesia.

A second delimitation relates to the mental content forensic brain-reading aims to disclose. Identifying thoughts, conscience, and religion without valid consent will violate the absolute *forum internum* of Article 9 ECHR. However, regarding present forms of brain-reading, the right to freedom of thought will hardly be relevant. In general, forensic brain-reading will not yield any information that allows for drawing inferences about the subject's religion, conscience, or thoughts in the meaning of Article 9 ECHR. But when they do, perhaps in the future, the *forum internum* of Article 9 ECHR will outlaw the non-consensual use of such brain-reading assessments.

Although not absolute, the right to respect for private life (Article 8 ECHR) and the freedom of non-expression (Article 10 ECHR) will further delimit and regulate the permissible use of reading brains. They require legal safeguards and boundaries to prevent from arbitrariness, abuse, and disproportionality. The level of legal protection will depend on a variety of factors. These include the privacy sensitivity of brain-reading data, possible risks of stigmatisation, the incriminating nature of brain-derived information, potentially chilling effects of reading people's brains, and the severity of the crime concerned and the public interest in convicting and preventing such crimes. Articles 8 and 10 ECHR are well equipped to be specified and tailored to the use of brain-reading in criminal law.

When brain-reading is used in the determination of a criminal charge, the privilege against self-incrimination could provide further, stricter protection. It protects against coercive brain-reading that requires cooperation of the subject. At the same time, brain-reading poses fundamental questions regarding the privilege's foundations. Volitionally coerced brain-reading will not typically threaten the first and second rationales of the privilege: preventing improper compulsion and avoiding miscarriages of justice. As such, brain-reading puts autonomy at the centre, raising the question of whether autonomy alone is strong enough to carry the weight of the right against self-incrimination. I have suggested it is not. Restricting autonomy is quite common and often legitimate in criminal law. To the privilege, autonomy appears mainly relevant in direct relation to (1) the prevention of improper compulsion and (2) the avoidance of wrongful convictions. But these two rationales do not apply in most cases of brain-reading. Therefore, we should be critical about whether considerations of autonomy alone can justify the legal protection afforded by the right against self-incrimination.

This study shows that, sometimes, brain-reading could violate the Convention in the determination of a criminal charge. Article 6 ECHR could then require procedural implications in order to preserve the fairness of the criminal proceedings. Brain-reading data that are obtained in breach of the privilege against self-incrimination should be excluded from evidence. Using such information at trial will render the proceedings as a whole unfair.

Where brain-reading violates an absolute right, the admission of the data so obtained will always raise serious issues regarding the fairness of the proceedings, even when the evidence was not decisive in securing a conviction. In case of torture and, arguably, if brain-reading violates the right to freedom of thought, the data so obtained must be excluded to preserve the overall fairness of the criminal proceedings. The use at trial of brain-reading evidence that has been obtained through inhuman and/or degrading treatment will at least violate the right to a fair trial if it had direct impact on the ultimate conviction or sentence.

The admission of brain-reading evidence obtained in breach of Article 8 ECHR shall not normally render the proceedings as a whole unfair. It is likely that a similar approach will apply to brain-reading in violation of Article 10 ECHR. Meanwhile, the precise procedural implications in this regard shall depend on the substantive approach that is yet to be developed regarding forensic brain-reading under Article 10 ECHR.

In conclusion, the European Convention on Human Rights will not as such prohibit coercive brain-reading in criminal law. Meanwhile, the Convention is well equipped to delimit the permissible use of present and future types of forensic brain-reading. In particular, the holistic legal protection of people's brains, their emotions, and mental states is anchored in the human rights and freedoms discussed in this book, each setting out their own normative limits. At the same time, introducing brain-reading in criminal justice entails novel challenges for European human rights law. It requires us to reconsider and specify decennial-old human rights in respect of emerging brain-reading technologies. To accomplish this challenging task, more research is needed. For this, the present book has identified four central themes of research that would advance the debate on brain-reading in criminal justice and beyond.

1. *Establish a central doctrine on the freedom not to express oneself under Article 10 ECHR.*
   The negative aspect of the right to freedom of expression – the freedom of non-expression – covers both present and future forms of brain-reading. However, this right is still underdeveloped in practice and in legal scholarship. Prior to specifying the freedom of non-expression to brain-reading technologies, it is necessary to establish a central conceptual theory on this freedom. This should at least entail discussion about the exact meaning and scope of this right, its conceptual foundations, and its relation to other convention rights, in particular to Articles 8 and 9 ECHR, and to the privilege against self-incrimination pursuant to Article 6 ECHR.
2. *Revalue the foundations of the privilege against self-incrimination.*

Under positive law, the privilege against self-incrimination has the ability to offer strict legal protection in respect of brain-reading that requires cooperation of a suspect. However, brain-reading technology raises fundamental questions regarding the rationales of this right. This calls for a debate about the sustainability of the privilege's foundations – particularly in view of technological means of investigation that will not typically entail a risk of improper compulsion nor of wrongful convictions. Among others, this debate should include the role of autonomy as a foundation of the right against self-incrimination.

3. *Develop a central human rights-based approach on different means of influences in relation to informed consent.*
   The European Convention on Human Rights has the ability to protect against present and future forms of non-consensual brain-reading. However, people may lose this human rights protection by consenting to brain-reading assessments. States could use different means of (indirect) influences in order to elicit consent to brain-reading in a criminal legal context, thereby circumventing a variety of human rights restrictions. In order for human rights to offer adequate and effective protection from brain-reading in criminal law, it should be clear when exactly consent in this context is valid and could negate human rights protection.
4. *Expand the procedural guarantees on the exclusion of unlawfully obtained evidence under Article 6 ECHR to violations of Articles 9 and 10 ECHR.*
   Brain-reading in criminal justice has the potential of violating the right to freedom of thought (Article 9 ECHR) and the right to freedom of expression (Article 10 ECHR). Traditional means of criminal investigation are not typically considered in light of these rights. As a consequence, no clear approach exists under Article 6 ECHR on the use at trial of evidence obtained in breach of Articles 9 and 10 ECHR. In order to guarantee fair criminal proceedings in cases of unlawful brain-reading, there is a need to develop a legal account on the use of evidence obtained in violation of the freedom of thought and the freedom of non-expression.

This book has shown that brain-reading in criminal justice poses challenging novel issues to the present framework of human rights in Europe. It provides a solid basis for further research on how we could effectively ensure human rights in the age of neuroscience and neurotechnology, safeguarding the values of human dignity and human freedom as are underlying the European Convention on Human Rights.

Bibliography

J. Aall, 'Waiver of Human Rights. Waiver of Procedural Rights According to ECHR Article 6', *Nordic Journal of Human Rights* 2011, 29(2–3), pp. 206–278.

K. Addo & N. Grief, 'Does Article 3 of the European Convention on Human Rights Enshrine Absolute Rights?', *European Journal of International Law* 1998, 9(3), pp. 51–524.

E. Aharoni et al., 'Neuroprediction of Future Rearrest', *Proceedings of the National Academy of Sciences* 2013, 110(15), pp. 6223–6228.

E. Aharoni et al., 'Predictive Accuracy in the Neuroprediction of Rearrest', *Society for Neuroscience* 2014, 9(4), pp. 332–336.

S. Alegre, 'Rethinking Freedom of Thought for the 21st Century', *European Human Rights Law Review* 2017, 2017(3), pp. 221–233.

A. Alimardani & J. Chin, 'Neurolaw in Australia: The Use of Neuroscience in Australian Criminal Proceedings', *Neuroethics* 2019, 12, pp. 255–270.

R. J. Allen & M. K. Mace, 'The Self-incrimination Clause Explained and its Future Predicted', *Journal of Criminal Law and Criminology* 2004, 94(2), pp. 243–293.

K. Aloui, A. Nait-Ali & M. S. Naceur, 'Using Brain Prints as New Biometric Feature for Human Recognition', *Pattern Recognition Letters* 2018, 113, pp. 38–45.

A. W. Alschuler, 'A Peculiar Privilege in Historical Perspective', in R. H. Helmolz et al. (eds.), *The Privilege against Self-incrimination: Its Origins and Development*, Chicago: University of Chicago Press 1997, pp. 181–204.

W. Ambach et al., 'A Concealed Information Test with Multimodal Measurement', *International Journal of Psychophysiology* 2010, 75(3), pp. 258–267.

W. Ambach & M. Gamer, 'Physiological Measures in the Detection of Deception and Concealed Information', in J. P. Rosenfeld (ed.), *Detecting Concealed Information and Deception: Recent Developments*, London: Academic Press 2018, pp. 3–33.

S. Anderson, 'Coercion', in E. N. Zalte (ed.), *The Stanford Encyclopedia of Philosophy* (https://plato.stanford.edu/cgi-bin/encyclopedia/archinfo.cgi?entry=coercion; Summer 2021).

S. A. Anderson, 'The Enforcement Approach to Coercion', *Journal of Ethics & Social Philosophy* 2011, 5(1), pp. 1–31.

R. Andorno, 'The Relevance of Human Rights for Dealing with the Challenges Posed by Genetics', in A. von Arnauld, K. von der Decken & M. Susi (eds.), *The Cambridge Handbook of New Human Rights: Recognition, Novelty, Rhetoric*, Cambridge: Cambridge University Press 2020, pp. 335–349.

P. S. Appelbaum, 'Assessment of Patients' Competence to Consent to Treatment', *The New England Journal of Medicine* 2007, 357(18), pp. 1834–1840.

P. S Appelbaum, C. W. Lidz & R. Klitzman, 'Voluntariness of Consent to Research: A Conceptual Model', *Hastings Center Report* 2009, 39(1), pp. 30–39.

Y. Arai-Takahashi, *The Margin of Appreciation Doctrine and the Principle of Proportionality in the Jurisprudence of the ECHR*, Antwerp, Oxford, and New York: Intersentia 2002.

A. J. Ashworth, 'Excluding Evidence as Protecting Rights', *Criminal Law Review* 1977, pp. 723–735.

A. J. Ashworth, 'Exploring the Integrity Principle in Evidence and Procedure', in P. Mirfield & R. Smith (eds.), *Essays for Colin Tapper*, New York: Oxford University Press 2003, pp. 107–125.

A. J. Ashworth, 'Human Rights: Article 3 – Article 6', *Criminal Law Review* 2007, pp. 717–721.

A. J. Ashworth, 'Self-incrimination in European Human Rights Law – A Pregnant Pragmatism?', *Cardozo Law Review* 2008, 30(3), pp. 751–774.

A. J. Ashworth, 'The Exclusion of Evidence Obtained by Violating a Fundamental Right: Pragmatism before Principle in the Strasbourg Jurisprudence', in P. Roberts & J. Hunter (eds.), *Criminal Evidence and Human Rights: Reimagining Common Law Procedural Traditions*, Oxford; Portland: Hart Publishing 2012.

A. J. Ashworth & L. Zedner, *Preventive Justice*, New York: Oxford University Press 2014.

L. Bachmaier, 'The European Court of Human Rights on Negotiated Justice and Coercion', *European Journal of Crime, Criminal Law and Criminal Justice* 2016, 26(3), pp. 236–259.

A. Baird, J. Kennett & E. Schier, 'Homicide and Dementia: An Investigation of Legal, Ethical, and Clinical Factors of Australian Legal Cases', *International Journal of Law and Psychiatry* 2020, 71, pp. 1–13.

T. Barkhuysen & M. van Emmerik, 'Right to an Effective Remedy', in P. van Dijk et al. (eds.), *Theory and Practice of the European Convention on Human Rights*, Cambridge: Intersentia 2018, pp. 1035–1061.

T. Barkhuysen et al., 'Right to a Fair Trial', in P. van Dijk et al. (eds.), *Theory and Practice of the European Convention on Human Rights*, Cambridge: Intersentia 2018, pp. 497–654.

B. D. Bartholow & D. M. Amodio, 'Using Event-Related Brain Potentials in Social Psychological Research', in M. D. Rugg & M. G. H. Coles (eds.), *Electrophysiology of Mind. Event-Related Brain Potentials and Cognition*, Oxford: Oxford University Press 1996.

A. J. Bauer & A. Just, 'Neural Representations of Concept Knowledge', in G. I. de Zubicaray & N. O. Schiller (eds.), *The Oxford Handbook of Neurolinguistics*, New York: Oxford University Press 2019, pp. 519–547.

T. Baumbach, 'Chilling Effect as a European Court of Human Rights' Concept in Media Law Cases', *Bergen Journal of Criminal Law and Criminal Justice* 2018, 6(1), pp. 92–114.

H. L. Bedard, 'The Potential for Bioprediction in Criminal Law', *The Colombia Science & Technology Law Review* 2017, XVIII, pp. 268–325.

H. K. Beecher, 'Some Fallacies and Errors in the Application of the Principle of Consent in Human Experimentation', *Clinical Pharmacology and Therapeutics* 1962, 3(2), pp. 141–145.

G. Ben-Shakhar, 'Countermeasures', in B. Verschuere, G. Ben-Shakhar & E. Meijer (eds.), *Memory Detection: Theory and Application of the Concealed Information Test*, New York: Cambridge University Press 2011.

G. Ben-Shakhar, 'Current Research and Potential Applications of the Concealed Information Test: An Overview', *Frontiers in Psychology* 2012, 3, Article 342.

J. Bentham, *Rationale of Judicial Evidence, Vol. 5*, collected by D. S. Berkowitz & S. E. Thorne, London: Hunt and Clarke 1978.

J. W. Berg et al., *Informed Consent: Legal Theory and Clinical Practice*, New York: Oxford University Press 2001.

M. Berman, 'The Normative Functions of Coercion Claims', *Legal Theory* 2002, 8(1), 45–89.

J. Bijlsma et al., 'Legal Insanity and Risk: An International Perspective on the Justification of Indeterminate Preventive Commitment', *International Journal of Law and Psychiatry* 2019, 66(September–October), pp. 1–6.

A. Biondi et al., 'Are the Brains of Monozygotic Twins Similar? A Three-Dimensional MR Study', *American Journal of Neuroradiology* 1996, 19(7), pp. 1361–1367.

R. J. R. Blair, 'Neuroimaging of Psychopathy and Antisocial Behavior: A Targeted Review', *Current Psychiatry Reports* 2010, 12(1), pp. 76–82.

R. J. R. Blair, 'The Neurobiology of Impulsive Aggression', *Journal of Child and Adolescent Psychopharmacology* 2016, 26(1), pp. 4–9.

D. Birks & T. Douglas (eds.), *Treatment for Crime: Philosophical Essays on Neurointerventions in Criminal Justice*, New York: Oxford University Press 2018.

M. J. Blitz, *Searching Minds by Scanning Brains*, Cham: Palgrave Macmillan 2017.

M. A. Bobes et al., 'Linkage of Functional and Structural Anomalies in the Left Amygdala of Reactive-Aggressive Men', *SCAN* 2013, 8(8), pp. 928–936.

L. Bomann-Larsen, 'Voluntary Rehabilitation? On Neurotechnological Behavioural Treatment, Valid Consent and (In)appropriate Offers', *Neuroethics* 2013, 6(1), pp. 65–77.

M. J. Bossuyt, *Guide to the 'Travaux préparatoires' of the International Covenant on Civil and Political Rights*, Dordrecht: Martinus Nijhoff Publishers 1987.

B. Bottalico & A. Santosuosso, 'Not Guilty by Reason of Insanity' in the Italian Jurisprudence', in S. Moratti & D. Patterson (eds.), *Legal Insanity and the Brain: Science, Law and European Courts*, Portland: Hart Publishing 2016, pp. 121–124.

M. T. Bradley et al., 'Leakage of Information to Innocent Suspects', in B. Verschuere, G. Ben-Shakhar & E. Meijer (eds.), *Memory Detection: Theory and Application of the Concealed Information Test*, New York: Cambridge University Press, pp. 187–199.

D. J. Brenner & E. J. Hall, 'Computed Tomography – An Increasing Source of Radiation Exposure', *The New England Journal of Medicine* 2007, 57(22), pp. 2277–2284.

T. Brown & E. Murphy, 'Through a Scanner Darkly: Functional Neuroimaging as Evidence of a Criminal Defendant's Past Mental States', *Stanford Law Review* 2010, 62, pp. 1119–1208.

R. Brownsword, 'Regulating Brain Imaging: Questions of Privacy, Informed Consent, and Human Dignity', in S. Richmond, G. Rees & S. J. L. Edwards (eds.), *I Know What You're Thinking: Brain Imaging and Mental Privacy*, Croydon: Oxford University Press 2012, pp. 223–244.

J. C. Bublitz, 'My Mind Is Mine!? Cognitive Liberty as a Legal Concept', in W. Hildt & A. G. Franke (eds.), *Cognitive Enhancement*, Dordrecht: Springer 2013, pp. 233–264.

J. C. Bublitz, 'Freedom of Thought in the Age of Neuroscience', *Archiv Für Rechts- Und Sozialphilosophie* 2014, 100, pp. 1–25.

J. C. Bublitz, 'Cognitive Liberty or the International Human Right to Freedom of Thought', in J. Clausen & N. Levy (eds.), *Handbook of Neuroethics*, Dordrecht: Springer Science + Business Media Dordrecht 2015, pp. 1309–1333.

J. C. Bublitz, '"The Soul Is in the Prison of the Body" – Mandatory Moral Enhancement, Punishment & Rights against Neuro-Rehabilitation', in D. Birks & T. Douglas (eds.), *Treatment for Crime: Philosophical Essays on Neurointerventions in Criminal Justice*, New York: Oxford University Press 2018.

J. C. Bublitz, 'The Nascent Right to Psychological Integrity and Mental Self-determination', in A. von Arnauld, K. von der Decken & M. Susi (eds.), *The Cambridge Handbook of New Human Rights: Recognition, Novelty, Rhetoric*, Padstow: Cambridge University Press 2020, pp. 387–403.

J. C. Bublitz, 'Freedom of Thought as an International Human Right: Elements of a Theory of a Living Right', in M. J. Blitz & J. C. Bublitz (eds.), *The Law and Ethics of Freedom of Thought*, Volume 1, Cham: Palgrave Macmillan 2021, pp. 49–101.

J. C. Bublitz, 'Novel Neurorights: From Nonsense to Substance', *Neuroethics* 2022, 15, Article nr. 7.

J. C. Bublitz & R. Merkel, 'Crimes against Minds: On Mental Manipulations, Harms and a Human Right to Mental Self-determination', *Criminal Law and Philosophy* 2014, 8(1), pp. 51–71.

W. Buelens, C. Herijgers & S. Illegems, 'The View of the European Court of Human Rights on Competent Patients' Right of Informed Consent: Research in the Light of Article 3 and 8 of the European Convention on Human Rights', *European Journal of Health Law* 2016, 23(5), pp. 481–509.

J. M. Burns & R. H. Swerdlow, 'Right Orbitofrontal Tumor with Pedophilia Symptom and Constructional Apraxia Sign', *Archives of Neurolaw* 2003, 60, pp. 437–440.

D. Bychawska-Siniarska, *Protecting the Right to Freedom of Expression under the European Convention on Human Rights. A Handbook for Legal Practitioners*, Strasbourg: Council of Europe 2017.

P. Catley & L. Claydon, 'The Use of Neuroscientific Evidence in the Courtroom by Those Accused of Criminal Offenses in England and Wales, *Journal of Law and the Biosciences* 2015, 2(3), pp. 510–549.

J. Chandler, 'The Use of Neuroscientific Evidence in Canadian Criminal Proceedings', *Journal of Law and the Biosciences* 2015, 2(3), pp. 550–579.

P. Chau, 'Excluding Integrity? Revisiting Non-Consequentialist Justifications for Excluding Improperly Obtained Evidence in Criminal Trials', in J. Hunter et al. (eds.), *The Integrity of Criminal Process: From Theory into Practice*, Oxford – Portland: Hart Publishing 2016, pp. 268–279.

A. L.-T. Choo, *Abuse of Process and Judicial Stays of Criminal Proceedings*, New York: Oxford University Press 2008.

A. L.-T. Choo, *The Privilege against Self-incrimination and Criminal Justice*, Oxford: Hart Publishing 2013.

S. E. Christ et al., 'The Contributions of Prefrontal Cortex and Executive Control to Deception: Evidence from Activation Likelihood Estimate Meta-analyses', *Cerebral Cortex* 2009, 19, pp. 1557–1566.

J. Christoffersen, *Fair Balance: Proportionality, Subsidiarity and Primarity in the European Convention on Human Rights*, Leiden: Martinus Nijhoff Publishers 2009.

L. Claydon, 'Brain-Based Mind Reading for Lawyers: Reflecting on Possibilities and Perils', *Journal for Law and the Biosciences* 2017, 4(3), pp. 594–598.

G. J. M. Corstens, *Het Nederlands strafprocesrecht*, bewerkt door M. J. Borgers & T. Kooijmans, Deventer: Wolters Kluwer 2021.

Committee on Bioethics of the Council of Europe, *Strategic Action Plan on Human Rights and Technologies in Biomedicine (2020–2025)*, Adopted by the Committee on Bioethics (DH-BIO) at Its 16th Meeting (19–21 November 2019).

Council of Europe, *Guide on Article 9 of the European Convention on Human Rights*, Strasbourg: Council of Europe/European Court of Human Rights 2020a.

Council of Europe, *The European Convention on Human Rights: A Living Instrument*, Strasbourg: Council of Europe/European Court of Human Rights 2020b.

J. N. Craig, 'Incarceration, Direct Brain Intervention, and the Right to Mental Integrity – A Reply to Thomas Douglas', *Neuroethics* 2016, 9, pp. 107–118.

P. Curry, D. Viernes & D. Sharma, 'Perioperative Management of Traumatic Brain Injury', *International Journal of Critical Illness and Injury Science* 2011, 1(1), pp. 27–35.

I. Van der Cruyssen et al., 'Is a Picture Worth a Thousand Words? Congruency between Encoding and Testing Improves Detection of Concealed Memories', *Journal of Applied Research in Memory and Cognition* 2021, doi.org/10.1016/j.jarmac.2021.03.001.

I. Dagogo & A. T. Shaw, 'Tumor Heterogeneity and Resistance to Cancer Therapies', *Nature Reviews Clinical Oncology* 2018, 15(2), pp. 81–94.

Y. M. Daly, 'Ireland: Curtailment of the Right to Silence through Statutory Adverse Inferences', *New Journal of European Criminal Law* 2021, 12(3), pp. 347–364.

C. Delfin et al., 'Prediction of Recidivism in a Long-Term Follow-Up of Forensic Psychiatric Patients: Incremental Effects of Neuroimaging Data', *PLoS ONE* 2019, doi.org/10.1371/journal.pone.0217127.

I. Dennis, 'Instrumental Protection, Human Right or Functional Necessity? Reassessing the Privilege against Self-incrimination', *The Cambridge Law Journal* 1995, 54(2), pp. 342–376.

S. Desmoulin-Canselier, 'Another Perspective on "Neurolaw": The Use of Brain Imaging in Civil Litigation Regarding Mental Competence', in A. D'Aloia & M. C. Errigo (eds.), *Neuroscience and Law: Complicated Crossings and New Perspectives*, pp. 529–547.

D. Dolinko, 'Is There a Rationale for the Privilege against Self-incrimination?', *UCLA Law Review* 1986, 33(4), pp. 1063–1148.

T. Douglas et al., 'Coercion, Incarceration, and Chemical Castration: An Argument from Autonomy', *Journal of Bioethical Inquiry* 2013, 10(3), 393–405.

T. Douglas et al., 'Risk Assessment Tools in Criminal Justice and Forensic Psychiatry: The Need for Better Data', *European Psychiatry* 2017, 42, pp. 134–137.

T. Douglas & L. Forsberg, 'Three Rationales for a Legal Right to Mental Integrity', in S. Ligthart et al. (eds.), *Neurolaw: Advances in Neuroscience, Justice & Security*, Cham: Palgrave Macmillan 2021, pp. 179–202.

D. Drewer & J. Ellermann, 'May the (Well-Balanced) Force Be with Us! The Launch of the European Counter Terrorism Centre (ECTC)', *Computer Law & Security* 2016, 32(2), pp. 165–204.

S. A. Drizin & R. A. Leo, 'The Problem of False Confessions in the Post-DNA World', *North Carolina Law Review* 2004, 82, pp. 892–1007.

A. T. Drysdale et al., 'Resting-State Connectivity Biomarkers Define Neurophysiological Subtypes of Depression', *Nature Medicine* 2017, 23(1), pp. 28–38.

P. J. Duffy, 'Article 3 of the European Convention on Human Rights', *International and Comparative Law Quarterly* 1983, 32, pp. 316–346.

J. Dukhart et al., 'Towards Increasing the Clinical Applicability of Machine Learning Biomarkers in Psychiatry', *Nature Human Behaviour* 2021, 5, pp. 431–432.

J. G. Edersheim, R. W. Brendel & B. Price, 'Neuroimaging, Diminished Capacity and Mitigation', in J. R. Simpson (ed.), *Neuroimaging in Forensic Psychiatry. From Clinic to the Courtroom*, Chichester: Wiley-Blackwell 2012, pp. 163–193.

S. J. L. Edwards, 'Protecting Privacy Interests in the Brain Images: The Limits of Consent', in S. Richmond, G. Rees & S. J. L. Edwards (eds.), *I Know What You're Thinking: Brain Imaging and Mental Privacy*, Croydon: Oxford University Press 2012, pp. 245–260.

J. Ellwanger et al., 'Detecting Simulated Amnesia for Autobiographical and Recently Learned Information Using the P300 Event-Related Potential', *International Journal of Psychophysiology* 1996, 23(1–2), pp. 9–23.

R. Encinas de Muñagorri & C. Saas, 'France. Is the Evidence Too Cerebral to Be Cartesian?', in S. Moratti & D. Patterson (eds.), *Legal Insanity and the Brain: Science, Law and European Courts*, Portland: Hart Publishing 2016, pp. 79–110.

M. D. Evans, *Religious Liberty and International Law in Europe*, Cambridge: Cambridge University Press 1997.

C. Evans, *Freedom of Religion under the European Convention on Human Rights*, New York: Oxford University Press 2001.

M. D. Evans & R. Morgan, *Preventing Torture: A Study of the European Convention for the Prevention of Torture and Inhuman or Degrading Treatment or Punishment*, New York: Oxford University Press 1998.

N. Eyal, 'Informed Consent', in E. N. Zalta (ed.), *The Stanford Encyclopedia of Philosophy* (Spring 2019 Edition).

R. Faden, T. L. Beauchamp & N. M. P. King, *A History and Theory of Informed Consent*, New York: Oxford University Press 1968.

M. J. Farah et al., 'Functional MRI-Based Lie Detection: Scientific and Societal Challenges', *Nature Reviews Neuroscience* 2014, 15, pp. 123–131.

M. J. Farah & S. J. Gillihan, 'Diagnostic Brain Imaging in Psychiatry: Current Uses and Future Prospects', *Virtual Mentor* 2012, 14(6), pp. 464–471.

N. A. Farahany, 'Incriminating Thoughts', *Stanford Law Review* 2012a, 64, pp. 351–408.

N. A. Farahany, 'Searching Secrets', *University of Pennsylvania Law Review* 2012b, 160, pp. 1239–1307.

N. A. Farahany, 'Neuroscience and Behavioral Genetics in US Criminal Law: An Empirical Analysis', *Journal of Law and the Biosciences* 2015, 2(3), pp. 485–509.

L. A. Farwell, 'Brain Fingerprinting: A Comprehensive Tutorial Review of Detection of Concealed Information with Event-Related Brain Potentials', *Cognitive Neurodynamics* 2012, 6, pp. 115–154.

L. A. Farwell & T. H. Makeig, 'Farwell Brain Fingerprinting in the Case of Harrington v. State', *Open Court* 2005, X(3), pp. 7–10.

L. A. Farwell, D. C. Richardson & G. M. Richardson, 'Brain Fingerprinting Field Studies Comparing P300-MERMER and P300 Brainwave Responses in the Detection of Concealed Information', *Cognitive Neurodynamics* 2013, 7, pp. 263–299.

R. Ó. Fathaigh, 'Article 10 and the Chilling Effect Principle', *E.H.R.L.R.* 2013, 3, pp. 304–313.

J. E. S. Fawcett, *The Application of the European Convention on Human Rights*, Oxford: Clarendon Press 1987.

S. Fazel et al., 'Risk of Violent Crime in Individuals with Epilepsy and Traumatic Brain Injury: A 35-Year Swedish Population Study', *PLoS Medicine* 2011, 8(12), pp. 1–8.

W. Federspiel, '1984 Arrives: Thought(crime), Technology, and the Constitution', *William & Mary Bill of Rights Journal* 2008, 16(3), pp. 865–900.

J. Feinberg, *The Moral Limits of the Criminal Law: Volume 3: Harm to Self*, New York: Oxford University Press 1989.

P. Ferrua, 'Neuroscientific Evidence and Criminal Trial', in A. D'Aloia & M. C. Errigo (eds.), *Neuroscience and Law: Complicated Crossings and New Perspectives*, Switzerland: Springer Nature 2020, pp. 403–414.

E. S. Finn et al., 'Functional Connectome Fingerprinting: Identifying Individuals Using Patterns of Brain Connectivity', *Nature Neuroscience* 2015, 18(11), pp. 1664–1671.

K. Flinterman, 'Compensation for Wrongful Conviction', in P. van Dijk et al. (eds.), *Theory and Practice of the European Convention on Human Rights*, Cambridge: Intersentia 2018.

F. Focquaert, K. Van Assche & S. Sterckx, 'Offering Neurointerventions to Offenders with Cognitive-Emotional Impairments: Ethical and Criminal Justice Aspects', in N. A. Vincent, T. Nadelhoffer & A. McCay (eds.), *Neurointerventions and the Law: Regulating Human Mental Capacity*, New York: Oxford University Press 2020.

F. Focquaert & M. Schermer, 'Moral Enhancement: Do Means Matter Morally?', *Neuroethics* 2015, 8, pp. 139–151.

L. Forsberg, 'Anti-libidinal Interventions and the Law', *Human Rights Law Review* 2021, 24(4), pp. 384–408.

E. Ford & N. Aggerwal, 'Neuroethics of Functional Neuroimaging in the Courtroom', in J. R. Simpson (ed.), *Neuroimaging in Forensic Psychiatry. From Clinic to the Courtroom*, Chichester: Wiley-Blackwell 2012, pp. 325–340.

R. Foqué & A. C. 't Hart, *Instrumentaliteit en rechtsbescherming*, Arnhem: Gouda Quint 1990.

D. Fox, 'Brain Imaging and the Bill of Rights: Memory Detection Technologies and American Criminal Justice', *American Journal of Bioethics* 2008, 8(1), pp. 34–36.

D. J. Galligan, 'The Right to Silence Reconsidered', *Current Legal Problems* 1988, 41(1), pp. 69–92.

M. Gamer, 'Mind Reading Using Neuroimaging Is This the Future of Deception Detection?', *European Psychologist* 2014, 19(3), pp.172–183.

M. Gamer, D. Kosiol & G. Vossel, 'Strength of Memory Encoding Affects Physiological Responses in the Guilty Actions Test', *Biological Psychology* 2010, 83(2), pp. 101–107.

G. Ganis et al., 'Lying in the Scanner: Covert Countermeasures Disrupt Deception Detection by Functional Magnetic Resonance Imaging', *NeuroImage* 2011, 55(1), pp. 312–319.

G. Ganis, 'Detecting Deception and Concealed Information with Neuroimaging', in J. P. Rosenfeld (ed.), *Detecting Concealed Information and Deception: Recent Developments*, London: Academic Press 2018, pp. 145–166.

G. Ganis & J. P. Rosenfeld, 'Neural Correlates of Deception', in J. Illes & B. J. Sahakian (eds.), *Oxford Handbook of Neuroethics*, New York: Oxford University Press 2011, pp. 101–118.

L. M. Gaudet, Brain Fingerprinting, Scientific Evidence, and *Daubert*: A Cautionary Lesson from India', *Jurimetrics* 2011, 51(3), pp. 293–318.

R. S. Gerstein, 'Privacy and Self-incrimination', *Ethics* 1970, 80(2), pp. 87–101.

J. Gerards, 'Pluralism, Deference and the Margin of Appreciation Doctrine', *European Law Journal* 2001, 17(1), pp. 80–120.

J. Gerards, 'How to Improve the Necessity Test of the European Court of Human Rights', *International Journal of Constitutional Law* 2013 11(2), pp. 466–490.

F. Gilbert, 'A Threat to Autonomy? The Intrusion of Predictive Brain Implants', *AJOB Neuroscience* 2015, 6(4), pp. 4–11.

G. M. Gkotsi & J. Gasser, 'Neuroscience in Forensic Psychiatry: From Responsibility to Dangerousness. Ethical and Legal Implications of Using Neuroscience for Dangerousness Assessments', *International Journal of Law and Psychiatry* 2016, 46, pp. 58–67.

A. L. Glenn & A. Raine, 'Neurocriminology: Implications for the Punishment, Prediction and Prevention of Criminal Behaviour', *Nature Reviews Neuroscience* 2014, 15(1), pp. 54–63.

A. L. Glenn, F. Focquaert & A. Raine, 'Prediction of Antisocial Behavior', in J. Clausen & N. Levy (eds.), *Handbook of Neuroethics*, Dordrecht: Springer 2015, pp. 1689–1701.

S. Goering et al., 'Recommendations for Responsible Development and Application of Neurotechnologies', *Neuroethics* 2021, 14, pp. 365–386.

D. Gomien, *Short Guide to the European Convention on Human Rights*, The Hague: Council of Europe Publishing 2005.

R. Goss, *Criminal Fair Trial Rights: Article 6 of the European Convention of Human Rights*, Oxford, Portland, and Oregon: Hart Publishing 2016.

R. P. Granacher Jr., 'Traumatic Brain Injury', in J. R. Simpson (ed.), *Neuroimaging in Forensic Psychiatry. From Clinic to the Courtroom*, Chichester: Wiley-Blackwell 2012, pp. 44–65.

H. T. Greely, 'Neuroscience-Based Lie Detection: The Need for Regulation', in E. Bizzi et al. (eds.), *Using Imaging to Identify Deceit. Scientific and Ethical Questions*, Cambridge: American Academic of Arts and Sciences 2009, pp. 45–55.

H. T. Greely & A. D. Wagner, *Reference Guide on Neuroscience*, Washington, DC: National Academies Press/Federal Judicial Center 2011.

R. K. Greenawalt, 'Silence as a Moral and Constitutional Right', *William & Mary Law Review* 1981, 23(1), pp. 15–71.

S. Greer, 'Is the Prohibition against Torture, Cruel, Inhuman and Degrading Treatment Really 'Absolute' in International Human Rights Law?', *Human Rights Law Review* 2015, 15, pp. 101–137.

M. S. Groenhuijsen & G. Knigge, 'Afronding en verantwoording. Algemeen deel', in M. S. Groenhuijsen & G. Knigge (red.), *Afronding en verantwoording. Eindrapport onderzoeksproject Strafvordering 2001*, Deventer: Kluwer 2004, pp. 3–186.

M. L. Gross, *The Brain Watchers*, New York: Random House 1962.

M. Hafner, 'Judging Homicide Defendants by Their Brains: An Empirical Study on the Use of Neuroscience in Homicide Trials in Slovenia', *Journal of Law and the Biosciences* 2019, 6(1), pp. 226–254.

S. Haller, 'The Role of Central and Medial Amygdala in Normal and Abnormal Aggression: A Review of Classical Approaches', *Neuroscience and Biobehavioral Reviews* 2018, 85, pp. 34–43.

E. Harmon-Jones & C. K. Peterson, 'Electroencephalographic Methods in Social and Personality Psychology', in E. Harmon-Jones & J. S. Beer (eds.), *Methods in Social Neuroscience*, New York: Guilford Press, pp. 170–197.

D. J. Harris et al., *Harris, O'Boyle, and Warbrick: Law of the European Convention on Human Rights*, New York: Oxford University Press 2018.

J.-D. Haynes et al., 'Reading Hidden Intentions in the Human Brain', *Current Biology* 2007, 17(4), pp. 323–328.

J.-D. Haynes, 'Brain Reading: Decoding Mental States from Brain Activity in Humans', in J. Illes & B. J. Sahakian (eds.), *Oxford Handbook of Neuroethics*, New York: Oxford University Press 2011, pp. 1–13.

Health Quality Ontario, 'The Appropriate Use of Neuroimaging in the Diagnostic Work-Up of Dementia: An Evidence-Based Analysis', *Ontario Health Technology Assessment Series* 2014, 14(1), pp. 1–64.

O. van der Heide et al., 'High-Resolution In Vivo MR-STAT Using a Matrix-Free and Parallelized Reconstruction Algorithm', *NMR in Biomedicine* 2020, 33(4), pp. 1–16.

P. de Hert & B.-J. Koops, 'Privacy is nog steeds een grondrecht: Pleidooi voor uitsluiting van onrechtmatig bewijs', *Ars Aequi* 2001, 50(12), pp. 972–975.

B. Holley, 'It's All in Your Head: Neurotechnological Lie Detection and the Fourth and Fifth Amendments', *Developments in Mental Health Law* 2009, 28(1), pp. 1–23.

M. B. Holloway, 'One Image, One Thousand Incrimination Words: Images of Brain Activity and the Privilege against Self-incrimination', *Temple Journal of Science, Technology & Environmental Law* 2008, XXVII(1), pp. 141–175.

X. Hu et al., 'Increasing the Number of Irrelevant Stimuli Increases Ability to Detect Countermeasures to the P300-Based Complex Trial Protocol for Concealed Information Detection', *Psychophysiology* 2012, 49(1), pp. 85–95.

X. Hu & J. P. Rosenfeld, 'Combining the P300-Complex Trial-Based Concealed Information Test and the Reaction Time-Based Autobiographical Implicit Association Test in Concealed Memory Detection', *Psychophysiology* 2012, 49(8), pp. 1090–1100.

R. C. Hughes, 'Law and Coercion', *Philosophy Compass* 2013, 8(3), pp. 231–240.

R. J. C. Huntjes, B. Verschuere & R. J. McNally, 'Inter-Identity Autobiographical Amnesia in Patients with Dissociative Identity Disorder', *PLoS ONE* 2012, 7(7), pp. 1–8.

A. J. Hurd, 'Reaching Past Fingerprints with Forensic Neuroimaging – Non-testimonial Evidence Exceeding the Fifth Amendment's Grasp', *Loyola Law Review* 2012, 58, pp. 213–249.

W. G. Iacono, 'Encouraging the Use of the GKT', in B. Verschuere, G. Ben-Shakhar & E. Meijer (eds.), *Memory Detection: Theory and Application of the Concealed Information Test*, New York: Cambridge University Press 2011.

M. Ienca, *Common Human Rights Challenges Raised by Different Applications of Neurotechnologies in the Biomedical Field*, Council of Europe, October 2021.

M. Ienca & R. Andorno, 'Towards New Human Rights in the Age of Neuroscience and Neurotechnology', *Life Sciences, Society and Policy* 2017, 13(5), pp. 1–27.

M. Ienca, P. Haselager & E. J. Emanuel, 'Brain Leaks and Consumer Terotechnology', *Nature Biotechnology* 2018, 36(9), pp. 805–810.

J. Illes et al., 'Ethical and Practical Considerations in Managing Incidental Findings in Functional Magnetic Resonance Imaging', *Brain and Cognition* 2002, 50(3), pp. 358–365.

P. Jacobs, *Force-Feeding of Prisoners and Detainees on Hunger Strike: Right to Self-Determination versus Right to Intervention*, Antwerpen: Intersentia 2012.

J. Jackson, 'Re-conceptualizing the Right of Silence as an Effective Fair Trial Standard', *The International and Comparative Law Quarterly* 2009, 58(4), pp. 835–861.

J. D. Jackson & S. J. Summers, *The Internationalization of Criminal Evidence. Beyond the Common Law and Civil Law Traditions*, New York: Cambridge University Press 2012.

M. Jalbrzikowski, 'Functional Connectome Fingerprinting Accuracy in Youths and Adults Is Similar When Examined on the Same Day and 1.5-Years Apart', *Human Brain Mapping* 2020, 41, pp. 4187–4199.

I. Jeandarme et al., 'Field Validity of the HCR-20 in Forensic Medium Security Units in Flanders', *Psychology, Crime & Law* 2017a, 23(4), pp. 305–322.

I. Jeandarme et al., 'PCL-R Field Validity in Prison and Hospital Settings', *Law and Human Behavior* 2017b, 41(1), pp. 29–43.

O. D. Jones, J. D. Shall & F. X. Shen (eds.), *Law and Neuroscience*, New York: Wolters Kluwer Law & Business 2014.

C. D. De Jong, *The Freedom of Thought, Conscience and Religion or Belief in the United Nations (1946–1992)* (diss. Maastricht), Antwerp, Groningen, and Oxford: Intersentia – Hart 2000.

M. A. Just et al., 'Machine Learning of Representations of Suicide and Emotion Concepts Identifies Suicidal Youth', *Nature Human Behaviour* 2017, 1, pp. 911–919.

M. A. Just, V. L. Cherkassky & D. Brant, 'Reply to: Towards Increasing the Clinical Applicability of Machine Learning Biomarkers in Psychiatry', *Nature Human Behaviour* 2021, 5, pp. 433–435.

M. A. Just, J. Wang & V. L. Cherkassky, 'Neural Representations of the Concepts in Simple Sentences: Conceptactivation Prediction and Context Effects', *NeuroImage* 2017, 15, pp. 511–520.

M. Karcz & P. J. Papadakos, 'Respiratory Complications in the Postanesthesia Care Unit: A Review of Pathophysiological Mechanisms', *Canadian Journal of Respiratory Therapy* 2013, 49(3), pp. 21–29.

K. S. Kassam et al., 'Identifying Emotions on the Basis of Neural Activation', *PLoS ONE* 2013, 8(6), pp. 1–12.

N. Kanwisher, 'The Use of fMRI in Lie Detection: What Has Been Shown and What Has Not', in E. Bizzi et al. (eds.), *Using Imaging to Identify Deceit. Scientific and Ethical Questions*, Cambridge: American Academic of Arts and Sciences 2009.

B. D. Kelly, 'Brain Imaging in Clinical Psychiatry: Why?', in S. Richmond, G. Rees & S. J. L. Edwards (eds.), *I Know What You're Thinking: Brain Imaging and Mental Privacy*, Croydon: Oxford University Press 2012, pp. 111–122.

K. A. Kiehl et al., 'Age of Gray Matters: Neuroprediction of Recidivism', *NeuroImage: Clinical* 2018, 19, pp. 813–823.

M. Kiener, 'Coercion', in E. Craig (ed.), *Routledge Encyclopedia of Philosophy* (Version 2, 2020).

M. Kilbride & J. Iuliano, 'Neuro Lie Detection and Mental Privacy', *Maryland Law Review* 2015, 75(1), pp. 163–193.

L. Kirchmair, 'Objections to Coercive Neurocorrectives for Criminal Offenders – Why Offenders' Human Rights Should Fundamentally Come First', *Criminal Justice Ethics* 2019, 38(1), pp. 19–40.

N. Knack, J. A. Chandler & J. P. Fedoroff, 'A Qualitative Study of Forensic Patients' Perceptions of Quasi-coercive Offers of Biological Treatment', *Behavioral Sciences and the Law* 2020, 38(2), pp. 135–151.

N. R. Koffemand, *(The Right to) Personal Autonomy in the Case Law of the European Court of Human Rights (nota opgesteld ten behoeve van de Staatscommissie Grondwet)*, Leiden: Leiden University 2010.

C. H. de Kogel & E. J. M. C. Westgeest, 'Neuroscientific and Behavioral Genetic Information in Criminal Cases in the Netherlands', *Journal of Law and the Biosciences* 2015, 2(3), pp. 580–605.

T. Kooijmans & P. A. M. Mevis, *ICT in the Context of Criminal Procedure: The Netherlands*, TLS/EUR/AIDP 2013.

E. J. Koops, *Verdachte en ontsleutelplicht: hoe ver reikt nemo tenetur?* Deventer: Kluwer 2000.

B.-J. Koops, 'S. en Marper tegen het Verenigd Koninkrijk, No. 13, Dec. 04, 2008', *European Human Rights Cases* 2009, 10(2), pp. 148–165.

E. J. Koops & L. Stevens, 'J. B. versus Saunders. De groeiende duisternis rond nemo tenetur', *Delikt & Delinkwent* 2003, afl. 3, pp. 281–294.

C. Korponay & M. Koenigs, 'The Neurobiology of Antisocial and Amoral Behaviour', in S. Moratti & D. Patterson (eds.), *Legal Insanity and the Brain: Science, Law and European Courts*, Portland: Hart Publishing 2016, pp. 10–39.

F. A. Kozel et al., 'Detecting Deception Using Functional Magnetic Resonance Imaging', *Biological Psychiatry* 2005, 58(8), pp. 605–613.

F. A. Kozel et al., 'Functional MRI Detection of Deception after Committing a Mock Sabotage Crime', *Journal of Forensic Sciences* 2009, 54(1), pp. 220–231.

C. J. Kraft & J. Giordano, 'Integrating Brain Science and Law: Neuroscientific Evidence and Legal Perspectives on Protecting Individual Liberties', *Frontiers in Neuroscience* 2017, 11, Article 621.

D. J. Kraphol, 'Limits of the CIT in Criminal Cases', in B. Verschuere, G. Ben-Shakhar & E. Meijer (eds.), *Memory Detection: Theory and Application of the Concealed Information Test*, New York: Cambridge University Press 2011.

R. Kuiper, *Vormfouten. Juridische consequenties van vorm verzuimen in strafzaken* (diss. Nijmegen), Deventer: Kluwer 2014.

E. Labkovsky & J. P. Rosenfeld, 'The P300-Based, Complex Trials Protocol for Concealed Information Detection Resists Any Number of Sequential Countermeasures against up to Five Irrelevant Stimuli', *Applied Psychophysiology and Biofeedback* 2012, 37(1), pp. 1–10.

M. Lamar et al., 'Dementia', in J. R. Simpson (ed.), *Neuroimaging in Forensic Psychiatry. From Clinic to the Courtroom*, Chichester: Wiley-Blackwell 2012, pp. 68–80.

S. Lamberigts, 'The Privilege against Self-incrimination: A Chameleon of Criminal Procedure', *New Journal of European Criminal Law* 2016, 7(4), pp. 418–438.

G. Lamond, 'The Coerciveness of Law', *Oxford Journal of Legal Studies* 2000, 20(1), pp. 39–62.

D. D. Langleben, D. F. X. Willard & J. C. Moriarty, 'Brain Imaging of Deception', in J. R. Simpson (red.), *Neuroimaging in Forensic Psychiatry. From Clinic to the Courtroom*, Chichester: Wiley-Blackwell 2012, pp. 217–236.

A. Lavazza, 'Freedom of Thought and Mental Integrity: The Moral Requirements for Any Neural Prosthesis', *Frontiers in Neuroscience* 2018, 12(82), pp. 1–10.

A. Lavazza, 'Technology against Technology: A Case for Embedding Limits in Neurodevices to Protect Our Freedom of Thought', in M. J. Blitz & J. C. Bublitz (eds.), *The Law and Ethics of Freedom of Thought*, Volume 1, Cham: Palgrave Macmillan 2021, pp. 259–287.

L. Lavrysen, 'System of Restrictions', in P. van Dijk et al. (eds.), *Theory and Practice of the European Convention on Human Rights*, Cambridge: Intersentia 2018, pp. 307–330.

R. A. Lawson, 'Hoe exclusief dient de 'exclusionary rule' te zijn?', in P. D. Duyx & P. D. J. van Zeben (eds.), *Via Straatsburg, Liber Amicorum Egbert Myjer*, WLP 2004, pp. 181–206.

M. A. Lemley & E. Volokh, 'Law, Virtual Reality, and Augumented Reality', *University of Pennsylvania Law Review* 2018, 166, pp. 1051–1138.

A. Leshinskaya et al., 'Neural Representations of Belief Concepts: A Representational Similarity Approach to Social Semantics', *Cerebral Cortex* 2017, 27(1), pp. 344–357.

A. Lester, 'Freedom of Expression', in R. St. J. Macdonald et al. (eds.), *The European System for the Protection of Human Rights*, Dordrecht: Martinus Nijhof Publishers 1993, pp. 465–491.

L. W. Levy, *Origins of the Fifth Amendment*, New York: Oxford University Press 1968.

S. Ligthart, 'Gedwongen brain imaging in de strafrechtspleging en artikel 3 EVRM: van analogie naar deductie', in A. K. Bosma & S. S. Buisman (eds.), *Methoden van onderzoek in het strafrecht, de criminologie en de victimologie*, Deventer: Wolters Kluwer 2018, pp. 51–66.

S. Ligthart, 'Coercive Neuroimaging Technologies in Criminal Law in Europe: Exploring the Implications for the Prohibition of Ill-Treatment (Article 3 ECHR)', in L. S. Reins (ed.), *Regulating New Technologies in Uncertain Times*, The Hague: T.M.C. Asser – Springer 2019a, pp. 83–102.

S. Ligthart, 'Coercive Neuroimaging, Criminal Law and Privacy: A European Perspective', *Journal of Law and the Biosciences* 2019b, 6(1), pp. 289–309.

S. Ligthart, 'Het recht tegen zelfincriminatie ex artikel 6 EVRM: Doorwerking van het nemo tenetur-beginsel in enkele gedachte-experimenten volgens de benadering van het EHRM en van de Hoge Raad', *Delikt en Delinkwent* 2019c, 3(16), pp. 216–234.

S. Ligthart, 'Coercive Forensic Neuroimaging and the Prohibition of Ill-Treatment (Article 3 ECHR)', in A. Waltermann et al. (eds.), *Law, Science and Rationality*, The Hague: Eleven 2020a.

S. Ligthart, 'Freedom of Thought in Europe: Do Advances in 'Brain-Reading' Technology Call for Revision?', *Journal of Law and the Biosciences* 2020b, 7(1), pp. 1-27.

S. Ligthart, 'Autonomie en privacy als rechtsgronden van het zwijgrecht en het nemo tenetur-beginsel?', *Nederlands juristenblad* 2021/2408.

S. Ligthart, T. Douglas, C. Bublitz & G. Meynen, 'The Future of Neuroethics and the Relevance of the Law', *AJOB Neuroscience* 2019 10(3), pp. 120–121.

S. Ligthart, T. Douglas, C. Bublitz, T. Kooijmans & G. Meynen, 'Forensic Brain-Reading and Mental Privacy in European Human Rights Law: Foundations and Challenges', *Neuroethics* 2020, doi.org/10.1007/s12152-020-09438-4, pp. 191–203

S. Ligthart, G. Meynen, N. Biller-Andorno, T. Kooijmans & P. Kellmeyer, 'Is Virtually Everything Possible? The Relevance of Ethics and Human Rights for Introducing Extended Reality in Forensic Psychiatry', *AJOB Neuroscience* 2021a, doi.org/10.1080/21507740.2021.1898489.

S. Ligthart, T. Kooijmans, T. Douglas & G. Meynen, 'Closed-Loop Brain Devices in Offender Rehabilitation: Autonomy, Human Rights, and Accountability', *Cambridge Quarterly of Healthcare Ethics* 2021b, 30(4), pp. 32–47.

S. Ligthart & G. Meynen, 'Zwijgen in de 21e eeuw: tijd voor herbezinning op het recht tegen zelfincriminatie?', in T. Kooijmans et al. (red.), *Op zoek naar evenwicht* (liber amicorum Marc Groenhuijsen), Deventer: Wolters Kluwer 2021.

S. Ligthart, G. Meynen & T. Douglas, 'Persuasive Technologies and the Right to Mental Liberty: The 'Smart Rehabilitation' of Criminal Offenders', in M. Ienca et al. (eds.), *Cambridge Handbook of Life Science, Information Technology and Human Rights*, New York: Cambridge University Press 2022.

S. Ligthart, T. Kooijmans & G. Meynen, '"Brain-Reading" in Criminal Justice and Forensic Psychiatry: Towards an Integrative Legal-Ethical Approach', in S. Ligthart, D. van Toor, T. Kooijmans, T. Douglas & G. Meynen (eds.), *Neurolaw: Advances in Neuroscience, Justice, and Security*, Cham: Palgrave Macmillan 2021a, pp. 121–142.

S. Ligthart, T. Kooijmans & G. Meynen, 'Neurorechten: wat doet Nederland ermee?', *Nederlands juristenblad* 2021b/1578.

M. Liljegren et al., 'Criminal Behavior in Frontotemporal Dementia and Alzheimer Disease', *JAMA Neurology* 2015, 72(3), pp. 295–300.

D. Linden, 'Overcoming Self-Report: Possibilities and Limitations of Brain Imaging in Psychiatry', in S. Richmond, G. Rees & S. J. L. Edwards (eds.), *I Know What You're Thinking: Brain Imaging and Mental Privacy*, Croydon: Oxford University Press 2012, pp. 123–135.

N. Lisofsky et al., 'Investigating Socio-cognitive Processes in Deception: A Quantitative Meta-analysis of Neuroimaging Studies', *Neuropsychologia* 2014, 61, pp. 113–122.

L. G. Loucaides, 'The Right to Freedom of Thought as Protected by the European Convention on Human Rights', *Cyprus Human Rights Law Review* 2012, 1(1), pp. 79–87.

G. Lukács et al., 'The First Independent Study on the Complex Trial Protocol Version of the P300-Based Concealed Information Test: Corroboration of Previous Findings and Highlights on Vulnerabilities', *International Journal of Psychophysiology* 2016, 110, pp. 56–65.

D. T. Lykken, 'The GSR in the Detection of Guilt', *Journal of Applied Psychology* 1959, 43(6), pp. 385–388.

D. T. Lykken, *A Tremor in the Blood: Uses and Abused of the Lie Detector*, McGraw-Hill Book Company 1981.

D. Lyons, 'Welcome Threats and Coercive Offers', *Philosophy* 1975, 50(194), pp. 425–436.

N. MacCormick, *Legal Right and Social Democracy: Essays in Legal and Political Philosophy*, New York: Oxford University Press 1984.

A. Maity et al., 'Detection of Hypoxia in the Early Postoperative Period', *Anesthesia, Essays and Researches* 2016, 6(1), pp. 34–37.

J. Marshall, *Personal Freedom through Human Rights Law? Autonomy, Identity and Integrity under the European Convention on Human Rights*, Leiden: Martinus Nijhoff 2009.

R. A. Mason & M. A. Just, 'Neural Representation of Physics Concepts', *Psychological Science* 2016, 27(6)904–913.

I. Matsuda, T. Ogawa & M. Tsuneoka, 'Broadening the Use of the Concealed Information Test in the Field', *Frontiers in Psychiatry* 2019, 10, doi.org/10.3389/fpsyt.2019.00024, pp. 1–10.

S. Matthies et al., 'Small Amygdala – High Aggression? The Role of the Amygdala in Modulating Aggression in Healthy Subjects', *The World Journal of Biological Psychiatry* 2012, 13(1), pp. 75–81.

N. Mavronicola, *Torture, Inhumanity and Degradation under Article 3 of the ECHR: Absolute Rights and Absolute Wrongs*, New York: Hart Publishing 2021.

S. McCarthy-Jones, 'The Autonomous Mind: The Right to Freedom of Thought in the Twenty-First Century', *Frontiers in Artificial Intelligence* 2019, 2(19), pp. 1–17.

S. McCarthy-Jones, 'Freedom of Thought: Who, What, and Why?', in M. J. Blitz & J. C. Bublitz (eds.), *The Law and Ethics of Freedom of Thought*, Volume 1, Cham: Palgrave Macmillan 2021, pp. 27–47.

C. McCrudden, 'Human Dignity and Judicial Interpretation of Human Rights', *The European Journal of International Law* 2008, 19(4), pp. 655–724.

J. McGregor, 'Undue Influence as Coercive Offers in Clinical Trials', in D. A. Reify & W. J. Riker (eds.), *Coercion and the State*, New York: Springer Science + Business Media B. V 2008, pp. 45–59.

J. McMillan, 'The Kindest Cut? Surgical Castration, Sex Offenders and Coercive Offers', *Journal of Medical Ethics* 2014, 40, pp. 583–590.

G. Mecacci & P. Haselager, Identifying Criteria for the Evaluation of the Implications of Brain Reading for Mental Privacy, *Science and Engineering Ethics* 2019, 25, pp. 443–461.

D. V. Meegan, 'Neuroimaging Techniques for Memory Detection: Scientific, Ethical, and Legal Issues', *American Journal of Bioethics* 2008, 8(1), pp. 9–20.

E. H. Meijer et al., 'The P300 Is Sensitive to Concealed Face Recognition', *International Journal of Psychophysiology* 2007, 66(3), pp. 231–237.

E. Meijer et al., 'A Comment on Farwell (2012): Brain Fingerprinting: A Comprehensive Tutorial Review of Detection of Concealed Information with Event-Related Brain Potentials', *Cognitive Neurodynamics* 2013a, 7, pp. 155–158.

E. H. Meijer et al., 'Detecting Concealed Information from Groups Using a Dynamic Questioning Approach: Simultaneous Skin Conductance Measurement and Immediate Feedback', *Frontiers in Psychology* 2013b, 4, Article 68.

E. H. Meijer et al., 'Memory Detection with the Concealed Information Test: A Meta-analysis of Skin Conductance, Respiration Heart Rate and P300 Data', *Psychophysiology* 2014, 51, pp. 879–904.

E. H. Meijer et al., 'Deception Detection with Behavioral, Autonomic, and Neural Measures: Conceptual and Methodological Considerations that Warrant Modesty', *Psychophysiology* 2016, 53, pp. 653–604.

E. H. Meijer & J. van Koppen, 'Lie Detectors and the Law: The Use of Polygraph in Europe', in D. Canter & R. Žukauskiene (eds.), *Psychology, Crime and Law: Psychology and Law: Bridging the Gap*, Hampshire: Ashgate Publishing Limited 2008, pp. 31–50.

E. H. Meijer & D. A. G. van Toor, 'Reading the Sleeping Mind: Empirical and Legal Considerations', in S. Ligthart et al. (eds.), *Neurolaw: Advances in Neuroscience, Justice, and Security*, Cham: Palgrave Macmillan 2021, pp. 101–120.

E. H. Meijer & B. Verschuere, 'Deception Detection Based on Neuroimaging: Better Than the Polygraph?', *Journal of Forensic Radiology and Imaging* 2017, 8, pp. 17–21.

E. H. Meijer & B. Verschuere, 'Detection Deception Using Psychophysiological and Neural Measures', in H. Otgaar & M. L. Howe (eds.), *Finding the Truth in the Courtroom: Dealing with Deception, Lies, and Memories*, New York: Oxford University Press 2018, pp. 209–224.

J. B. Meixner, 'Liar, Liar, Jury's the Trier? The Future of Neuroscience-Based Credibility Assessment in the Court', *Northwestern University Law Review* 2015, 106, pp. 1451–1488.

J. B. Meixner & J. P. Rosenfeld, 'Countermeasure Mechanisms in a P300-Based Concealed Information Test', *Psychophysiology* 2010, 47(1), pp. 57–65.

J. B. Meixner & J. P. Rosenfeld, 'A Mock Terrorism Application of the P300-Based Concealed Information Test', *Psychophysiology* 2011, 48(2), pp. 149–154.

J. B. Meixner & J. P. Rosenfeld, 'Detecting Knowledge of Incidentally Acquired, Real-World Memories Using a P300-Based Concealed-Information Test', *Psychological Science* 2014, 25(11), pp. 1994–2005.

J. B. Meixner Jr., 'Admissibility and Constitutional Issues of the Concealed Information Test in American Courts: An Update', in J. P. Rosenfeld (ed.), *Detecting Concealed Information and Deception: Recent Developments*, London: Academic Press 2018, pp. 405–429.

M. F. Mendez, 'The Unique Predisposition to Criminal Violations in Frontotemporal Dementia', *Journal of American Academy of Psychiatry and the Law* 2010, 38(3), pp. 318–323.

R. Mertens & J. B. Allen, 'The Role of Psychophysiology in Forensic Assessments: Deception Detection, ERPs, and Virtual Reality Mock Crime Scenarios', *Psychophysiology* 2008, 45, pp. 286–298.

G. Meynen, 'A Neurolaw Perspective on Psychiatric Assessments of Criminal Responsibility: Decision-Making, Mental Disorder, and the Brain', *International Journal of Law and Psychiatry* 2013, 36(2), pp. 93–99.

G. Meynen, 'Legal Insanity and Neurolaw in the Netherlands: Developments and Debates', in S. Moratti & D. Patterson (eds.), *Legal Insanity and the Brain: Science, Law and European Courts*, Portland: Hart Publishing 2016a, pp. 137–168.

G. Meynen, *Legal Insanity: Explorations in Psychiatry, Law and Ethics*, Switzerland: Springer 2016b.

G. Meynen, 'Brain-Based Mind Reading in Forensic Psychiatry: Exploring Possibilities and Perils', *Journal of Law and the Biosciences* 2017, 4(2), pp. 311–329.

G. Meynen, 'Forensic Psychiatry and Neurolaw: Description, Developments, and Debates', *International Journal of Law and Psychiatry* 2018, doi.org/10.1016/j.ijlp.2018.04.005.

G. Meynen, 'Ethical Issues to Consider before Introducing Neurotechnological Thought Apprehension in Psychiatry', *AJOB Neuroscience* 2019, 10(1), pp. 5–14.

G. Meynen, 'Neuroscience-Based Psychiatric Assessments of Criminal Responsibility: Beyond Self-Report?', *Cambridge Quarterly of Healthcare Ethics* 2020, 29, pp. 446–458.

R. N. Mhuircheartaigh et al., 'Cortical and Subcortical Connectivity Changes during Decreasing Levels of Consciousness in Humans: A Functional Magnetic Resonance Imaging Study using Propofol', *The Journal of Neuroscience* 2010, 30(27), pp. 9095–9102.

F. Michael et al., *Consensus Report of the APA Work Group on Neuroimaging Markers of Psychiatric Disorders*, American Psychiatric Association 2012.

S. Michalowski, 'Critical Reflections on the Need for a Right to Mental Self-determination', in A. von Arnauld, K. von der Decken & M. Susi (eds.), *The Cambridge Handbook of New Human Rights: Recognition, Novelty, Rhetoric*, Padstow: Cambridge University Press 2020, pp. 404–411.

G. Miller, 'fMRI Lie Detection Fails a Legal Test', *Science* 2010, 328, pp. 1336–1337.

P. Mirfield, *Silence, Confessions and Improperly Obtained Evidence*, New York: Oxford University Press 1997.

S. Mohnke et al., 'Brain Alterations in Peadophilia: A Critical Review', *Progress in Neurobiology* 2014, 122, pp. 1–23.

A. Mohr et al., 'The Similarity of Brain Morphology in Healthy Monozygotic Twins', *Cognitive Brain Research* 2002, 20(1), pp. 106–110.

G. Monina, 'Article 15. Non-admissibility of Evidence Obtained by Torture', in M. Nowak, M. Birk & G. Monina (eds.), *The United Nations Convention against Torture and Its Optional Protocol (2nd Edition): A Commentary*, New York: Oxford University Press 2019, pp. 417–440.

S. Moratti & D. Patterson (eds.), *Legal Insanity and the Brain: Science, Law and European Courts*, Portland: Hart Publishing 2016.

S. Morse, 'New Neuroscience, Old Problems', in B. Garland (ed.), *Neuroscience and the Law. Brain, Mind, and the Scales of Justice*, New York: American Association for the Advancement of Science 2004, pp. 157–198.

S. J. Morse, 'Diminished Capacity, Neuroscience, and Just Punishment', in S. Richmond, G. Rees & S. J. L. Edwards (eds.), *I Know What You're Thinking: Brain Imaging and Mental Privacy*, Croydon: Oxford University Press 2012, pp. 155–172.

S. J. Morse & A. L. Roskies (eds.), *A Primer on Criminal Law and Neuroscience*, New York: Oxford University Press 2013.

W. Muller, 'Bewijs verkregen als gevolg van bedreiging met foltering: is een 'giftige vrucht' wel altijd een verboden vrucht?', *NJCM-Bulletin* 2009, nr. 1, pp. 22–41.

J. M. Muñoz, 'Chile – Right to Free Will Needs Definition', *Nature* 2019, 574, p. 634.

J. Murdoch, *Protecting the Right to Freedom of Thought, Conscience and Religion under the European Convention on Human Rights*. Strasbourg: Council of Europe 2012.

E. R. D. Murphy & J. Rissman, 'Evidence of Memory from Brain Data', *Journal of Law and the Biosciences* 2020; lsaa078, doi.org/10.1093/jlb/lsaa078.

E. Myjer, 'Onrechtmatig maar niet unfair: De gebugde drugshandelaar', *NJCM-Bulletin* 2000, 25(7/8), pp. 1255–1261.

E. Myjer, *Van Duimschroef naar bloedproef*, Preadvies NVVR, Deventer: Kluwer 1978.

M. V. Nadal, 'Artificial Intelligence and 'Pseudonymity': The Government Presents the First Version of the Digital Rights Charter', *NeuroRights Initiative* 17 November 2020 (www.nri.ntc.columbia.edu, visited on 15 May 2021).

T. Nadelhoffer et al., 'Neuroprediction, Violence, and the Law: Setting the Stage' *Neuroethics* 2012, 5(1), pp. 67–99.

T. Nadelhoffer & W. Sinnott-Armstrong, 'Neurolaw and Neuroprediction: Potential Promises and Perils', *Philosophy Compass* 2012, 7(9), pp. 631–642.

G. Nahari & G. Ben-Shakhar, 'Psychophysiological and Behavioral Measures for Detecting Concealed Information: The Role of Memory for Crime Details', *Psychophysiology* 2011, 48(6), pp. 733–744.

R. M. Nelson et al., 'The Concept of Voluntary Consent', *The American Journal of Bioethics* 2011, 11(8), pp. 6–16.

S. Nishimoto et al., 'Reconstructing Visual Experiences from Brain Activity Evoked by Natural Movies', *Current Biology* 2011, 21(19).

R. Noggle, 'The Ethics of Manipulation', in E. N. Zalta (ed.), *The Stanford Encyclopedia of Philosophy* (Summer 2020 Edition).

J. Nouwt, 'Reasonable Expectations of Geo-privacy?', *SCRIPTed – A Journal of Law, Technology & Society*, 5(2), 375–403.

L. Noyon et al., 'Integrating Neuroscience in Criminal Law: The Dutch Situation as an Example', *International Journal of Forensic Mental Health* 2019, 18(3), pp. 281–291.

R. Nozick, 'Coercion', in S. Morgenbesser, P. Suppes & M. White (eds.), *Philosophy, Science, and Method Essays in Honor of Ernest Nagel*, St. Martin's Press 1969, pp. 440–474.

K. M. Nugent, 'Practical Legal Concerns', in J. R. Simpson (ed.), *Neuroimaging in Forensic Psychiatry. From Clinic to the Courtroom*, Chichester: Wiley-Blackwell 2012a, pp. 255–273.

K. M. Nugent, 'Neuroimaging and the Constitution', in J. R. Simpson (ed.), *Neuroimaging in Forensic Psychiatry. From Clinic to the Courtroom*, Chichester: Wiley-Blackwell 2012b, pp. 275–302.

D. M. O'Brien, 'Fifth Amendment: Fox Hunters, Old Women, Hermits, and the Burger Court', *Norte Dam Law Review* 1978, 54(1), pp. 26–72.

P. O'Callaghan & B. Shiner, 'The Right to Freedom of Thought in the European Convention of Human Rights', *European Journal of Comparative Law and Governance* 2021, 8(2–3), pp. 112–145.

K. O'Driscoll & J. P. Leach, '"No Longer Gage": An Iron Bar through the Head Early Observations of Personality Change after Injury to the Prefrontal Cortex', *BMJ* 1998, 317, pp. 1673–1647.

F. P. Ölçer, 'Illegally Obtained Evidence in European Treaty of Human Rights Law (ETHR)', *Annales de la Faculté de Droit d'Istanbul* 2008 40(57), pp. 65–153.

F. P. Ölçer, 'The European Court of Human Rights: The Fair Trial Analysis under Article 6 of the European Convention of Human Rights', in S. C. Thaman (ed.), *Exclusionary Rules in Comparative Law*, Dordrecht: Springer Science + Business Media 2013, pp. 371–399.

D. Ormerod, 'ECHR and the Exclusion of Evidence: Trial Remedies for Article 8 Breaches?', *Criminal Law Review* 2003, Feb., pp. 61–80.

M. Oshana, 'How Much Should We Value Autonomy?', *Social Philosophy & Policy Foundation* 2003, 20(2), pp. 99–126.

A. Osugi, 'Daily Application of the CIT in Japan', in B. Verschuere, G. Ben-Shakhar & E. Meijer (eds.), *Memory Detection: Theory and Application of the Concealed Information Test*, New York: Cambridge University Press 2011.

J. Paasonen et al., 'Functional Connectivity under Six Anesthesia Protocols and the Awake Condition in Rat Brain', *NeuroImage* 2018, 172, pp. 9–20.

D. A. Pardini et al., 'Lower Amygdala Volume in Men Is Associated with Childhood Aggression, Early Psychopathic Traits, and Future Violence', *BIOL Psychiatry* 2014, 75(1), pp. 73–80.

M. S. Pardo, Neuroscience Evidence, Legal Culture, and Criminal Procedure, *American Journal of Criminal Law* 2006, 33(3), pp. 301–337.

S. Pardo & D. Patterson, *Minds, Brains, and Law. The Conceptual Foundations of Law and Neuroscience*, New York: Oxford University Press 2015.

K. J. Partsch, 'Freedom of Conscience and Expression, and Political Freedoms', in L. Henkin (ed.), *The International Bill of Rights: The Covenant on Civil and Political Rights*, New York: Columbia University Press 1981, pp. 209–245.

R. Pattenden, 'Admissibility in Criminal Proceedings of Third Party and Real Evidence Obtained by Methods Prohibited by UNCAT', *The International Journal of Evidence & Proof* 2006, 10, pp. 1–41.

I. Peçi, *Sounds of Silence* (diss. Groningen), Nijmegen: WLP 2006.

J. Peth, G. Vossel & M. Gamer, 'Emotional Arousal Modulates the Encoding of Crime-Related Details and Corresponding Physiological Responses in the Concealed Information Test', *Psychophysiology* 2012, 49(3), pp. 3980–390.

T. W. Picton, 'The 300 Wave of Human Event-Related Potential', *Journal of Clinical Neurophysiology* 1992, 9(4), pp. 456–479.

J. Pillai & M. R. Sperling, 'Interictal EEG and the Diagnosis of Epilepsy', *Epilepsia* 2006, 47(1), pp. 14–22.

B. Pirker, *Proportionality, Analysis and Models of Judicial Review*, Groningen: Europa Law Publishing 2013.

K. M. Pitcher, *Judicial Responses to Pre-trial Procedural Violations in International Criminal Proceedings*, The Hague: T.M.C. Asser Press 2018a.

K. M. Pitcher, 'Rights-Analysis in Addressing Pre-trial Impropriety: An Obstacle to Fairness?', in J. D. Jackson & S. J. Summers (eds.), *Obstacles to Fairness in Criminal Proceedings: Individual Rights and Institutional Forms*, Oxford: Hart Publishing 2018b, pp. 273–300.

K. M. Pitcher & M. Samadi, 'Integriteit als perspectief bij de rechterlijke reactie op vormverzuimen', *DD* 2018/59, pp. 731–746.

R. A. Poldrack et al., 'Predicting Violent Behavior: What Can Neuroscience Add?', *Trends in Cognitive Science* 2018, 22(2), 111–123.

A. Pivaty et al., 'Opening Pandora's Box: The Right to Silence in Police Interrogations and the Directive 2016/343/EU', *New Journal of European Criminal Law* 2021a, 12(3), pp. 328–346.

A. Pivaty et al., 'Strengthening the Protection of the Right to Remain Silent at the Investigative Stage: What Role for the EU Legislator?', *New Journal of European Criminal Law* 2021b, 12(3), pp. 427–448.

A. Pivaty, P. ter Vrugt & D. de Vocht, *Policy Report Netherlands*, EmPriSe Project 2021.

J. Pugh, 'Coercion and the Neurocorrective Offer', in D. Birks & T. Douglas (eds.), *Treatment for Crime: Philosophical Essays on Neurointerventions in Criminal Justice*, New York: Oxford University Press 2018, pp. 94–116.

J. Pugh, *Autonomy, Rationality, and Contemporary Bioethics*, New York: Oxford University Press 2020.

J. Purshouse, 'The Reasonable Expectation of Privacy and the Criminal Suspect', *Modern Law Review* 2016, 79(5), pp. 871–884.

A. C. Pustilnik, 'Neurotechnologies at the Intersection of Criminal Procedure and Constitutional Law', *University of Maryland Legal Studies Research Paper* 2012, 61, pp. 1–20.

M. E. Raichle, 'An Introduction to Functional Imaging in the Context of Lie Detection', in E. Bizzi et al. (eds.), *Using Imaging to Identify Deceit. Scientific and Ethical Questions*, Cambridge: American Academic of Arts and Sciences 2009.

M. E. Raichle, 'What Is fMRI?', in M. S. Gazzaniga & J. S. Rakoff (eds.), *A Judge's Guide to Neuroscience: A Concise Introduction*, California: University of California 2010.

A. Raine, *The Anatomy of Violence: The Biological Roots of Crime*, New York: Pantheon Books 2013.

S. Rainey et al., 'Is the European Data Protection Regulation Sufficient to Deal with Emerging Data Concerns Relating to Neurotechnology?', *Journal of Law and the Biosciences* 2020, 7(1), pp. 1–19.

B. Rainey, P. McCormick & C. Ovey, *The European Convention on Human Rights*, New York: Oxford University Press 2021.

M. Redmayne, 'Rethinking the Privilege against Self-incrimination', *Oxford Journal of Legal Studies* 2007, 27(2), pp. 209–232.

D. A. Reify & W. J. Riker (eds.), *Coercion and the State*, New York: Springer Science + Business Media B.V 2008.

J.-F. Renucci, *Article 9 of the European Convention on Human Rights: Freedom of Thought, Conscience and Religion*, Strasbourg: Council of Europe 2005.

G. Richardson, 'Coercion and Human Rights: A European Perspective', *Journal of Mental Health* 2008, 17(3), pp. 245–254.

S. Richmond, 'Introduction', in S. Richmond, G. Rees & S. J. L. Edwards (eds.), *I Know What You're Thinking: Brain Imaging and Mental Privacy*, Croydon: Oxford University Press 2012, pp. 1–10.

J. M. Rickli & M. Ienca, 'The Security and Military Implications of Neurotechnology and Artificial Intelligence', in O. Friedrich et al. (eds.), *Clinical Neurotechnology Meets Artificial Intelligence. Advances in Neuroethics*, Cham: Springer 2021, pp. 197–214.

A. van Rijn, 'Freedom of Expression', in P. van Dijk et al. (eds.), *Theory and Practice of the European Convention on Human Rights*, Cambridge: Intersentia 2018, pp. 765–811.

S. L. Risacher & A. J. Saykin, 'Neuroimaging in Aging and Neurologic Diseases', in S. T. Dekosky & S. Asthana (eds.), *Handbook of Clinical Neurology, Vol. 167, Geriatric Neurology*, Amsterdam: Elsevier B. V. 2019, pp. 191–227.

C. K. Roberts, *Reconceptualising the Place of the Forum Internum and Forum Externum in Article 9 of the European Convention on Human Rights* (diss. University of Bristol), Bristol 2020 (electronic version).

P. Roberts, 'Excluding Evidence as Protecting Constitutional or Human Rights?', in L. Zedner & J. V. Roberts (eds.), *Principles and Values in Criminal Law and Criminal Justice: Essays in honour of Andrew Ashworth*, Oxford: Oxford University Press 2012, pp. 171–190.

P. Roberts & A. Zuckerman, *Criminal Evidence*, New York: Oxford University Press 2010.

D. Rodrigues-Amorim et al., 'Schizophrenia: A Review of Potential Biomarkers', *Journal of Psychiatric Research* 2017, 3, pp. 37–49.

J. P. Rosenfeld, 'Brain Fingerprinting': A Critical Analysis', *The Scientific Review of Mental Health Practice* 2005, 4(1), pp. 20–37.

J. P. Rosenfeld, 'P300 in Detecting Concealed Information', in B. Verschuere, G. Ben-Shakhar & E. Meijer (eds.), *Memory Detection: Theory and Application of the Concealed Information Test*, New York: Cambridge University Press 2011, pp. 63–89.

J. P. Rosenfeld (ed.), *Detecting Concealed Information and Deception: Recent Developments*, London: Academic Press 2018.

J. P. Rosenfeld, 'P300 in Detecting Concealed Information and Deception: A Review', *Psychophysiology* 2020, 57(7).

J. P. Rosenfeld et al., 'Simple, Effective Countermeasures to P300-Based Tests of Detection of Concealed Information', *Psychophysiology* 2004, 41(2), pp. 205–219.

J. P. Rosenfeld et al., 'The Complex Trial Protocol (CTP): A New, Countermeasure-Resistant, Accurate, P300-Based Method for Detection of Concealed Information', *Psychophysiology* 2008, 45(6), pp. 906–919.

J. P. Rosenfeld et al., 'Review of Recent Studies and Issues Regarding the P300-Based Complex Trial Protocol for Detection of Concealed Information', *International Journal of Psychophysiology* 2013, 90, pp. 118–135.

J. P. Rosenfeld et al., 'Evidence Suggesting Superiority of Visual (Verbal) vs. Auditory Test Presentation Modality in the P300-Based, Complex Trial Protocol for Concealed Autobiographical Memory Detection', *International Journal of Psychophysiology* 2015a, 96(1), pp. 16–22.

J. P. Rosenfeld et al., 'Superiority of Pictorial versus Verbal Presentation and Initial Exposure in the P300-Based, Complex Trial Protocol for Concealed Memory Detection', *Applied Psychophysiology Biofeedback* 2015b, 40(2), pp. 61–73.

D. R. Rosell & L. J. Siever, 'The Neurobiology of Aggression and Violence', *CNS Spectrums* 2015, 20, pp. 254–279.

A. L. Roskies, 'Brain Imaging Techniques', in S. J. Morse & A. L. Roskies (red.), *A Primer on Criminal Law and Neuroscience*, New Yok: Oxford University Press 2013a, pp. 37–74.

A. L. Roskies, 'Other Neuroscientific Techniques', in S. J. Morse & A. L. Roskies (red.), *A Primer on Criminal Law and Neuroscience*, New Yok: Oxford University Press 2013b, pp. 75–88.

A. L. Roskies, 'Mind Reading, Lie Detection, and Privacy', in J. Clausen & N. Levy (eds.), *Handbook of Neuroethics*, Dordrecht: Springer 2015, pp. 679–695.

M. Ruiz-Blondet, Z. Jin & S. Laszlo, 'CEREBRE: A Novel Method for Very High Accuracy Event-Related Potential Biometric Identification', *IEEE Transactions on Information Forensics and Security* 2016, 11(7), pp. 1618–1629.

S. E. Rushing, D. A. Pryma & D. D. Langleben, 'PET and SPECT', in J. R. Simpson (red.), *Neuroimaging in Forensic Psychiatry. From Clinic to the Courtroom*, Chichester: Wiley-Blackwell 2012, pp. 3–26.

E. Rusconi & T. Mitchener-Nissen, 'Prospects of Functional Magnetic Resonance Imaging as Lie Detector', *Frontiers in Human Neuroscience* 2013, 7, pp. 1–12.

M. Russo et al., 'Evaluation of Accuracy and Reproducibility of a Relocatable Maxillary Fixation System for Fractionated Intracranial Stereotactic Radiation Therapy', *Journal of Medical Ration Sciences* 2016, 63, pp. 41–47.

J. Ryberg, 'Punishment, Pharmacological Treatment, and Early Release', *International Journal of Applied Philosophy* 2012, 26(2), pp. 231–244.

J. Ryberg, 'Neuroethics and Brain Privacy: Setting the Stage', *Res Publica* 2017a, 23, pp. 153–158.

J. Ryberg, 'Neuroscience, Mind Reading and Mental Privacy', *Res Publica* 2017b, 23, pp. 197–221.

J. Ryberg, *Neurointerventions, Crime, and Punishment*, New York: Oxford University Press 2020.

W. Sententia, 'Neuroethical Considerations: Cognitive Liberty and Converging Technologies for Improving Human Cognition', *Annals of the New York Academy of Sciences* 2004, 1013, pp. 221–228.

S. E. Stoller & P. R. Wolpe, 'Emerging Neurotechnologies for Lie Detection and the Fifth Amendment', *American Journal of Law and Medicine* 2007, 33(2), pp. 359–375.

A. Sbrizzi et al., 'Fast Quantitative MRI as a Nonlinear Tomography Problem', *Magnetic Resonance Imaging* 2018, 46, pp. 56–63.

W. A. Schabas (ed.), *The Universal Declaration of Human Rights: The Travaux Préparatoires*, New York: Cambridge University Press 2013.

E. Shaw, 'Offering Castration to Sex Offenders: The Significance of the State's Intentions', *Journal of Medical Ethics* 2014, 40, pp. 594–595.

F. X. Shen, 'Neuroscience, Mental Privacy and the Law', *Harvard Journal of Law & Public Policy* 2013, 36, pp. 653–713.

F. X. Shen, 'Law and Neuroscience 2.0', *Arizona State Law Journal* 2016, 48, pp. 1043–1086.

J. R. Simpson (ed.), *Neuroimaging in Forensic Psychiatry. From Clinic to the Courtroom*, Chichester: Wiley-Blackwell 2012.

B. van der Sloot, 'How to Assess Privacy Violations in the Age of Big Data? Analysing the Three Different Tests Developed by the ECtHR and Adding for a Fourth One', *Information & Communication Technology Law* 2015, 24(1), pp. 74–103.

R. Smith-Bindman et al., 'Radiation Dose Associated with Common Computed Tomography Examinations and the Associated Lifetime Attributable Risk of Cancer', *Archives of Internal Medicine* 2009, 169(22), pp. 2079–2086.

P. Sommaggio et al., 'Cognitive Liberty. A First Step Towards a Human Neuro-rights Declaration', *BioLaw Journal* 2017, 3, pp. 27–45.

P. Sommaggio & M. Mazzocca, 'Cognitive Liberty and Human Rights', in A. D'Aloia & M. C. Errigo (eds.), *Neuroscience and Law: Complicated Crossings and New Perspectives*, Switzerland: Springer Nature 2020, pp. 95–111.

S. Sottiaux & G. van der Shyff, 'Methods of International Human Rights Adjudication: Towards a More Structured Decision-Making Process for the European Court of Human Rights', *Hastings International and Comparative Law Review* 2008, 31(1), pp. 115–156.

S. A. Spence et al., 'Behavioural and Functional Anatomical Correlates of Deception in Humans', *Neuroreport* 2001, 12(13), pp. 2849–2853.

S. A. Spence et al., 'Muchausen's Syndrome by Proxy' or a 'Miscarriage of Justice'? An Initial Application of Functional Neuroimaging to the Question of Guilt Versus Innocence', *European Psychiatry* 2008, 23(4), pp. 309–314.

S. Sutton et al., 'Evoked-Potential Correlates of Stimulus Uncertainty', *Science* 1965, 150(3700), pp. 1187–1188.

A. M. Staffaroni, 'Neuroimaging in Dementia', *Seminars in Neurology* 2017, 37(5), pp. 510–537.

L. Stevens, *Het nemo-teneturbeginsel in strafzaken: van zwijgrecht naar containerbegrip* (diss. Tilburg), Nijmegen: WLP 2005.

L. Stevens, 'Het nemo-teneturbeginsel als containerbegrip? Een beschouwing van de koers van het EHRM naar aanleiding van het Jalloh-arrest', *Delikt & Delinkwent* 2007/54, pp. 682–697.

L. Stevens, 'Gedwongen biometrische toegangsverschaffing is niet in strijd met nemo tenetur', *Nederlands juristenblad* 2019/315, pp. 400–403.

M. Susi, 'Novelty in New Human Rights. The Decrease in Universality and Abstractness Thesis', in A. von Arnauld, K. von der Decken & M. Susi (eds.), *The Cambridge Handbook of New Human Rights: Recognition, Novelty, Rhetoric*, Padstow: Cambridge University Press 2020, pp. 21–33.

A. Sweeney et al., 'Multimodality Cranial Image Fusion Using External Markers Applied via a Vacuum Mouthpiece and a Case Report', *Strahlentherapie und Onkologie* 2003, 179(4), pp. 254–260.

G. Szmukler & P. S. Appelbaum, 'Treatment Pressures, Leverage, Coercion, and Compulsion in Mental Health Care', *Journal of Mental Health* 2008, 17(3), pp. 233–244.

P. M. Taylor, *Freedom of Religion: UN and European Human Rights Law and Practice*, New York: Cambridge University Press 2005.

M. Thommen & M. Samadi, 'The Bigger the Crime, the Smaller the Chance of a Fair Trial? Evidence Exclusion in Serious Crime Cases under Swiss, Dutch and European Human Rights Law', *European Journal of Crime, Criminal Law and Criminal Justice* 2016, 24, pp. 65–85.

S. K. Thompson, 'The Legality of the Use of Psychiatric Neuroimaging in Intelligence Interrogation', *Cornell Law Review* 2005, 90, pp. 1601–1638.

S. K. Thompson, 'A Brave New World of Interrogation Jurisprudence', *American Journal of Law & Medicine* 2007, 33, pp. 341–357.

M. Timonen et al., 'The Association of Preceding Traumatic Brain Injury with Mental Disorders, Alcoholism and Criminality: The Northern Finland 1966 Birth Cohort Study, *Psychiatry Research* 2002, 113(3), pp. 217–226.

D. A. G. van Toor, 'Het nemo-teneturbeginsel: Rechtspraak van het Europese Hof voor de Rechten van de Mens en de Hoge Raad vergeleken', *Tijdschrift voor Bijzonder Strafrecht & Handhaving* 2016, (1), pp. 28–43.

D. A. G. van Toor, *Het schuldige geheugen? Een onderzoek naar het gebruik van hersenonderzoek als opsporingsmethode in het licht van eisen van instrumentaliteit en rechtsbescherming* (diss. Nijmegen), Deventer: Wolters Kluwer 2017.

D. A. G. van Toor, 'Het nemo-teneturbeginsel bij digitale opsporingsbevoegdheden: oproep tot discussie over fundamentele bezinning van de normering van het opsporingsonderzoek in een digitale context', *Tijdschrift voor Bijzonder Strafrecht & Handhaving* 2021, nr. 2, pp. 89–100.

L. Tortora et al., 'Neuroprediction and A. I. in Forensic Psychiatry and Criminal Justice: A Neurolaw Perspective', *Frontiers in Psychology* 2020, 11(222), pp. 1–9.

S. Trechsel, *Human Rights in Criminal Proceedings*, New York: Oxford University Press 2005.

G. Treglia et al., 'Diagnostic Performance and Prognostic Value of PET/CT with Different Tracers for Brain Tumors: A Systematic Review of Published Meta-Analyses', *International Journal of Molecular Sciences* 20(19), 2019.

J. I. Turner & T. Weigend, 'The Purposes and Functions of Exclusionary Rules: A Comparative Overview', in S. Gless & T. Richter (eds.), *Do Exclusionary Rules Ensure a Fair Trial? A Comparative Perspectives on Law and Justice*, Cham: Springer 2019, pp. 255–282.

UN Special Rapporteur on Freedom of Religion or Belief, *Report on the Freedom of Thought*, 5 Ocotber 2021, A/76/380.

B. Vermeulen & H. Battjes, 'Prohibition of Torture and Other Inhuman or Degrading Treatment or Punishment', in P. van Dijk et al. (eds.), *Theory and Practice of the European Convention on Human Rights*, Cambridge: Intersentia 2018, pp. 381–424.

B. Vermeulen & M. Roosmalen, 'Freedom of Thought, Conscience and Religion', in P. van Dijk et al. (eds.), *Theory and Practice of the European Convention on Human Rights*, Cambridge: Intersentia 2018, pp. 735–764.

B. Verschuere, G. Ben-Shakhar & E. Meijer (eds.), *Memory Detection: Theory and Application of the Concealed Information Test*, New York: Cambridge University Press 2011.

B. Verschuere & E. Meijer, 'What's on Your Mind? Recent Advances in Memory Detection Using the Concealed Information Test', *European Psychologist* 2014, 19(3), pp. 162–171.

N. A. Vincent, 'Neuroimaging and Responsibility Assessments', *Neuroethics* 2011, 4, pp. 35–49.

N. A. Vincent, T. Nadelhoffer & A. McCay (eds.), *Neurointerventions and the Law: Regulating Human Mental Capacity*, New York: Oxford University Press 2020.

J. Vorhaus, 'On Degration – Part One: Article 3 of the European Convention on Human Rights', *Common Law World Reviews* 2002, 31, pp. 374–399.

K. de Vries, 'Right to Respect for Private and Family Life', in P. van Dijk et al. (eds.), *Theory and Practice of the European Convention on Human Rights*, Cambridge: Intersentia 2018, pp. 667–734.

A. Wagner et al., *fMRI and Lie Detection: A Knowledge Brief of the MacArthur Foundation Research Network on Law and Neuroscience*, The MacArthur Foundation Research Network on Law and Neuroscience 2016.

J. Waldron, 'Torture and Positive Law: Jurisprudence for the White House', *Columbia Law Review* 2005, 105(6), pp. 1681–1750.

N. Walker, 'Ethical and Other Problems', in N. Walker (ed.), *Dangerous people*, London: Blackstone 1996, pp. 1–12.

B. F. Wall et al., *Protection of Pregnant Patients during Diagnostic Medical Exposures to Ionizing Radiation. Advice from the Health Protection Agency. The Royal College of Radiologists and the College of Radiographers*, London: Health Protection Agency 2009.

L. Waller et al., 'Evaluating the Replicability, Specificity, and Generalizability of Connectome Fingerprints', *NeuroImage* 2017, 158, pp. 371–377.

J. Wang et al., 'Identifying Thematic Roles from Neural Representations Measured by Functional Magnetic Resonance Imaging', *Cognitive Neuropsychology* 2016, 33(3–4), pp. 257–264.

J. Wang, V. L. Cherkassky & M. A. Just, 'Predicting the Brain Activation Pattern Associated with the Propositional Content of a Sentence: Modeling Neural Representations of Events and States', *Human Brain Mapping* 2017, 38(10), pp. 4865–4881.

A. Wertheimer, *Coercion*, Princeton: Princeton University Press 1987.

A. Wertheimer & F. G. Miller, 'There Are (STILL) No Coercive Offers', *Journal of Medical Ethics* 2014, 40(9), pp. 592–593.

B. Williamson, 'Brain Data: Scanning, Scraping and Sculpting the Plastic Learning Brain through Neurotechnology', *Postdigital Science and Education* 2019, 1, pp. 65–86.

J. Witzel, 'Implications of Neuroimaging for Dangerousness Assessment', in J. R. Simpson (ed.), *Neuroimaging in Forensic Psychiatry. From Clinic to the Courtroom*, Chichester: Wiley-Blackwell 2012, pp. 195–200.

N. D. Woodward & C. J. Cascio, 'Resting-State Functional Connectivity in Psychiatric Disorders', *JAMA Psychiatry* 2017, 72(8), pp. 743–744.

Y. Yang et al., 'Localization of Deformations within the Amygdala in Individuals with Psychopathy', *Archive of General Psychiatry* 2009, 66(9), pp. 986–994.

R. Yuste et al., 'Four Ethical Priorities for Neurotechnologies and AI', *Nature* 2017, 551.

R. Yuste, J. Genser & S. Herrmann, 'It's Time for Neuro-rights', *Horizons* 2021(18), pp. 154–164.

D. Zimmerman, 'Coercive Wage Offers', *Philosophy & Public Affairs* 1981, 10(2), pp. 121–145.

J. Zijlmans et al., 'The Predictive Value of Neurobiological Measures for Recidivism in Delinquent Male Young Adults', *Journal of Psychiatry & Neuroscience* 2021, 46(2), pp. 271–280.

K. Zukotynsk et al., 'PET/CT of Dementia', *American Journal of Roentgenology* 2018, 211(2), pp. 246–259.

Index

www.ingramcontent.com/pod-product-compliance
Lightning Source LLC
LaVergne TN
LVHW011807200926
848484LV00005B/1098

* 9 7 8 1 0 0 9 2 5 2 4 3 0 *